Mike Alfreds

Mike Alfreds was born in London and trained as a director at Carnegie Mellon University in Pittsburgh. He lived in the USA for eight years, during which time he worked for MGM Studios in Hollywood, was artistic director of Theatre West, Tucson, and then of the Cincinnati Playhouse-in-the-Park. For five years he worked in Israel where he became artistic director of the Jerusalem Khan Theatre. He has also worked in Australia, New Zealand, Canada, Germany, Norway, China and Mongolia. In the UK, he founded Shared Experience and ran it for thirteen years. He was artistic director of Cambridge Theatre Company, later renamed Method & Madness, and has directed for the Royal Shakespeare Company, Shakespeare's Globe, the Royal National Theatre, where he was an associate director, and for several regional repertory theatres. He has staged over two hundred productions, and won awards both abroad and in the UK. He has adapted novels and stories for the stage, devised performances and translated the texts of several of his productions. He maintains a parallel career as a teacher. He was a senior lecturer at Tel Aviv University and on the staff of LAMDA. He frequently gives courses on acting, directing, improvising and storytelling. He is the author of *Then What Happens? Storytelling & Adapting for the Theatre*, also published by Nick Hern Books.

DIFFERENT EVERY NIGHT

Freeing the Actor

Mike Alfreds

NICK HERN BOOKS
London
www.nickhernbooks.co.uk

A Nick Hern Book

Different Every Night
first published in Great Britain in 2007
by Nick Hern Books Limited
The Glasshouse, 49a Goldhawk Road,
London W12 8QP

Reprinted 2009, 2010, 2011, 2012, 2013, 2014, 2015

Cover designed by Peter Bennett
Typeset by Country Setting, Kingsdown, Kent, CT14 8ES

Printed and bound by CPI Group (UK) Ltd, Croydon, CR0 4YY

A CIP catalogue record for this book
is available from the British Library

ISBN 978 1 85459 967 4

MIX
Paper from
responsible sources
FSC® C013604

For
PHILIP OSMENT
best of collaborators

To
ACTORS
for years of pleasure
with many thanks, some frustration and lots of love

CONTENTS

3 PREPARATION

4 THE WORK: REHEARSAL, PRODUCTION, PERFORMANCE

FOREWORD

PAM FERRIS

Most of what I am as an actress I owe to Mike Alfreds. He gave me the language and the tools I needed for my craft.

When I met him in 1976 I had been acting professionally for ten years, and although I'd had no formal training, I thought that all the classes I'd been to, and books I'd read, had given me my own 'Way of Working'. How wrong I was. I was just muddling through.

The slow and sometimes painful process of taking on board Mike's system seemed, at first, to threaten that vague thing I called 'Instinct', and I've since seen other actors struggle and sometimes reject his work for fear of damaging their mysterious internal processes. But if you trust the work, not just intellectually but viscerally, it liberates a powerful creativity that makes old-fashioned 'Instinct' look a shambolic hit-and-miss affair.

I remember clearly my feelings before the first performance of *The Arabian Nights*. The rehearsal period had felt like a series of exercises, all enjoyable and enriching, but without the goal-orientated focus I was used to. Nothing was set. No moves. No agreed way of saying a line. Nothing. There was too much freedom, and I felt really insecure. But I also knew that inside I had a huge resource of knowledge about the characters I was to play, the world they lived in and most important of all – what they wanted.

Understanding what a character wants and embodying it fully is the challenge. It took me about a year of continuous work for the knowledge to seep through from my brain to my whole being, and it makes me sad when young actors think that just to know the words 'Action' or 'Objective' is enough. I get even sadder when I work with some directors – I wish they knew who they were – who have some sort of intellectual theory about theatre, but no idea how to put it into practice. I hope they read and digest this book soon.

Over a period of years I came to enjoy that empty/full feeling before stepping on stage and I love it still. There is nothing so exciting for me as the push and pull of battling out a well-written scene with another actor. It's like an improvisation with carefully worked-out parameters, but within those limits, it's as free as any football match. I believe an audience knows when actors are 'in the moment' and Mike's work fosters that freedom more than any director I know.

I haven't worked with Mike for many years now, but I still find myself comparing other directors with him. I'm always a little shocked by their lack of rigour, their vagueness, their willingness to accept second best. Mike's pursuit of excellence drives him on and I'm proud to have travelled some of that journey beside him.

ACKNOWLEDGEMENTS

The following people gave me invaluable comment,
criticism and encouragement: Laurence Boswell, Tony Graham,
Robert Hale, Jenny Harris, Glynn MacDonald, Barbara Marchant,
Philip Osment, Sue Parrish, Peter Thomson and Annabelle Winograd.
To them all, my warmest thanks. And to Nick Hern
for remarkable patience – twenty-three years' worth in fact.

For the happiness of being a writer or an actor, I would bear the dislike of my family, I'd bear deprivation, disappointment, I'd live in an attic and eat only coarse bread, I'd endure dissatisfaction with myself and awareness of my own imperfections, but, in return, I would demand fame . . . real, resounding fame . . . (*She covers her face with her hands.*) I feel dizzy . . . Oooooof! . . .

> Nina, a would-be actress, in the second act of *The Seagull*

I performed senselessly . . . I didn't know what to do with my hands, I didn't know how to stand on stage, I couldn't control my voice. You've no idea how it feels to know you're acting badly . . . Now, I'm not like that . . . I act with enjoyment, with enthusiasm, I become intoxicated on stage and I feel beautiful . . . Now I know, I understand . . . that in our work . . . what matters isn't fame, isn't glamour, not the things I dreamt of, but the capacity to endure. To bear your cross and have faith. I have faith and it's not so painful, and when I think about my calling, I'm not afraid of life.

> Nina, an actress, in the fourth act of *The Seagull*

A PRACTICAL GUIDE

PURPOSE

The book has two subjects. The first is how I direct. The second is the relationship between actors and directors. Combining them, this book suggests ways for us to collaborate. But techniques and processes risk becoming arbitrary unless they're framed within some cohesive 'philosophy' of what theatre is. Specific methods of preparation and rehearsal should logically derive from – and aim towards the fulfilment of – what we believe makes theatre intrinsically what it is, rather than something else. What follows then is my vision of what theatre is or could be, and how I try to achieve it: ways of working and ways of thinking about work; practice and theory; *modus operandi* and *modus vivendi*.

ORGANISATION

In the *first part*, I set out my wares, which include my own learning curve, my idea of theatre's purpose, its vital elements and the broad belief system that frames how I function.

The *second* describes in detail the concepts of the techniques I use in rehearsal, with examples of how they work.

The *third* describes the work of the pre-production period: preparing the text, planning the rehearsals and casting.

The *fourth* describes the practical application of those techniques from the first day of rehearsal to the final performance, together with consideration of some technical matters.

The *fifth* describes the troubleshooting that accompanies the rehearsal work and offers some ethical considerations in connection with this.

The *sixth*, a brief coda, consists of a résumé of the main principles guiding the work, a glossary for quick reference and some suggestions for further reading (which, together, could spare you reading the rest of the book).

STYLE

GENDER

'Actor' refers to both genders. I use 'actress' when it seems appropriate to make that distinction. To avoid the self-consciousness of alternating even-handedly between *she* and *he, him* and *her, hers* and *his* or of even more self-consciously trying to compensate for centuries of injustice by 'privileging' *she, her* and *hers*, or of using either the laborious *he-or-she* or the ugly, unpronounceable *s/he*, I'm attempting to stick to *they, them* and *their.*

TYPEFACE

Points of emphasis, foreign terms and titles are in *italics*. SMALL CAPITALS indicate topics that are dealt with fully further ahead in the text and more concisely in the glossary.

FOOTNOTES

The footnotes are not vital to the flow or understanding of the main text. They're asides in which I've succumbed to the urge to elaborate on detail, illustrate a point from my own experience or indulge in a diatribe on matters adjacent to what I'm currently pursuing.

ADDRESS

Most of the time, I'm addressing the director; but sometimes I talk to the actor and at all times, of course, to the reader.

DEFINITIONS

PLAY

Although I refer consistently to plays, the techniques I describe can, with intelligent adjustments, be applied equally well to devised work and adaptations of non-dramatic material.

STAGE

When I refer to the 'stage', it implies any space where acting takes place.

THEATRE

Within the text I of course describe in considerable detail what I believe theatre to be, but I'll define it here briefly as an event in which one group of human beings, in the presence of another group of human beings and on their behalf, transform themselves into yet another group of human beings who pursue objectives through actions that involve them in conflict.

ART

Where I use the words 'art' or 'artist', it's not in any elitist sense, but rather to suggest the aspiration to create something of excellence.

PRACTICAL WORK

PREPARATION — REHEARSAL TECHNIQUES — EXERCISES — IMPROVISATIONS

All practical work is set in boxes and is found in the central three sections. Anyone can go directly to these, should they wish, and ignore the verbiage surrounding them.

INTERPRETATION

The interpretive suggestions I make for the choice of actions and objectives in my examples of text analysis are just that, reasonable conjectures, and in *no way* meant to be definitive.

PLAY REFERENCES

I'm focusing mainly on Chekhov's *Seagull* and, to a lesser extent, his *Cherry Orchard* to illustrate techniques and processes. The translations are my own. Along the way, I refer to other classic texts that I trust are reasonably familiar.

ARGUMENT

To pursue my argument for a particular way of working as vividly as possible, I deliberately contrast it with a completely different tradition of going about things. But, in theatre practice, things are never quite so cut-and-dried as this might imply. For example, when discussing the interpretation of plays, I stipulate that there are two basic approaches: one – that I criticise – imposes a concept on the text; the other – that I espouse – allows the text to reveal itself. Of course, directors don't neatly divide up on one side or the other. They practise their craft in endless variations on a spectrum between these two extremes. But wherever directors fall along this continuum, I'm suggesting that they should be examining their true intentions (why they work the way they do). I'm fully aware of the necessary pragmatism imposed on us by the circumstances of most of the theatres we work in. But I see no point in letting us off the hook with excuses for not doing the work we should be doing. Similarly, in order to make my point firmly when I describe certain behaviour patterns of actors and directors, I sometimes amalgamate several connected tendencies into one syndrome.

HEALTH AND SAFETY WARNINGS

Health Warning: Danger from Words

This is a book about theatre. That means it's first and foremost a book about acting. But a book about acting is a contradiction in terms. Acting means doing. It's as it says, active, physical. Actors are athletes. A book of acting techniques is a poor substitute for experiencing them on stage or in the rehearsal room. It won't work like a manual for building a garden shed, from which, if you follow the instructions accurately, you'll get predictable results. To expect predictable results from an actor is as unrealistic as expecting a garden shed to build itself. It's also undesirable. Actors are, paradoxically, their own instrument: they are at once artist and creation, doer and done-to, fingers and keyboard, feet and football, programmer and programme . . . Like the rest of us, they live inside themselves. There's no way in which they can extract themselves from the delusion of objectivity under which we all seem to exist, in order to observe themselves from the outside. We'd like to think we operate predominantly through common sense and reason, but the larger part of our functioning is autonomic and unconscious. Therefore, there's a limit to how much control actors can have over their creative – unconscious – selves.

Human beings – and who should be more in touch with their humanity than actors? – are holistic: bodies, feelings, needs, thoughts are not discrete elements that can each be dealt with independent of the others. We're hard-wired by billions of nerve cells that interconnect in ways we still scarcely understand. The danger of reading a lot of words about acting is that it may lead you to believe that learning to act is a matter of using your head, that ratiocination will solve the problems of acting. This isn't so. Words are helpful only so far as they point you towards other areas of understanding – experiential, visceral, in the muscle, in the gut. What's clear is that too many words can disconnect us from the rest of ourselves: from our physicality, our spontaneity, our instinct, our imagination – those very channels, in fact, that might tap those unconscious parts of ourselves where true creativity lies dormant, waiting to be woken up. Too much discussion blocks action. Too much talk encourages evasion. Actors become head-bound and their instincts immobilised.

Nor is language always precise enough to pinpoint the nuances of motives, feelings and impulses involved in acting. Besides, people translate what they hear and what they read subjectively within their own frames of experience. Most often, the intellectual understanding comes *after* the doing and experiencing. The sequence is: *do, experience, then understand*. This is a problem for many directors who love words and love listening to themselves using them. Inevitably they ask actors for direct results, making their appeal from head to head, bypassing the rest of an actor's holistic self on the way. So I would suggest, for the good of your artistic health – especially if you're an actor, *more* especially if you're a director – that while reading this book, you periodically remind yourself that the ultimate aim of all these words is to activate the instinct.

However, true to myself as a director, I'd love *these* words to be 'heard'. I'd love them to be useful to both actors and directors and of interest to anyone curious about acting.

Safety Warning

LIVE ACTORS: HANDLE WITH CARE. AVOID BLOCKING CURRENTS OF ENERGY.

I
INTRODUCTIONS

CURRICULUM VITAE

I'm a director. I've staged some two hundred productions in about fifty years. Once I did as many as twelve in a year; now I restrict myself to no more than two. Most of my life I've spent running companies or being in some way involved with the same group of actors over a sustained period. Parallel with this I've maintained a career as a teacher both of directors and of actors. I've translated and adapted many of the texts of my productions. I was born in the United Kingdom, trained in the United States and have worked in eight other countries.

As a child, I wanted to act. Rotting in some attic – or so I hope and pray – is a home movie of me, aged six, impersonating Carmen Miranda, in a turban of real fruit and a towel, with multi-coloured plastic rings, the sort for identifying chickens, dangling from my ears. My first stage appearance – or half appearance – was as the third of a trio of bluebells in a school pantomime. We wore gauzy blue costumes with floppy hats. Due to the incompetence of the first bluebell, or her malice, I barely got out of the wings. (Big disappointment of parents: 'Why didn't you push?') In the following year's school play, I was promoted to the role of Amundsen, of whom I'd never heard, and had one line: 'My name is Amundsen and I'm going to get to the South Pole before anyone else.' Then, bearing the Norwegian flag, I had to run in a circle faster than the boy playing Scott who was running around in the opposite direction with the Union Jack. Auntie Bea, the headmistress who conducted rehearsals, asked me what I'd eaten for lunch. 'Cod,' I replied. 'Well, you're acting like a stuffed cod,' she said. (Directors, our jibes go deep and last for years.) At grammar school, I played Madam Wang in *Lady Precious Stream* and Raina in Shaw's *Arms and the Man*. I was probably appalling – but I read well. There was a one-act verse play whose name I've forgotten, something on the lines of *Phoebe or The Spartan Maid* in which I played the title role in a borrowed maid's uniform. It was some arch 1920s parody of Greek Tragedy, but whatever it was went right over my head. I was about to be relieved of *travestie* by playing Jaques in *As You Like It* (my voice was breaking), but the performance dates conflicted with my Bar Mitzvah. So my official break with drag was delayed until I joined a local amateur group a couple of years later, for whom, good Jewish boy that I was, I played – in a church – St Cuthman in Christopher Fry's *The Boy with a Cart*. I was so nervous that all I can remember is inverting words, making hills roll down stones. An actors' agent, a friend of the family, came to see the performance. She arranged a screen test for me to play the boy king Ptolemy in a film version of Shaw's *Caesar and Cleopatra*, starring Vivien Leigh with whom I was totally smitten. I was so overcome by terror that on the scheduled day I pretended to be ill. The agent, undaunted, gave me a copy of Stanislavsky's *An Actor Prepares*, of which, ironically, I could then make neither head nor tail. This key that eventually unlocked some basic truths about acting for me remained unturned on my bookshelf for ten years. I continued to perform with the local amateur group with increasing self-consciousness.

My growing awkwardness on stage chimed with, or maybe was the reason for, my new ambition to become a playwright. From the age of eleven I'd become a regular theatregoer, so that by the age of eighteen, when I went off to do my National Service, I'd seen a lot of productions and read a lot of plays. At that time, London theatre was uncomplicated – just the West End plus a couple of what were then called Little Theatres, specialising in gloomy foreign muck. Consequently, I saw a lot of light comedies (a genre which, like intimate revue, has long since passed away). I have a file with the yellowing first few pages of my earliest attempts at playwriting which begin: 'Act One Scene One. A Country House. Through the French windows enters . . . ' I thought *Hay Fever* and *Private Lives* were the funniest plays imaginable and read them over and over again. When my mother, some years later, rather unwisely asked Noël Coward to read a play of mine, he did so and wrote back suggesting 'he try writing one off his own bat'.

Directing, then called producing, meant little to me, although I was aware of Peter Brook and did see several of his earliest productions, including *Ring Round the Moon* which I precociously didn't find as stylish as I'd been led to expect. I was already starting to develop a critical eye of my own and – though I then couldn't have stated it in this way – a sense of theatrical truth. During this period I saw Peggy Ashcroft in *The Deep Blue Sea* and Sam Wanamaker and Michael Redgrave in *Winter Journey* (the English title for Clifford Odets' *The Country Girl*), and was profoundly stirred by the deep sexuality of her performance and the spontaneity and danger of theirs. I saw the Oliviers in *The School for Scandal*, which revealed that classic texts could be immediate and accessible. Their playing of the 'screen scene' unveiled another thrilling possibility: comedy and tragedy could exist within the selfsame moment.

When I ended up in the RAF in Singapore, I started a film club and began reading about film direction. I was excited by the discovery that the manipulation of composition, light and movement could suggest meanings beyond their literal purposes. I understood that film (and by implication theatre) could be about more than its surfaces. 'One of those bells that now and then rings' rang for me. *This* was what I wanted to do. Direct. Films.

So instead of returning to the UK, I managed, with laborious cutting of red tape, to get myself demobbed in Singapore and took a cargo boat across the Pacific to Hollywood. I got work at MGM as an office boy in the *Tom & Jerry* cartoon department; then, after two weeks, made gloriously rapid promotion onto the

Main Lot as an apprentice in the Publicity Department. I thought there was no stopping me. There was. My attempts to move myself yet further, into the Production Department, came to nought. My days were spent giving VIPs special tours of the studio, which, as well as taking them onto the sound stages to watch shooting and to be photographed with none-too-willing stars, included showing them dresses that Garbo had worn in *Camille* and pointing out Elizabeth Taylor in the commissary. My evenings, however, were spent directing for one of the theatre companies that mushroomed around Los Angeles, providing potential showcases for the thousands of aspiring movie stars that came West in the unreasonable hope of being discovered. My first production was of a one-act play by Tennessee Williams called *Hello From Bertha*, about a whore dying of a broken heart in a New Orleans brothel – a long way from my native Maida Vale! Nevertheless, it won 'The Southern California Theatre's Jesse Lasky Award for Best Production' and seemed to confirm me in my third choice of career. My next endeavour was an ambitious triple bill. It comprised an adaptation, by me, of a Kenneth Tynan piece on bullfighting, *The Death of Manolete*, and a translation, by me, of Cocteau's *The Human Voice*, a one-act play for a woman and a telephone, in which I cast a Swedish actress who planned to be the next Ingrid Bergman. (In the perilous shoals of Hollywood she sank without trace.) The third item was a farce by Molnar called *One, Two, Three*, for which, during the inter-mission, I – single-handed – converted the seating from an end-on configuration to one in-the-round. The evening was successful but long, a description that has accompanied much of my work down the years.

It was successful enough to encourage me to take off and study in New York and subsequently at Carnegie Mellon University in Pittsburgh, then Carnegie Insti-tute of Technology, in whose theatre department I began to learn my craft and to whom I am, as they say, eternally grateful. The training was intense and intensive, firmly balanced between practice and theory. We worked eighteen-hour days, acting, directing, building scenery, making costumes, writing plays, stage manag-ing, assistant-directing, preparing research papers, analysing texts and – as neophyte directors – doing endless exercises in composition, focus, balance and picturisation. While training, I found, to my dismay, that my instinct for directing, which had served me so well up to this point, sank under the weight of the techniques I was acquiring. For a while, my work was correct, but unsponta-neous. Over time, I absorbed these techniques and eventually, to my relief, my instinct resurfaced, strengthened by my new skills. I came to realise that in theatre the absorption of processes takes its own good time and cannot be hurried. I learned that it's useless, apart from being quite wrong, to expect immediate results from actors, except of the most practical sort.

In the summer vacations, I went as a stage manager to a summer stock theatre in Kennebunkport, Maine, which did a different musical, operetta or opera each of its eleven weeks. The director for the season had to leave early, and I was offered the last two shows to direct which I did well enough to be asked back as director for the following season. I learned to deal with a large cast of some forty performers, to focus on essentials, communicate precisely and to get a show on efficiently in record time – approximately nine hours. Mornings were devoted to music rehearsals and staging dance numbers. I got to block the first half of the show on Wednesday afternoons, the second on Thursday afternoons and pull the whole thing together on Friday afternoons. Saturdays there were matinees, so we couldn't rehearse. Mondays, we did technicals and, the next day, dress rehearsals in a state of hysteria, weeping with helpless laughter and sobbing with frustration. By some miracle, every Tuesday-night opening was as smooth as the proverbially unruffled lake.

When I graduated, a group of student colleagues and myself set up a winter stock theatre in Tucson, Arizona, which lasted an ill-fated single production. Then, at 26, I became artistic director of the Cincinnati Playhouse-in-the-Park where I directed fourteen plays in nine months, including *Hamlet*, *The Seagull*, *Hedda Gabler*, *Volpone*, *Heartbreak House*, *La Ronde*, *A View from the Bridge*, *The Servant of Two Masters*, Ionesco's *The Chairs* and Sartre's *No Exit*. Some of these plays became part of a personal repertoire that I've since directed frequently, with ever-increasing pleasure. I had a permanent company and learned painfully to deal with the challenges of several Methodised actors. Their moments of truth were stunning, but were always about themselves and not their characters. I also learned to work out my daily rehearsal schedules according to who had slept with whom the night before and who had broken up with whom. My job, unofficially, included rushing downtown to the Greyhound Bus Station in the middle of the night to drag actors off departing buses when they'd suddenly decided they just had to get back to New York. It was a period of intense apprenticeship for a very young artistic director. My learning curve was steep. I came to understand that directing was as much about dealing with people as with texts.

When I started directing, I worked conventionally, blocking the actors. I had a clear idea of how every moment should be played and tried to push the actors towards these very detailed results which I then set. I had, I believe, a good instinct for what was meant by the word 'style' and was meticulous in my research and preparation. However, part of my training had been in The Method, at its peak at that time, and amidst its confusions and indulgences, I was struck by the recurring exhortations to 'Play the moment', 'Be in the moment.' I was also greatly thrilled by reading accounts of the rehearsal processes of Stanislavsky, Vakhtangov, Tairov and Meyerhold. Their conditions of work seemed to come from another planet where they had access to full costumes and scenery from the start of rehearsals and worked on one production for as long as they needed, sometimes for more than a year – a far cry from our prevailing one-to-four-week schedules. I had taken a directing class in New York at the now defunct American Theater Wing, given by a playwright, Joseph Kramm, whose claim to fame was a play called *The Shrike*. Twice a week we brought in scenes we'd prepared, begging and borrowing actors wherever we could. After we'd shown them, he would ask the actors what their objectives were. Almost without fail, when the scenes were replayed, they came vividly to life, their previously blurred images pulled sharply into focus. Another of those profound bells tolled the good tidings that objectives were vital to the life of theatre. Through these various influences, I gradually discovered greater and greater freedom in working with actors. From Kramm, I also discovered that good plays were not just what they literally seemed to be about, but were metaphorical.

I came back to England in 1962. The theatre there beckoned with an exciting new energy emanating from the Royal Court. When a good Cincinnati lady had come up to me gushing, 'I just love Isben', I did begin to wonder what I was doing in the Mid-West. I came back to England. And promptly stopped working. Despite my three-year training, some forty productions and the fact that I'd run three companies, I was treated as if I'd just dropped off the moon. I had an interview with Hazel Vincent Wallace, then a doyenne of the English repertory system, who ran the Sybil Thorndike Theatre in Leatherhead. 'You've done quite a lot,' she conceded grudgingly and then, as if she were holding up a dead rat, 'but in *America*!' Within six months, from an ebullient and confident 28-year-old, armed with good reviews and a fairly impressive résumé (American for CV), I became a bitter-and-twisted recluse, full of resentment towards the British theatre establishment, who let me know that I was already passé and that they were only interested in recent Oxbridge graduates. That resentment and sense of not really belonging has never entirely left me. The first directing job I did get, a dreadful Peter Ustinov play called *Photo Finish*, at the Churchill Theatre, Bromley, was conducted for its two weeks' rehearsal with icy politeness between myself and the cast, who let me know that they were having no truck with any American nonsense like improvisation and seemed mainly concerned as to whether they were going to be centre stage, lit in surprise pink or special lavender. I swore to myself that if this was English theatre, I wanted none of it.

I did a variety of odd jobs. I was one of a bevy of stage managers for a *Night of a Thousand Stars*, an annual charity event at the London Palladium. It was a Night of the Thousand Humiliations for me. I upset John Mills and was the only one not wearing a dinner jacket. I knew nothing of the rigid etiquette then still pervading English theatre, where stage management mirrored a below-stairs class structure, the company stage manager functioning as the butler, and assistant stage managers ordered around like tweenies. I caught sight of Edith Evans rehearsing, hatted, gloved, suited and bejewelled as if for lunch at Claridges. At Frinton Rep, I steered a husband-and-wife team called Hannah Watt and Roderick Lovell through their adaptation of *Les Liaisons Dangereuses* in which they played all the roles. They were a handsome, imposing couple, rather large and rather old for the cast of decadents and innocents they'd chosen to embody.

I assisted on a musical called *What Goes Up!* at the Theatre Royal, Stratford East, notable for its very jolly company and the aura of Joan Littlewood which I imagined permeated the very walls around us. The production had nothing to do with her company, Theatre Workshop, but I did, with awe, glimpse her one day, through the half-open door of her office, wearing what looked like a knitted tea cosy. I also directed some small-scale touring operas, including *Die Fledermaus* for a company run by two rather hearty ladies, one of whom went rock-climbing between singing bouts, the other, a lady-in-waiting with very long arms and a limply regal handshake, who played the piano; she had to sit quite far from her instrument to do so. I directed a touring production of *La Traviata* for the Welsh National Opera and had digs in Cardiff with a Mrs Price who used to keep her lodgers up-to-date by reading them items from the morning paper. 'Ngaio Marsh, the novelist, has died,' she informed us all as we chewed our way through eggs, beans, bacon, fried bread and sausages. Most of my time, however, I spent in a bedsit, watching my hairline recede and convincing myself my life was over.

I slowly regained my creative health when I began teaching and directing at LAMDA (The London Academy of Music and Dramatic Art). While there, I came to discover that I was a natural teacher and began to take the steps that evolved into the way I structure my work today. As soon as I started teaching, certain things about the nature of acting, which were still confusing me when I left Carnegie Tech, suddenly became clear. I realised (another bell rang!) that during the three apparently fallow years in which I'd scarcely worked, the unconscious had somehow been freed to solve problems that up to then had eluded conscious solution. This led me to certain ideas about the essentially anti-creative nature of accepted rehearsal structures, more of which later. While at LAMDA, I was hugely influenced by Philip Hedley who was also teaching there. He showed me a lot of liberating techniques from East 15 Acting School and Stratford Theatre Royal, run, of course, by the lady in the tea cosy. Her productions, alive, freewheeling, honest, spontaneous and, in the best sense of the word, popular (never populist), and those of William Gaskill, meticulous, honed to their essentials and equally honest, were strong influences on me at that time and have, I hope, remained so.

My time at LAMDA was interspersed with occasional sorties into rep. Some people, rather discouragingly, still think that *Lady Be Good*, a Gershwin musical I directed at the old Marlowe Theatre in Canterbury, is the best thing I've ever done! While at LAMDA, I collaborated with their singing teacher, Anthony Bowles, a multi-talented musician, on two musicals for the students; I contributed the book and lyrics. One of them played at the Edinburgh Festival from where, thanks to excellent reviews, it was taken up by a West End theatre management who wouldn't let me direct it. For two years of innumerable rewrites and a mediocre provincial tryout, we spent a life of misery in the hope that our suffering would be compensated by fame and fortune when the production reached London. It eventually staggered into the West End, unrecognisable from the show it had first been. It received the sort of notices one could only wish for one's worst enemies. The period involved with this show introduced me to a theatre that was about the abuse of power, the humiliation of actors and, possibly, ways of creating a tax loss. Seeing, at last, my name outside a West End theatre was like ashes in my mouth. It was a turning point for me. The possibility of success weighed against a world apparently devoid of decency, I decided, was an unequal trade-off. I knew then that I wanted to work only where I could try to do what I believed in with like-minded people. Career (success, money) would have to take second place to vocation. The glamour of the West End was a mirage left over from the theatregoing days of my childhood. Since then, forming my own companies is one of the ways I've tried to create my own terms and conditions of work.

After five healthy and productive drama school years, I decided that LAMDA was becoming a cosy womb from which I would never be delivered if I stayed any longer. I somehow knew that clinging to security leads nowhere but backwards. You have to trust that if one door closes, another will open. Sometimes, you have to initiate that possibility by firmly closing one of those doors behind you, yourself. With regrets and immense gratitude, I left LAMDA with no jobs in view, no reputation to speak of, but a growing knowledge of how to work and a great confidence in what I believed theatre should be.

I was unemployed for three months, and then I went to work in Israel. For some while, a lot of offers had been beckoning me in that direction until I thought that maybe some Old Testament deity was nudging me rather heavily to go, not before time, and check out my Jewishness. Oded Kotler, an actor who ran The Actors' Stage, then the most interesting alternative company in Tel Aviv, had seen my work at LAMDA, where his wife had been a student, and gave me my first opportunities there. I was made welcome, learned Hebrew, soon got my own company and theatre, the Jerusalem Khan, created a lot of original material, had a warm response to my work, won prizes and, most important, was able to develop the techniques and processes I'd begun at LAMDA. This was helped in no small way by the Israeli tradition of immensely long rehearsals, inherited from its roots in Russian theatre, the thrilling accounts of which had so inspired me at the start of my career. A sort of creative longing had unexpectedly come full circle. I now consider long rehearsals a necessity and a right, not something for which you should express gratitude, as so many actors, well-meaning but erroneous, think they should ('We're so lucky!' they cry when they discover they have five weeks rather than four). I become anxious and aggrieved if I have anything less than ten weeks. A long way from those weekly musicals in Kennebunkport! Though from them I know I can get a show on in short order should the necessity arise. One project at the Khan, a political documentary about Jerusalem, got me into trouble with various authorities. A newspaper editorial described me as 'foreign poison', and arts journalists who had professed themselves my advocates retreated clumsily from my requests for support. For a while, I had a very faint taste of what it must feel like to be a dissident in a dictatorship. I was vindicated when the Yom Kippur War, a few months later, proved the foresight of our show which, amongst other matters, questioned the public assumption that since 1967, under Israeli authority, the Palestinian population had never had it so good.

For five years I had managed to retain my English calm amidst excitable Levantine temperament, but when I found myself starting to scream at actors and throw props at them (more effective than words), I decided, once more with regret and gratitude, to be on the move again. Yahweh, incidentally, had not revealed Himself to me.

I came back to London very confident in my abilities to start my own company alongside the many alternative theatre groups that were then driving the theatre forward at that time. I formed Shared Experience and ran it for thirteen years. Peter James, then artistic director of the Crucible Theatre in Sheffield, had seen my work in Israel and generously gave me the opportunity, budget and space to launch the company from his theatre. Our first show, telling stories from *The Arabian Nights*, was a tremendous success and got us unusually rapid revenue funding from the Arts Council of Great Britain. The early years of Shared Experience were the most creative of my career. We did one project a year and had long rehearsal periods as well as long tours in which we continued to develop our work. We won awards and an enthusiastic following. I made what I think were genuine discoveries about creating an ensemble, solving complex acting problems, telling stories, adapting novels, playing Chekhov and, most important of all, realising the purpose for the company: my belief that you need nothing else but actors in order to create good theatre. For five years, we did shows in any space we were offered, without any design or technology whatsoever. It was theatre at its purest, stripped to its vital elements: actors and audience sharing the same evenly lit and totally empty space, with the actors transforming themselves into other people in order to act out whatever material – be it story, improvisation or play – we had chosen to perform for the audience.

Eventually, the company became trapped in its own structures and on an Arts Council touring treadmill. At the moment when we were getting the greatest recognition, our work, I felt, was becoming less interesting. I left Shared Experience for the National Theatre, lured there by a vision of art *and* career. At that time there was a policy of directors with their own companies producing repertoires within the National's framework. First, I directed a successful *Cherry Orchard* for the Ian McKellen–Edward Petherbridge company. Then Peter Hall offered me a company of my own. Whereupon I had two four-hour flops: *The Wandering Jew*, adapted from an immense nineteenth-century popular French potboiler, and *Countrymania*, a trilogy by Goldoni, that emptied, respectively, the Lyttelton and the Olivier Theatres. The following year, I worked in China, Australia, New Zealand and Canada, a period rich in experiences. When I came back to London, I felt *persona non grata*, out in the theatrical cold, and did a variety of rather undistinguished jobs from which I learned nothing.

I had never been happy freelancing, so when I had the chance to run the middle-scale touring Cambridge Theatre Company (later converted to Method & Madness) I grabbed it. Naively, I now see, I thought that I could change the nature of what was acceptable in middle-scale theatres and spent almost a decade increasingly ruing my miscalculation. Despite a very joyful collaboration with playwright Philip Osment, resulting in four fine plays; despite two stimulating co-directing stints, one with Neil Bartlett, the other with David Glass, both of whom taught me a lot, as I'd hoped when I invited them to team up with me (my work was rewardingly refreshed by observing it within the context of theirs); despite half-a-dozen engrossing adaptations, and winning a TMA Director-of-the-Year Award, it was a downhill struggle. Eventually, in our eighth year, total lack of support from the touring circuit, ranging from indifference to unsheathed hostility, forced us – after twenty months of the very special three-year project we'd initiated – to disband the ten actors who had courageously pledged themselves to it. I spent a further few months trying to reimagine – reinvent – the company, then gave up and resigned.

I found myself surprisingly happy without a company – words I never believed I'd hear myself even think. I'd been released from the concerns of budgets and bookings, and Arts Council demands for mission statements and staff evaluations, quarterly returns, annual reports, three-year business plans, five-year assessments, marketing policies and 'gesture' education schemes, all the increasingly time- and energy-consuming burdens of most artistic directors. I was free to come and go as I wished and to respond to a variety of offers, both at home and abroad. One from Mark Rylance at Shakespeare's Globe gave me the chance to begin to learn about Shakespeare and to tackle the challenging potential of the Globe stage. There, I encountered what up to then I'd only experienced in Israel – audiences that exercised their right to be part of the performance.

This seems not to be a time for companies. But I still believe that the best theatre comes from a committed ensemble. And what follows will, I hope, explain why.

THE PRIMACY OF THE ACTOR

The Reason Why

Theatre is predominantly the domain of actors. We speak tautologically of live theatre; we proclaim 'live-ness' as its greatest attraction. Rightly so, for without any life there's no theatre, at least not theatre that honours its true nature. And no one brings the theatre to life – or, to be more accurate, brings life to the theatre – but actors. Before actors come on stage, everything about theatre is abstract, theoretical, potential. Actors are the ones who make theatre *happen*, who *turn ideas into experience*. They're the artists through whom all other elements of theatre are mediated: they embody the playwright's words and the director's intentions; a good set is incomplete until actors inhabit it; it is actors who make contact with the audience. Actors are the *sine qua non* of theatre.

In fact, actors are its *raison d'être*. We go to the theatre *because of them*. Actors are more than mere executors of other people's ideas. More vitally, *and in their own right*, they manifest the extraordinary human phenomenon of acting: the ability to embody another person. I believe that at the deepest level of our theatregoing experience, we long to witness this special evidence of our humanity in action. Apart from actors and audiences, everyone else in theatre (and therefore everything else except what actors do) is expendable.

A Little List

Quite some time ago, on one of those not infrequent occasions when I become convinced that live theatre has finally died but just won't lie down, I *sat* down and made lists of what different performance disciplines had to offer. I wanted to discover what was unique – or whether there *was* anything unique – to theatre. What, if anything, made theatre truly itself? Did it have its own purity? Or, as I suspected, might it be no more than a collection of elements begged, borrowed and stolen – or dumped on it – from other art forms?

I'd begun to doubt its validity as a medium. What vitality could it have for a present-day audience? Compared to film, for example, it seemed slow and clumsy; the component parts and participatory skills of most productions were of far too variable a standard, and rarely integrated seamlessly enough to command the sort of absorption achieved so seductively by film. Other burgeoning forms of media seemed to deal much better with anything theatre had to offer. Quite possibly, like many other institutions that we're brought up to look on as eternal facts of life, theatre had, after some two-and-a-half-thousand years, actually passed its sell-by date and should be dispensed with and disposed of. I wasn't too happy with this conclusion; hence the list-making.

My lists confirmed that most of the elements that go to make up theatre could be found elsewhere. I arrived at a fairly standard definition: theatre could be created when two lots of people came together at the same time in the same place, in order for one lot to present something, more or less prepared, to the other lot. It was – that already stated platitude – *live*. So what was new! And so what! Didn't classical and rock concerts, recitals, stand-up comedy, lectures, busking, circus, sports events, even political rallies, fulfil these requirements?

What *did* distinguish it from those other sorts of events, however, was that in theatre *one of the groups of people transformed themselves into yet another group of people before the very eyes of their audiences*. Theatre offered the phenomenon of actors becoming other people, creating the amazing double reality of being themselves in this performance space at this moment and simultaneously other people in another place at another time; being both *here now* and *there then*. But what benefit was to be gained by actors transforming themselves in front of an audience rather than, say, giving a performance on film, shot, lit and edited to perfection? Just that: the audience experienced the transformation simultaneously with the actors. *The audience and actors shared in an act of imagination.* The two groups were brought together by this duality.

This, then, was the essence of theatre, what made it unique and defined its purity. People talk about the magic of theatre, a lazy phrase I don't much admire, but if theatre does have any 'magic', it is our complicity – actors' and audiences' – in an act of imagination, in this double experience of believing that something is happening *when it really isn't happening at all.*[*]

———

The Most Human of the Arts

Theatre is the most human of the arts. Its basic material is three groups of people: audiences, actors and characters – the first two groups complicitly combining their imaginations to create the third, sharing in the double process of transforming the here-and-now into the there-and-then, and bringing the there-and-then into the here-and-now. (This actor in this theatre at this moment is playing Hamlet in Elsinore in some imagined past and making me believe that I am watching Hamlet here in Elsinore now.) This is what theatre does: makes what isn't there, be there; what doesn't exist, exist. I am completely caught up in the

---

[*] By comparison, anything filmed requires no participatory imagination from its audiences in order to exist; pretty much everything has already been done for them; it has been decided in advance exactly what they should see. And anything filmed seems always in the past. This is the possible reason that film seems the most convincing medium for realism: *what we look at must be real because it must actually have happened in order to be filmed.*

story unfolding before me and *at the same time* know that I'm in a theatre watching actors. Both audience and actors are doing two things at once: the human beings on stage are objectively doing their job as actors while subjectively living their characters' lives; the human beings in the audience are objectively appreciating the actors' skills, while subjectively being moved by the characters' stories. This duality is what makes theatre theatre.

The actor is demonstrating our extraordinary human capacity for empathy. In this respect, the only difference between actor and audience is that of degree. Every person is born with the instinct to act and the potential to imagine. The actor has the particular talent to *embody* this act of imagination. The audience responds by augmenting and detailing this imagined world and its characters by means of *their own imaginations*, framing them within the context of their own lives. Ideally, all members of the audience create their own performance, each one recognising and interpreting it from an individual perspective and understanding. This is *genuine* audience participation. All those involved in this shared experience, both actors and audiences, fulfil themselves individually and communally. The actors offer a suggestion, the audience develops it. The actors initiate a transaction, the audience completes it. *Actors and audience bond in a shared act of imagination.*

Audience Participation

In the early, purist, storytelling days of Shared Experience (the actors in their own clothes, in a totally empty, technology-free space, in constant white light that they shared with the audience), we did a ten-hour, four-part performance of Dickens's *Bleak House*. When we began work on this thick novel, it offered us many possible interpretive directions to pursue: the expressionist (Kafka-esque), labyrinthine world of the law; the, then, very right-on, satirical attack on an entrenched establishment; documentary social realism (abused children, poverty); a thriller (this was the first English novel to portray a detective, the first 'who–done–what'); and the psychologically astute autobiography of its heroine. It was also comic, at times to the point of slapstick; and it was sentimental. Which avenue should we go down, which was the tone that should dominate? After long deliberation, it seemed invidious to reduce such rich material to any one interpretive colour. We decided to embrace the book in its entirety to the limits of our collective abilities. When we at length performed it, members of the audience would say to us 'How Kafkaesque!', 'It's so politically relevant!', 'Ah, what a lovely story!', 'What a terrific thriller!', 'I haven't laughed so much in ages!' . . . A French woman summed up the point completely by thanking us 'for allowing me to see my own show'.

At another level of experience, too, audiences had been able to use their imaginations. People, meeting me later, would express their admiration for 'the wonderful lighting in *Bleak House*'. When I assured them that they had watched the show in constant white light without a single change of cue, they insisted on distinct memories of candlelight, chandeliers, firesides, fog and gas lamps in the street. From the evidence we'd put before them, members of the audience had not only made their own personal interpretation of the material, they'd also visualised their own performance. They'd been given the space in which to stretch their creative muscles. The greater the intrusion of other elements (sets, music, lighting) into the relationship between actors and audience, the less the audience's imagination is engaged. Depending on the amount of 'production', audiences shift on a sliding scale from active collaborators to passive consumers. Howard Barker wrote that musical comedy is the most fascistic form of theatre, by which I presume he meant that its ingredients beat the audience into submission by bullying them into preconceived reactions. I think *any* show that tells the audience what to think, what to feel, and how to react, that prods and nudges them as to when they should laugh, cry or sit-up-and-get-the-message, is fascistic.

The application of rigour, on the principle of less is more, is a way of trying to recover theatre's true source of vitality, rediscovering its purity, reinventing its unique nature. Here's a quote from a very fine French director, Jean Vilar:[*]

> *Imagination . . . is that boundless realm which the stage, and only the stage, can represent.* And that is why . . . the stage must be unlimited, unconfined and, if possible, bare. Then the imagination of playwright, spectator and actor delights and rejoices . . . The theatre must be reduced to its simplest – and most difficult – expression: the stage actor or, more precisely, the acting. Hence the stage must not be turned into a crossroad of all the arts . . . The designer must be put in his place . . . Music should be used only when the script explicitly calls for music . . . *In short, all effects should be eliminated which are extraneous to the pure and Spartan laws of the stage, and the production reduced to the physical and moral action of the players. (My emphases.)*

The Three-Dimensional Medium

We live in an increasingly two-dimensional world. We spend more and more time gaining our experience by means of flat screens – computer, television, cinema. There are days when I, who am neither TV surfer nor internet anorak, can spend one third of my waking day looking at virtual reality. Theatre, by contrast, is three-dimensional. For someone raised on two-dimensional images, it must be confusing to participate in a three-dimensional world. It is an innately more complex experience and it demands more interpretative initiative. A rounded person gives

[*] Jean Vilar was the artistic director of the TNP (Théâtre National Populaire) in the 1950s and '60s and the founder of the Avignon Festival.

off more signs and information than a flat one. A dedicated screen-watcher has to (re)discover how to become a stage-watcher in order to deal with the less selected, less controlled complexity of three-dimensional life. It requires more effort than pressing a remote control button or tilting an image. It needs alert and inventive watching – piecing together the evidence into your own narrative. And you can't rewind. You have to travel with a performance at its own rate.

Whatever theatre once was, it now has to exist within the context of these technological media. Which means that it cannot avoid comparing itself with them. Which should mean that theatre ought to exploit those of its elements that make it unique. Instead, it seems to suffer from a sense of inferiority and feel required to justify its existence by borrowing the exciting technology from the new forms of media. By dressing up in other people's clothes, it hopes to retain – regain! – its status, to reverse its dwindling appeal. But, in fact, by allowing alien elements to dominate, it becomes less and less itself without becoming anything other than a dissatisfying hybrid.[*]

This is ultimately self-defeating on three counts: first, however much theatre pursues technology, it cannot aspire to the fluidity and rightness of that technology's existence within its own natural context; second, it will encourage a new audience to believe that theatre is just another of the many branches of technological entertainment and to expect more and more (and better) of the same; third – and most critical – it smothers actors, depriving them of their life, which is the only true life of the theatre.

I don't at all say that technology should never be used, but *it needs to be thought about*, rather than desperately and somewhat mindlessly seized upon as a means of restoring theatre's 'sexiness'. Consider how appropriately Robert Lepage utilises technology to enhance the humanity of his material. It becomes his servant, rather than the other way round. His technology exemplifies the language of theatre: metaphor, transformation, imagination. Compare this with the use of technology, say, in a production such as *The Coast of Utopia*, Tom Stoppard's trilogy at the National Theatre, where the use of moving projections were literal – the contemporary equivalent of realistically painted backdrops[**] – and not in the least metaphorical or transformative or imaginative.

---

[*] There used to be something called 'Total Theatre' that employed a hodgepodge of anything that was going: film, puppets, masks, music, mime, dance, circus tricks, the technology of the time as well as actors and texts; the understanding being that this must be the best sort of theatre as it had everything in it, including, if necessary, the kitchen stove. In reality, these productions were a sort of curiosity, never completely satisfying, one element clumsily annulling and voiding another.

[**] These are merely a more sophisticated version of the rear projections that were fashionable in the '6os, until rightly dismissed as being lazily two-dimensional solutions for a three-dimensional world.

The Dangerous Medium

Theatre can only be really vibrant when it concentrates on what it does best and what it has – which is immediacy and freedom. *Theatre is potentially subversive because it is rough and unpredictable* (if only most of its practitioners would refrain from trying to tidy it up). Anything filmed can never be rough or unpredictable, even if the film-maker allows unexpected images to come before the camera. However the images are achieved, they're finally contained by the necessity of cutting. Chance moments become enshrined in the editing. So it unspools (or whatever digital film does) irrespective of its audience and cannot be other than what it was before it was shown on a screen. Because there's no danger of the actors breaking out of the screen, audiences can watch even the most disturbing images in the secure knowledge they'll come to no harm (that might be why horror films work so well). The film has no immediate life and so we watch it in a dream or state of reverie. It's notable that even in a crowded cinema, we have very little sense of community, of sharing an experience with others. Theatre is potentially more dangerous. Because it's actually taking place at the very moment it's being watched, there's the possibility that anything could happen. Nudity on stage is far more disturbing because the intimacy is real: the actors on a stage are vulnerable; actors on a screen are not. And so we can never really watch a play in the same private dream-state that we do a film. We're all there, actors and audience alike, with our shared awareness of our shared live-ness; theatre is much more a social and collective experience. In the cinema, you snuggle back in your seat; in the theatre, you sit up.* When we come out of a cinema, we're often still in our dream; we walk along streets that are now an extension of the film. When we come out of a theatre (assuming the work is good), we have a greater sense of experiencing the life in ourselves, we feel energised. Theatre *is* open to the unexpected because of the presence of actors who cannot be edited, cannot be controlled beyond a certain point. Live actors – if only most of them would acknowledge this potential in themselves – are dangerous because they're raw, at any moment capable of bursting beyond the confines of theatrical decorum. By dangerous, I don't mean that they should threaten the audience with acts of sex-and-violence but that they have the possibility (rarely taken) of extending our experience of what they're enacting to heights and depths of the most intense and intimate revelation; *to shock us with truth.*

The Intimate Medium

Technology can cater for millions at a go. Out of sheer practicality, theatre can only be seen by hundreds at any one time. Any theatre much larger than a thousand starts to dissipate its human-scale experience. I myself want to get up close and personal with the actors. I want to experience their breathing, their sweating.

---

* The director, Tyrone Guthrie, wrote in his book, *In Various Directions*, that audiences should sit on hard benches to watch theatre productions with appropriate alertness.

Because of scale, theatre can't be other than elitist. It's true that a musical performed all over the world for a generation will have eventually been seen by millions. But each one-off experience is for the few. And so the specialness of that intimacy needs to be explored and exploited to the full. Intimacy is a vital component of the theatre experience.

The Interactive Medium

Technology makes great claims for interactivity. But the simple, neglected fact is that theatre's the truly interactive medium. Interaction is part of its condition. Just by sitting, observing and responding in the most natural way, an audience creates interaction with the stage. Depending on the format of a production, this can be developed by any degree to the point where the audience actually goes into the performance space and mingles with the performers or the performers invade the auditorium. Technology will never achieve that degree of interactivity for the simple reason that its essence is based on bringing something from a distance in space and time. Even as voyeurs of the goings-on in the Big Brother house, we can never see more than we're shown, we can never really be there. Imagine how much more excitingly prurient it would be actually to spy on the inmates through holes in the wall.

The Ephemeral Medium

Every performance is born and dies within its chosen length. It cannot be recorded, held, locked. Theatre has as much to do with time as with space. Possibly more. The ephemerality of theatre is yet another reason not to pursue the futile attempt to recreate what has already happened. We can do this no more than we can recreate a moment in our actual lives; any experience has too many variables beyond our control. Isn't the desire to recreate, say, a rapturous experience of love-making totally ruined by that desire. You can never quite repeat what's gone. Even athletes, gymnasts, dancers – all those who are skilled at using their bodies with the utmost precision and technical control – cannot guarantee to bring their bodies repeatedly to the exact same state just by their determination to do so. During a performance, we're all growing older together, actors, audience – and characters. The transience of theatre is part of its uniqueness, its poignancy. As soon as it's happened, it's gone.[*] (Photographs, recordings and written accounts can never recreate the actual experience.) Its only trace remains subjectively in our unreliable memories.

---

[*] I have a theory that if film spontaneously combusted after it was screened and couldn't be replayed, it would eventually become – for many people – like theatre, another branch of literature, evaluated through its screenplays.

The Transcendent Medium

Over a hundred years ago, the advent of electric light and theories of the unconscious brought naturalism to the theatre. But film and TV can 'do' naturalism far more convincingly. Those nice plays that fed the theatre for most of the twentieth century with their 'sort-of' realism are now as dead as dodos. Theatre is metaphorical and imaginative, suggestive – never literal. Personally, I love naturalism from time to time, but the sort of inner naturalism – something akin to the intensity of an Ingmar Bergman close-up – that allows a 'baring of the soul'. This goes hand in hand with the intimacy of small spaces and the ability of actors to transcend themselves: their potential to explode the confines of the expected and accepted and to transport us beyond our normal world. Only actors can do this – not directors, writers, designers and technicians, who can only prepare the ground for take-off.

What I'm proposing places a huge onus on actors. They have to be more than mere entertainers, charmers, interpreters; they must be dedicated craftspeople, artists, who understand that it's their job to expose their humanity to our gaze. This demands actors of prodigious bravery with exceptionally high performance skills that ensure nothing inhibits the release and expression of such revelation. That's what theatre has to offer. And it's possible that most actors don't want to go anywhere near this. The sense of fulfilment could be extraordinary, but the personal cost for many might be too high. *But for theatre to be viable as a unique experience in its own right, that is perhaps what has to happen.*

The Human Medium

I think of the actor as a sort of sacrificial being who, on our behalf and for our benefit, undergoes a sequence of experiences, terrifying, tragic, sad, funny, ridiculous, joyful, celebratory, as though saying to us, 'This is what life's like, isn't it? Do you recognise this? Have you ever thought of life in this way?' The actor manifests our capacity to be vulnerable and daring, sensitive and strong, perceptive and compassionate, to be expressive and to be beautiful. The actor not only stimulates our empathic imagination but also reminds us of our inexhaustible potential as human beings. We all have something of everyone else within us.

If theatre has a purpose, I believe it is this: the revelation and confirmation of the heights, depths and breadth, the multi-dimensional richness, of our shared humanity.

———

The Actor's Job

No boredom is comparable to the tedium that can smother us in the theatre. It's not just a manner of speaking when we say we're dying of boredom, that we're bored to death. Boredom in the theatre really does seem to threaten us with imminent mortality, no doubt because we're being deprived of the very thing we came to the theatre for: a strong dose of undiluted, unpolluted vitality: human energy – *a fix of life itself.* *

When I watch a performance in this state of torpor, I'm overcome by the point-lessness of what's taking place. Why is he pouring a drink, why does she perch on the arm of that chair, why on earth are they crossing and recrossing the stage, why in heaven are they saying those words with such strange emphases, what in hell do those strange gestures mean, what is this meaningless ritual? *What's going on?* My disbelief remains firmly unsuspended. I'm trapped in some Sartrean inferno where hell is not just other people but, specifically, actors who have abandoned the purpose of their craft.

Since actors create the life of theatre, the responsibility for this state of affairs lies firmly on their shoulders – not just on their shoulders in fact, but in their whole being. Good theatre only happens when the actors are doing their proper job: play-ing with immediacy, with vulnerability, which means with complete honesty. We've all seen enough deadly performances of Shakespeare to know that the play, alone, is *not* the thing – even with Armani suits and ravishing lighting.** Have you ever come away from seeing a play for the first time, saying, 'What a wonderful play' and in the same breath, 'The actors weren't good, though'? We can't do without good actors. Bad acting can kill a good play (think of the painful productions of classics we've all endured). On the other hand, good acting can make a mediocre play seem good (take your pick), at least while it's happening. Actors frequently save a writer's bacon, to say nothing of creating a director's reputation!

Building a Home v. Renting Space

Good theatre is hard to achieve. The occasions on which it *is* good are rare, but when they do happen, they're so life-enhancing that they make it worth risking more of those other – deadly – performances in the hope that once again some-thing intensely human will occur. I can count on maybe twice the fingers of both

---

* If energy were the equivalent of drink, our daily intake would no doubt be a wide range of beverages, some more nourishing, some less; some more or less intoxicating; some more or less diluted. But when we went to the theatre, we'd expect the purest, most distilled liquids: the freshest water, the maturest whisky, the finest champagne.

** In *The Empty Space*, Peter Brook coined the term *deadly theatre* to identify the frequent, but not always easily recognisable, experience of a production that is actually dead. Because of the prestige attached to it (classics, stars), high production values (pretty frocks) and deliberately ingratiating performances, the audience can be fooled into believing it's alive.

hands such occasions, spaced over a lifetime's theatregoing, that have – mercifully – given me periodic shots of renewed belief in theatre and reminded me why I first so wanted to be a part of it.

Three of them, conveniently, occurred within a very short space of time in 1975: the Market Theatre from Johannesburg's *Sizwe Banzi is Dead* at London's Royal Court Theatre; *L'Age d'Or* by Le Théâtre du Soleil at their home in La Cartoucherie outside Paris; and a very early preview off-Broadway of *A Chorus Line* at the Public Theater. Subsequently, reflecting on why these three experiences of theatre – a play, a devised piece and a musical – had seemed so exhilarating, I realised that what these very different productions had in common was the unique involvement of the actors in their creation. Athol Fugard had collaborated with his cast of two on a play that reflected their own lives in Apartheid South Africa. The French company's collaboration, distilling a *Commedia* vision of contemporary society, centred on the plight of North African immigrants. The performers in the musical had contributed their autobiographies to the construction of a show about the lives of Broadway dancers. The actors in all three shows wanted the audience to appreciate something both intensely personal to them and at the same time greater than them. Their sense of ownership intensified their commitment to the performance. These three shows reinforced my conviction that actors are the vital force of theatre – and vividly so if they are given the opportunity.

Something of this extra sense of excitement can occur when actors are the original interpreters of a new play. Even if they have had no official input into the text, they will inevitably have contributed to its first performance.* This sense of ownership cannot exist in quite the same way in the performance of an extant text, no matter how great the play or how fine the production. The actors in these cases inevitably function more as interpreters than as creators. When you're part of the creation of a production, you're building your own home; when you interpret, you're renting space. This doesn't mean that revivals don't have their own validity; past achievements are a source of inspiration, the launching pad from which we can take off into the future. We can only seriously build our present on our past, otherwise our foundations for the future will be very shaky. But it *does* mean that, in all circumstances, actors should be allowed the maximum creative space to ensure that those texts live to their fullest.

---

* The sequence of actors who have worked at the Royal Court Theatre since its inception half a century ago as a promoter of new writing tends, for the most part, to be actors who do their proper job well. There have been periods when groups of them have seemed like an unofficial repertory company there. This can't always be said for those who appear at our other theatrical institutions. After all, it must be difficult for the actor playing yet another Macbeth not to be thinking 'How am *I* going to play him? What can *I* do with the role?', rather than to ask himself 'What's in the play?'. The truer the actor to the play, the freer he is. Pursuing the text to the best of one's understanding demands good practice, whereas concern for oneself encourages bad.

Live Theatre, Open Theatre

When I formed Shared Experience Theatre Company, it was to prove that to make theatre all you needed were actors with a story to tell and an audience to tell it to.* And these were the terms on which we began our explorations: actors and audience in constant mutual awareness; the actors' transformations effected right in front of the audience; the dual nature of theatre (simultaneously here-and-now and there-and-then); the actors' and audience's shared act of imagination; the actors' freedom to create and respond freely at each performance. The actors were the central creative energy of the performance, so it was imperative to strip away all the accretions of theatre practice which, while appearing to help them, were in fact disguising their true identity, encouraging their own evasions and hiding them and the audience from each other with the complicit pretence that, from each other's point of view, neither was there. Costumes, make-up, scenery, lighting, blackouts, sound effects, curtains, proscenium arches, darkened auditoriums, wings, masking, the actors' custom of abandoning the performance for the dressing-room when they weren't in the action – all these seemed to impede the revelation of what made theatre theatre. Lighting and sound scores (especially music) manipulated the audience and reduced the actors' purpose in being there; their imagination and that of the audience were, much of the time, deprived of their function. Nor was a play vital to a performance. Many other sources of material could be valid, from narrative poetry to improvisation, and these could be expressed through many forms – mime, dance, song and so on . . . These realisations cleared my theatrical decks of a lot of clutter. I began to see a way in which theatre could have its own validity.

Since theatre *was* live, how wasteful, let alone perverse, not to exploit that uniqueness, not to investigate fully what it *really meant* for theatre to *be* live. Since human beings were the most important element of theatre and actors the generating force of a performance, it seemed illogical not to take advantage of human unpredictability. Theatre should be treated as a living process rather than a product pre-packaged for passive consumption. The more traditional treatment of the actor as a reasonably intelligent robot, programmed to repeat more-or-less the same vocal, physical and emotional patterns night after night, denied the only thing that theatre actually had to offer: life. When we live fully, we're creative, spontaneous, curious, enterprising, responsive to others . . . Theatre, to be theatre, had to express these qualities. In brief, *the performance had to be open-ended, not fixed.*

It seemed, too, a distortion to give so much emphasis to the other elements of theatre before the central power of the actor had first been developed and

---

* I include story as a natural adjunct to the actors' transformation into characters; after all, once they've been evoked, what are those characters supposed to do if they have no story?

exploited to the full.* Maybe that's why so much theatre seemed so hollow behind its slick exterior. Cynical directors could disguise the lack of life in their actors by the vibrancy of music, lighting and, increasingly, high-technology. Edna Everage used to wave a bright chiffon scarf at those in the audience she identified as 'foreign persons'. 'They're happy with a bit of colour and movement,' she would say, vigorously flapping it in their direction.

There's no point in pursuing an ideal of external, polished perfection in a medium that simply doesn't offer that sort of possibility. Things can go wrong (a source of challenging possibilities to a lively actor) in a way that can never happen, say, with film. The actor is a vulnerable human being, both fallible and capable of inspired resourcefulness. Technology, too, has a way of sabotaging a performance: revolves jam; computerised lighting boards can take on a life of their own and decide to run through their entire sequence of cues in rapid succession. But unlike actors, technology cannot adapt or improvise its way out of a mishap. Audiences, too, have a will of their own (though you might never know it from their often lemming-like conformity) and the energy of their collective concentration has a huge influence on the nature of a performance in a way that can never happen in a cinema, unless movie-goers took to invading the projection booth. At their crudest, audience members arrive late and leave early; some have all too identifiable laughs; theatrical moments can be so alarming that some have been known to faint! At their most sensitive, entire audiences can hold their collective breath and give the actors the most thrilling sense of a shared experience. All this inevitably draws attention to the double reality of theatre. *Theatre is essentially a rough medium. It can never be completely controlled. Because it's live, life has a way of breaking in on it. Therefore it would seem logical to welcome this element of uncertainty, of possibility, of the unexpected; to embrace life's intrusions creatively, rather than trying to block them out.*

As part of the audience, I could feel our collective discomfort during a realistic production when a well-known actor's hat fell from his lap to the floor. He never attempted to pick it up but sat trying to pretend it hadn't happened. The hat lay there commanding greater and greater focus from the audience the longer it remained undealt with, sucking all the energy out of the moment, a dumb but embarrassingly expressive condemnation of the falsity and deadness of this performance in which spontaneous life had been denied.

A theatre production is repeated for a certain period of time during which the actors continue to lead their lives, have experiences, grow and change. So why

---

* If this sounds like a puritanical diet of empty spaces, I'll qualify this by saying that the voluptuousness of design (that includes sound) can be wonderful, but must be absorbed into the fabric of the actors' work so that they are always in creative control of it and not, as so often happens, swamped by it (*see*: PRODUCTION).

shouldn't they also be able to do so within their roles? The actor's growth and change in real life should feed the life of the character; subsequent insights that were not realised during rehearsals (and of course what doesn't get discovered in rehearsal is immeasurable and unknowable) should be allowed their expression within any performance in which they materialise.

An open-ended performance becomes exponentially richer. Beyond the actor's own personal discoveries is the stimulation provoked by partners who are similarly making new choices that of course demand new responses. Actors who play truthfully can't help but accommodate each other's fresh impulses, which automatically create further fresh moments. There is also, as noted, the stimulation of different audiences at each performance who by their particular collective perception may reveal new aspects of their performance to the actors and elicit fresh responses from them.[*] This cross-fertilisation, this complex of fresh stimuli, creates a proliferation of details, textures, perceptions; *the experience of life itself*.

Open-ended playing would seem the natural way for the actor to proceed, but common practice is counter-intuitive and prefers to set things. The reason for this is the fear of vulnerability: the actor's fear of exposure and the director's feared loss of authority (*see*: ACTORS AND DIRECTORS in UNCLOGGING THE WORK). But if theatre isn't vulnerable, it's not human. If a production is drilled to within an inch of its life, even that inch of life eventually dies in automatic repetition and mechanical energy.

If a production is sealed off after it opens, if directors feel it's their main business to get the show up to scratch for the press night,[**] if actors are condemned to repeat more or less the same pattern of performance night after night, all they can do is refine and polish what already exists. A long-running production, un-nurtured, can easily become a slick and empty display. Actors, having a deep instinct for survival, rapidly develop an effective muscle memory that can easily take over without their even realising they've gone onto auto-pilot. I know of actors, who, in the middle of performances of long runs, have suddenly forgotten what scene they're in – somewhat like waking abruptly out of a dream – or, rather, finding themselves in a nightmare!

---

[*] Before we gave our first performances of *The Arabian Nights* (in fact, the very first performances of Shared Experience), we assumed – hoped – the audience might find the material funny, surprising, sexy, delightful. They did indeed find it all these things. We were happily thrown, however, when the audience's response told us they also found it moving, tender and affirmatively erotic. Those early audiences taught us a lot about our material, taught us to appreciate the range of what we'd achieved.

[**] This estimate of what really matters is compounded by most theatres where, after this all-important date, the director has to fight for any time with the actors.

Often, literally *right after* a final performance, actors suddenly realise how a scene or aspect of character that evaded them through the entire run *could have been played*. Once released from the strictures of the fixed production, their unconscious creativity is unblocked and – too late – they're free to imagine and create! Why should a human being be forced to become little more than a sophisticated copying machine? The actors' creativity should be continuously at play for the entire life of the performance. There's no limit to the discoveries that imaginative and open actors can make. There's no such thing as a definitive performance. If there were, audiences wouldn't return again and again to see the same plays.

I believe, in fact I *know* from my own practice, that a production can be developed through rehearsals in such rich depth that the WORLD OF THE PLAY becomes profoundly absorbed into the actors' psyches. They feel so familiar with this world, its space, its conventions and the relationships within it, that it gives them the security to play openly and freely every night. The external structure of fixed patterns and deliveries is replaced by strong inner structures. Each performance should be a *disciplined* improvisation in which the *'what'* (text and, to a certain degree, ACTIONS and OBJECTIVES) remains unchanged, but the *'how'* (the execution of these) can vary. *This is not change for the sake of change, but for the sake of being alive and true to each moment as it occurs.* Tonight is not like last night and certainly not like a rehearsal several weeks ago. The performance is open to the possibility of increased fluidity, sudden revelation, greater intensity, *creative joy*. Such exhilaration is not only the experience of the actors, but also transfers itself to the audience. They'll probably believe that what they're seeing is what every other audience has seen, but, without understanding its source, they'll certainly experience the vitality and freshness of a genuinely creative moment.

If actors know in advance how their partners are going to deliver a line or play a moment or, indeed, how they themselves are going to respond to that line or moment, there can be no spontaneity, no surprise, no risk and therefore no true creativity – the actor is safe, playing a facsimile of what once was. What was truthful and spontaneous in rehearsal dies a little each time it's repeated. However skilfully an actor contrives to keep a repeated pattern alive, there comes a time – after a few days, a couple of weeks, maybe a month if they're lucky – when it's going to become stale and then dead. The laws of entropy and diminishing returns kick in. All that's left is the external representation of a moment, while the impulse that created it has withered away. An actor cannot pretend to be spontaneous (*vide* the rictus, the fake, strained, grimacing energy of some musical-comedy performances). Honesty only occurs *when something really happens between actors for the first time*. Everything else is no more than very skilful repetition. And though adroit skills of delivery may fool many people much of the time, the audience deserves at very least the occasional possibility of experiencing those thrilling moments that seem mostly to happen during rehearsal. Then the performance grabs us by the lapels and we find ourselves sitting forward in our seats drawn into the action with a totally different sense of alive-ness.*

If it isn't totally clear by now, I define theatre as an artistic medium in which the essential element are actors who, in front of an audience, transform themselves into other people, spontaneously and openly acting out stories; and in which everything else serves to enhance this phenomenon. What follows describes ways of supporting and reinforcing this particular vision.

---

* A few years ago there was a production of *A Doll's House* at the Playhouse in which Janet McTeer played Nora. I have no idea exactly how open or closed the production was (I sense it was more the former than the latter), but she kept playing moments of such inspired immediacy that made me quite literally sit forward in my seat with excitement and anxiety for the fate of a character in a play that I'd read and seen more times than I can remember. These experiences, far too rare, renew one's faith in the power of theatre. Great work is, quite simply, inspiring; mediocre work is reductive – it robs you of energy.

PERMANENT TRAINING

The Mystery of Rehearsals

Sometimes, in the middle of a rehearsal, when the actors are playing some sophisticated version of Grandmother's Footsteps (this is what we get up to in rehearsal), or when one of them is incoherently demanding attention for a problem that appears to have nothing to do with the work in hand, or when I'm suddenly hit by the total unreality of a scene being worked on so earnestly, I wonder what on earth we're all doing in this room. Outside, the rest of human-kind – useful, responsible citizenry – goes about its business while we stay indoors, exploring our feelings and motivations. Working in the theatre can feel like an exercise in irrelevance and self-indulgence.

What goes on in a rehearsal remains a mystery to everyone but the participants. Even directors know very little about each other's work because they rarely observe each other in action. If they *are* curious, they tend to get an actor into a corner and enquire in an offhand way how such-and-such a director goes about his or her business. Actors, after all, are the ones who should be in the know. With luck, they'll have worked with quite a few directors. However, for various reasons – they may be called to rehearsal only for their own scenes and not have a sense of the whole; they may be too absorbed in themselves to take in what's happening around them; the work may be too chaotic to bear description – it's frequently the case that their view of rehearsals is selective or partial. Often, quite simply, it's difficult to explain what's going on.

This has nothing to do with a desire for mystification, but everything to do with the nature of the work, which is the complex relationship between a group of people struggling to create something three-dimensional, living and breathing, out of an idea – at most, from a two-dimensional page. A large part of rehearsal is a search, and while nothing appears to be happening, it is then, more likely than not, that something is developing beneath the surface. This can be boring for an uninformed observer (sometimes for the participants too). But rehearsals are not about entertaining whoever's there. Of course, rehearsals should be carried out in a spirit of *creative play*, but we're there to work, not to amuse ourselves. When things are going well, the former rewards us with the latter. When actors do suddenly burst into flower, it may well be the result of the previous week's drudgery and frustration. The casual observer can never understand the full implication of that moment. Many laypeople's idea of an actor, if they have one at all, is of someone out of whom character, emotion and 'timing' pour effort-lessly and to order. The cliché, 'How *do* you remember all those words?' suggests that all they can pinpoint as the actor's actual job is the learning of text; everything else is presumed to come naturally.

———

Actor Training

This false impression of how actors work is compounded by the boast of certain actors, mainly from earlier generations, that they haven't had any training ('Never had a class in my life!'), the implication being that you either 'have it' or you don't, and those that study do so because they, less talented beings, need the help and, what's more, theories about acting get in the way of the natural actor. They tell you that what they've learned, they learned on the job, which means, mostly, that they've picked up (bad) habits, tricks and short cuts, reductive ways of saving their skins rather than releasing their creativity. No doubt, some talented actors succeed without formal training, but they're the exceptions rather than the rule.

Crudely, what drama schools used to teach or what actors would pick up learning on the job were largely a set of external techniques for making sure their faces could be seen and their voices heard. When I studied theatre in the States at Carnegie Mellon, we had three acting teachers, one of whom was an actress who had played Abbie in the original production of O'Neill's *Desire Under the Elms*, and was rumoured to have been his mistress. In her classes, we used to repeat, *ad nauseam*, exercises which involved opening and closing doors, looking out of windows, kneeling and standing, all with our upstage foot slightly ahead of the downstage foot, props held in our upstage hand, so that we would be more open to the audience. Whenever we moved upstage, we had to do so on a complicated and totally artificial S-curve so that as much as possible of our face was turned to the audience for as long as possible while executing this manoeuvre. There was certainly a degree of common sense about these rather narrow skills, but they are hardly intrinsic to the complex business of acting and, if necessary at all, would be so at the end of the work, not at the start. In work on text, she subjected us to rigid line-readings with great emphasis put on stressing the right word. Again, if the actor hasn't found the logic of a speech through the truthful playing of the scene, this might function as a last resort. There was the great day when a student had to deliver the line: 'When the sun shines on the Riviera, it's raining in Merthyr Tydfil.' 'No, dear,' said our mentor whose name was Mary Morris, 'you're not contrasting Riviera with Merthyr Tydfil sufficiently.' 'When the sun's shining *on the Riviera*, it's raining *in Merthyr Tydfil*.' 'Good, dear, but now you've forgotten to compare sun and rain.' 'When *the Sun's Shining on the Riviera, it's Raining in Merthyr Tydfil*.' 'I can't hear "When", dear.' '*When The Sun's Shining On The Riviera, It's Raining in Merthyr Tydfil*'. 'No, no, no, dear – now you're HITTING EVERY WORD!'

What was considered learnable was a series of external skills; all the rest, the inner life, was presumed to be the natural talent of the actor for which no training was any use whatsoever. ('Touch it and the bloom is gone.') I've known actors who superstitiously don't want to know how they work ('Don't tell me what I was doing!' they scream), as though self-knowledge would pull down the entire edifice of their careers. Acting can never be an exact science but there *are* techniques for negotiating scenes, developing the imagination, releasing emotions and focusing the will. Acting schools are now considerably more enlightened than they were, so it's possible for actors – and it behoves them – to learn the tools of their trade in a coherent manner rather than piecemeal, 'on the job'. But two or three years of drama school should be just the beginning of a lifetime's development.

Other performers – singers, dancers and musicians – know they cannot sing, dance or play an instrument without intense and specialised training. Indeed, their lives are accompanied by continuous coaching, study and exercise. (Dancers know that if they don't take a daily class, their muscles will seize up.) Whatever their natural talent, it needs skills and structures to release its potential. Actors know little of such rigour. A human being's potential is inexhaustible, but most actors seem to settle for a sort of competence. Their potential remains largely unchallenged. Indeed, most casting directors and many directors, too, abet this; they want actors for exactly what they've done before and exactly as they are. They like the security of a known product. For them, actors are a commodity like soap powder, the more predictable the better, and the less they confuse their possible employers with options and choices, the better. The profession is ecologically wasteful, destructive. It uses up its most valuable resource (actors), but does nothing to nurture or replenish what it devours. It's an unspoken assumption that there will always be a constant flow of fresh actors coming on stream. But, like cod or oil, the source may one day dry up; people who might have the urge to act may realise what a mug's game it is for the majority of the profession and curb their impulses. Some of the larger theatre organisations talk about furthering the actors' training, but make little more than perfunctory gestures in that direction. Nobody gives a damn about an actor's growth. So actors have to take the fate of their development into their own hands.

This contrast in attitude to training lies largely in the perceived demands of different performance skills. Anyone can see that to sing, dance or play an instrument requires exceptional abilities well beyond the norms of everyday life. It's given to relatively few, say, to dance Petipa, sing Wagner or play Liszt. You have to master incredibly demanding techniques and then keep on top of them for the rest of your career. And, to a certain degree, you cannot cheat. At very least, you have to be seen to get on point or heard to hit that note right in its centre. On the other hand, all that actors are seen to do, mostly, is talk and walk about, displaying attitudes and emotions common to us all. In theory, anyone can do what actors do. This in a way is true: part of the actor's job *is* to reveal what is common to us all.

However, they should do so in a way that is heightened, selected and resonant. The Victorian actor, William Macready, unexpectedly, has something to say on the subject:

> One of the disadvantages incident to the pursuit of the theatrical act is the supposed facility of its attainment, nor is it less cheapened in public estimation by the general assumption of the ability to criticise it. How frequent, to questions of opinion on other arts, are the evasive answers, 'I am no judge of poetry'; 'I have never studied pictures'; 'I do not know much about sculpture.' Yet the person confessedly ignorant on these subjects, would be at no fault in pronouncing a decisive judgement on 'the youngest of the sister arts where all their beauty blends!' [i.e. acting!] . . . It surely needs something like an education for such an art and yet that appearance of mere volition and perfect ease, which cost the accomplished artist so much time and toil to acquire, evidently leads to a different conclusion with many, or amateur acting would be in less vogue.

Employable dancers nowadays must have a practical knowledge of many disciplines – classical ballet, Graham, jazz, tap, Laban, acrobatics, for starters . . . Can actors similarly offer their directors competence in, say, Stanislavsky's physical actions, Michael Chekhov's psychological gestures, Laban's efforts, Meyerhold's biomechanics. Grotowski's cat, Meisner's repetitions and Boal's forum techniques . . . ? (And would many directors know to ask for any of these?) The irony is that by comparison, actors, who work with their entire being – body, voice, emotion, will and interpretative skill, *whose job, I believe, is ultimately the most demanding* – hardly train at all. This may account for the rapturous and endless applause that greets dance and opera performances and rarely finds its way to straight theatre.[*] Possibly I idealise the rigour of other disciplines, but from where I stand, that particular grass often looks greener.

---

[*] The ecstatic response to some 'physical theatre' (but all theatre's physical) is maybe a corollary of this. The more energy the performers appear to be expending – no matter how unskilful the execution – the greater the audience's approval. Who screams and cheers after displays of delicacy? But I fear these are barbaric times. The audience wants blood; the more the performers hyperventilate and perspire, the more the audience likes it. They can see they're getting their money's worth. The response to some performances is more akin to that of onlookers who crowded the ballrooms of Depression America to watch marathon contestants collapse on the dance floor. I, for one, certainly don't want to see the effort; it tells me that the performers don't know their job.

The Art That Conceals Art

The good actor's art is the art that conceals art. The naturalness, the effortlessness that Macready refers to, takes extraordinary skill and dedication. Unfortunately, just because acting for the most part appears to consist of walking and talking (remember: all that other stuff – emotion, 'mimicry' – are supposed to come just naturally), actors themselves are complicit in undervaluing their own craft. They aren't much good at talking about their work and they don't much help matters when they do. When interviewed, they indulge in anecdotes about dropping props, 'drying' (forgetting lines) or 'corpsing' (laughing uncontrollably when something goes wrong on stage – a sort of hysteria), all of which merely trivialises their work. Revealing their private superstitions, the lucky charms that accompany them to their dressing-room tables to be wedged in their dressing-room mirrors, only compounds this. They may gush indiscriminately about the talents of their colleagues or writhe in agonies of incoherence, attempting to describe the indescribable – their private processes. At such moments, they come across as arch or pretentious, narcissistic or downright stupid. This is not totally their fault. The process of acting *is* elusive, hard to define, and whatever language does exist is notoriously imprecise. ('It feels like . . . '; 'I have a sense of . . . ') There is inevitably much use of the words 'I', 'me', 'my' connected to words like 'feeling' and 'instinct', that adds unfairly to the image of the actor as totally self-absorbed. But as actors are their own instrument, what else *can* they talk about? Unlike music and dance, which – as a bottom line of communication – do at least have concrete vocabularies, theatre has no common language from which to start work (apart from simple instructions like 'stage left', 'stage right' – and some actors have problems even with those). If I were to ask twenty actors and directors what they understood by, say, an action or a beat, I'd be likely to get twenty different replies. Even a request for more energy isn't as precise as it might seem. Whenever I watch session musicians coming together for the first time, I envy their ability to make some immediate sense of the music they're playing. What pleasure, what a relief, to be able to come to the first day of rehearsal, tap your baton and have the actors make good sense of their text and look as if they were working together. But it can take a long time before a group of actors show any semblance of coherence individually or collectively. The musical director at least has the starting point of a basic common language with the musicians. The director has to work out a separate way of communicating with each member of the cast or of initiating a language they all can share. And both take time.

Directors are just as guilty of dereliction of duty as actors are. Most have even less formal training than actors and learn their jobs on the job, mainly at the expense of the actors. If it's easy to walk and talk, it's even easier to tell other people how to do so. It's not difficult to talk a good directorial job; words come cheap. It's less easy to do one.

It's a sort of miracle that productions ever come to fruition, let alone achieve any degree of excellence. You could describe many rehearsal experiences as a group of people who have probably never before worked together, cooped up for far too brief a period in a frequently disagreeable, dark, dirty and noisy space, without a shared language or a shared vision of what they believe theatre to be, in order to create something as profound and complex and as intimate as a performance. Some people stagger through rehearsals by an arbitrary and inconsistent mixture of moment-to-moment decisions ('Wouldn't it be a good if . . . ', ' . . . fun if . . . ', 'Here, why don't we . . . ', 'How about if you . . . ') or of superstitious routines that, with some actors, pass for technique ('I always take a long walk in the park', 'I have to know my moves before I learn my lines', 'I can't work without the real props', 'I find the character when I get the right shoes'). These are really nothing more than habits of limited usefulness that have grown into delusional crutches.

No, acting is not an exact science, but if other professions proceeded with the same lack of a shared language, knowledge and rigour, buildings would crash, bridges collapse and patients die on operating tables as a matter of daily routine. Actors are physical, emotional, mental – and, if you like, even spiritual – athletes; they should treat themselves as such and those that work with them should treat them with appropriate care, expectations and demands. Acting at its best is an act of bravery. Nothing lies between actors and their audiences' observation of every aspect of their physicality, taste, sensibility and intelligence. To face such scrutiny, the actor needs to be master of many skills.

Acting is hard. That some actors seem to compound this fact with the determination not to continue to develop their skills seems a form of complacency, if not insanity. Or fear – fear of having to learn things that might disturb their sense of themselves and how they already function. True, it must be painful to face the fact that for many years you could have been going about your work in a far more creative and productive way than you actually do. It can be more comfortable to avoid this sort of realisation. This is not dissimilar to the sort of trauma a lot of acting students go through in their first year of study, when they're forced to realise that acting has nothing to do with their fantasies of what it might be – showing off (those inclined to comedy), going on an emotional binge (those inclined to tragedy) and having lots of fun, money and fame.

The process by which an actor creates a performance is mysterious, elusive. I could never say that I understand precisely how a particular actor, even one I know well, actually thinks and feels and imagines. I can make reasonable guesses, which come from experience and sympathetic observation. I work with the faith bred of trial and error that if I offer a series of suggestions or instructions (input), the actor will more often than not produce a series of appropriate responses (output). The more I develop a shared language with the actor, the more reliable this process becomes.

———

A Way of Working

I believe that there *can* be a shared language and a shared process of work, *certainly as a point of departure*, and that if a group of people understands each other's language and processes, we save time, avoid a lot of unnecessary confusion and gain greater coherence. For better or for worse, I've evolved a way of working. I don't want to call it a method as that tends to lead to confusion with 'The Method' with which it has only a passing connection. Let's call it a process of work. This process has evolved over a long period in which I've begged, borrowed and stolen other people's exercises or modified them to my own requirements. I've also invented many of my own. As time's gone on, I've jettisoned some procedures that grew less useful. Some have been elbowed out by others I found more specific or that dug deeper. Some I've simply grown out of; good in themselves, they've gone stale for me. There's been a continuous movement and adjustment, elaborating something here, simplifying something there, replacing, reordering, rethinking. For most of the time, this, too, has been a living process.

Each step of the way has its particular purposes.* But each step should be taking the actors on an ultimately coherent journey. There exist innumerable excellent exercises and improvisations, but you have to know why you're using them. An exercise may be good in itself, but it also has to have relevance to the context in which it's placed. A particular exercise can take on a different emphasis depending on how and when it's set up. I've observed some directors starting rehearsals with games and improvisations, all great fun, then abruptly halting them at some point in the schedule, never to refer to them again, as they embark on a totally conventional pattern of rehearsal. This brings virtually nothing to the actual performance and leaves the actors with a feeling of *coitus interruptus* or, at least, of precious time having been wasted. Gestures are being made to a way of working that is neither really understood or quite trusted. *But improvisatory work and training have to be continuously blended throughout the rehearsal in a sustained manner so that the actors' techniques and discoveries become organically embedded in the development of the performance.* Working on a text through exercises, improvisations and non-linear techniques is radically different from working one's way, more traditionally, from scene to scene, mainly though discussion, and requires a totally different mindset. Discussion usually means negotiating on behalf of a preconceived result. *The route of improvisation is a search for possibilities.*

I've evolved this work in an attempt to serve and honour as fully as possible the actors' autonomy and humanity. I've sought ways to provide them with the greatest

---

* Most good exercises have more than their one obvious purpose. For example, breaking down the play into actions is ostensibly to make the actors conscious of the concept of action, about what they are doing to each other. But in addition, it allows them to experience the surface journey of each scene and, accumulatively, the play; it brings them into the habit of good contact with each other; it gets them moving freely in the space; it reveals character traits . . . and so forth.

creative space appropriate to each project, in which to maximise their imagination and expressiveness, living in the moment, continuously spontaneous, growing and deepening in their roles to the last moment of the final performance.

——

More Words of Warning

A few beginning directors have sat in on some of my rehearsals and then immediately tried, too literally, to apply the processes they'd observed – with disastrous results. It's clear they hadn't fully digested the intentions behind what they'd seen, and had only dealt with the surface. I'm aware that, in an attempt to avoid this happening with readers, I may have detailed the instructions for some rehearsal techniques more elaborately than might be wished. But I'm trying to be as precise, as specific as possible in their description. I suggest that anyone interested in trying them out should take the time to absorb them calmly and thoroughly before embarking on their practical application.

What I'm describing in this book is a way of working I developed for myself. *All the choices, structures and sequences are what I created to solve my own personal artistic aims.* I'm in no way advocating a system that must be slavishly followed. By all means, embrace the spirit of the work but (a) use only those processes that seriously connect with you, that you understand in some depth and can therefore justify for your actors; and (b) use them in any order that makes sense to you and in any way that blends with your own processes. You may quite possibly find fresh applications for them. I'm not saying, 'You must do it this way', but, rather, I'm encouraging you to think along similar lines about theatre and to develop your own rehearsal processes that will release the actors' creativity in a form of theatre that's *genuinely alive*.

2
CONCEPTS

PROCESS V. RESULT

Stanislavsky Turns Gently in His Grave

I want to define the principle concepts of the techniques I use in rehearsal before I describe the actual process of putting them into practice. Some of them are based on Stanislavsky's System of Physical Actions, and of course you can read about that in many other books, not least his own. Most acting books refer to his techniques in some degree and most drama schools do deal with them, but I'm always suspicious as to how thoroughly. I've met few actors for whom the playing of actions and objectives is second nature, as I believe it should be. Most actors know about them, but seem to regard them as something interesting you might apply now and then, rather than essential to the craft of acting. Actors will say to me, 'Oh, yes, such-and-such a director used them with us. M'm, very good!' But, no, they haven't used them since. I think one reason that actors don't use them as a matter of course is that objectives and actions implicitly deny the possibility of a repeatable result. If you genuinely play an action, you can never exactly reproduce a moment you've played before. The principle of an action is process-orientated rather than result-orientated.

Fresh Air v. Stale Air

I stated at the start of this book that theatre is by its nature live. But that doesn't mean any old live-ness. It's not enough for actors to drag their bodies on stage and repeat some learned patterns of behaviour. That act alone doesn't guarantee the particular quality of life necessary to give theatre its vitality – or validity. It merely offers us the equivalent of poor-quality air recycled into the cabins of some airlines. Good acting functions differently. Understanding the distinction between acting by result (closed, dead) and acting by process (open, live) is fundamental to the creation of real life on stage and impinges on everything else to be discussed. You cannot play an action spontaneously if you already know how you're going to do it. All actors, I'm certain, would tell you they do sincerely try to play each moment as if for the first time. But surely it's easier and more natural to play it, not *as if* it were for the first time, but actually *for* the first time.

What and How

Of course, the actor can't avoid knowing *what* will happen next and *what* is about to be said. But in performance the *how* is the thing that matters. The *how* gives the *what* its vitality and specificity. We can read the *what* at home. The *what* (the play) is a blueprint, not the thing itself. We return continually to see certain plays in the hope of discovering something new about them. This can only mean that each time we revisit a classic, we expect the actors to provide us with something fresh about the text, characters and situations; for no one else but the actors can do that: invest the basic *what* with a fresh *how*. Directors can – and do, with their designers – fill the stage with visual clues as to how we might look anew at a text and, of course, point the actors in certain interpretive directions; but *only the actor can play the specific, detailed, moment-to-moment choices*, choices which are frequently too subtle, too instinctive, too fleeting and too complex for verbal explication and are therefore, in a sense, *beyond the director's reach and exclusively the business of the actor.*

Any scene and any line of text can be played in an infinite number of ways; we know there's no such thing as a definitive performance. So if the text is always legitimately open to interpretation and if the interpretation can vary from production to production (in fact we expect it), why shouldn't it vary from per-formance to performance *within* one particular production. What law of theatre dictates that each production is allowed only one choice of interpretation per line or per moment!

Stanislavsky's work supports this flexibility. It's based on the simple perception that in life we're driven by WANTS – needs and intentions that motivate us to carry out a range of actions in an attempt to fulfil those WANTS. As in life, so in the theatre: the actor-character functions in exactly the same way. This way of play-ing is based on intention rather than result. Actors working this way ask a differ-ent question from that asked by actors who fix their performances: '*What* does my character want at this moment?' as opposed to '*How* shall I play this moment?': process versus result; open versus closed. The former *allow the how to reveal itself from moment to moment*; the latter *decide in advance on the how for the foreseeable future of the production*, either by choosing from several options that emerged in rehearsal, or by discussion (i.e. negotiating) with the director and other actors in the scene ('If you play your line like that, then I can play mine like this!'). Such a choice often depends on the determination of the person with the highest status rather than on the requirements of the text. This is a reductive option; a denial of the actor's full creative potential (a potential that even some actors deny them-selves) or a refusal to accept it. Moments pregnant with who-knows-how-many rich possibilities are reduced by ego and fear to the false security of one.

Process and Results in Practice

Process-led actors build an internal structure of intentions and actions that liberates them dynamically through time and space. Result-led actors build an external structure of moves, business and line-readings that imprisons them in time and space; what feels to them like security is actually constraint. Process-led actors pursue objectives through actions that spontaneously release whatever feelings are aroused in them by those actions and by their partners' reactions to them. Result-led actors repeat predetermined patterns and try to inject planned simulations of emotions into them. (Emotion is a can of worms I'll open up in due course.) Process-led actors think in character. Result-led actors think about themselves (how they're doing). Actors who play results may give performances that are intelligent (well analysed and well shaped), but incomplete (unfulfilled and unembodied). The external form, devoid of the inner life that created it, becomes a repeated formula, life-*like* but actually life-*less*.* What you get is what you see and what you hear. Such performances tend to lack dimension or subtext. They're exclusively linear. They offer the top line of the score, without any harmonics, any counterpoint, any orchestral richness. You get the simplistic, the obvious, the predictable, the cliché, rarely the revelation or the surprise. One reason why theatre so often seems dull is because the audience is ahead of the actor; they know what the actor is going to play before the actor plays it. At a head-based level of experience, they're as familiar as the actor with the conventionally accepted clichés of how people behave in particular situations. But we're all different, complicated and unpredictable. The actor who works through process is likely to produce an unpredictable choice, one that is revelatory and yet inevitable – because *it's true to that moment and that performance and that performer.*

Sarah and Eleonora

George Bernard Shaw, who wrote about acting with great perspicacity, describes these two sorts of actors by comparing and contrasting the performances of Eleonora Duse and Sarah Bernhardt in the title role of *Magda* (the English title of Hermann Sudermann's *Heimat*), both of whose productions of that play were fortuitously playing in London at the same time: Duse – process, spontaneity, experiencing the role; and Bernhardt – result, calculation, displaying herself in the role. I quote at length from his review in *The Saturday Review* for 15 June, 1895.

> The contrast between the two Magdas is as extreme as any contrast
> could be between artists who have finished their twenty years apprenticeship** to the same profession under closely similar conditions.
> Madame Bernhardt has the charm of jolly maturity, rather spoilt and
> petulant, perhaps, but always ready with a sunshine-through-the-clouds
> smile if only she is made much of . . . her complexion shews (*sic*) that
> she has not studied modern art in vain. Those charming roseate effects
> which French painters produce by giving flesh the pretty colour of

* Again, this is the Deadly Theatre that Peter Brook identified and defined in *The Empty Space.*

** I doubt there are now many actors who would consider even the first three years of their professional work as an apprenticeship or ever think of themselves as apprentices.

strawberries and cream . . . are cunningly reproduced by Madame Bernhardt . . . She paints her ears crimson and allows them to peep enchantingly through the few loose braids of her auburn hair . . . Her lips are like a newly-painted pillar box; her cheeks, right up to the languid lashes, have a bloom and the surface of a peach; she is beautiful . . . and entirely inhuman and incredible . . . nobody believing in it, the actress herself least of all. It is so artful, so clever . . . and carried off with such a genial air that it is impossible not to accept it with good-humour . . . one is not sorry to have been coaxed to relax one's notions of the dignity of art . . . The coaxing suits well with the childishly egotistical character of her acting, *which is not the art of making you think more highly or feel more deeply, but the art of making you admire her,* pity her, champion her, weep with her, laugh at her jokes . . . *and applaud her wildly when the curtain falls.* It is the art of finding out all your weaknesses and . . . fooling you. And it is always Sarah Bernhardt in her own capacity who does this to you. The dress, the title of the play, the order of the words may vary; but the woman is always the same. *She does not enter into the leading character: she substitutes herself for it.*

All this is precisely what does not happen in the case of Duse, *whose every part is a separate creation.* When she comes on stage, you are quite welcome to take your opera glass and count whatever lines time and care have so far traced on her. They are the credentials of her humanity; and she knows better than to obliterate that significant handwriting beneath a layer of peach-bloom . . . Duse is not in action five minutes before she is a quarter of a century ahead of the handsomest woman in the world. I grant that Sarah's elaborate Mona Lisa smile, with the conscious droop of the eyelashes . . . not only appeals to your susceptibilities, but positively jogs them. And it lasts quite a minute, sometimes longer. But Duse, with a tremor of the lip which you feel rather than see, and which lasts half an instant, touches you straight on the very heart . . . Every idea, every shade of thought and mood expresses itself delicately but vividly to the eye . . . there will be no difficulty in understanding the indescribable distinction which Duse's acting acquires from the fact that *behind every stroke of it is a distinctively human idea* . . . Sarah did not trouble us with any fuss about the main theme of Sudermann's play, the revolt of the modern woman against the ideal of home which exacts the sacrifice of her whole life to its care . . . Duse, with one look . . . nailed it to the stage as the impending dramatic struggle before she had been five minutes on the scene. (*My emphases.*)

Shaw goes on like this for almost six pages. The whole review is worth reading.*

A Thought Experiment

Let's imagine the performance of a truly excellent actor, who has skill, charm, wit, expressive physical and vocal capacities; who observes people perceptively and is capable of recreating such observations; who, during the rehearsal period, has made a truthful and committed emotional and intellectual search of the text to discover fresh insights into the role. That actor then, from all those discoveries, has selected and polished a sequence of choices, deemed to be the most appropriate, exciting, satisfying and logical, to link into a performance that will then be more or less repeated for however long the play runs. It would seem to contain everything needed for excellent theatre. Indeed, it does have everything, *except the one thing that makes theatre what it is, that makes theatre unique: it lacks life.* Which means it lacks the truth that comes with immediacy, it lacks the possibility of spontaneous response to others, it lacks creativity in the moment, it lacks surprise, risk, initiative, adventure, lacks everything that brings it alive, everything by which we live from moment to moment. It might as well have been played on film. An artefact is displayed for us but, despite the fact that it moves in space, *nothing is actually happening.* It is not real, it is a simulacrum, a substitute; it is, in fact, a form of virtual reality; not really there, but the formalised memory of something that happened elsewhere (in the rehearsal room). It is not a creation but a re-creation; it cannot therefore be other than a demonstration and, in consequence, self-regarding. *Without playing a genuine action, the actor can do nothing else but demonstrate what he or she already found and shaped in rehearsal.* All this fine and serious work has been locked into a result. And that is what we get, *the remains of the work and not the work itself.*

The Fixed and the Flexible

The nonsense with all this, of course, is that, even in productions that are rigidly fixed, performances do minutely vary. This is because even actors wedded to this concept of acting are, despite themselves, simply not robots and couldn't, even if they wanted to, remain exactly the same. Consequently, actors talk about good nights and bad nights. Bad nights for them are when things *do* change, which they equate with things going wrong! Shows get imperceptibly slower or faster, begin to lose or blur details, the balance of moments shifts. With these actors, variations do not occur within *a creative context*, but by default, that is to say by mistake, out of the actors' control. These changes often cause disagreements ('Why did you move on that line? It totally throws what I do.') or dilemmas ('Oh, that was rather good, do you think we could keep it?'). Such thoughts are irrelevant, indeed inconceivable, for actors whose work is process-orientated, whose imperative is to respond specifically to whatever happens at each moment and to embrace change

---

* In fact, all his reviews are worth a read. He has an extraordinary understanding of what constitutes good acting. He's also very funny. Compare and contrast with our current providers of dramatic evaluation.

as a creative fact. They therefore would never be thrown by what a partner did since that is in fact their need, their stimulation, the *nourishment* of their performance; nor would they consider 'keeping' something, however special that moment had been. *Any future playing of the scene is unlikely ever to build in exactly the same way to that moment*; so they continue to act openly in the anticipation that this moment (and any moment) may contain something equally – or even more – special to be released by the spontaneity of their playing. After all, permanent change is a part of life.

WANT! DO! FEEL!

The 'System'

At its simplest, the Stanislavsky 'system' is: WANT, DO, FEEL.

I want something. Therefore I do something. Consequently I feel something.

What I WANT is an OBJECTIVE. What I DO is an ACTION. What I FEEL is of course an EMOTION.

I want something, but wanting alone will achieve nothing; I have to *do* something about it. To pursue what I want, I have to put my want into action, I have to engage with the world, which means engaging with other people who (I believe) could give me what I want. And this means *doing things* to them, *making an impact* on them, *affecting* them in such a way that *they give me what I want*. Otherwise, I remain passive, internally static, not the best condition for dramatic purposes.

Two Examples

AN EXAMPLE FROM ACTUALITY

Let's say my *objective* is *to persuade actors to embrace the principles of acting that I'm describing in this book*. So to (try to) make this happen, I have to put a series of tactics into action. Technically, I put a series of active verbs into action:

> I *study, read* and *observe* material connected with my ideas; I *develop* and *nourish* my theories; I *assemble* them as coherently as I can; I *seek out* confirmation from other practitioners, past and present; I *corroborate* my work with theirs; I *eliminate* as many contradictions in my arguments as I can and *justify* those I can't to the best of my ability; I *enthuse* about my beliefs to my company of actors and *clarify* any grey areas; I *apply*

appropriate techniques so that I can *guide* them though rehearsals; I *instruct* them, I *urge* them, I *exhort, encourage, demonstrate, define, explain argue, debate, proselytise, suggest, provoke* . . . I *write* a book! I'm doing a whole complex of ACTIONS, large and small, long-term and short, in order to gain my objective – to get actors to work in a particular way (i.e. applying objectives and action!).

How do emotions fit into this equation?

If, having executed all these actions, I find that the actors *dismiss* my ideas, *deride* my enthusiasm, *resist* my blandishments, *express indifference to* my beliefs, *reject* my exercises, *denounce* Stanislavsky as out-of-date or *walk out* on me, I feel angry, frustrated, depressed, humiliated, unhappy, resentful, insecure . . . In short, I have a series of what I'd call *bad* feelings. If, on the other hand, the actors *express enthusiasm* for what I have to say, *work* with a will, *absorb* every pearl that drops from my lips, *extol* Stanislavsky's insights, *embrace* the process and *ask* for more, I feel happy, relieved, joyful, proud, excited, confident, triumphant, loving, complacent . . . I have a series of *good* feelings.

The point is that, *whatever the emotions I feel, they occur spontaneously, automatically, autonomically.* I can do nothing deliberate to elicit a particular feeling (except in the general sense that I lead my life in an attempt to be happy rather than unhappy). They come as a result of my efforts to pursue what I want; they arise in response to the success or failure of my objective. They surface unbidden and frequently *unexpected as to kind and degree* – it isn't always the expected emotion in a particular circumstance that emerges.

AN EXAMPLE FROM 'THE SEAGULL'

In the following scene, Trigorin's OBJECTIVE is *to persuade Arkadina to release him from their relationship* so he can establish one with Nina. Arkadina's OBJECTIVE is *to prevent him from leaving her* or, to rephrase it, *to hold on to him*. She responds with a full battery of tactics (ACTIONS) to get him to change his mind. She succeeds. The scene is a good example of playing a wide range of ACTIONS to get what you want.

A SCENE FROM ACT 3 OF 'THE SEAGULL'
BETWEEN ARKADINA AND TRIGORIN

TRIGORIN (*to Arkadina*). Let's stay one more day! ([1]*Arkadina shakes her head.*) Let's stay!

ARKADINA Darling, [2]I know what's holding you here. [3]But try to exercise some self-control. [4]You're a little drunk, [5]sober up.

TRIGORIN You be sober, too, be understanding, be reasonable, I beg of you, look at it like a true friend . . . (*Presses her hand.*) You are capable of sacrifice . . . Be my friend, let me go . . .

ARKADINA (*highly agitated*). [6]Are you so infatuated?

TRIGORIN I'm drawn to her! Perhaps she is exactly what I need.

ARKADINA [7]The love of some provincial little girl? [8]Oh, how little you know yourself!

TRIGORIN Sometimes people go through their lives sleepwalking, here I am, talking to you, but it's as if I'm asleep, and dreaming of her . . . I'm possessed by sweet, wonderful dreams . . . Let me go . . .

ARKADINA (*trembling*). [9]No, no . . . I'm an ordinary woman, you mustn't talk to me like that . . . Don't torture me, Boris . . . I'm terrified . . .

TRIGORIN If you wanted to, you could be extraordinary. Young, enchanting, poetic love, carrying you into a world of dreams – this is the only thing on earth that can bring you happiness! I've still never experienced such love . . . When I was young, I never had time, I was so busy, haunting publishers' doorsteps, struggling to survive . . . Now, it's here, this love, it's come at last, it's calling to me . . . What sense in running away from it?

ARKADINA (*angrily*). [10]You've gone mad!

TRIGORIN Let me!

ARKADINA [11]You're all conspiring to torment me today. ([12]*She cries.*)

TRIGORIN (*holds his head in his hands*). She doesn't understand! She won't understand!

ARKADINA [13]Am I already so old and ugly that one can talk to me about other women without embarrassment? ([14]*She embraces and kisses him.*) [15]Oh, you're raving mad! [16]My beautiful, wonderful . . . [17]the last page of my life. (*18She kneels at his feet.*) 19My joy, my pride, my rapture . . . (*20She embraces his knees.*) 21If you abandon me, even for an hour, I'll not survive, I'll go mad, my marvel, my magnificence, my sovereign . . .

TRIGORIN Somebody may come in. (*He helps her to her feet.*)

ARKADINA 22Let them, I'm not ashamed of my love for you. 23My treasure, my reckless boy, you want to go berserk, but I won't have it, I won't let you . . .

(*24Laughs.*) 25You're mine . . . you're mine . . . This forehead is mine, these eyes are mine, and this beautiful, silky hair is mine, too . . . You're all mine. 26You're so talented, so intelligent, the best of today's writers, you're Russia's only hope . . . You have such sincerity, simplicity, freshness, healthy humour . . . With one stroke, you can convey the essence of a character or a landscape, your people are like life. Oh, it's impossible to read you without rapture. 27Do you think this is all 'incense'? That I'm flattering you? Well, look me in the eyes . . . look . . . Do I look like a liar? 28So you see, I'm the only one capable of appreciating you, the only one who tells you the truth, my darling, my divine man . . . 29You're coming? Yes? You won't leave me?

TRIGORIN I have no will of my own . . . I've never had a will of my own . . . Flabby, spineless, always submissive – how could a woman ever find this attractive? Take me, carry me away, but don't let me go a step out of your sight . . .

ARKADINA (*to herself*). 30Now he's mine. (*Very casually as if nothing had happened.*) 31Do stay if you want . . . 32I'll go by myself, and you can come later, in a week. 33There's really no need for you to hurry back, is there?

TRIGORIN No, let's go together.

ARKADINA 34As you like. Together, then, together . . .

A BREAKDOWN OF ARKADINA'S ACTIONS

1. She shakes her head/refuses/indicates 'No!'

2. She informs him she's on to him/knows what he's up to

3. She advises him to pull himself together

4. She points out to him that he's drunk

5. She orders him to sober up

6. She questions the degree of his attraction to Nina

7. She mocks his feelings/reduces his love for Nina to an infatuation

8. She sneers at Nina's suitability as a partner for him

9. She blames him for her suffering and vulnerability/plays victim

10. She accuses him of losing his judgement

11. She complains that everyone's against her

12. She cries (to arouse his guilt)

13. She challenges him to admit she's old and ugly (to embarrass him, exacerbate his guilt)

14. She embraces and kisses him

15. She accuses him of madness

16. She praises him ecstatically

17. She confesses he's the last page in her life/her last chance for love

18. She kneels at his feet

19. She intensifies her praise of him

20. She embraces his knees

21. She threatens him with responsibility for the state of her sanity and existence

22. She announces she's proud enough of their love for it be seen publicly/warns him she won't give up quietly

23. She states her determination to exert control over him

24. She laughs

25. She stresses her total ownership of him

26. She extols his brilliant talent

27. She dares him to accuse her of false flattery/lying to him

28. She insists that he acknowledge she's the only one who understands him (to tap his needy vanity)

29. She coaxes him to concede he's staying with her

30. She reassures herself she's managed to keep him*
31. She agrees he should stay if he want to
32. She suggests he follow her in a week's time
33. She points out he has no need to hurry
34. She accepts what he wants

A NOTE ON THE ACTIONS

Arkadina demonstrates great flexibility (*warns, threatens, refuses, accuses, praises, complains, cries, laughs, embraces* . . . and so on) in pursuing her objective. Trigorin has been pursuing his own series of ACTIONS, but with considerably less skill or variety, mainly appealing to her sympathy; until his OBJECTIVE changes from *trying to persuade her to release him to that of trying to modify her behaviour* ('*Somebody* may come in'). Her ability to break his OBJECTIVE and the breadth of her ACTIONS compared to the narrowness of his, are the reasons she's the more likely of the two to win her OBJECTIVE.

A NOTE ON ARKADINA'S EMOTIONAL LIFE IN THE SCENE

* 'Now he's mine' (30) gives an indication of how Arkadina feels after all this effort. The line is totally open to interpretation, but suggests possibilities such as relief, exhaustion, regained confidence, exultation, self-satisfaction . . . or a mixture of any of them. *But whatever she does feel now must be influenced by what she's gone through up to this moment when Trigorin gives in.* She's obviously been experiencing a stream of emotions throughout the body of the scene: anger maybe, resentment, disgust, jealousy, panic, despair, grief, uncertainty, insecurity, humiliation, determination, hope . . . ebbing and flowing through her with varying degrees of intensity. Because these feelings are out of the actor's control – EMOTION *being spontaneously aroused by the interplay of* ACTIONS *and* OBJECTIVES – they will fluctuate considerably from performance to performance. It's inevitable, therefore, that this line ('*Now he's mine*') will produce a different outcome every time it's played. And rather than trying to put a label on the emotions – a very subjective and approximate (and unhelpful) procedure – it would be better to concentrate on her action and allow what the actor's experiencing to inform *how* she expresses it (*see*: EMOTION).

RECAPITULATION OF WANT! DO! FEEL!

We attempt to achieve our *objectives* by pursuing *actions* whose success or failure cause spontaneous *feelings* to be aroused in us. Or, stated the other way round: we experience spontaneous *feelings* as a result of pursuing *actions* in an attempt to achieve our *objectives*. If we achieve them – good feelings; if we fail – bad feelings.

I want, I do, I feel. This is the 'system' in a nutshell. It is simple, obvious, and *it is how we function in life.* Any good psychological techniques we apply on stage are conscious recreations of how we function naturally. They create *specific, recognisable behaviour* in the actor from which the audience is able to recognise, interpret or intuit what is going on within the character. *This liberates actors from any need to demonstrate or 'explain' their characters.*

Want: Objectives

Definition

Objectives are wants. Every moment in our waking lives (and our sleep, too, if dreams have any meaning) we're in a state of want. They accompany us from womb to tomb. We are drawn through our lives by a mesh of intertwined wants, long-term and momentary, all travelling together, over varying periods of time.

You want: to be a celebrity, to have a cup of tea, to find someone to love, to pay a bill, to change your life, to buy some clothes, to settle an argument, to borrow some money, to lead an honourable life, to recall the past, to take a holiday, to be left in peace, to feed the ducks, to prove yourself a good friend, to catch up on the gossip, to avoid confrontation, to get your own back, to learn the tango, to find that missing document, to recover from a painful relationship, to find the meaning of life, to get sympathy, to justify your behaviour, to have the last word, to win forgiveness . . .

All such wants dictate how we behave, that is to say, what we actually do. In this respect, characters in plays are no different from people in real life. The difference lies in the nature of stage objectives, which should be more selectively interesting than the rather shapeless collection of wants that we carry around within us (more about finding love than having a cup of coffee – although in the right context, even wanting a cup of coffee can have its dramatic uses, for example in Act One of *The Cherry Orchard*).

The above list comprises different sorts of wants. *There is, in fact, a hierarchy of objectives.* So let's start with the most practical and immediate.

Scene Objectives

Definitions

A scene objective is what a character wants and is trying to obtain from the other characters throughout a specific portion of text. Indeed, an objective is what initially brings a character on stage. Without a strong purpose to come into a scene, a character really has no dramatic reason to be there. A character can have more than one objective during a scene. A UNIT, however, is usually defined by a single objective. The quantity and duration of objectives can vary. If a character's objectives seem to be changing too frequently, it might indicate an uncertainty on the playwright's part. *What the characters want from each other in a scene – their objectives – gives the scene its structure.* Scene objectives are the most immediate of the objectives in the hierarchy, the most practical and accessible.

I mentioned taking a directing class in New York taught by the playwright Joseph Kramm. After we students had shown him our scenes, he would, as a matter of routine, ask the actors what their objectives were, clearly a question we tyro directors hadn't asked. The actors seemed able to reply with great precision as to what their characters wanted. He would then instruct them to play the scene again, this time making sure they fully engaged with those objectives. And, as I've said, on every occasion (or so it seems in retrospect), the situation being played became clearer and each scene acquired a dramatic vitality that it hadn't displayed the first time around. It became compellingly watchable, suspenseful – you wanted to know what would happen next (although, of course, you already *knew* that!). Experiencing this, I felt that I'd been granted the revelation of a serious theatrical truth: *actors cannot play scenes if they haven't endowed their characters with intentions (objectives).*

Think of it in this way: characters are unhappy or dissatisfied with their current situation and want to change it. They want to improve it, to rectify it in some way. *Pursuing an objective means trying to change the situation.* The situation can only be changed through the medium of another or other characters who (you believe) hold the key to that change. To change your situation, *you need to change the other characters. That is the event of the scene.* Your love is ignored – you want it acknowledged. You're owed money – you want it repaid. You're in a bad relationship – you want out. You have low self-esteem – you want reassurance. You feel guilty – you want forgiveness. More specifically: A ignores your love – *you want A to acknowledge your love.* B owes you money – *you want B to repay you the money.* You're in an unhappy relationship with C – *you want C to agree to end it.* You have low self-esteem – *you want D to make you feel better about yourself.* You feel guilty about something you did to E – *you want E to forgive you.* Essentially, you're unhappy and you *want to be happy,* you're unfulfilled and *want fulfilment,* you're dissatisfied and *want satisfaction.*

Think of it another way: pursuing an objective always means *trying to get something from someone else*. It's a two-way operation – you do something to other people in order to get something back from them. Young actors, when they first play objectives, tend to focus only on the first half of the transaction, bulldozing their way through a scene with lots of energy, but not allowing anything to come back at them from their partners, which of course renders the playing pointless. If I'm trying to have some sort of effect on you, i.e. *to get you to give me money, to get you to declare your love, to get you to forgive me*, I must stay open to your responses. How else can I know whether I'm getting what I want from you and whether I need to change my approach? If your response is not proving what I hoped for – if I'm *not* getting what I want – I can adjust the way I pursue my objective; *I can change my tactics*, i.e. my actions – more of which later. Good scenes have continuous adjustments and varying tactics. That's what keep them interesting. You already have such an example in the scene where Arkadina persuades Trigorin to stay with her.

Objectives and Conflict

You do things to other people *in order to get what you want from them*. At the same time, they'll be doing something to you *in order to get what they want from you*. The struggle to change the situation, and the conflict of clashing objectives are the dynamic of drama. Without struggle and conflict, there's no drama.*

Objectives and Plot

Objectives ensure that the plot is kept clearly on track. Objectives drive the characters forward to pursue their stories. *Objectives create plot.*

Objectives and Contact

The solution to the majority of problems for actors is almost always in the other actors, not in themselves. Objectives create a need to engage with other characters. Objectives, fully committed, ensure that actors are always in truthful contact with their partners so that *something actually happens between them*. Objectives ensure that actor-characters' focus is on their partners and not on themselves. Asides or soliloquies create a need for actor-characters to make contact with audiences; their objectives are to get some response from the audience: sympathy, support, understanding, complicity . . .

---

* Of course there are situations in which a non-human agent is causing the unhappiness, such as a snowstorm, an accident, an outbreak of war, an illness, but these are the devices of melodrama and are usually the framework for more interesting conflicts; they are also much more the material of film (*see*: OBSTACLES). Most Performance Art is devoid of drama. It has all the externals of theatre (lighting, staging, movement, sound, music – rich visuals and aurals) but none of the internal life.

Objectives as Scenic Fuel

Objectives are strategies. They are the fuel that ignites characters into action. Objectives generate actions. You cannot literally play an objective. *Your objectives stimulate you to play actions.* (Actions are the only thing an actor can actually play.) Think of it like this: objectives are *propelling/moving/thrusting/urging/driving/ shoving/hurling/kicking/pushing/pulling/drawing/shifting/leading/coaxing/luring/ seducing/encouraging/guiding/prodding you into appropriate action.*

Objectives are Holistic

Objectives do not just emanate from the head. They are not solely the result of conscious decision. They often stem from the unconscious. Characters are not always aware of their objectives. That is why actors have to embody them so deeply that, like lines, they become a natural part of their performance and need no longer be thought about. They should be holistically all-consuming, imagined so fully that they create an inner state of need that permeates an actor's entire being.

Objectives and Balance

Unfulfilled objectives are part of the condition in which characters exist. Actor-characters should feel incomplete, unfinished, in a state of dissatisfaction which only the success of their objectives can rectify. As objectives rarely or only briefly succeed (there'd be no drama if they did), characters are always, in a sense, off-balance. *Being off-balance creates suspense; it is a creative state.* Balance, in contrast, creates harmony and eliminates drama.*

Objectives and Lateral Thinking

I said objectives are strategies. In certain circumstances, characters feel that if ever they're going to get what they want, they'll need to manipulate the person from whom they want it, to handle that person with extreme caution. This can also happen at an unconscious level. Such manipulation involves the application of lateral thinking and an imagination of some wit to manoeuvre the other character (or characters) into the right frame of mind to concede to their wishes. This often means approaching the matter indirectly, circling around it, even appearing to retreat from the very thing that's wanted. As I've already indicated, the mistake inexperienced actors often make is to feel they're not playing their objectives unless they do so head-on, at full blast, with maximum energy and attack. Even accepting that they're playing truthfully and with intensity, a frontal attack, if overused, becomes an obvious and uninteresting choice. That way of playing only applies when the conflicts in a scene become unambiguously explicit and directly confrontational. Actors who apply an imaginative approach to their objectives create far more thrilling theatre. Technically, they are using interesting tactics (*see*: ACTIONS) in their attempt to succeed.

* Eugenio Barba convincingly elaborates on this in *The Paper Canoe.*

Le Mot Juste: Intention, Mission, Goal . . .

People often insist on using competing terminologies for an objective. If you prefer, you can think of an objective as:

a *want* to be got;	a *desire* to be sated;
an *intention* to be gained;	a *target* to be hit;
a *mission* to be accomplished;	an *aim* to be achieved;
a *goal* to be attained;	a *problem* to be solved;
a *destination* to be reached;	a *need* to be answered;
a *purpose* to be fulfilled;	a *task* to be done;
a *longing* to be assuaged;	a *drive* to succeed;
a *hunger* to be satisfied;	a *stake* to be won.

All these words – *objective, intention, mission, goal, destination, purpose, longing, hunger, desire, target, aim, problem, need, task, drive, stake* – are encompassed by the word *want*. The word is unimportant so long as you understand the idea behind it. The sign is unimportant so long as you understand what's signified.[*]

An Example of Objectives

A SCENE FROM ACT 3 OF 'THE SEAGULL'
BETWEEN KONSTANTIN AND ARKADINA

KONSTANTIN [1]Living in the country's not healthy for him [*i.e. his uncle, Sorin*]. He broods. Mama, if you would suddenly feel generous and lend him one-and-a-half, two thousand roubles, he could live in town for a whole year.

ARKADINA I haven't any money. I'm an actress not a banker.

Pause.

KONSTANTIN [2]Mama, change my bandage. You do it so well.

ARKADINA (*takes iodine from the medicine cabinet and bandages from a drawer*). The doctor's late.

---

[*] Among the adherents to particular acting systems there can be a certain amount of wilful semantic confusion, of pedantic nit-picking about precise terminology. Often through lack of real understanding, they cling to the word rather than the spirit. This is unhelpful. Arguments over words immediately get actors out of their bodies and into their heads, where we'd prefer them not to be.

KONSTANTIN He promised to be here by ten. It's midday already.

ARKADINA Sit down. (*Takes off his bandage.*) You look as if you're wearing a turban. A stranger in the kitchen yesterday asked what nationality you were. It's almost entirely healed. Just a little bit left. (*Kisses his head.*) While I'm away, you won't go click-click again?

KONSTANTIN No, Mama. That was a moment of insane despair when I couldn't control myself. It won't be repeated any more. (*He kisses her hand.*) You've got such clever hands. I remember long ago when you were still working in State Theatres – I was very small then – there was a fight in our courtyard, a washerwoman was badly beaten up. You remember? She was picked up unconscious . . . you used to visit her with medicine and wash her children in a tub. You must remember?

ARKADINA No. (*She puts on a new bandage.*)

KONSTANTIN Two ballet dancers lived in the same house then . . . They used to visit you for coffee . . .

ARKADINA That I remember.

KONSTANTIN They were very religious. (*Pause.*) Lately, these last few days, I've loved you as tenderly and as fully as I did as a child. I've no-one left beside you. [3]Only why, why do you let yourself be influenced by that man?

ARKADINA You don't understand him, Konstantin. He has a fine character.

KONSTANTIN However, when he was informed I was about to challenge him to a duel, his fine character didn't prevent him from playing the coward. He's leaving. Ignominious flight!

ARKADINA What nonsense! I asked him to leave myself. You may not like our intimacy, but you're a clever and intelligent person and I have the right to demand that you respect my freedom.

KONSTANTIN I respect your freedom, but please don't deny me the right to think what I like about this man. Fine character! You and I are on the verge of having a fight because of him, while he's sitting somewhere, in the drawing room or in the garden, laughing at us . . . contributing to Nina's 'development', trying to convince her once and for all that he's a genius.

ARKADINA You enjoy saying unpleasant things to me. I respect this man and I ask you to refrain from speaking ill of him in my presence.

KONSTANTIN And I do not respect him. You want me to think him a genius too, but, forgive me, I can't lie, his work makes me sick.

ARKADINA That's envy. People without talent but with pretensions to it have nothing better to do than abuse real talent. Some consolation, I must say!

KONSTANTIN (*sarcastically*). Real talent! (*Angrily.*) [4]I'm more talented than all of you, if it comes to that. (*Tears the bandage from his head.*) You hacks, you lovers of stale routine have grabbed all the first places in art, and consider only what you do to be real and legitimate, everyone else you try to stifle and suppress. I don't recognise you people! I don't recognise you or him!

ARKADINA Decadent!

KONSTANTIN Go back to your lovely theatre and act in your rotten, worthless plays!

ARKADINA I have never acted in such plays. Leave me alone! You aren't capable of writing even a third-rate vaudeville skit. Petit Bourgeois from Kiev! Parasite!

KONSTANTIN Miser!

ARKADINA Tramp! ([5]*Konstantin sits down and cries quetly.*) Nonentity! (*She walks up and down agitatedly.*) Don't cry. There's no need to cry . . . (*Cries.*) Don't . . . (*Kisses his forehead, cheeks and head.*) My darling child, forgive me . . . Forgive your sinful mother. Forgive this wretched creature.

KONSTANTIN (*hugging her*). If only you knew! I've lost everything! She doesn't love me and I can't write any more . . . all my hopes have vanished . . .

ARKADINA Don't despair . . . Everything will work out. He's going away, she'll love you again. (*She wipes his tears.*) Enough. We've made it up now.

KONSTANTIN (*kissing her*). Yes, Mama.

ARKADINA (*tenderly*). Make it up with him, too. No need for a duel . . . Now is there?

KONSTANTIN Alright . . . Only, Mama, don't force me to see him. It's hard for me . . . more than I can bear.

KONSTANTIN'S OBJECTIVES DURING THE SCENE

1 (a) To encourage his mother to give her brother some money; (b) to elicit from her some show of concern for her family.

2 (a) To get her to be the mother he remembers (to nurse him, to share childhood memories with him); (b) to get her to demonstrate her love for him by her willingness to be his exclusively; (c) to return to a secure place in his childhood; (d) to become a child again.

3 (a) To make her break up her relationship with Trigorin; (b) to reclaim his mother for himself.

4 (a) To make her understand how much he despises her sort of theatre; (b) to humiliate her professionally; (c) to get her to acknowledge/bow down to his superior artistry.

5 (a) To share his unhappiness with her; (b) make her feel guilty.

(1) + (2) + (3) have the overall objective of trying to get his mother to become exclusively his again.

(4) + (5) have the overall objective of wanting to punish her for not doing so.

NOTES ON THE OBJECTIVES

These objectives are of course interpretive: the 'a's are obvious at a surface level; the 'b's, 'c's and 'd' probe deeper. Note that the same objective can usually be phrased in a variety of ways (e.g. 2c or d); often, actors will find a particular choice of words more stimulating to their imagination than another.

An objective also often implies one or more corollaries (e.g. 2b, c & d; 4b & c). The actor can choose to let one of these dominate, but whatever he chooses to play should contain all the implications of the others. Whichever one he does emphasise will give the scene a different tone and texture.

Through-Lines

Definition

The next level in the hierarchy of objectives is the through-line. This is the character's main objective through the story (play) and links all that character's scenes and behaviour with a dramatic logic. *It is the character's essential plot-drive through the play.* In the Aristotelian sense, this is what gives a drama its cohesion – the character's pursuit of an all-encompassing goal, which they may (comedy) or may not (tragedy) achieve. It should inform every scene in which the character appears and, therefore, each scene objective. The sum of the scene objectives should add up to the through-line. *The through-line both generates plot and functions in response to the circumstances of the plot.*

Sometimes, towards the end of the play, circumstances force the characters to adjust or change their through-line. The last scenes of a play are often about how the characters deal with the success or failure of their through-lines.

Sometimes, a through-line doesn't kick in until activated by a circumstance, usually early on, in the play.

A through-line could also be defined as the way in which the character's SUPER-OBJECTIVE (coming up next) motivates and guides the character through the specific circumstances of the play in which the character finds itself.

The through-line is also known as the *main-line-of-action.* It could also be called *the play objective.*

SOME THROUGH-LINES

Nina – to succeed as an actress [*The Seagull*]

Torvald – to contain his wife within what he believes a wife's role should be [*A Doll's House*]

Claudius – to rule safely, therefore to control Hamlet [*Hamlet*]

Oedipus – to discover the cause of, and therefore end, the plague in Thebes [*Oedipus Rex*]

Hamlet – to avenge his father's death [*Hamlet*]

Hedda Gabler – to exert influence over Eilert Lövborg [*Hedda Gabler*]

Nora – to keep her secret from her husband, Torvald [*A Doll's House*]

Arkadina – to hold on to everything she possesses, particularly Trigorin [*The Seagull*]

NOTES ON THE THROUGH-LINES

The first four through-lines exist before the play begins. The last four hover potentially at the start of the play until clearly activated by specific circumstances, respectively:

The Ghost's injunction to Hamlet to avenge his death

Thea Elvsted's news of Eilert Lövborg's rehabilitation

Krogstad's threat to reveal Nora's secret

Nina's appearance in Konstantin's play

SOME ADJUSTED THROUGH-LINES

Hamlet's – from his sense of futility concerning his previous actions – *to resign himself to his fate*

Oedipus's – once he discovers that he himself is the cause of the plague (because of his unwitting acts of patricide and incest) – *to punish himself/to appease the Gods*

Hedda Gabler's – once her attempts to influence Lövborg threaten her either with social disgrace or subjugation to Judge Brack's will – *to kill herself as the only way out of this impasse*

Nora's – once she is disillusioned by Hjalmar's response to her 'secret' – *to (leave home and children and) test her ability to live independently*

Torvald's – once he discovers that he no longer has any power over his wife – *to preserve their marriage by acceding to Nora's wishes in anyway he can*

Arkadina and Nina keep their through-lines going to the very end of the play; Claudius keeps his until his death.

The adjusted through-lines are of course influenced by the characters' super-objectives.

Super-Objectives

Definition

Most comprehensive of all in the hierarchy of objectives, super-objectives are characters' *life-wants*, their overarching drive through life. They extend beyond the duration of the play in which the characters live out that part of their lives: conceivably, they exist before the play begins and, assuming the character is still alive at the end of the play, continue afterwards. *Super-objectives define character; through-lines define plot.*

A super-objective is usually stated in very general terms, and deals with large concepts such as *to want to:*

conquer the world;	avoid commitments;
embrace all that life offers;	belong somewhere;
hide from life's vicissitudes;	seek justice;
be a good person;	find love . . .

It informs a character's journey through life, both a goal and a guide to conducting one's life. In the play, the super-objective influences all the choices that characters make – their through-lines and therefore their scene objectives. That means *characters create plot* – as they should.

Suicide

Our own lives are motivated by some overarching drive, though what that might be would be hard for most of us to identify. It is usually broad enough to allow us a reasonable flexibility of choices as we move through the varied circumstances of our existence. If one desired avenue closes for us, we are able to see the possibility of others. The concept of super-objectives may become clearer by looking at people who take their own lives. Suicides have super-objectives that are too narrow, too specific to leave them room for much manoeuvre. When we hear of someone's suicide, we often find it hard to understand; to us, their life seemed happy and fulfilled. Nevertheless, whatever it is that they wanted from life must at some point have become an impossible goal – or so they *felt* it to be. What for us would have been a minor setback seemed for them the end to any hope of obtaining their super-objective.

In the early '60s, among the celebrity cast list of the Profumo Affair was an osteopath called Stephen Ward, who had found his way into the circle of the rich and well-connected. As something of a scapegoat for the whole scandal-filled business, he was brought to trial for living off the earnings of prostitutes and pimping for his socialite client-friends. After he heard the judge's summing up, before the actual verdict (he *was* subsequently found guilty), he took an overdose. A psychiatrist's report put forward the view that because, during his trial, none of the great and the good, who had availed themselves of his various services and purported to be his friends, had come forward to give evidence on his behalf, he believed that he would never again be *persona grata* in that particular society. Sensing (rightly or wrongly) that there was no future possibility for himself in a world he wanted to be part of more than any other, he did away with himself. His super-objective (something along the lines of '*to belong to/be accepted by the rich and famous*'), being an unusually narrow one, left him no options. The cause of this sense of hopelessness may well have been unconscious.

In *The Seagull*, Konstantin is an example of a dramatic character with a narrow life-drive, focused exclusively on one person. His super-objective is to win his mother's love and respect. Chekhov brilliantly flags this up for us by giving him, soon after he first appears, a long diatribe about his mother; then, just before his final exit to shoot himself, a few last words of concern for her. From Nina's visit, he realises that he will never be a great writer and this (in *his* mind) removes any hope of ever winning his mother's love. Without her reassurance of his worth, he has total lack of self-esteem. Deprived of this – or the hope of it – he cannot continue to live. Whether this is unconscious (in which case, his *conscious* despair is fixated on his failure as a writer, with *no awareness* of his deeper need to succeed) or whether it is conscious (in which case, his despair comes from his certainty that his mother's love can now never be won) is a matter of interpretation. I would probably opt for the former; Konstantin, like most of the other characters in the play, exhibits very little self-knowledge. Fortunately for us and for drama, most people and most characters have broader drives.

Chicken and Egg

Discovering the super-objective is a chicken-and-egg process. The super-objective defines the character's choice of objectives from scene to scene. The sum of the scene objectives reveals the super-objective. Either, from your overall sense of the character's movement through the play, you can make a reasonable conjecture as to the super-objective, then work through each scene objective, testing it against your conjecture. Or you can decide on your scene objectives as you work through them, one at a time, and see what super-objective they cumulatively suggest. You are working from the general to the particular or from the particular to the general. In practice, you'll probably work from both. There's a certain amount of pulling and pushing as you adjust your scene objectives to fit in with your conjectural super-objective, or as you modify your super-objective to accommodate your scene objectives. It's an ongoing process. If, for example, the objectives in a few scenes seem to have no connection with the others, either you need to adjust your super-objective to accommodate them, or rework those scene objectives until they seem to connect with the super-objective. (In a poorly written play, this problem may well be the writer's lack of consistency or understanding of action, in which case the actors and director have to do a lot of smart man-oeuvring to bring the scenes into an artistically integrated whole.)

SOME SUPER-OBJECTIVES

Hedda Gabler – to exert power in a male-dominated world (*through-line*: by having influence, first over her husband's possible political career, then over Eilert Lövborg) [*Hedda Gabler*]

Oedipus – to (be seen to) be a powerful and responsible ruler (*through-line*: by discovering and destroying the cause of the plague that is ravaging the citizen of Thebes, the city-state he rules) [*Oedipus Rex*]

Ranyevskaya – to (go where she can) find unconditional love (*through-line*: by being accepted unreservedly back into the bosom of her family) [*The Cherry Orchard*]

Imogen – to exist in truth and loyalty (*through-line*: by finding a way to be reunited with her husband, Posthumus) [*Cymbeline*]

Nora – to experience herself as an independent human being within the confines of a male-dominated society (*through-line:* by keeping her secret of forging a signature to save her husband's health) [*A Doll's House*]

Konstantin – to win his mother's love and respect (*through-line*: by impressing her with his talent as a writer) [*The Seagull*]

Nina – to embrace life to the full (*through-line*: by becoming an actress) [*The Seagull*]

Arkadina – to receive the world's adulation (*through-line*: by holding on to all she possesses: looks, career, youth, money, lover . . .) [*The Seagull*]

The Language of Super-Objectives

A super-objective can be stated in many ways: Ranyevskaya's could be, simply, *to be loved; to live for love; to gain everyone's love; to be adored.* Nina's, *to experience everything that life has to offer, to explore life to the full, to seize life in all its dimensions* . . . It very much depends on what combination of words stimulates an actor's imagination. Even though there may be subtle shifts of emphasis in differ-ent rewordings, it's more important that a super-objective is phrased in a way that energises the actor. Anyway, there's no such thing as a definitive super-objective.

Like all objectives, its interpretation is a matter of informed and reasonable conjecture, and more constructive if expressed through language that triggers the actor's creativity.

Super-Objective as Synthesiser

The super-objective is where the head meets the viscera. The actor is making discoveries about the character's drives in the sweat of rehearsal through scene objectives, and analysing and synthesising this information intellectually through super-objectives.

The Embodiment of Super-Objectives

The super-objective is not playable. It is both too generalised and usually unconscious. The purpose of the super-objective is to give aesthetic integrity and structure to a role. At a deep level, it can resolve a character's apparent contradictions. Although a super-objective is not playable, it must nonetheless be psychosomatically absorbed into the actor's organism, so that eventually it functions creatively at a semi-conscious level. It defines how the character looks at life – the character's world-view and values – and should find expression in the character's physical life. As human beings are holistic, the way of absorbing a super-objective into the essence of the role is through physical work (*see*: EMOTION AND BODY and TECHNIQUES TOWARDS CHARACTERISATION).

The Super-Objective of Plays

In a good play, the sum of the characters' super-objectives reveals the play's super-objective (or theme). This must make sense as plays can only be about the characters that exist in them. Themes are not mental constructs somehow hovering above a text. They're ingrained in the characters' journeys and aspirations (stories) that create the play. So what the characters want and do *must* contain (and reveal) the play's themes – what it's 'about'.

In *Cymbeline*, all the characters are motivated by loyalty or disloyalty: parent and child, husband and wife, master and servant, ruler and subject, citizen and country, descendant and ancestors, man and Gods. They divide into three groups: those who operate by disloyalty and betrayal and are ultimately destroyed; those who act with unwavering loyalty; and those who lapse into disloyalty but are ultimately redeemed by repentance with their loyalty implicitly renewed. These last two groups are rewarded by reunion and reconciliation. The play's theme might be stated: *Those people who lead their lives with loyalty and fidelity win love and redemption.*

In *Hedda Gabler*, all the characters, but one, are governed by bourgeois respectability and the fear of scandal which encourages them to keep low profiles. They can only operate behind and through other people (they don't enter by the front door, but, in Ibsen's words, by 'the rear entrance'). For example, Hedda tries to be the power behind the throne, first of Tesman, then of Lövborg; Tesman researches other men's work; Thea Elvsted inspires Lövborg to write, and hopes to do the same for Tesman; Judge Brack operates by entering other people's marriages – 'the third in a triangle'; even Aunt Julie looks after her sick sister until she dies, whereupon she starts looking around for another sick person to tend. In counterpoint, the exception, Eilert Lövborg, is motivated by his defiance of society and is the cause of most of the other characters' through-lines in the play. The theme might be: *In a bourgeois society, dominated by fear of scandal, people avoid overt action and dare operate only through or behind others.*

In *The Three Sisters*, all the characters are looking for a place where they can belong – geographically, socially, professionally, domestically, emotionally and, quite simply, by having a room of their own. In fact, the subject of rooms recurs over and over again through the play. Rooms become a metaphor for the need to belong somewhere. The soldiers are periodically on the move to another army base and always living in temporary quarters (rented rooms); Natasha wants to move up in the world and takes over the Prozorov household, pushing the sisters out of their rooms to make room for her babies; Andrei wants a life free of responsibilities and hides in his room, playing the violin, trying to avoid the problems, largely of his making, that engulf his family; Irina who longs for some idealised form of work, keeps changing jobs throughout the play as she and Olga are slowly pushed out of the house by Natasha; Anfisa, the old nurse, despite Natasha's threat to get rid of her, ends up rejoicing in having a room of her own at the school where Olga has moved . . . The theme might be: *In a period of social disruption and radical change, most people are searching for a place were they can belong.*

In *The Seagull*, the theme might be: *Most people create performances of the failures and disappointments of their lives in order to render the pain more tolerable.* There is also a sub-motif in the way the characters batten on art to give themselves some sort of prestige. They use art, not as a means of genuine creative expression, but as a means to solve some other need (status, image, celebrity, money, admiration . . .). Nina is the exception. She comes to realise that art is not, as she'd once thought, about acquiring fame, but about acquiring the honesty (and therefore strength) to cope with life.

Super-Objectives v. Through-Lines

Super-objectives are character-driven and more concerned with inner needs – hopes, longings, ambitions. *Through-lines* are more involved with externals – events, situations, contexts. *Super-objectives* are ingrained in their characters, whatever their story might be, and are the prime instigators of plot. *Through-lines* are specific to the concrete circumstances of the play and are plot-driven.

Counter-Objectives

Definition

Finally, the *counter-objective*. This is a critical character-driven need that is almost equal in strength to the *super-objective*, but works in opposition to it. *The counter-objective* causes characters to be in conflict with themselves. We live with inner contradictions. We can have needs that pull us away from our *super-objective* – from the very thing we most want. That's why, often, we remain with our ambitions unfulfilled. At times, it may take patience and perceptive analysis to decide which is a character's *super-objective* and which their *counter-objective* (*see*: OBSTACLES).

Some Examples of Counter-Objectives

I've suggested that Hedda Gabler's *super-objective* is to exert power in the world. In her closed and male-dominated society, the only route she sees open to her is through her influence over a man. By marrying Tesman, she hopes to manoeuvre him into some political or high academic position. However, as the daughter of a general, she has an overvalued perception of herself. She is a snob, a product of the *haute bourgeoisie*, its values and conventions, and her *counter-objective is to remain aloof from others, and*, it goes without saying, *to avoid scandal*. These two large objectives collide when, failing to shift Tesman, she becomes embroiled with Eilert Lövborg, a man to whom scandal easily adheres. Her involvement puts her under the power of Judge Brack. Caught between the Scylla of threatened disgrace and the Charybdis of being under someone else's power, which excludes the possibility of exerting any power of her own – her super-objective, that is – she 'sees' no alternative but suicide.

In *The Cherry Orchard*, Lopakhin's *super-objective* is to belong to the world of Ranyevskaya, more specifically, to be accepted by her (he probably has an unconscious childhood-fixated love for her). For the first half of the play, he's trying to help her to save her estate. But in the third act, he buys the estate for himself. His motive for buying it, his *counter-objective*, is *to avenge the injustices done his family who were serfs on her family's estate, to get amends for the wrongs done them*. By an act against the woman whose acceptance he so deeply desires, he ends up destroying any chance of gaining the very thing he wants, his super-objective.

In *The Seagull*, Konstantin's *super-objective* is to win the love and respect of his actress mother. *His counter-objective is to prove that his talents and ideas about theatre will make her see the vulgarity and mediocrity of hers.* She, of course, is totally committed to her sort of theatre, a necessity in her life, possibly *the* necessity. His blindness to her needs puts him on a course of action that antagonises her and totally precludes any chance of his gaining his super-objective. When he finally 'sees' the inadequacy of his writing, he tears all of it up (a metaphorical suicide) and then shoots himself.

Also in *The Seagull*, Arkadina's *super-objective* is to receive the world's adulation. *Her counter-objective is to hang on to all that she has*: her income, her appearance, her career, her 'youth', her lover. She's reached an age when she fears that everything that's made her what she is will start to erode or be taken from her unless she defends it. This makes her ungenerous and demanding, creating tension in others rather than the adoration she craves. So, despite the routine flattery that comes her way, she is in a continual state of dissatisfaction, irritation and anger. In each of the first three acts, she loses her temper!

RECAPITULATION OF OBJECTIVES

The super-objective is the character's overarching purpose in life; *the through-line* is the character's purpose through the context of the play; *the scene objective* is the character's purpose from situation to situation. *Super-objectives* motivate *through-lines* that motivate *scene objectives*. *The counter-objective* is a strong character drive in conflict with *the super-objective*.

Do: Action and Actions

A Mnemonic

Active Actors Actually Enact Actions & Activities in an Actuality, (Acting Out, Acting Up, Acting on Impulse, Acting as If, Acting the Fool, Putting On an Act, Getting In On the Act, Getting Their Act Together,) Reacting and Interacting, to Activate the audience – even to DistrAct them!

The Essence of Theatre

The profound nature of theatre, its essence, is action – not language, not image, nor the interpretation of great texts, not political engagement, but action. Action is how theatre expresses itself. *The purpose of theatre is the revelation of action and revelation through action.* The life of theatre is created by characters in action, that is to say, acting out their lives through meaningful and revelatory deeds and behaviour.

The Actor's Art

Action can only be – well – activated by human beings. That's why actors are the *sine qua non* of theatre. *The actor's art is the art of action.*

Technically, *actions are what characters do to try to achieve their objectives; therefore actions are what actors play.* Playing actions is the actor's main task. It's what actors do. This is their job. This, technically, is all they *can* play. In *True and False*, his book about acting, David Mamet – if I understand him – believes that the playing of actions encompasses *everything* a good actor need do.

To repeat: actions are what characters carry out in order *to try to get what they want.* They use them *to change their current situation, to improve* or *rectify* it in some way. In good drama, that situation is always dependent upon other characters. Therefore, to achieve the desired change, *characters* have to effect a change in *other characters.* Which means that *actors* have to effect a change in *other actors.* They can only achieve this by pursuing actions.

Many actors don't play actions. That's why many performances are inartistic. By which I mean that these actors' focus is not on wanting to move the story forward through meaningful, imaginative and imperative action – which means through seamless, active contact with their partners – but on other preoccupations, such as affecting the audience with aspects of their performance: their ability to communicate difficult texts, their capacity for expressive emotion, their 'comic timing', their charm, their vitality, the wit of their choices, the virtuosity of their skills and so forth – totally the wrong sorts of objectives, even if executed with honest intentions on behalf of the playwright and the play. Wrong because they are implicitly saying 'Look at me acting', rather than just acting.* 'Good' actors also use such skills, *but in the service of their actions*, as the means to an end, rather than as ends in themselves.

'Bad' actors may be tempted to believe there are other things they should 'play', such as character, mood, style . . . But this sort of acting is essentially demonstrative rather than active. *Character, mood, atmosphere and style will quite naturally be created if actors play their actions and objectives within the context of their* GIVEN CIRCUMSTANCES. 'Bad' actors invite the audience to watch them trying to move, amuse, disturb, enlighten and delight them. 'Good' actors invite the audience to watch their characters struggling to work out the story of their lives through action. They trust that by playing actions truthfully and imaginatively, they *will* move, amuse, disturb, enlighten and delight their audiences.

There is a world of difference between an actor who plays a result and one who plays an action: a result strikes a single note; an action resonates with infinite harmonic possibilities. Actors who play results can do no other than display themselves in their performance because what they're playing has nowhere to go; results and demonstrations are essentially dead ends. This sort of acting is inevitably – even if unintentionally – narcissistic because its outcome is to show off the actor. By contrast, actors who play actions generate energy and spontaneous life

---

* This is exactly what Shaw is criticising in Bernhardt's performance.

with their partners. Actors who are absorbed in themselves draw attention to themselves. Actors utterly absorbed in playing their actions will utterly absorb the audience in the play.

———

Action and Text

Sets, lighting, music, sound, costumes, *mise-en-scène* cannot supply action. The text itself can only provide the possibility for it. Good plays offer the opportunity for lively, meaningful and varied action. Natural playwrights instinctively conceive and write in actions. Plays often don't work because they lack the potential for action. Playwrights who have a lot to say and say it through words rather than through action create, oxymoronically, static drama – an impossible object. Characters should talk, not to score points for the writer, but because what they say is part of their actions in pursuit of their objectives. Dialogue is one of several means employed by characters to get what they want. (Others might be physical expression, gesture and attitude, demeanour, behaviour, 'business', activities, degree of energy, appearance . . .)

Action and Plot

Actions are the steps along the spine – the through-line – of the plot. *Actions turn story into drama.*

Action and Space

To fulfil their actions, actors, whose bodies are trained to be flexible and spontaneously responsive, instinctively employ appropriate physicality. Actions will move them naturally and dynamically through space, both in relationship to their partners and to their environment. Spontaneous actors don't have to be told, nor need to set, where or how they move. The need of the action will motivate their physical life as well as their psychological life. The two – the physical and the psychological – are intertwined. The physical is the manifestation of the psychological, the one can't happen without the other. By playing actions, actors automatically bring the whole physical world of the play alive: not only their own bodies, but the space around them, the objects they handle, the clothes they wear, the other actors on stage . . .

Action and Time

Actions move the characters through time; actions pull them forwards in pursuit of their objectives. The sum of their actions is their journey through the play. Theatre is as much concerned with time as with space. When actors play actions, they and the audience live through an event together. By contrast, actors who play results or demonstrate their acting are essentially static. Watching that sort of performance is experiencing dead time. That is why so much theatre can feel heavy and tedious, why even short shows seem to take for ever. We have difficulty in sustaining our concentration. It's because *nothing is happening, nothing engages, nothing's in action.**

Action and Dynamics

In matters of volume, tempo and rhythm, actions proceed with the appropriate energy that each moment dictates. Actions create natural dynamics; the intensity of the dynamic depends on how much energy the actor-characters feel they need to invest in each action, how high they place the stakes of their objectives. Any other means of achieving energy is generalised and false. Directorial exhortations for 'More energy!' or to play 'Louder!', 'Faster!' induce forced and mechanical performances. Actions endow a performance with appropriate, organic energy, with specificity and with life.

Action and Character

Actions reveal character. The type of actions they employ reveals something of their psychology. What they *do* is more likely to tell us what sort of people they are, rather than what they say, which usually tries to disguise the fact. A character's tendency periodically to resort to certain types of action is a clue to personality. The actor might find that a character *argues* a lot or *flatters* a lot or *boasts* a lot. In *The Three Sisters*, Olga frequently *complains*. In *The Seagull*, Konstantin keeps *criticising* his mother. In *The Cherry Orchard*, Lopakhin continually *exhorts* the others to embrace his business plans. Such actions are clues towards characterisation. After all, we *are* what we do. What we do makes us what we are.

Action and Contact

Actions ensure that actor-characters contact each other. To play actions truthfully, actors have to be in genuine contact with one another. They must truly affect each other, not merely as character to character, *but as actor to actor* – no polite

---

* It's worth noting that, unlike a novel or film, theatre rarely, if ever, succeeds, when it disrupts our normal experience of time. I can think of no theatre equivalents of *Last Year in Marienbad*. Even experiments, like J.B. Priestley's Time Plays are more about 'What if . . . ', offering alternative developments to a story. Plays that move 'backwards', like *Betrayal* or *Merrily We Roll Along*, do, at least, move consistently in one direction. Plays that cover many years and deal with generations rarely have the dramatic impact and punch of plays that happen within a contained period. We want to stay with the same characters, not jump to their descendants. Shakespeare totally ignores the logic of time, allowing events that happen in swift succession and those that logically would occur over longer periods of time to coexist, so that we always have a sense of immediacy. We never question their literal impossibility, because of the power of his *dramatic action*. There's something to be said for the Classical Unities of Time, Place and Action. Because we're experiencing a play as it happens in front of us, our sense of 'real time' is very powerful.

pretence at contact. Actors have to have the courage to engage with one another. Playing actions truly and fully makes this inevitable.

Action and Emotion

Actions lead to feeling. As I've said, the need and the effort exerted in pursuing actions – and their success or failure in achieving the objectives that have initiated them – generate *spontaneous and therefore truthful feelings* in the actor. If actors are not in action, what passes for their emotional life will of technical necessity be dredged up, simulated, contrived, strained and often clichéd.

Actions as Tactics

Whether you agree or not with the perception that we are by nature manipulative in everything we do, the fact is that *actions are tactics* we employ to get what we want. (Objectives are strategies.) The more flexible we are tactically, the more likely we are to succeed. Actors who play unvaryingly the self-same actions throughout a scene become uninteresting and unrevealing (unless this is clearly meant to be an aspect of character). It's hard for an audience to sustain its attention; we find we've stopped listening and are barely watching. Not only is it uninteresting; more to the point, it's unreal. In life, we are infinitely varied in the ways we relate to each other, there seems no end to the range of our human expressiveness as we interrelate. Therefore it's somewhat perplexing that actors, human beings who in their actual lives will be quite naturally full of expressive variety, can become creatures of such limited colours on stage. This is often the result of planning. Actors who make decisions in advance inevitably close off access to their imagination and to unexpected possibilities. By making prior choices, their heads limit them to what is obvious and clichéd, what is consciously available to them. Actors who play spontaneously will automatically play with variety and freshness, because they've dared to leave themselves open, uncensored, to what instinctively occurs.

The objective of a scene should stimulate actors to a wide variety of tactics (actions) on its behalf. These tactics should be in direct response to the reactions they are eliciting from their partners in the scene. Actors should be continuously adjusting with appropriate, fresh actions to the OBSTACLES that are presented to them. (Refer back to the scene in *The Seagull* between Arkadina and Trigorin, in which she is continuously adjusting her actions to his.)

Not only do a succession of varied actions create liveliness, so will *the variety of ways in which the same action or tactic can be played*. Even if an actor has planned an action, so long as it's only the *what* of the action rather than the *how* that has been decided upon, it can still be played with spontaneity. Think of the incalculable number of ways in which you can, for instance, *threaten* someone or *disagree* with them.

Action as a Constant

Actions are the actors' constant factor in performance. They are the source of their strength and security: literally and metaphorically their lifeline. A sequence of actions is the actor-character's journey through the play. You could see them as beads threaded on a string, except that this is too static an image; slightly better is to think of them, as I've suggested, as numerous vertebrae that compose the long spine that supports the complete skeleton of the play. Or, simply, think of them as steps on the play's journey. Actions are playable right from the start of rehearsals. On the first day, it's possible for actors to play them with complete commitment, even before they have much or any knowledge of character, objectives, or GIVEN CIRCUMSTANCES. The actors play the situation from themselves to the best of their understanding.

For a simple example, the first scene of *The Seagull*, deals with Medvedenko's declaration of love to Masha and her rejection of him. His first line, 'Why do you always go around in black?' is clearly a question. So his action is to *ask, find out, question, enquire.* This is undeniable. The actor playing Medvedenko at this point probably knows nothing certain about his character, nor exactly what his objective is; nor what the GIVEN CIRCUMSTANCES are. Nevertheless, *he can still play the action,* using whatever ideas he does have at this point about his character and the scene; or simply by playing from himself – what this situation might mean to him. What he uses is unimportant, *so long as he plays an action.* Whatever he does use, he is still playing the basic situations of the scene (e.g. *asking* that question) and thus learning its basic structure. By the end of rehearsals, this action will still be the same (*to ask, find out, question, enquire*), but by then it will be informed and conditioned by the appropriate GIVEN CIRCUMSTANCES of the play: character, environment, story, relationships and so forth. The vertebrae will have acquired muscles and tendons, joints and tissue, veins and arteries, skin and fat, blood and genes. But the bones themselves, no matter what new conditions affect them, will be a constant; they may become arthritic, bruised, even broken, but they will always be there.

———

An Analysis of Actions

In this speech of Lopakhin's from the first act of *The Cherry Orchard*, his scene objective is *to persuade Ranyevskaya and Gayev to build dachas on their estate and rent them out in order to pay off their debts.*

LOPAKHIN ADDRESSING RANYEVSKAYA AND GAYEV
IN ACT I OF 'THE CHERRY ORCHARD'

LOPAKHIN I want to tell you something very pleasant, encouraging . . .
(*Glances at his watch.*) I'm leaving now, no time to talk . . . So, in two or
three words. As you know, your cherry orchard is up for sale to pay
your debts, the auction's set for the twenty-second of August, but you
needn't worry, my dear, sleep peacefully, there's a solution . . . Here's
my plan. Please listen! Your estate is only fifteen miles from town, the
railway runs nearby, and if the cherry orchard and land along the river
were divided into summer lots and then leased out for summer villas,
you'd have, at the very least, an annual income of twenty-five thousand
roubles . . . From each summer visitor you can get at least twenty-five
roubles annually per each two-and-a-half-acre lot, and if you announce
it immediately, I guarantee you anything you like that, by autumn,
you won't have a single piece of land left, everything will be taken. In
one word, I congratulate you, you're saved. The location is wonderful,
the river is deep. Just one thing, of course, it needs to be tidied up,
cleared . . . let's say, for example, you tear down all the old buildings,
this house here which has become worthless, and cut down the old
cherry orchard . . . Up to now, there have only been landowners and
peasants in the country, but now summer residents are appearing. Every
town, even the least big, is surrounded by summer villas. It's likely that
in about twenty years, your summer residents will have multiplied
enormously. Now he only drinks tea on his veranda, but soon he may
take up cultivating his two-and-a-half acres and then your cherry
orchard will become happy, rich, splendid . . .

Some of the many actions he uses to pursue his objective in this speech are:

To *encourage them* to listen to him
To *remind them* of their situation (debt)
To *put their minds at ease / reassure them* that there is a solution
To *get* and *keep their attention*
To *detail for them* the ideal nature of their family estate to become real estate
    for rentable dachas
To *emphasise for them* the certainty of success if they take this line of action
To *inform them* as to how much they could earn
To *stress for them* the popularity of such dachas
To *assure them* of a new class of potential customers
To *paint a picture for them* of future happiness and abundance

From Action to Objective: Revealed and Hidden Objectives

The actions in a scene lead towards the discovery of the scene objective. Some actions in a scene can very clearly reveal the scene objectives motivating them, such as Lopakhin's in this speech. This is because it's directly connected to the plot and the situation the characters find themselves in. However, many actions function at a less obvious level of intention. In *The Three Sisters*, Olga, the eldest of the three, frequently *complains*. These are her complaints, scattered throughout the first three acts:

OLGA'S COMPLAINTS IN 'THE THREE SISTERS'

(Act 1) I'm at school every day and then giving private lessons till evening, so I've got a constant headache and my thoughts are like an old woman's. Really, during the four years I've been teaching, I've felt, day by day, drop by drop, my strength and youth draining out of me . . . I've got old, very thin, probably because I get upset with the girls at school . . .

(Act 2) I'm worn out. Our headmistress is ill and I'm deputising for her. My head, my head aches, my head . . . My head aches, my head . . . Andrei lost . . . the whole town's talking . . . I'll go and lie down . . . My head aches, my head . . .

(Act 3) How dreadful it is! I'm sick of it! . . . I'm tired, I can hardly stand on my feet . . . I shan't be headmistress . . . I'll refuse. I can't . . . I haven't the strength . . . Forgive me, I can't bear it . . . Everything went dark before my eyes . . . Maybe we were brought up strangely but I can't bear that sort of thing. An attitude like that oppresses me, it makes me ill . . . I simply give up . . . Any rudeness, even the slightest . . . upsets me . . . I've aged ten years tonight . . .

What is she up to? What's her objective? She's letting people know she's worn out and feels that she's aged. But why? The actor playing Olga will probably have to search harder than the actor playing Lopakhin needs to in his scene before she discovers what's motivating her character. Her actions are not connected with an obvious plot so much as with some internal needs of character that possibly even she herself isn't totally conscious of. There appears to be a gap between her need and others' seeming indifference. No one ever offers any response to these complaints of hers. What *does* she want? Attention? Sympathy? Love? To be noticed as an individual rather than as a schoolmistress?

The audience will not experience these expressions of pain and unhappiness as a serious revelation of a character in crisis *unless the actor transforms the character's portrayal of herself* (tired, prematurely aging, having a headache) *into actions that reach out for a response from the other characters*, rather than merely demonstrating them as naturalistic character traits, illustrations of tiredness and so forth . . .

————

Some Technical Concerns about Actions

TYPES OF ACTION

There are two basic categories of action:

> Physical (external) actions: e.g. *pushing, pulling, pointing, gesticulating, sighing, weeping, laughing, knitting, cooking* . . .

> Psychological (internal) actions: e.g. *threatening, coaxing, praising, obeying, ordering, denying, reproaching, reassuring, clarifying, refusing, encouraging, confiding* . . .

ACTIONS, GRAMMAR AND SEMANTICS

Actions are defined by (mainly) active, transitive verbs. Some enterprising practitioners have brought out a dictionary of actions.[*] But some of the verbs listed there are not always *playable* actions. There are certain groups of verbs that can't function as actions.

1. *Verbs which imply result or achievement* such as: *seduce, persuade, convince, surprise, stimulate, frighten* . . . These express *an already completed action*, the successful result of other actions (such as *urge, coax, tempt* . . .) and are usually employed in the past tense e.g. *I persuaded him; I seduced her; I surprised them.* In the present tense they usually describe an attribute of a person e.g. *I persuade people to buy my products; he surprises people by his resourcefulness; she seduces young men on a regular basis; his presence frightens me* . . . These are not playable as actions. How can you persuade someone before they've actually been persuaded? In the process of *trying to* persuade someone, you can have no idea whether you'll succeed or not. Such verbs technically function as objectives (wants) – e.g. *I want – therefore I try – to persuade you* – which then invoke into play specific actions such as *suggest, beg, explain, flatter, coax, tempt, exhort, challenge* . . . Such actions as these, effectively executed, may eventually succeed in *persuading* someone.

2. *Verbs of emotion and relationship* such as *hate, love, regret, revere, suspect, doubt* . . . These are actually emotional states of being: *I love you, he hates her* are not actions; they're usually sustained over a long period of time. To become active they have to be specified as *I declare my love, reveal my hatred, share my dislike, offer my regret, express my admiration, accuse you of my suspicions, air my doubts* (in fact, what the character *is doing* with the emotion).

---

[*] *Actions – The Actors' Thesaurus* by Marina Caldarone and Maggie Lloyd-Williams.

3. *Verbs of secret intention* such as *lie, deceive, trick, mislead, confuse.* You cannot play *I lie to you, I confuse you.* (Again, these function as objectives: e.g. *I want to deceive him.*) You have to play the action that you're employing to effect the lie or deception. That is to say, *you play the action you want the other characters to 'see' and accept.* Instead of 'I *pretend* that I was at home last night', the action might be something like: *I inform you* I was at home last night, *I assure you* I was at home last night, *I give you proof* . . . , *I insist* . . . , *I confirm* . . . , *I repeat* . . .

4. Some purists are resistant to the use of prepositions with verbs, but it's perfectly acceptable to use such verbal phrases as 'sympathise *with*', 'confide *in*', 'run something *by*', 'defer *to*', 'retreat *from*', 'size *up*', 'laugh *at*' and so forth.

5. Even if the verb used is *not obviously transitive towards another person* (e.g. *conjecture, ponder, realise, conclude* . . .), it must always be played transitively, for *the benefit of* and *to* the other actor-characters in the scene. For example, Lopakhin, in the opening scene of *The Cherry Orchard*, *recalls* or *reminisces about* Ranyevskaya. Dunyasha, his partner in the scene, has no text specifically responding to his recollections. This sort of situation tends to encourage actors, wrongly, to treat such texts as soliloquies to be acted by and for themselves. But the actor playing Lopakhin must always play this action *for* Dunyasha. She's in the room with him, so he can't avoid that fact and merely talk to himself.[*]

LOPAKHIN AND DUNYASHA
IN THE OPENING SCENE OF 'THE CHERRY ORCHARD'

LOPAKHIN Lyubov Andreyevna's been living abroad for five years. I've no idea what she's like now . . . She's a good person. Easy, simple. I remember, when I was a boy of about fifteen, my father – he had a store here in the village then – he punched me in the face and blood poured out of my nose. The two of us had come onto the estate for something or other and he was a bit drunk. Lyubov Andreyevna, I remember it like now, she was still a slender young girl, she brought me to the washstand here in this very room, the nursery. 'Don't cry, little peasant,' she says, 'it will be better in time for your wedding' . . . (*Pause.*) Little peasant . . . True, my father was a peasant, as for me, here I am in a white waistcoat and yellow shoes. A pig in a pastry shop. Only, I'm rich, lots of money, but however you look at it, a peasant's a peasant . . . (*He thumbs through the book.*) Here I was, reading this book and didn't understand a word. Tried reading and fell asleep.

DUNYASHA (*after a pause*). The dogs didn't sleep all night, they can feel their masters are coming.

---

[*] The scene between Konstantin and Sorin in the first act of *The Seagull*, in which Konstantin talks a lot and Sorin says very little, could similarly fall into this trap.

NOTES ON THIS SCENE

He could restate his action: *to share my memories of Ranyevskaya with Dunyasha*. But this might slightly overstate their relationship and encourage the actor to play the text in a too overly frontal way, rather than allowing his need for contact with her to be more subtly expressed.

This is an example of extremely delicate writing, where what Lopakhin wants from Dunyasha is not immediately obvious. As one grows familiar with the play, it becomes clear that he's extremely nervous about meeting Ranyevskaya after so many years. It clearly matters to him a lot. He has left his business affairs and made a train journey from Kharkov especially to welcome her home. He wants to be the one to give her the advice that will save her family estate from auction. Then he has to hurry to catch his train back. He is anxious to make a good impression on her, to be accepted by her, to have her appreciate how much he wants to reciprocate the kindness she showed him when his nose bled; at some level he probably wants to win her 'love'. He's unsure whether she'll recognise him. He's also very conscious that he still looks and behaves 'like a peasant', or so he thinks. He castigates himself for having already damaged her first impression of him by falling asleep and failing to go with the others to greet her at the station. Hence his anxiety.

Often, in a state of unease, we can find ourselves talking to complete strangers about the most personal matters. While waiting in a doctor's surgery, we may give the person next to us the most intimate details of the symptoms that are currently worrying us. We don't do this deliberately, consciously anticipating some solution from them. But at an intuitive level, we feel the need to unburden our anxieties for the sympathetic ears of another human being who might somehow reassure us that all will be well. I would suggest that something like this is happening to Lopakhin in this scene with Dunyasha. Possibly, at some submerged level, he feels he can unburden himself to Dunyasha because they're both peasants. His objective, unconsciously, is probably along the lines of: *to elicit something from her – sympathy, agreement, possibly reassurance that Ranyevskaya will still remember him and, still feel the same affectionate concern for him that she once demonstrated when he was a boy* . . .

But it would be precipitate to try to pin this down too early in rehearsal. Therefore you need an action that is true to the scene but doesn't force the actors to run before they can walk. *I recall or I reminisce* are perfectly sufficient, appropriate and accurate actions, so long as the actor plays them with an awareness of Dunyasha's presence; and so long as the actor playing Dunyasha responds to what he's saying. Eventually, between them, as they start to know their characters and understand the scene, they will discover the subtler levels of actions and objectives underpinning it. But whatever Lopakhin is finally playing, he will nevertheless *always, at a 'surface' level, be reminiscing about or recalling an incident from his youth.*

I've gone into what might seem like excessive explanation about this brief moment in the play. But it's to emphasise the point that, *early in rehearsals, the best way into a text is to use the simplest, least interpretive action, rather than cluttering yourself with complicated guesswork that could well turn out to be inaccurate.*

I would advise actors and directors not to let any bullying constraints issued by the Action Police inhibit them from using an occasional intransitive verb, so long as they play it *to* and *for* their partners in the scene!

What and How: Discipline and Freedom

The *what* is clearly the text the playwright has created: the words for the characters to speak and the stage directions for them to carry out. *The what is the incontrovertible body of facts* about the characters, their world and the details of the plot. The characters in *The Seagull* are undoubtedly living during the last years of the nineteenth century in Czarist Russia. Konstantin definitely directs Nina in his play. She indisputably acts in it. He indubitably stops the performance when his mother loudly comments on it. He unarguably lays a dead seagull at Nina's feet. She irrefutably runs away to Moscow, has an affair with Trigorin and a child with him, who dies. Trigorin does go back to Arkadina. Nina does become an actress. Konstantin does have some short stories published under a pseudonym and he does shoot himself. So *what* the characters do and say are constant and unchanging, never to be altered or ignored.

The *how* is the manner in which the actors play their actions (and therefore how they play the text). *The how is open to change* and totally in the actors' domain. The variation in the playing of *hows* is predicated on what happens between the actors during any performance. From performance to performance (and rehearsal to rehearsal, of course) the *how* may alter, from the subtlest shift to the most radical change.

The *what* holds the actors in the scene, gives them a spine and eliminates tendencies towards caprice and arbitrariness. The *what* provides the *how* with the security of defined parameters within which the actors are free to explore possibilities, respond with spontaneity and allow their imaginations to take flight. *The what gives actors discipline and control; the how gives them creative freedom.*

Actions and Verbs

The *what* includes – to a less fixed degree – the choice of objectives and actions. In many cases, what they are is clear and indisputable, but their choice, nonetheless, will always be a matter of some interpretation. They are vulnerable to the imprecision of language and to an actor's subjective understanding of words. They are therefore open to a certain degree of variation.

Let's take the action *to admonish*. Is it radically different from the actions *to chide, rebuke, reprimand, tell off, haul over the coals, have on the carpet, reprehend, reprove, upbraid*? Does it also imply *blame, warn, reproach . . .*? For all of us, a particular verb or verbal phrase may have some slight subtlety of implication that differentiates it from the others and makes it seem a more appropriate choice. But whatever the nuanced difference might be, we all understand at a non-verbal level the 'area' of the action that has to be played. To insist on an 'exact' choice of verb may render the actor totally head-bound. This is why, beyond a certain point, it's counterproductive for a director to be too prescriptive in defining the words of an action or objective. A word that excites the imagination of one person may be a very damp squib for another. You may want to *castigate* me, I may prefer to *chastise* or even *chasten* you. You may feel you can physically inhabit the word *rebuke* more imaginatively; I may find *admonish* more creatively stimulating.

Actions: To Plan or Not to Plan?

Are actions meant to be worked out in advance and firmly set – or not? As we will see when we come to the application of actions early in the rehearsal process, the actors can and do work out actions suggested by the text at their least interpretive – most factual – level. However, they never become locked into an idea of *how* they will be performed. The actions function as tendencies that are open to spontaneous variation or change depending on the way a scene develops during a performance. Such variations are influenced by where the actors find themselves emotionally in the heat of playing and, above all, by the need to deal with the responses of their partners, which will almost certainly vary from show to show. Most of the time, the initial actions, which should have become instinctively embedded in the actors' psyches and bodies, will stay reasonably close to the 'world' of their initial analysis (the 'worlds' say, of *admonishing* or *threatening* or *complaining . . .*). But the more the actors immerse themselves in the play and the more they discover about their material, they may well find that on occasions they shift to very different actions. If actors have a sudden flash of fresh insight into an action, they can then play it, secure in the knowledge that their partners are ready to respond to whatever they are offered. They important thing is that they do play an action.

Even if the early choice or interpretation of an action (the *what*) does remain, it's still open to be played in a wide range of expressive ways (the *how*). If I *do* choose to *admonish* you, I may do so with more or less aggression, more or less regret, more or less self-righteousness, more or less sympathy, more or less impatience . . . I may admonish you staying firmly seated, I may move about restlessly or stand over you threateningly or face you challengingly, or I may take you by the arm and walk you about while I admonish you . . .

The analysis of actions helps to hold the actor in the *logic* of a scene (the *what* of discipline) while giving them a secure foundation from which they can develop, grow and change 'in the moment' of performance (the *how* of creative freedom).

RECAPITULATION OF ACTIONS

Theatre is the Art of Action – Action is the Art of the Actor

Actions are what the character does and what the actor plays. In fact, it is the only thing an actor can play. It provides the life and truth of the performance. Even before actors know anything much about their characters or the WORLD OF THE PLAY, they can still play, through actions, each situation with truth and intelligence to the best of their understanding. Gradually they will enrich these actions with their growing knowledge of the WORLD they're learning to inhabit through the process of rehearsals. So, when or if in doubt, the actor's security is in action. It is always there to hold the actor in the scene and to ensure a continuity of truthful contact with partners. By playing actions, actors make discoveries about a scene. *Without actions, the performance flies apart. Nothing happens between actors.* There is no event. We end up with demonstrations of acting, displays of emotion and mood and line-reading – nothing but generalisations and results.

Actions are *absorbent*, imbibing all the other elements of the play. (This I'll explain fully when we get to POINTS OF CONCENTRATION.) Whatever is needed – the revelation of character, the motivation of objectives, the influence of GIVEN CIRCUMSTANCES – is contained within the playing of an action.

Theatre is the art of action because actions, played with truth and wit, ensure the fluency of the physical, emotional, intellectual and aesthetic life of the performance. Actions are central and essential to the craft of acting. They connect with every area of an actor's work: intention, contact, energy, tempo, rhythm, emotion, space, time, movement, gesture, vocal expression, story, plot, theme, characterisation . . . *Actions unite them all in a single resonant form of expression.*

Beats

An action can conceivably last the duration of a play (e.g. Oedipus's through-line *to discover the cause of the plague*). At this level, it is too generalised to be playable. It becomes more like a guide pointing the actor-character in the direction of more detailed actions; in fact, it really functions like an objective. Such actions break down into successively smaller, more digestible actions. These are called beats.[*]

A beat is an action at its most precise and unable to be broken down any further. A new beat occurs with every transition, with the slightest change of thought, and can be as short as an intake of breath or an exclamation. However, its criterion is not its length, but its *indivisibility. Beats are what actors actually play.* The concept of beats is to alert actors to be specific and consequently gives due weight to details of text that they may tend to ignore or dismiss as of little or no significance, such as Shakespearian 'O's, that are frequently thrown off without much thought or intention, when not totally ignored.

Let's say an actor plays the action: *to greet some friends.* This may have several components, such as *hailing them from the distance, showing surprise, exclaiming with delight, shaking hands, embracing, patting arms and shoulders, asking after their health, nodding with interest at their news* – and so on. These are beats. The larger action (*greeting friends*) is comprised of a lot of smaller actions (beats), all of which must be fully honoured.

As an example, here is a breakdown of beats from the opening dialogue of *The Seagull*. The slashes (/) represent transitions and therefore the start of a new beat. Note that punctuation is *not* necessarily a guide to defining beats. When breaking down a text into beats, you must ensure that each beat is *a complete thought or idea.*

BEATS IN THE OPENING SCENE OF 'THE SEAGULL'

MEDVEDENKO *Beat/*Why are you always in black?

MASHA *Beat/*I'm in mourning for my life. *B/*I'm unhappy.

MEDVEDENKO *B/*But why? *B/*(*Ponders.*) *B/*I don't understand . . .
*B/*You're healthy, *B/*your father's not rich, *B/*but he's comfortable.
*B/*My life's much harder than yours, *B/*I only get twenty-three roubles
a month *B/*and then from that they take something for the pension
fund, *B/*but I don't wear mourning.

---

[*] Beats should not be confused with Stanislavsky's *bits*. These are closer to units and are dealt with in Bella Merlin's excellent *The Complete Stanislavsky Toolkit.*

B/They sit down.

MASHA *B/*It isn't a question of money. *B/*Even a pauper can be happy.

MEDVEDENKO *B/*In theory yes, *B/*but in practice it works out so: *B/*myself, *B/*my mother, *B/*two sisters *B/*and a little brother *B/*all on a salary of twenty-three roubles. *B/*People need to eat and drink? *B/*Need tea and sugar? *B/*Need tobacco? *B/*It's hard to make ends meet.

——

When Actions Become Objectives: the Layering of Actions and Beats

The through-line – or main line-of-action – is the largest action in a play; a beat is the smallest. Between the two, there can exist simultaneous layers of actions, becoming more and more precise as they're successively broken down, until there are no further actions to be revealed. In this process, *each action that generates a more precise action automatically becomes the objective that motivates that action.* To play accurately, actors can break down scenes into detailed beats. To understand the idea of layered actions, let's analyse a short exchange between Konstantin and his uncle Sorin from Act One of *The Seagull.*

KONSTANTIN AND SORIN IN ACT ONE OF 'THE SEAGULL'

SORIN Why is my sister out of sorts?

KONSTANTIN Why? Bored. Jealous. She's already against me, against the performance, against my play, because that novelist of hers might take a fancy to Nina. She knows nothing about my play but already she hates it.

SORIN (*laughs*). You're the one who's inventing things, really! . . .

KONSTANTIN She's put out that on this little stage Nina will be the one to have the success and not she. A psychological oddity – my mother. Undeniably talented, intelligent, capable of sobbing over a book, of reeling off all of Nekrassov by heart, of nursing the sick like an angel, but just try praising Duse in her presence. Oh-ho-ho! You must only praise her, write about her, rave, rant, go into raptures over her extraordinary performance in *Camille* or *The Haze of Life*, but here in the country she doesn't get these narcotics, so she's bored and bad-tempered, we are all her enemies, we are all to blame.

ANALYSIS OF THE DIALOGUE FOR LAYERS OF ACTIONS
THAT BECOME OBJECTIVES

When Konstantin first enters, his *scene objective* is to ensure that everything is ready for the performance of his play. Consequently some of his
actions are: *to get rid of the audience members (Masha and Medvedenko)*
who have arrived too early; to warn his stagehand, Yakov, to be back on time
from his swim; to show off his unique stage setting to Sorin; to express his anxiety
that Nina might not show up; to ensure all the special effects are ready . . . and
so on. When his uncle, Sorin, referring to his mother, the actress Arkadina,
asks him: *Why is my sister out of sorts?*, this triggers a new action: *to prepare*
himself for – or steel himself against – his mother's likely criticism of his play.
This action still remains within his overall scene objective: *to ensure that*
everything is ready for the performance (which includes his own state of
mind and anticipation of the audience's reaction). It also generates his
need to explain why she might criticise his play. So his action becomes: *to*
blame his mother's jealousy as the cause of her criticism. (He believes that his
mother can't bear anyone else to be involved in theatre, especially pretty
young women like Nina.) In order to justify this attack on his mother, his
action then becomes: *to itemise the reasons for her jealousy.* This action
proliferates a sequence of specific actions – *beats* – that specify those
reasons. These beats are the bottom line: they generate no further actions,
and are *what the actor actually plays. Each preceding action has become the*
objective of the fresh action it generated. The scene breaks down as follows:

BREAKDOWN OF KONSTANTIN'S ACTIONS-TURNED-OBJECTIVES

(SCENE OBJECTIVE:)   I *want* to make sure that everything is ready for the
performance of my play
so my *action* in this section of the scene is:
(therefore) *I prepare myself for my mother's likely criticism of my play*
which becomes the *objective*:
I *want* to prepare myself for my mother's likely criticism of my play
which generates the *action*:
(therefore) *I blame my mother's likely criticism on her jealousy*
which becomes the *objective*:
I *want* to blame my mother's likely criticism on her jealousy
which generates the *action*:

(therefore) *I justify my accusation by itemising the reasons for her jealousy* which becomes the *objective*:

I *want* to justify my accusation by itemising the reasons for her jealousy

which breaks down into the following detailed actions – beats – that specify the reasons for her jealousy:

*Beat 1/*Why? *B2/*Bored. *B3/*Jealous. *B4/*She's already against me, against the performance, against my play, because that novelist of hers might take a fancy to Nina. *B5/*She knows nothing about my play, *B6/*but already she hates it. *B7/*She's put out that on this little stage Nina will be the one to have the success *B8/*and not she. *B9/*A psychological oddity – my mother. *B10/*Undeniably talented, *B11/*intelligent, *B12/*capable of sobbing over a book, *B13/*of reeling off all of Nekrassov by heart, *B14/*of nursing the sick like an angel, *B15/*but just try praising Duse in her presence. *B16/*Oh-ho-ho! *B17/*You must only praise her, *B18/*write about her, *B19/*rave, *B20/*rant, *B21/*go into raptures over her extraordinary performance in *Camille B22/*or *The Haze of Life*, *B23/*but here in the country she doesn't get these narcotics, *B24/*so she's bored *B25/*and bad-tempered, *B26/*we are all her enemies, *B27/*we are all to blame.

These beats cannot be broken down any further or smaller.

A PYRAMID OF ACTIONS

Each of these beats is informed by and carries the intentions of all the layers of Actions–Turned–Objectives within which it is ensconced:

I (want to) ensure everything is ready for the play, therefore

> I (want to) prepare myself for my mother's likely criticism of my play, therefore

>> I (want to) blame any such criticism on her jealousy, therefore

>>> I (want to) justify my accusation by itemising the reasons for her jealousy, therefore

>>> I play Beats 1 – 27.[*]

---

[*] Compare this with the section: A PYRAMID OF TITLES in PREPARING THE TEXT.

NOTES ON THE BEATS

These 27 beats are indivisible. They are the bottom line. *They are what the actor plays.* Each beat is a new thought and played as a fresh and specific action.

When breaking down a text for beats, you must ensure that each beat is *a complete thought or idea*. For example: *B23/but here in the country she doesn't get these narcotics* cannot be split into two, because *'but here in the country'* on its own doesn't mean anything. A conditional sentence such as *If you do such-and-such, I'll do such-and-such* is one beat; because *'If you do such and such'* by itself has no meaning, it's an incomplete idea. You can recognise a beat by whether it makes sense played on its own.

However, in some cases, the beat that has gone before can support *a subsequent beat*, e.g. *B7/She's put out that on this little stage Nina will be the one to have the success* supports *B8/and not she*. And *'not she'* takes its full meaning from the previous beat. Or, in *B12/capable of sobbing over a book*, the word *'capable'* supports the sense of the two subsequent beats: *B13/of reeling off all of Nekrassov by heart*, and *B14/of nursing the sick like an angel*.

In many cases, actors have an interpretive choice as to how to break up some sequences. For example, *B21 & 22* could be played as one beat *'go into raptures over her extraordinary performance in Camille or The Haze of Life'*. If the actor lumps the titles of the two plays, *Camille* and *The Haze of Life*, together as one beat, that is a justifiable choice and maybe he could run them together dismissively. However, by splitting them into two, he has the possibility of getting extra mileage for his contempt for her sort of theatre by characterising each play with a different sort of mockery.

Konstantin could also play *Beats 10-14* and *Beats 17–22* as one beat each. But if so, he similarly loses the possibility of several different shifts of thought, variety of expressive colours and revelations of his own psychology. The more detailed the beats, the more vivid the performance. We, the audience, are being kept on the *qui vive*, continuously alerted to new information, continuously refreshed and surprised. A positive side effect of this attention to the specificity of beats is that *language becomes more vivid* without any self-conscious demonstration on the part of the actor.

IMPORTANT: Konstantin must play all these beats, actions and objectives *to and for Sorin* (he is the only other person in the scene).[*] So, to state

---

[*] Refer back to the discussion of Lopakhin's scene with Dunyasha in FROM ACTION TO OBJECTIVE in the section on ACTIONS, in which one character has what is virtually a monologue, to which the other character makes very little response or none at all.

> them absolutely accurately, we need to add some more words to his objectives, along the lines of: *I want you, Uncle, to agree with/sympathise with/support me* – in blaming my mother's jealousy as the reason for her likely criticism of my play.

This no doubt seems inordinately elaborate, but I want to stress that to be detailed, specific and truthful, the actor has to play accurately rather than approximately. *He does not necessarily have to think this process through or work it out intellectually.* It's usually sufficient for him to arouse in himself the intention: *I want to prepare for the performance* – or *I want to prepare myself for my mother's likely criticism* – in order to launch himself into a creative, active state in which he'll go through this process instinctively, possibly making some of the choices I've suggested here, in all likelihood making others of his own. But if he doesn't, he always has this structure and method of analysis to fall back on for guidance and support. Actors very easily become generalised, especially under emotional pressure.

Infinite Possibilities

The text will of course suggest some choices of action, but not necessarily all the possibilities. As I've said before and will no doubt repeat frequently, a line, a speech, a scene can be played in an infinity of ways. Finding a way to say a line of text is *not* the ultimate purpose of a performance; it is, *rather*, using that line of text to pursue the character's objectives through action. Their dialogue is just one tool (though probably the main one) used by characters to assist them in attempting to get what they want. *Planning or working out how to say a line is deadly. Using a line in order to pursue an objective is lively.* The *how* should happen instinctively in the moment.

And, as I've already said, even if an actor has 'decided' on an action, there is *not just one way* of playing it. Konstantin's action *'to blame'* can be played in many ways: the *how* of blaming has endless possibilities. He can blame his mother with reproach, with regret, sarcasm, defensiveness, resentment, defiance . . .

His *hows* will largely depend on the other actor in the scene – in this case, on Sorin and the way he reacts to Konstantin's need for his support. Sorin's actions and attitude to each beat will influence *how* Konstantin plays his next beat. It will depend on whether Sorin agrees with him, or tries to avoid being drawn into criticising his own sister, or tries to laugh off his accusations, or expresses his disapproval, or his embarrassment . . . and so forth. In short, the actor playing Konstantin responds specifically and spontaneously to what he's getting back from his partner.

So you can see how much potential mobility, flexibility and variation there is in the playing of the smallest moment; and, correspondingly, I hope you can see how artificial and how limited planned choices of *how* to play a moment or line must be.

Despite such close analysis, you are *never* instructing actors *how* they should play a beat. *You never ask for a result.* You use the concept of beats to point out (a) that they've missed a transition, or (b) that they're in danger of becoming generalised because of running several beats together, or (c) you're encouraging them to explore the smallest beats for greater variety and more detail, or (d) for the possibility of an apparently unimportant beat yielding unexpected dividends.

Obstacles

Obstacles stand in the way of the character's objectives. They are what characters have to overcome in order to gain their objectives. Consequently, obstacles create conflict, the lifeblood of drama. They come in three modes:

1. External Obstacles

First, the external obstacle: this comes from outside the action and is usually a matter of chance – an avalanche, earthquake, traffic jam, coincidence, war, fire, famine, drought . . . These are usually the material of melodrama or heavily plot-driven cinema. Sometimes the conduct of the Gods comes into this category if it appears unmotivated by anything other than caprice. Usually these obstacles are metaphorical and provide a context for other, more interesting personal conflicts.

2. Obstacles Created by Others

Second, the obstacle caused by other people: people who don't want to give you what you want, or want something from you that you don't want to give them. This is the central device of drama. Sometimes the conflict is overt such as that, say, between Stanley and Blanche in *A Streetcar Named Desire* or that between Konstantin and Arkadina in *The Seagull*. Sometimes it is, initially, more hidden, such as the one between Hedda Gabler and Thea Elvsted or between Lopakhin and Ranyevskaya in *The Cherry Orchard*. In many cases, you could say that *one character's objective is another character's obstacle.*

3. Inner Obstacles

Third, the obstacle from a conflict *within* the character itself: this is the most sophisticated and complex for the actor. The obstacle can be a trait within the character – prejudice, selfishness, low self-esteem – that inhibits the pursuit of the very thing the character wants. The *counter-objective* exists totally in this category. Characters don't automatically proceed in a straight line towards what they want. They can be pulled in other directions and do in fact pursue their *counter-objectives* in direct opposition to their *super-objectives*. Think how often in your own life, you fail to pursue something you really want because of some other need that takes you in the opposite direction. (You want the job but you also want to avoid rejection – so you don't go for the interview.) Characters are often unaware of their obstacles in this third category.

SOME OBSTACLES

Konstantin (*super-objective*: to win his mother's love and respect); *some obstacles*: his lack of confidence in himself; his lack of social skills; his inability to pursue a career/earn a living; the blindness of his need for his mother's love; his inability to understand her situation and her needs; his contempt for her sort of theatre; his rejection by Nina; his talent for self-dramatisation; the failure of his play; his emotional self-righteousness; his double jealousy of Trigorin; and his *counter-objective*: to prove himself a revolutionary writer . . .

Arkadina (*super-objective*: to receive the world's adulation); *some obstacles*: Nina's youth and freshness; her own fears of getting old, losing her looks and therefore the roles for which she is known, losing her career, losing her status, losing her lover; losing her money, being unsupported; the threat to her financial situation from her family's requests for money; her guilt at not dealing sympathetically and generously with her son and brother; Trigorin's interest in Nina; her boredom in the country; and her *counter-objective*: to hang on to what she has at all costs . . .

It is important that the *actor* recognises what the character's obstacles are, even if the *character* doesn't always register them consciously. An awareness of the obstacles will encourage the actors to play with greater variety. Each new obstacle should elicit a new sequence of actions from the character who faces it.

The Hierarchy of Actions and Objectives

A Text is a Score

A text is a score potentially composed of detailed OBJECTIVES, ACTIONS and BEATS
that lie dormant awaiting the actor. The actor translates the language of dialogue
and stage directions into the language of OBJECTIVES, ACTIONS and BEATS.

RECAPITULATION

The Super-Objective exists before – and continues beyond – the play. This is
the character's main goal in life. It is character-driven and motivates ▶

The Through-Line – the main objective that the character is pursuing
through the specific circumstances of the play. This is plot-driven. It is also
known as The Main Line of Action. It breaks down into ▶

The Scene Objectives – what the character *wants* from situation to situation,
scene to scene. The sum of these should constitute the through-line and
help reveal the super-objective. They break down into – or more accurately
are – the motivations for playing ▶

The Actions – what the character *does* in order to achieve those objectives.
These in their most detailed manifestation are ▶

The Beats – the most precise actions. *These are what the actor actually plays.*

[*The Counter-Objective* exists on the same terms as the super-objective but
is in conflict with it. This is an important drive in the character's life. This
is also character-driven.]

[*The Obstacles* – whatever conflicts with an objective.]

EXAMPLES OF THE HIERARCHY OF OBJECTIVES AND ACTIONS:
LOPAKHIN IN 'THE CHERRY ORCHARD'

His Super-Objective: To be accepted (appreciated/loved) by Ranyevskaya
and her world

His Counter-Objective: To get reparation/revenge for the injustices done to
his family who were serfs

His Through-Line: To help Ranyevskaya save the estate

His Adjusted Through-Line: To gain her forgiveness for buying the estate
himself

SCENE FROM ACT ONE OF 'THE CHERRY ORCHARD'

LOPAKHIN I want to tell you something very pleasant, encouraging. (*Glances at his watch.*) I'm leaving now, no time to talk . . . So, in two or three words. As you know, your cherry orchard is up for sale to pay your debts, the auction's set for the twenty-second of August, but you needn't worry, my dear, sleep peacefully, there's a solution . . . Here's my plan. Please listen! Your estate is only fifteen miles from town, the railway runs nearby, and if the cherry orchard and land along the river were divided into summer lots and then leased out for summer villas, you'd have, at the very least, an annual income of twenty-five thousand roubles.

GAEV Excuse me, what nonsense!

RANYEVSKAYA I don't quite understand you, Yermolai Aleksyeyevitch.

LOPAKHIN From each summer visitor you can get at least twenty-five roubles annually per each two-and-a-half-acre lot, and if you announce it immediately, I guarantee you anything you like that, by autumn, you won't have a single piece of land left, everything will be taken. In one word, I congratulate you, you're saved. The location is wonderful, the river is deep. Just one thing, of course, it needs to be tidied up, cleared . . . let's say, for example, you tear down all the old buildings, this house here which has become worthless, and cut down the old cherry orchard . . .

RANYEVSKAYA Cut down? Forgive me, my dear, you don't understand a thing. If there's something interesting, even remarkable, in the entire Province, then it's our cherry orchard.

LOPAKHIN The only remarkable thing about the cherry orchard is that it's big. The cherries make an appearance only once every two years and then there's nothing to be done with them, nobody buys them.

GAEV This orchard is mentioned in the Encyclopaedia.

LOPAKHIN (*glancing at his watch*). If we don't come up with something,, don't reach a decision, then on the twenty-second of August, the cherry orchard, as well as the entire estate, will be auctioned off. Take courage. Do it! There's no other way out, I swear to you. None, none.

FIRS In the old days, about forty – fifty years ago, they used to dry the cherries, soak them, pickle them and make them into jam, and they used to . . .

GAEV Keep quiet, Firs.

FIRS And they used to send the dried cherries by cartloads to Moscow and
Kharkov. There was money then. And the cherries were soft, juicy,
sweet, fragrant . . . Then they had a method of . . .

RANYEVSKAYA And where's that method now?

FIRS Forgotten. No one remembers.

S-PISHCHIK (*to Ranyevskaya*). What's happening in Paris? How are things?
Did you eat frogs?

RANYEVSKAYA I ate crocodiles.

S-PISHCHIK Think of that . . .

LOPAKHIN Up to now, there have only been landowners and peasants in
the country, but now summer residents are appearing. Every town, even
the least big, is surrounded by summer villas. It's likely that in about
twenty years, your summer residents will have multiplied enormously.
Now he only drinks tea on his veranda, but soon he may take up
cultivating his two-and-a-half acres and then your cherry orchard will
become happy, rich, splendid . . .

GAEV (*exasperated*). What nonsense!

AN ANALYSIS OF THE SCENE

Lopakhin's *scene objective* in the above sequence:

> To convince Ranvevskaya to sell off some of her estate and with the
> proceeds to build summer villas that will generate rents to pay off
> the family's debts.

His *obstacles* in this sequence:

> His low self-esteem (he feels like a peasant in her company:
> uneducated, unrefined, not knowing how to behave or how to talk);
> his more profound awkwardness around her because of his buried
> feelings for her; Ranyevskaya's apparently faint recollection of him
> (as opposed to his vivid childhood memory of her – she's on stage
> for a good fifteen or twenty minutes without addressing a word to
> him though she has spoken to everyone else, including the servants;

he's the one who has to initiate a conversation with her); her inability even to conceive of his suggestions as viable solutions; his inability to understand her point of view; his embarrassment at the jokes and gossip about his non-existent 'engagement' to Varya; his busy schedule (he has a train to catch); the fact that he missed greeting her at the station because (like a peasant) he fell asleep . . .

His *actions* in this sequence:

(His first speech): *To promise her good news. To explain to her why he has to be succinct. To calm any anxiety she has. To remind her of the situation. To get her attention. To point out to her the suitability of the property for the transaction he has in mind. To encourage her by predicting the financial rewards of such a transaction.*

(His second speech): *To impress upon her the certain financial rewards. To urge her to act promptly for maximum success. To congratulate her. To praise/make her see the location's viability. To advise clearing the place up by tearing and cutting down whatever is no longer of any use.*

(His third speech): *To refute Ranyevskaya's unrealistic idea of the cherry orchard.*

(His fourth speech): *To warn her of the risk she takes by not making a decision. To urge her to be courageous. To insist there's no other way out for her. To reiterate this.*

(His fifth speech): *To describe to her the contemporary social situation. To inspire her with his vision of the future.*

His *beats* in his first two speeches are:

LOPAKHIN *Beat1/*I want to tell you something very pleasant, *B2/*encouraging. *B3/(Glances at his watch.) B4/* I'm leaving now, *B5/*no time to talk . . . *B6/*So, *B7/*in two or three words. *B8/*As you know, your cherry orchard is up for sale *B9/*to pay your debts, *B10/*the auction's set for the twenty-second of August, *B11/*but you needn't worry, my dear, *B12/*sleep peacefully, *B13/*there's a solution . . . *B14/*Here's my plan. *B15/*Please *B16/*listen! *B17/*Your estate is only fifteen miles from town, *B18/*the railway runs nearby, *B19/*and if the cherry orchard and land along the river were divided into summer lots and then leased out for summer villas, you'd have, at the very least, an annual income of twenty-five thousand roubles.

GAEV /Excuse me, /what nonsense!

RANYEVSKAYA /I don't quite understand you, Yermolai
Aleksyeyevitch.

LOPAKHIN *B20/*From each summer visitor you can get at least
twenty-five roubles annually per each two-and-a-half-acre lot,
*B21/*and if you announce it immediately, I guarantee you
anything you like that, by autumn, you won't have a single piece
of land left, *B22/*everything will be taken. *B23/*In one word,
I congratulate you, *B24/*you're saved. *B25/*The location is
wonderful, *B26/* the river is deep. *B27/*Just one thing, *B28/*of
course, it needs to be tidied up, *B29/*cleared . . . *B30/*let's say, for
example, you tear down all the old buildings, *B31/*this house here
*B32/*which has become worthless, *B33/*and cut down the old
cherry orchard . . .

The point of this very detailed structure of actions and objectives is to give actors
a practical, creative, open-ended technique to fall back. Should their instincts fail
them anywhere within the process, instead of throwing their hands in the air and
dumping everything in the director's lap, crying 'I don't know what I'm doing!'
(not an infrequent *cri du coeur*), they can, by asking themselves enough questions,
come up with provisional choices of actions to be tried and discarded until they
arrive at an approach that seems appropriate for that part of the text that's
causing them trouble.

———

Commitment to Actions and Objectives

Super-objectives and objectives are *not* just mental guides, they must also be
fulfilled physically and sensuously. They need the total commitment and concentration of the actor. Actors who commit to embodying objectives and playing
actions *lose all self-consciousness.* I stress again: they become *fully absorbed* in what
they're doing and *therefore absorbing to the audience.* Without actions and objectives, there is only indicating, commenting, demonstrating, playing results and
playing for effect, all of which add up to untruthful – therefore bad – acting.

Feel: Emotion

The Unactability of Emotion

Stanislavsky's search was to discover how an actor could produce truthful, spontaneous emotion in performance. When he began his exploration of acting, despite his admiration for such actors as Salvini and Rossi, he was, presumably, exposed to predominantly what we used to call ham actors – performers with grand gestures and even grander voices, demonstrating their emotionality with great *élan* but not much truth. To display themselves and their emotional expressiveness was the purpose of their craft. Nowadays, with more than a century of film and half-century of television behind us, we're unlikely to see acting so overtly fake. (However, I'd contend that there's still acting on display that is essentially doing the same thing, albeit by subtler and more sophisticated means.)*

The last chapter of Stanislavsky's *An Actor Prepares* is called 'On the Threshold of the Subconscious'. He understood that emotions cannot be summoned up to order. In our own lives, we have little control over how we feel. When we're depressed, we can't just 'snap out of it'; if we're angry, it takes time to calm down. How on earth, then, can an actor – truthfully – fall madly in love at 8.30, become overwhelmed with jealousy at 9.00, be filled with hatred at 9.30 and die of despair

---

* Naturalistic – as distinct from truthful – acting is a matter of fashion. We tend to confuse the two or see them as synonymous; understandably, because in contemporary naturalism we're seeing and hearing, superficially at least, behaviour, language, clothes and environments that mirror our own. But naturalism is as much a style as any other, and vulnerable to the manners of the moment. If you revisit the films of actors you admired in the past, you may be in for huge disappointments. James Dean, who seemed to be the last word in naturalism – truth itself – when I first saw him in *East of Eden*, looks, years later, immensely mannered, a compound of tics and self-conscious inarticulacy. Ironically, Raymond Massey, who next to him (he played his father) had then seemed rather stolid and dull, can now be seen to be playing in a more durable manner. Garbo, certainly compared to the actors around her, originally seemed 'real', full of imaginative psychological details and spontaneity. Now she is clearly playing in a rather *souffrante*, drooping manner, vocally in a minor key, very much within a Romantic convention. I once saw a brief clip of Duse, by then quite an old woman, but it was hard even to glimpse the naturalness that was so admired in her heyday and so extolled by Shaw. She seemed very stiff and restrained. I also saw Olga Knipper on film, again when she was old. She had been Chekhov's leading lady (as well as his mistress and wife) and had created the main women's roles in his four great plays. Here she was playing Ranyevskaya in scenes from *The Cherry Orchard*. She was very much the theatrical grande dame, discharging emotion with total lack of charm and no concern at all for her partners. Garrick? Siddons? Irving? Maybe we should be thankful we're spared glimpses of *them* on film. We can still imagine them in any way we choose. The criterion is not whether any acting is naturalistic, but whether it is truthful. Any style of acting can be truthful. It is a matter of transforming a truthful impulse into a particular form without losing the truth *en route*, and of believing in that reality (*see*: WORLDS).

at 10.15? Emotions aren't on tap like water, to be turned on and off at will. They have to be coaxed from the unconscious. He discovered that playing objectives and actions was a way to open up the psycho-physical channels through which they might *possibly* emerge.

Emotion in performance is a paradoxical matter, of considerable confusion to many practitioners. Acting is not about 'being emotional' and 'trying to feel'. It's about doing. Nevertheless, we expect actors to express true emotions, and when appropriate, strong and vivid ones. But an actor *cannot play* an emotion. Emotion, how and what we feel, is *an outcome*: the outcome either of succeeding or failing to get what we want. If actors pursue their objectives by playing appropriate actions honestly and openly, that's to say, trying genuinely to affect their partners and, in turn, allowing themselves to be affected by their partners' responses, then *feelings will quite naturally be aroused without any conscious effort*. In fact, through-out a performance, actors, by playing a continuous, seamless flow of actions, should consequently experience a seamless flow of feelings that shift and adapt to the ever-changing circumstance in which they're evoked. Our emotional state is never static, it's always adjusting in degree and quality and kind.

States of Pure Feeling

The only exception to the concept of being constantly in action may be those rare moments when we're suspended at the extreme peak or trough of an emotion whose intensity engulfs us to the exclusion of everything else: a moment, say, when we're overawed by the beauty of a view and can do nothing but experience that sensation; or we are stunned into shock by sudden bad news and remain im-mobilised, beyond tears or any sort of response. Those are states of pure feeling, momentarily beyond objectives and actions, into which nothing else can intrude.[*]

I once had the chance to revisit a Chinese theatre company I'd worked with some years earlier. I'd never expected the likelihood of seeing them again, and presumably they'd never expected me to reappear. They insisted on laying on one of those generous Chinese 'banquets' to mark the occasion. I sat at the table, surrounded by the warmth of people wanting to express their pleasure at seeing me again and by many hands pressing food onto my plate. For a moment, some sunlight lit up the rather shabby room where we were all squeezed together. Sud-denly, I was overwhelmed by a sense of complete joy. I could still hear, distantly, the sound of everyone laughing and chattering around me but I felt that I had levitated out of myself and was suspended in time. I could do nothing else but give myself to the intensity of that feeling. I have no idea how long it lasted. Then it gently subsided. For the rest of the day and for some time afterwards, I went

---

[*] Even in these cases, it could be said that we still commit some sort of action, albeit one beyond our conscious control: in the first example we *surrender ourselves* to the beauty of the moment; in the second, we *numb ourselves* against pain.

around saying to myself, 'That was happiness! That was real happiness!' According to Dylan Evans, in his book, *Emotion*, I was experiencing what the Japanese call '*amae*', for which there is no equivalent word in English. It means something along the lines of 'comfort in another person's complete acceptance' – a sense of joy in belonging, of being wanted.

I would suggest that such intense and extreme moments, rare enough in life, are even less likely in a performance. However, such an occurrence is not beyond the realms of possibility. It's more likely to be so in the heat of rehearsal when the actors have none of the self-consciousness connected with performance. I heard Imelda Staunton, in an interview about her role as the eponymous amateur abortionist in the film, *Vera Drake*, discussing an improvisation when, totally unanticipated by her – neither as character, nor as actor – the police showed up at her home to arrest her. She described not being able to breathe, feeling that she was about to die. Presumably, and impressively, she totally believed herself within the circumstances of her role, and underwent such a state of pure emotion. Whether she could have responded to such a moment as intensely and freshly, performance after performance, had she been doing it on stage, I have no idea. Nevertheless, this condition of total belief is what actors should ideally be aspiring to at all times.

Emotional Recall: Pros and Cons

During my training in the States, we did exercises on emotional recall, the purpose of which was just that – to bring back a previously experienced state of intense feeling. I have the distinct image of us seated around the room, heads in hands, elbows on knees, straining to squeeze feelings out of ourselves as though we were all in the throes of acute constipation. Rather than trying to dredge up the feeling itself, we should have been trying imaginatively to recreate the physical circumstances of the situation containing the feeling we wished to recall. Feelings can be evoked by concrete, sensory memories: the sound of a ticking clock, the sight of rain running down a windowpane, the smell of freshly brewed coffee, the feeling of a rough woollen sweater, the taste of a madeleine, you know, that sort of thing . . . I'm sure everyone, in an intensely emotional moment in their life, has experienced the sensation of time seeming to slow to a halt and their senses becoming fixated on some such available sensory image. Clearly, these moments penetrate deep into our psyches and lie there doggo, forgotten, until particular circumstances provide the necessary trigger that cause them to resurface to our consciousness. I was once driving along a street in London when I suddenly felt a surge of the sort of excitement that is aroused when you're looking forward to an especially pleasurable event. I was so surprised by this that I tried to figure out what on earth could have caused such an access of feeling on an ordinary day with nothing especially pleasurable ahead of me. I eventually narrowed down the cause to the combination of the grinding sound of double-decker buses revving up and the sunlit sight of a 1930s block of flats evoking the excited anticipation I used to feel as a very young child when I was brought up to London for a day's treat. (No doubt to see a film starring Carmen Miranda.)

Exercises for emotional recall can be helpful for acting students as a way of stretching their emotional muscles. But now, for several reasons, I find them, even accurately executed, unhelpful in working on a performance. They evoke feelings connected to a specific personal experience that may only be remotely analogous to the emotional context of a particular scene. Therefore this work is not only emotionally inappropriate for the scene in question, it also involves the actors in imagining circumstances unconnected with the WORLD OF THE PLAY. It further implies that the actors are anticipating *how* they think they should feel in the scene and have automatically closed off the chance of allowing something more specific and spontaneously true to emerge in the moment. You really cannot slide the emotions from one experience across to another, even seemingly similar, situation. A particular state of emotion is never identically repeatable.

Emotionalism

Emotionalism occurs when actors are busy showing you how emotional they can be; no doubt at times very effective and impressive to the easily impressed, as those ham actors must have been in their heyday. It is, self-indulgently, more about the actor than the role. Some actors produce tears very easily and will do so at the drop of a hat. Demonstrating emotional availability is not the business of acting. Emotional availability should be placed at the service of expressively pursuing appropriate actions and objectives.

You cannot force emotions to appear. Some actors, however, insist on trying to do just that. If you observe tendons standing out on an actor's neck, tightness in the head and shoulders, stiff gestures, an increasingly red face, a choked or squeezed voice, shortness of breath or no breath at all – symptoms that have no recognisable connection with any emotion, and only communicate tension (rather than the desired intensity) – you're watching a bad actor, or, at least, a desperate, misguided one.

Block v. Flow

Some actors, mistakenly, try to play scenes in emotional blocks: 'This is my "angry" scene', 'This is my "sad" scene', and the like. What they achieve is a generalised display of how they think an emotion should look. Being unnatural, this is frequently accompanied by signs of strain. Unfortunately, these false expressions of emotion – or, more accurately, these expressions of false emotion – are often accepted by audiences as (a convention for) the real thing. You see a lot of such effort and tension in performances of Shakespeare where the actors realise the emotional stakes are vertiginously high but aren't in the creative state to reach them organically. Certainly, every *Lear* storm scene I've ever seen has ended up as an exercise in rant – strained, generalised and incoherent. The frequent reason for this is that the actors are more preoccupied – or daunted – by the emotional peak they're psyching themselves up to scale, rather than trusting that the sequence of beats contained in the scene, played specifically, would release an organic flow of feelings to accompany them on their upward climb. However intense an emotion, it's never static, but constantly shifting in quality and degree.

Release v. Restraint

In most states of high emotion, we are released. So released, in fact, that many emotional states are accompanied by the release of bodily fluids from several possible orifices. There's no strain in losing your temper, bursting into tears, cursing the Gods or laughing ecstatically. They may be highly energetic and full of intensity, but they are not executed through tension.* They are in fact necessary *releases*. Our problem is that culturally we're so used to restraining our emotions, that *we confuse the constriction with the release.* To some degree, some of us (the British) are still influenced by that Victorian legacy that decreed displays of emotion to be an embarrassingly vulgar loss of control we should never impose on others. Displays of emotion(alism) in nineteenth-century theatre were formulaic, codified and therefore contained within some sort of aesthetic decorum. They were never messy or ugly – or real.

I think that nowadays it's particularly difficult for actors who live in potentially violent, crowded cities easily to release themselves. As we move around the streets, we tend – women especially and understandably – to give away little that might draw unwanted attention to us. In the Tube, we sit facing each other like zombies. Whatever we're feeling and thinking, we keep our face muscles firmly under control.** How anxious we are in case the 'nutter' talking to himself in the corner might come and sit next to us! We've taught our bodies to disconnect the expression from the emotion. And then, in rehearsal, actors are expected to reverse this emotional vasectomy and maintain themselves in a continuous flow of expressiveness, to release those muscles they've learned to keep firmly gripped, to relearn what was once a natural process. It's of no help for actors to reply, as they often do when I complain that I can't see anything happening, 'Well, I *was feeling* it.' Audiences aren't clairvoyants, and it's only through our behaviour (what is expressed by our bodies – which includes our faces and our voices) that we can be 'read'.

---

* Intensity good; tension bad. The one is vital to theatre; the other destructive.

** This situation may be exacerbated by the fact that the bulk of most actors' employment is now in television where actors, more used to working on stage, are often exhorted not to 'act', not to 'do' anything, not to 'show' anything!

Generalised Emotion and Emotional Clichés

A theatregoing friend I hadn't seen for some while announced that he now only goes to opera (!) and film. 'Theatre?' he replied to my inquiry, 'Who wants to see those same old emotions being trotted out again and again?' His remark initially left me feeling rather defensive; then deflated, for I had to acknowledge the justness of his comment. Actors, for a large part, don't observe life, they take their observations from theatre or film or – younger actors nowadays – from television soaps; their performances are based on other performances, twice or more times removed from actuality. For actors unwilling to observe 'real' people or to get in touch with their own behaviour, a repertoire of well-wrought emotional clichés stands in for the real thing and these are unfortunately accepted by many audiences as such. Displays of emotion are reduced to expressions almost as formalised as those codified in the nineteenth century by François Delsarte in his system of gestures: the choked-back tears with twitching cheek muscles while staring into the middle distance (incipient distress), the smooth, tight-lipped smile (incipient violence) . . . The complexity and variety of human expressiveness is reduced to a few handy, recognisable signs. The actors are not in the creative state to allow spontaneous emotion to be released, so they resort to what is most readily available: what they've done before and what they've seen other actors do in similar circumstances. Of course, these forms of emotional expression do – or once did have – a basis in reality. And if they're executed with commitment, they will elicit some residue of the feeling that initially caused them. This is because our somatic and psychic experiences are totally interconnected (i.e. movement can induce feeling just as much as feeling can induce movement – more on this later). But they're now being mass-produced, coming off the assembly line rather than being handcrafted. And even if such forms of expression do evoke some sensation of genuine feeling in the actor, they have been imposed *on* the scene rather than discovered *in* the scene at the moment of playing. This accounts for the lack of freshness, that clichéd quality which so bores my friend with its wearying sense of *déjà vu*.

Misguided (and misguiding) directors instruct actors with unspecific adjectival requests to *be* angry or sad, less frenzied or more suspicious. But what degree of anger exactly? What sort of sadness? What exactly is frenzy? In what way suspicious? Generalised directing gets generalised acting.* Better to change such loose

---

* A lot of acting in Shakespeare is generalised, often because the actors don't really understand what they are saying in any depth or detail; and if you don't understand what you're talking about, it's almost impossible to be specific in your intentions or feelings. Peter Brook, in *The Empty Space*, brilliantly pinpointed this:

> Of course, nowhere does the Deadly Theatre install itself so securely, so comfortably, so slyly as in the works of William Shakespeare. The Deadly Theatre takes easily to Shakespeare. We see his plays done by good actors in what seems the proper way – they look lively and colourful, there is music and everyone is all dressed up, just as they are

demands for emotional states into suggestions for playable actions, such as: 'threaten him with a punch on the nose if he does it again'; 'get her to sympathise with your feeling of loss'; 'try to pull yourself together so you can communicate more clearly'; 'check out his story thoroughly'.

If actors aren't having a good night, straining to reach some required or imagined emotional state only moves them further out of touch with themselves. In a sense, there's no point in actors worrying about emotion. It will either be there or it won't. All actors can do is to pursue their objectives and carry out their actions truthfully to the best of their abilities, focusing on good contact with their partners, and allowing whatever feelings that do emerge *to* emerge without censorship or inhibition – and in whatever form they take.

Accepted Emotional Truth and Experienced Emotional Truth

I heard an actor in a radio interview, eager to demystify the process of acting, referring to David Mamet writing in *Truth and False* that the actor's job is to stand in the right place, say the lines and tell the truth. She threw off the quote as though it were a matter of obvious common sense, some support for a no-nonsense approach to acting. Yes, it's easy enough to stand in the right place and say the lines, but the problem is the bit about telling the truth. If telling the truth on stage were so easy, I with a million others would be packing the theatres every hour of every day that God gives us. And I wouldn't feel compelled to fill so many pages in an attempt to offer possible ways in which actors might work towards some expression of it. I repeat: what is accepted as the real thing – truthful acting – is mainly a collection of well-executed formulas.

But we do know the real thing when it happens. Truly truthful acting makes us sit up and pay attention; truthful acting turns us hot and cold, makes us sweat, makes us blush, makes us gasp, makes our stomachs churn, makes us hold our breath, makes us laugh with joy, gives us a sudden, intense sense of breathing sharp clean air, of being thrillingly alive and in touch with our humanity. And how often do we experience such sensations in the theatre?

supposed to be in the best of classical theatres. *Yet secretly we find it excruciatingly boring* – and in our hearts we blame Shakespeare, or theatre as such, or even ourselves. To make matters worse, there is always a deadly spectator, who for special reasons enjoys a lack of intensity and even a lack of entertainment, such as the scholar who emerges from routine performances of the classics smiling because nothing has distracted him from trying over and confirming his pet theories to himself . . . Unfortunately, he lends the weight of his authority to dullness and so the Deadly Theatre goes on its way. (*My emphasis.*)

Unfortunately, some critics seem to have learned nothing from this celebrated book, and are still unable to distinguish between what's dead and what's alive.

Emotion and Culture

In the extremes of primal emotion – those that transcend cultural values (fear, for instance, surprise, anger, disgust . . .), all human beings behave – that is, our bodies function – in exactly the same, autonomic way. In anger, for example, the blood rushes to our heads and our foreheads jut forward. When we're afraid, we recoil, bending at the waist in an attempt to make ourselves smaller, protecting with one arm the vulnerable areas of our bodies, at the same time thrusting out the other to ward off the source of the threat. I've worked a lot on melodrama, one condition of which is that the characters make no effort to hide what they're feeling, but totally give in to the expression of their emotions at their fullest and most intense. Investigating this genre, we found ways for the actors to exercise so that eventually the expression of emotions that we normally experience only in situations of extreme intensity became truthful and natural for them. (I take melodrama seriously.) In exploring the extremes of big emotions, all the actors' bodies would tend to move in basically the same way for a particular state. So it was possible to define very accurately the physical tendencies of various peaks or depths of emotion. (One interesting aside from this work was the striking visibility of the armpit!)

All human beings have the capacity to experience the same feelings. (How else could we identify with characters from the past or in foreign plays or novels – or even real people! – when their circumstances and values are so different from ours?) It may seem that people of one culture experience certain feelings more intensely than those of another, or even experience emotions exclusive to themselves. This is not the case. This perception occurs because an emotion and the expression of that emotion are not synonymous. *Culture dictates what values we put on particular feelings* – those that we admire, those we disapprove of, those we are encouraged to display, those we are expected to hide. Depending on when or where we were brought up, we have, or would have had, very different attitudes towards loud lamentations at funerals, stiff upper lips, weeping men, honour killings and suicide caused by social disgrace. Dare we assume that the woman who withholds tears at her child's funeral feels any less grief than the mother who throws herself weeping on the coffin of hers? These are entirely matters of cultural indoctrination, absorbed from birth.* Let me refer back to my experience of

---

* Steven Pinker, in *The Blank Slate*, gives the example of the Ifaluk people (a Micronesian culture) that apparently have no word for or concept of our *anger*, but experience what they call *song*: 'a state of dudgeon triggered by a moral infraction such as breaking a taboo or acting in a cocky manner. It licenses one to shun, frown at, threaten, or gossip about the offender, though not to attack him physically.' In simple terms, it indicates that culturally, we take offence at different things. Whatever we call it, the fundamental mental-emotional mechanism is the same. In *How the Mind Works*, he makes a similar point, this time referring to Darwin's research for *The Expression of the Emotions in Man and Animals*, in which Darwin writes: 'The same state of mind is expressed throughout the World with remarkable uniformity . . . evidence of the close similarity in bodily structure and mental disposition of all the races of mankind.'

amae in China: Dylan Evans conjectures that the reason that the Japanese have a single word for an emotion that requires several words to identify it in English (joy in a sense of belonging, being valued and accepted) is because of the difference in cultural attitudes to the group and the individual, the Japanese being far more concerned to fit in with their community than English individualists. *But anyone can experience the emotion.* In my lifetime, attitudes to guilt, shame or sexual openness have changed totally – they now barely cause a tremor: politicians brazenly deny obvious lies when once they would have blushed deeply at being caught using the wrong knife! Now the demand for sexual ubiquity requires Jane Austen's lovers to appear in wet clothes to reassure a present-day audience that they do have sex organs.*

So: we can distinguish between primal feelings of such intensity that transcend cultural conditioning and in which we all behave alike, and those feelings that have been culturally structured to express themselves according to the values and rules of that society. This means that actors working on material both foreign and from the past, should, as part of their research and transformation, train their psycho-physiological systems to learn new behaviour patterns and responses, much as I've indicated in my remarks on melodrama. This work requires serious rehearsal time (*see:* TECHNIQUES TOWARDS CHARACTERISATION in the REHEARSAL process).

Emotion and Body

There are two fundamental approaches to acting: working from the inside-out, in which the inner life (thoughts, feelings, objectives) influences the outer life (physical behaviour); or vice versa, outside-in, when the state of the body can induce feelings and thoughts. When I was training in the States, the Actors Studio and the Method were at their height, and I was totally indoctrinated into the former approach. Both are valid, of course, and actors with a healthy mix of the two at their disposal will find themselves with more options and greater flexibility. No point in becoming doctrinaire one way or the other about this. But over the years, I've come to believe that, for certain situations, there is far greater efficacy in using the body to get in touch with inner experience. Any movement we make, the smallest gesture, evokes some feeling, autonomically connected with it. Often, by committing yourself totally to a physical action, you will make a more direct and natural contact with your need, thoughts and feelings than by trying to think or 'feel' your way into them. There are various techniques (many devised by Michael Chekhov) that help actors to embody their super-objectives

---

* There is a discouraging contemporary inability or unwillingness to identify with anything that isn't 'just like us', a total collective failure of imagination that, more and more, forces characters from period plays into modern dress, for fear that the audience won't otherwise recognise them as human beings. A way of trying to attract disaffected youth into the theatre is to give them more of what they already experience. This strikes me as patronising and reductive.

and their emotional life. I describe some of these approaches in both the CHAR-
ACTER and WORLD OF THE PLAY strands of the REHEARSAL process.

Our bodies' cross-culturally shared expression of certain prime emotions is proof
of the holistic interconnection between our physical and emotional lives. Particular physical patterns become unconsciously connected with particular feelings.
If we recreate those physical patterns, they reactivate those feelings. In this way,
we can either engage or limit particular feelings and attitudes. For example, if you
collapse your chest, you'll be unable to express aggression or self-assertion; if you
stick it out (a predominantly male assumption of cool to keep uninvited intimacy
at bay), you'll find it difficult to make contact with anyone or, interestingly, to take
in what is being said to you (it creates a sort of tension in the ears). Examining
such examples, we are practising reverse engineering, working backwards from
our physical state to discover the feelings – and therefore motives – that produced
it. Originally, of course, the inner life initiated the external behaviour. People who
want to keep a low profile, will instinctively take up as little space as possible ('I'm
not really here'). Feeling socially inadequate or insecure, depressed or worried,
they aren't likely to display much physical assertion. Collapsing the chest is one
way of achieving this. They are not consciously doing this; the body instinctively
knows to put itself into this state. Similarly, someone who tries to avoid unwanted
familiarity will, by pushing out the chest, signal to others to keep their distance.
This is a pseudo-aggressive stance, not actually threatening but pretending to be:
by pushing the chest forward, the head automatically gets pulled back, indicating
an unwillingness to engage. The chest is saying 'Keep away', the head, 'I don't want
to get involved with you'. (Quite different from the menace of a jutting forehead.)

Every gesture contains within it some previously learnt experience. Our emotions
are not abstractions floating about in the ether, they are actually in our bodies.
Many repressed feelings are locked in our muscles. Once, in rehearsal, during a
Feldenkrais movement class,[*] two actresses who were lying on their backs with
legs bent and knees up like the rest of the company, burst into tears after carrying
out the instruction to open and release their thighs. What had those thigh muscles
been holding that was being released along with their thighs? Skilled Alexander
teachers can relate the frequent occasions on which the apparently simple placing
of a hand on a particular muscle of the person they're teaching can cause
extraordinarily vivid releases – of tears, laughter, trembling, sighs, euphoria.

I did an adaptation of James Elroy's novel, *The Black Dahlia*, an especially violent
thriller which demanded huge reserves of stamina and energy from the actors. To
this end, the company did daily circuit training, increasing the number of circuits

---

[*]   Moshe Feldenkrais was a Russian-born Israeli who developed a system of movement based
on the development of detailed self-awareness of how one habitually uses one's body, taking
nothing for granted, e.g. where do you place your feet when you sit in a chair, forward or under
you, how wide apart and so forth . . . and what difference does that make for you . . . ?

and the duration of each station every few days. At the end of these sessions, the actors' eyes were vibrantly alive, their skins clear and they themselves unusually present – the energy and power vibrating from them was tangible. Sometimes, at this point, instead of letting them rush off to have a pee, drink water and wipe away the sweat, I would send them straight back into a scene. They were so released, so free, that their emotional life was totally available. Strong feelings poured naturally from them without a trace of strain or tension. Acting suddenly seemed so easy! Everyone got very excited about the possibility of doing circuits as a pre-show warm-up once we started touring. Unfortunately, this idea faded: the practicalities of pre-show preparation got in the way and the actors lost the habit – and the addiction! I had to observe rather sadly that their performances, however excellent, never quite matched the electricity and release of those rehearsal sessions. It also suggests that great performances require the most extraordinary combination of high energy and total release (not a hint of reserve, caution or inhibition) that is beyond the reality of most performance conditions. But the point I'm making here is the extraordinarily thrilling impact the actors' physical life had on their emotional life.

Two Levels of Emotion

From this, we can see that there is the theatrical possibility of recreating feelings by working backwards, as it were, from our bodies. This might seem totally to contradict my earlier premise that emotion is a result of thwarted or successful objectives that can only be achieved through spontaneous, unplanned playing of actions. *However, there are two quite different levels of emotional experience.* We must distinguish between *short-term* and *long-term* feelings.

From our individual natures and nurture, we each have tendencies to favour particular states of mood or feeling; we have some dominant emotional basis from which we function. Someone obsessive and anally retentive, for example, will spend a large percentage of their life in a state of *angst*, worried, uneasy, fussing over apparent trivialities. Someone who sees themselves as a victim will much of their time live in a state of distrust, suspicion, both hostile and defensive, oversensitive to anything that could be interpreted as a sneer or a smear. These are *long-term* states, deeply absorbed within the person's psyche. Let us assume that actors playing characters with such tendencies personally inhabit quite different emotional worlds from their creations. If they proceed to play 'from themselves', rather than adapting their inner life to that of their characters, the resulting moment-to-moment choices will always be skewed, always slightly 'off'. In the long term, through their careers, such actors will seem to be playing, again and again, the same part from the same emotional base (always playing 'themselves'), whatever the role. But if they can change the tendency of their inner emotional states to what they understand is more appropriate for the characters they're creating, they will be more likely to suit the demands of the play (rather than making the play suit them). One way of achieving this change is by working from your experience of other people, from your study of the outward manifestations of their inward states. By close observation and then accurate assumption of the physical life that organically releases such feelings, actors can provide themselves with an emotional basis with which they engage in the actions of the play. Acquiring a pattern of physical behaviour will help to put the actor into a suitable area of feelings, and with them, thoughts, values and attitudes, that is the character's long-term habitation. There are many techniques for doing this that I describe as part of the rehearsal process (*see*: CHARACTER; WORLD OF THE PLAY).* *With time, actors absorb this physicality as naturally as their lines; it becomes an organic function of their performance. They 'live' in character.*

But there are emotions aroused by specific circumstances from moment to moment, encounter to encounter, that are very much the outcome of objectives and actions, and that cannot be prepared for by physical behaviour. These circumstantial or situational moments play spontaneously off the ground bass of the prevailing emotional tendencies of the character. I've quoted at some length the Act 3 scene from *The Seagull* in which Arkadina refuses to release her lover, Trigorin. If you can imagine Arkadina, not as the self-absorbed, energetic, demanding woman she is, but as someone wise and thoughtful, the scene would be played from a very different emotional basis and the moment-to-moment playing of the scene would consequently be totally dissimilar. *Even though, in both cases, the actions and the emotions created by the situation would be more or less the same, their expression would be completely different.* The way someone wise and thoughtful deals with their jealousy is quite unlike that of someone impulsive and selfish. This reiterates *exactly* one reason why emotional recall or pre-planned emotion – dredged up from the actor's personal experience and injected into a scene – is useless. The emotional ground bass of the actor is not the same as that of the character, therefore the experience and expression of the same emotion will be totally different.

We can see how the two levels of emotional experience interact: the spontaneous, immediate emotional states which arise because of the moment-to-moment circumstances are informed by the broader, more general emotional tendencies of character.

Categories of Feeling

Probably this is a good place to make a small semantic point. We are always in some state of feeling. Emotions and moods are two opposing ends of a continuum in the general category of feelings. Emotions are usually passions (rage, joy, despair) or very strong feelings (anxiety, resentment); moods are more sustained

---

* This approach also applies to states of feeling that characters might be prone to fall into under certain influences, such as music, or the change of seasons; these tend to be moods rather than big emotions – sadness, restlessness, Weltschmerz, nostalgia, contentment and so on.

states towards the lighter end of the emotional scale (contentment, restlessness, nostalgia, sadness). And then we use the word feeling for more low-level experiences: we feel tired, amused, perplexed . . . Of course, these cannot be absolute categories. Different states blur into each other. I can slide from a mood of pleasant weariness to a state of profound tiredness and from that to wanting to weep from exhaustion. There is no precise moment when we can claim someone moved from intense irritation to anger and from anger to rage any more than we can say exactly on which day someone became bald. *We are constantly in process, in flow, not in a sequence of strung-together results.*

Characters' Feeling v. Audiences' Feelings

Some actors play the emotion that the audience are likely to feel. They are responding *to* the scene, rather than participating *in* it – a very different matter. The audience should be moved differently from the characters. Actors who make such choices tend to play sentimentally. They are also doing the audience's job for them.

Emotion Inside Rehearsal but Outside the Text

Acting is an emotional business. A good actor is constantly vulnerable. In the pressure of rehearsal, a lot of feelings, with little or nothing to do with the content of the work, but *because* of the work, can come to the fore. At times, the rehearsal room has to be a safe place where an actor can release pent-up emotion. It can be healthy as long as it doesn't become a self-indulgence. A sensitive director should make space for such occurrences, neither indulgent – which only encourages more of the same – nor going into a state of denial – which leaves matters unresolved for everyone. In Canada, I once worked with an actor who seized every opportunity to become hysterical and had continuously to be calmed down by the rest of the company. It was all exciting stuff, but did nothing for her performance. God knows what she thought acting is for! Acting is certainly not a branch of therapy unless you're deliberately participating in forms of psycho-drama.

Mask v. Face

There has been a continuous debate down the centuries as to whether an actor should experience emotions or simulate them, whether to present the Face or a Mask. The degree of simulation ranges from a totally externalised sequence of expressions (what we might call posturing and face-making) to our contemporary, more subtle emulation. Denis Diderot's eighteenth-century *The Paradox of Acting* is all for Mask; William Archer's late nineteenth-century refutation, *Masks or Faces?*, is all for Face. Shaw's comparison of Duse and Bernhardt that I've already referred to, exemplifies the debate. He goes into great detail about their comparative performances and ends with a description of Duse blushing:

She began to blush; and in another moment she was conscious of it, and the blush was slowly spreading and deepening until, after a few vain efforts to avert her face . . . she hid her face in her hands. After that feat of acting I did not need to be told why Duse does not paint an inch thick, I could detect no trick in it: it seemed to me a perfectly genuine effect of the dramatic imagination . . . I must confess to an intense personal curiosity as to whether it always comes spontaneously.

He comes down clearly on the side of the Face. And so, you may have gathered, do I!

Given Circumstances

A scene does not only comprise its structure of objectives and actions and the dialogue employed in their execution. There is also the context within which those actions and objectives are played out. This context is created by given circumstances.

Given circumstances are any facts, events and conditions that influence the situation taking place. They can range from the environmental (time of day, weather, season, location . . .) to the cultural (period, ethnicity, social structure, social conduct, politics, religion, fashion, entertainment . . .) and through to the personal and historical (what has happened in the past, what might be about to happen, daily routines, relationships, careers, celebrations, arrivals and departures . . .). In *The Cherry Orchard*, they range from the Emancipation of the Serfs to the sweets in Gaev's pocket. Writers choose the time and place of their plays for good reasons. Why does *The Cherry Orchard* begin in the small hours of a cold May morning? Why does the last act of *The Three Sisters* take place out of doors in October? Why does *A Doll's House* take place at Christmas? These conditions are established to influence the characters in some pertinent way (for us to discover) or to throw more light on them.

The plays of Ibsen and Chekhov, particularly, are dense with given circumstances, those of Shakespeare, surprisingly light. In Ibsen there are usually two actions unrolling simultaneously – what has happened in the past and what's unravelling in the present. What's happened in the past is a given circumstance for what is happening in the present. In *A Doll's House*, for example, Nora's forgery of her father's signature to raise money for her husband's health impinges on her behaviour in the present. When Krogstad threatens to tell her husband the truth, that threat becomes an all-engulfing given circumstance for Nora. That the play takes place at Christmas isn't only an irony for the audience, it's another given circumstance that must affect the characters' actions: the conjunction of a time of festivity and the threat of exposure puts Nora under pressure that manifests itself, for example, in the hysteria of her tarantella rehearsal.

All given circumstances will affect *how* the actors play their objectives and actions. (For the way in which given circumstances are actually absorbed by the actors into the body of their performances, see POINTS OF CONCENTRATION in REHEARSAL TEXT WORK.)

Note that given circumstances are *factual* and have nothing to do with value judgements (nice, nasty, clever, stupid . . .) or adjectival, emotional descriptions (suspicious, romantic, shy, daring . . .). Such opinions are subjective and generalised.

Feelings as Given Circumstances

The emotions evoked in one scene become part of the given circumstances that affect how an actor plays the following scene. There's an immensely satisfying short sequence in the second act of *The Three Sisters* when Vershinin is called away because of some problem with his wife. Masha's frustration at losing his company is turned into anger against Anfisa when the old nurse starts fussing about Vershinin not drinking his tea before he left. Anfisa, in turn, takes out her grievance against Masha's anger by shouting at Andrey through the closed door of his room. A flow of feelings accompanies the actor-characters on their journey through the play, the feelings aroused at one moment affecting how the actions will be played in the next.

Examples of Given Circumstances

THE FIRST ACT OF 'THE CHERRY ORCHARD'

Here are some of the main given circumstances that apply to *all* the characters in the first act of *The Cherry Orchard*:

1. It is about 3 a.m. on a morning in May.

2. It is cold outside, but warm indoors.

3. The cherry orchard is in bloom.

4. The action takes place in the nursery.

5. Ranyevskaya is returning home, penniless, to her estate after five years in France.

6. She left home after the death of her husband and then the death by drowning of her little son, Grisha, both of which occurred during the period in which she was having an affair.

---

7. She has been living with her lover, who has pursued her, first to Monaco where she had to nurse him through an illness, then to Paris where he took all her money and abandoned her.

8. She left her daughter, Anya, who was then twelve, on the estate for those five years, during which she hasn't seen her.

9. Anya with her governess, Charlotta, has travelled to Paris to bring her destitute mother home.

10. The three of them, plus Yasha, a former peasant from the estate who went to Paris with Ranyevskaya and is now her valet, have been travelling back by train for three sleepless days.

11. Lopakhin has come from Kharkov to welcome her home.

12. Lopakhin, now a wealthy businessman, is the son of serfs who once worked on this estate.

13. Semyonov-Pishchik, a neighbouring landowner, who is always trying to borrow money, has also come to greet her.

14. Trofimov, a student who had been Grisha's tutor at the time of his death, has reappeared on the estate.

15. Varya is Ranyesvskaya's 'adopted' daughter and runs the household.

16. Gaev is Ranyevskaya's older brother who lives on the estate.

17. Yepikhodov is the estate clerk.

18. Dunyasha, who is about the same age as Anya, is a maid.

19. Everyone from the estate has been up all night awaiting their return and gone to meet their train at the local station (except Dunyasha, Yepikhodov, Lopakhin, who fell asleep, and Trofimov, whom Varya has deliberately excluded from the welcoming party).

20. During Ranyevskaya's five-year absence, some retainers have left the estate or died.

21. The estate is heavily in debt and will be auctioned off in August if the debts are not paid.

22. The cherry orchard was once productive and profitable!

There are many other *given circumstances* that apply to characters individually, for example: Ranyevskaya bathed Lopakhin's wounds in the nursery when, as a boy, he had been beaten by his drunken father.

THE FIRST ACT OF 'THE SEAGULL'

These are the main given circumstances that apply to *all* the characters:

1. The action takes place on the edge of a lake on Arkadina's estate.
2. It is a summer evening.
3. The weather is very close (a storm is likely).
4. The moon is rising.
5. A stage has been erected on the edge of the lake, with a view of the lake and moon when the curtain rises.
6. Konstantin is presenting a play he has written and that Nina will perform.
7. The estate is not productive, and absorbs more money than it earns.
8. Konstantin's mother, Arkadina, is a famous actress, making her annual summer visit to the estate from Moscow.
9. Her lover, a famous novelist, Trigorin, is visiting the estate for the first time.
10. Nina is the daughter of neighbours who try to keep her away from the 'Bohemia' of Arkadina's estate.
11. The estates surrounding the lake were once the scene of parties and a vibrant social life.
12. Masha is the daughter of Polina and Shamraev, who is the estate manager.
13. Dorn, a bachelor, is the 'local' doctor, who has known the family since he was a young man.
14. Sorin is Arkadina's brother and Konstantin's uncle.
15. He is a retired mid-ranking bureaucrat (state councillor in a legal department).
16. He is in poor health.
17. Konstantin has no money and wears worn-out clothes.

Some individual *given circumstances* that not all the characters might know:

1. Medvedenko is a poorly-paid schoolmaster with responsibility for his mother, two sisters and a little brother.
2. He is in love with Masha.
3. He walks four miles each way to see Masha.
4. Masha is in love with Konstantin.
5. Dorn and Polina have had an affair.
6. Nina wants to be an actress.
7. Konstantin wants to be a writer.
8. He is in love with Nina.

RECAPITULATION

Actor-characters are motivated by *objectives*. To try to achieve those *objectives*, they have to play *actions*. Playing *actions* means having an effect on the other actor-characters. Success or failure in playing those *actions* will automatically cause them to experience *emotions*: 'good' feelings if they succeed, 'bad' feelings if they fail. Throughout a scene, they will experience a continuous flow of emotions accompanying and affecting the playing of their *actions*. In the pursuit of their *objectives*, they will have to overcome *obstacles*: resistance, opposition, dilemmas. *Obstacles* create *conflict*. *How* actor-characters carry out their *actions* will be influenced by *given circumstances* – the conditions and contexts in which they find themselves. *Objectives, actions, obstacles and given circumstances are the vital elements of acting.*

3
PREPARATION

THE PURPOSE OF PREPARATION

Two Approaches to Preparation

Directors, you might consider your preparation to be the more important and creative half of your work, in which you visualise the production that you will then bring to fruition in rehearsal. In crude terms, you plan what you want and then get the actors to flesh it out. I have a feeling that I was implicitly taught this way; as part of my thesis, I had to complete a full production on paper with every detail of blocking meticulously set down. And my earliest productions were executed pretty much according to a pre-planned scheme – until I saw the error of my ways.

Rather, you might consider the preparation in a totally different light, one in which you gather all the information you can glean from your material until you're sufficiently primed *to begin exploring it together with the actors in rehearsal.* Only then will you be ready to discover what the production might be like. If you chance to have what most theatre people still tend to call the luxury – but I'd call the right – of adequate rehearsal time, it might be perfectly possible to launch your voyage of discovery from an almost blank page. But, at very least, you do need a starting point from which the actors can explore with some focus. Which does imply *some* thoughts about the material, if nothing more than what about it first whetted your creative juices.

Two Areas of Preparation

There are two parts to preparation: the first is to get to know your material (the text) and anything that will throw further light on it (the research); the second, to make a provisional map of the rehearsal journey you think might be most sympathetic to the development of what you've discovered about the material. Both must be considered as first steps only, with the understanding that new ideas are going to manifest themselves throughout rehearsal which may well require you to loosen your grip on those you embarked with. It's quite startling to find that a scene that you thought you understood perfectly well on the page only makes sense when you start working on it with the actors. The danger is that the wrong sort of preparation – making decisions, planning results – can inadvertently lead you into 'good ideas' which you're then loathe to let go of, despite their evident unsuitability in practice. On some occasions, gratifyingly, initial thoughts do prove sympathetic, and the discoveries you continue to make in rehearsal reinforce that initial vision. On others, original ideas, tested in action, prove uncongenial and require a radical rethink. Most often, the ideas you start with transmute gradually and naturally into something quite different, in which only traces of its origins may be faintly perceived in the eventual production.

So the idea of preparation is to arm yourself with (a) knowledge of the material ('This is what I know *so far*') and (b) possible ways of structuring the rehearsals ('This is how we *might* approach the work').

PREPARING THE TEXT

Respect for Texts

It's inevitable that if you work on a text, you interpret it. But it's the degree and manner of that interpretation that's at issue. The theatre is not a forum for the interpretation of plays. Its aim is to bring them alive – a surprisingly different concept. Conferences provide the opportunity for people so inclined to gather together and debate theory. 'Talking' an interpretation is considerably easier than 'walking' it.*

Just as you're trying to avoid imposing on actors, endeavouring to give them space for their creative autonomy, so, in a similar spirit of collaboration, you should approach a text, allowing it to release its own life and imagined WORLD. Potentially it's a living organism, waiting to be brought to life, not to be smothered at birth by inappropriate ideas.

Some directors – from above and outside the text, as it were – often impose a concept on it, forcing it to conform to an existence for which it has little affinity, squashing, squeezing, cutting and generally abusing it, rather like the Ugly Sisters mutilating their feet to force them into glass slippers that were clearly never meant for them. Directors should make love to texts rather than forcing themselves on them, listening to what the play is saying rather than hearing what they want to hear ('She said "No", but I know she didn't mean it').

---

* Early in my career, I tried to execute what seemed potentially exciting academic interpretations of plays I was currently directing. In every case, they didn't work. Some of the ideas were, quite simply, unplayable, that is, not translatable into practical or scenic language; or they required the actor to carry such a freight of complicated subtext that the audiences were probably left more bemused than enlightened. This was the case in a production of *Hamlet* that was heavily influenced by John Dover Wilson's *What Happens in Hamlet*, particularly his theory of why two versions of *The Mousetrap*, one mimed, the other spoken, were performed for Claudius. It was wonderfully convincing on paper, but unfortunately not so in action.

It can be hard to avoid the temptation of an attractive preconception of a production. By preconception, I mean some striking idea or image you've got from a play's reputation without having fully studied the play, or possibly from a quick skim through it, or from being stimulated by just one of its aspects. It means that when you do get around to studying the text in depth, you've already decided how you're going to do it. You're in no frame of mind to allow the play to reveal itself to you; your brain's already hard at work looking for ways to justify the concept you've no doubt fallen in love with and are determined not to give up. (Of course – fair's fair – there *is* always the chance that such initial images may organically grow and flower with the progress of rigorous study.)

Against Interpretation Redux

A more arduous approach, but an infinitely more rewarding one, is to try to become one with the play, to immerse yourself in the material, steeping yourself in it, letting it engulf you, allowing yourself to find out what you've learned about the play only when you return to the surface, saturated with your experience of it; more arduous, because it takes longer, requires more patience, more rigour and may not initially provide you with a smart, neat idea. It may never supply you with an 'idea' at all, but take you into a world of complexities and contradictions. This may sound counter-intuitive, but the more you let the play speak to you, the more deeply imaginative you will find your own contribution. It will not limit your creativity. Quite the opposite. Because you're trying to become one *with* the material rather than doing something *to* it, you develop an intimacy with it, you learn to breathe with it, so that in time it organically releases its buried associations. It must be more productive to collaborate with what *is* there, rather than deny, distort or fight it.

Working from the disciplined frame of what irrefutably *is in* the play, you have secure parameters from which to launch your conjectures and from them, your imagination. Defined parameters will stimulate your imagination. Too much freedom can leave you flounderingly spoilt for choice. Doing whatever you want can lead you to behave capriciously, like a spoilt child whose boundaries have never been set. We're familiar with productions that have had enormous sums of money thrown at them; what you see is all that money can buy, except imagination – which can't be bought. The discipline of facts points the way to freedom. A good play has more than enough information to generate innumerable possibilities; a great one, an infinity. By this route, the actors, too, will be at one with the play, not feeling torn, as they often are, between writer's text and director's concept.

Ethics and Empathy

You can create theatre without scripted plays, but if you do choose to direct one, you should respect it. Apart from the practical and logical benefit of being in tune with your material, there's the ethical matter of whether you have the right to do whatever you like with someone else's 'intellectual property'. You cannot do what you want with the work of living writers without their permission, nor for seventy years after their death without the permission of their estates. But the longer a writer's work has been in the public domain, the more we feel it's fair game to do to it whatever we fancy. It's true, of course, that the more distant the culture, the more difficult it is to understand what the writer's intentions were or what the play says. We cannot (and shouldn't bother trying to) recreate the theatrical conditions we believe operated, say, four hundred years ago; there's no way we can respond to the play in the same way as its original audience. We can only work from within our own inescapable cultural perceptions. We can't think like Elizabethans; there's too much subsequent knowledge that gets between us and them. But we should respect some basic underlying principles of what that culture was like, *try* to put our heads into that space (after all, that should be a large part of the creative pleasure) and acknowledge the expression of the eternally human that's no doubt attracted us to work on the piece.

It depends how free you feel to stand on the shoulders of others, frequently giants, for your own advancement.* I've always chosen to direct a play because I was excited by the material (and the mind that created it) and, quite simply, wanted to share the particular pleasures I derived from it. If you don't like certain material, why do it? If it doesn't speak to you, how can *you* speak to it? You are, then, working against all your better instincts as well as against the material. Your empathic imagination can only extend so far.

I do understand, of course, that, at times, it's a practical necessity for you to accept less than appealing material because you need the job and the experience. And, then again, there are writers against whom you feel you ought to measure oneself – or should learn to love. Through the challenge of working on them, you might find you come to do so.

In principle, what I'm talking about is the ethical way in which you make choices. If you rush rather indiscriminately from one project to the next, working on them cynically with your eye on one career move after another, you'll end up losing touch with your own feelings, taste, judgement and, worse, your own talent. Recently, I heard of a director about to direct a hitherto unproduced play by a writer of some stature. Was he excited by it? It's alright, he shrugged. But he felt it was a choice that would get him attention. There are directors who, with the utmost

---

* I recently came away from a production of a 'classic' that seemed to have been executed out of loathing for both the play and the playwright, as though we now know everything there is to know about them and what we do know is no longer worth knowing. Whatever makes the play great had been replaced by directorial ego. I suppose the desire to cut a writer down to size and force a re-evaluation might be a justification for doing a production. But, to my mind, gutting the life out of a play and inserting the deadliest piece of deadly theatre in its place is – if not exactly immoral – certainly an *a*moral act.

efficiency and intelligence, can turn their hand to virtually any play in any genre. But their productions, highly professional though they are, tend to remain anonymous, without inner conviction, let alone passion. Their creative hearts are simply not in them.

The Infinitude of Great Plays

We keep returning to great plays because we instinctively believe that there's always something as yet undiscovered to be revealed. I believe this is true.* And I believe, too, that if you explore the material with genuine rigour, the conjunction of what you find filtered through your individuality, your human uniqueness, must create something fresh. It's a matter of having the courage to keep sailing into the unknown, steering your way past the reassuring Scylla of yet another stodgily conventional revival, past the tempting Charybdis of dressing the play up in fashionable clothing, on and on until you find yourself on the shores of a truly new world.

Sometimes, when I'm working on a production and am beginning to know the play, I find my imagination has begun visualising a performance I'd long to experience if I went to see the play performed. Often it's something I've never quite seen before, something I have a sense of – a hunch about – but can't quite define. Most of the time, I rarely manage to realise these hunches, but the attempts are healthy and exciting. Sometimes, you do manage to advance a little way along this creative road. When I saw the *L'Age D'Or* created by Le Théâtre du Soleil in their amazing space at La Cartoucherie, I was overcome by a sort of joyful surprise and a sense of fulfilment. I experienced, totally realised, the shadowy glimpse of a vision (a contemporary *Commedia*) that had lain for years, very faint and unfocused, far to the back of my mind. I felt – far too infrequent in theatre – that I'd come home. A very special form of *déjà vu*.

Over a long span of years, I've redirected several plays by Chekhov. Each time I do them, I try as much as is possible to clear the decks and start from scratch, as

---

* This doesn't mean casting about for topical relevance to shove into them, so that, all of a sudden, *Henry V* is about Tony Blair, and then – who'd've thought it? – *Richard II* turns out to be about Tony Blair, too; and *Henry VI* is about Bosnia, *Richard III* about Iraq, and Saint Joan appears to be a suicide bomber . . . On and on it goes. Critics usually find such tacks useful as smart little hooks on which to hang their reviews. But this sort of interpretation is essentially trite. It creates a slight frisson for jaded senses and smacks self-consciously of theatre people desperately trying to prove they belong to the real world just like everyone else. If you want to deal with contemporary issues, by all means deal with them, but this way of treating rich texts is reductive. Great plays are capable of expanding and resonating in many directions, allusive, complex, layered. Audiences are quite capable of seeing contemporary relevance for themselves, without having it simple-mindedly spelled out for them and rammed down their throats. They become straitjacketed by this fascistic tendency to tell them what to think, totally depriving them of their right to interpret and create their own performances.

though the plays were totally new to me. The results are not necessarily different: I'm going in more or less the same direction, what I originally discovered is rarely invalidated, but – and it's a *big but* – each time, I find I'm being led further into the seemingly bottomless depths of Chekhov's creativity. What I first found is being reinforced by more and more realisations. Because I'm getting closer to a sense of Chekhov's creative impulse and feeling increasingly confident with the material, I'm encouraged to relax my directorial grip, as it were, and open myself up unreservedly to what the text is suggesting: I see more connections, more details, more relevance, more corollaries to the main themes, all merging exponentially until I sense that there's too much to be achieved within any one production. *The more I learn to trust the text, the more I trust myself as a director.* At successive periods in your life, you find you have fresh understandings and new sympathies. (With *The Seagull*, I started out identifying with Konstantin; now I identify with Sorin!) When you spend your life with a play, your experience of it inevitably grows. Conductors spend much of their careers playing the same repertoire; why not directors? I recommend it.

Two Approaches to Text

In the preparation of the text, there are two essential approaches: the subjective and the objective.

In the former, which should be your initial encounter with the material, you must allow yourself to respond to the text quite spontaneously, letting it move you, amuse you, confuse you, stimulate your imagination in the most open way possible, trying to eliminate all preconceptions and received ideas, resisting the impulse immediately to start fixing ideas about how you'll direct it (to quell the rising panic that you won't have any). Read it for sheer enjoyment, for its sensuousness, for its story. Try to read it non-judgementally. This is a good exercise in self-discipline. Allow the material to release images for you without instantly seizing and squeezing them into some shape. If they're any good, they'll stay with you. If they vanish, they won't have had much substance. Read it in this way as many times as you find possible or useful. Let it sift through your imagination. Keep a record of your responses. Your instinctive early responses, unmediated by what you think you *ought* to do, or what you think *might be* the thing to do, are often the most perceptive.

After which, you must switch modes and become as coolly *objective* as possible. You want to find out what in the text are incontrovertible facts, not subject to interpretation – the foundation stones on which you will build your edifice, the stepping stones to set you on your journey, the discipline from which you'll find freedom.

You should then compare the subjective responses you noted with your analytical evaluations. Struggle with that juxtaposition until they blend into some holistic vision of what direction *you might aim in*. If you've initially read the play responsively, not imposing yourself on it and blurring it with preconceptions[*], you may well be gratified to see that a lot of your instinctive reactions have been confirmed by your analysis. Instinct is no more than the combination of natural ability and experience.

Text v. Research

This analytical work has two sources of material: one intrinsic to the play, that is, the text itself; and the other extrinsic to it, your research. Research takes you into three worlds: that in which the play is set, that of the writer in which it was written, and that of its critical reception. But the text must always be your prime source of knowledge. Research is obviously useful to orientate you within the WORLD OF THE PLAY, especially if that world is culturally or stylistically remote. However, too much information or inappropriate information, no matter how fascinating, can get in the way of what the play actually needs. You may be tempted to force into the performance intriguing morsels of research that the text simply cannot digest. (We've all experienced biographies, in which the authors simply have to give you every detail of what they've uncovered, consequently blurring the book's focus.) Research is good for knowledge that is *pertinent* to the material in the play. Similarly, with literary criticism, be wary of other people's opinions. It's perfectly possible, of course, to come upon an insight that illuminates the material for you in a way you'd never have seen for yourself. The risk, of course, is that all opinions are subjective, interpretive and clearly not factual. You cannot know from how close and accurate a 'reading' of a text such opinions are derived. The opinions of others are also very much influenced by the *zeitgeist* in which they were formed. It's easy to be seduced by an attractive but inappropriate idea that may well distort your vision of the play. So these areas of potential information, misinformation and disinformation must be approached with a certain wariness.

---

[*] With classics and very well-known work, there are inevitably a lot of received ideas that attach themselves to texts like barnacles to the hulls of ships, and need to be scraped away. Never accept them as truths; in many cases, they're totally inaccurate. They're often based on early receptions of a play that was quite misunderstood at the time of its first appearance. Some people (who don't much go to the theatre) will still tell you that Chekhov's plays are slow and boring and nothing happens in them. Chekhov himself complained that Stanislavsky's productions dragged things out, overlaid them with unnecessary naturalistic effects and leaned to the heavy at the expense of the light. The plays' first woolly translations into English and consequently vague productions also have a lot to answer for in reinforcing this false but clinging reputation. In fact, the plays are filled with plots and action and characters of a Slavic temperament that rarely permit them to be slow or boring! Some people dismiss Ibsen's *Ghosts* as a dated play about syphilis. Syphilis may be part of the subject matter of the play, but that is not what the play is *about*. The play is permanently modern, *about* the way in which the *mores* of a culture encourage us to lie and how those lies destroy us.

Ninety per cent of the most useful information comes from the text itself. Before you have the facts, you cannot start making any assumptions. So, to aid your analysis, there are ways of taking the text apart (*see*: DECONSTRUCTING THE TEXT) that force you to examine all aspects of it equally – not favouring some at the expense of those that attract you less – in order to discover what is factually incontrovertible. *Having an idea about a play needs to derive from a thorough knowledge of the play.* Then you can proceed with reasonably justified confidence, rather than bluff.

To Cut or Not to Cut

I find it difficult to cut the text of plays I'm working on. I've always believed it was beholden on someone bringing a play alive to bring it alive whole. There is some sort of responsibility or obligation to be true to the material – and therefore to the writer. Of course, times change. Some parts of plays have become incomprehensible. Or we no longer find aspects of them politically appropriate. We are now less patient. We're in some ways quicker on the uptake. Since the advent of technology in entertainment, we've all seen – and heard – in one form or another, more stories than we could possibly count. Who can estimate how many more we've experienced than theatregoers of a pre-technological era? Nevertheless, if we're dealing with playwrights of undoubted talent, genius even, we should be making an effort to understand what they had in mind when they were writing those sections that we're tempted either to dismiss as no longer of relevance to us or to remove in the interest of saving time. As my familiarity with a text develops, I gradually find justification for almost every word. And whenever I do cut, it's always with the feeling that I'm avoiding a challenge and betraying the writer, that I'm cheating, taking the line of least resistance, in short, with a feeling of failure, never of accomplishment.*

---

* Whenever I direct *The Cherry Orchard*, I always restore some cuts made by Chekhov at Stanislavsky's request after its first performances – presumably because he couldn't make those pieces of text work. Those cut sections make total sense to me, both in terms of character and of formal structure, in every way better than what replaced them. Specifically, at the opening of the second act, Charlotta, seated with Yasha, Dunyasha and Yepikhodov, reveals her desolate sense of anonymity, something that seems psychologically inappropriate for someone of some insight and wit to do in the presence of that foolish threesome, for whom she clearly has only contempt. And they don't relate to her at all. In the earlier version, she is not present in the scene, which works much better for them without her interpolations. Her self-revelation comes in a scene cut from the very end of the act, in which she imparts her life story, at greater length, to Firs – who is deaf! Here it's possible for her to speak aloud of her emptiness without fear of exposure. It's not surprising that Stanislavsky might have had difficulty with this scene. It reads like something out of Beckett, almost absurdist – a vision of life as a meaningless bad joke. (If Chekhov had lived to create more plays, maybe his writing would have developed in this vein.) And formally, the second act has a better shape in its original structure. First there are the trio of 'servant-clowns' – to a degree, parodies of their 'masters', Ranyevskaya, Gayev and Lopakhin, who soon enter and replace them – another trio. Then most of the other characters appear, creating the equivalent of an orchestral *tutti*. After which there's a duet

Cutting Shakespeare is a complicated problem. Personally, whenever I embark on one of his plays, I have to admit to a sinking feeling as I prepare to face his clowns. I find them for the most part unfunny, their jokes, once they've been glossed and you see that they do have some wit, far too complicated to clarify for a contemporary audience.* But there they are, those clowns with their function and place in the play needing validation. So you learn to love them! Then there are words that we no longer use or, more confusing, words that have changed their meaning. Recently, working on *Much Ado About Nothing*, I found the word 'sad' chiming throughout the play, creating potential distortion of both psychology and atmosphere. Its actual meaning is much closer to 'serious', a very different matter. In certain cases, if possible, I'm prepared to substitute a contemporary word with the same syllabic value and close enough in sound to the original. I'd say that this is being truer to the original than retaining a word that is now actually misleading. And we have no idea if any version of Shakespeare's plays, say, the inordinately long *Hamlet*, was his final word on the subject. Was it a conflation of all the versions available to its first publishers? Was a play a moveable feast, dependent on the exigencies of the circumstances of its performances in London or on tour and open to cuts and rewrites? Directors have to study hard and then make decisions about which parts of a text make more or less dramatic sense to them.

I suppose cutting can be justified in those writers whose style is excessive; who write in an uncontrolled flurry of vehement passion and rarely return to them in more objective mode. The precision and economy of texts by writers like Beckett, Pinter or Chekhov absolutely forbid any messing around, whereas with O'Neill, say, or Strindberg, there might be a case for editing. On the other hand, I've seen several productions of *Long Day's Journey Into Night* and the uncut performances were consistently much more satisfying than the cut versions, that, in fact, always felt longer! That relentless family war of attrition needs the space and time that O'Neill has given it to work out its full emotional impact. Some plays need their

---

between Anya and Trofimov who talk ardently and naively about the future and, finally, this other duet, between Charlotta and Firs, who talk confusedly of the past. A totally satisfying pattern. Also cut were some brief crossover scenes between Anya and Trofimov and between Varya and Charlotta that help to fill in some useful details of relationships and plot (e.g. Anya's visit to her great aunt). It's a good idea for directors to read, if available, earlier drafts of plays. You never know what gems of insight might be lurking in them. Also, it's not always possible to know if the final version of a play *was* totally to the writer's approval. You can read about Tennessee Williams's concern over the last act of *Cat on a Hot Tin Roof* that he rewrote at the insistence of his director, Elia Kazan – and which he subsequently replaced with the original.

* That crude convention really isn't good enough that encourages actors to play Shakespearean jokes with nods and winks and nudges or, in the case of sexual jokes, to clutch their groins or mime masturbating in order to indicate for the audience that (a) the line *is* a joke and (b) a 'dirty' one at that! It only encourages a compliant sheep-like audience to bleat obligingly even though there's no way – unless they've studied the text – that they can understand the actual joke; only that they know it's meant to be funny and dutifully respond as instructed.

four hours. Edward Albee, in the original preface to *Who's Afraid of Virginia Woolf?* made the point that a play takes as long as it takes. (However, forty-five years on, he has considerably shortened it!)

What I'm suggesting is that you should cut with great care and, despite the pragmatic nature of theatre, not just for expediency or from ignorance or out of laziness. If you've deemed a play worth directing, sweat a bit and honour it!

Deconstructing the Text

A Detective Story: the Tip of the Iceberg

The text of a play is an unsolved mystery, a detective story, or at least material that requires detective work. The writer has given us the tip of the iceberg, the surface of an imagined WORLD, comprised only of dialogue and stage directions from which we have to deduce everything else. Who are the characters who say and do these things? Why do they say and do them? What is the nature of this WORLD? The words on the page are the only clues we have to a fuller understanding of the play; they provide the code we must break in order to perform it. Therefore it's important to identify the clues (definite facts) from which we can start to make *reasonable conjectures*.

Reverse Engineering

The search for clues involves deconstructing the text: that is to say, conducting reverse engineering, taking the play apart to find out how it is made and then reassembling it, by which time it will be informed by the insights we've gained in the process. There are two essential purposes in breaking down the text: to understand its structure; and to gather information on character. In the former, the text is broken down into sections and units which, together with acts and scenes, are given titles. In the latter, it is sifted for lists of information concerning the characters, which are then further sifted for connections, similarities and contrasts (*see*: CHARACTER in REHEARSAL). We are in search of deep structures that aren't necessarily apparent from a linear reading. What we find will lead us to matters of theme and form. Unless we understand how the text functions, we're in no position to create a production from it.

Titling the Acts

Wood and Trees

One of the obstacles that beset actors and directors is the urge to be different, to create something fresh and surprising, especially when dealing with a classic text. This is understandable and not necessarily an unworthy intention, especially when you consider the unending revivals of the same 'great plays' (of which there are surprisingly few – one of the reasons for their frequency). But it does exacerbate a tendency to fail to see the wood for the trees. The search for originality does encourage the rejection of what seems obvious. However, if you really want to be different, a more secure way is to start from what *is* obvious and simple and by stages proceed to the unexpected and complex. From some of the many productions of *The Three Sisters* I've sat through, it would be hard to know that the first act revolves around a young woman's birthday – to be precise, her saint's day celebration – so sunk in Chekhovian depths and mired in emotional complexities are the cast and characters; similarly with *The Cherry Orchard*, in the first act of which a woman arrives home after a three-day train journey and a five-year absence, without much trace of tiredness or genuine reunion to be seen. In both cases, these facts are, of course, mentioned in the text, but not actually embodied in the cast, who are usually off on their own individual trips down Psychology Lane. But Chekhov has chosen these details of time and place for good dramatic reasons – maybe as a base from which to intensify the very complexities and subtleties so eagerly sought by the cast; at very least to provide a suitable context to contain narrative and reveal theme and character.

So I find it useful – and a simple way into a script – to give each act or scene a title that sums up, factually, free from interpretation and implied motivations, the essential situation that holds the act together and from which its various actions stem. In *The Cherry Orchard*, of course, the big event which holds the first act together is, as stated, Ranyevskaya's return. In *The Three Sisters*, it is Irina's birthday (and within that, the visit of the new battery commander, Vershinin). The first act of *The Seagull* revolves around the performance of Konstantin's play. But to stress the sense of action and forward motion, I prefer to give the title a complete sentence. So:

TITLES FOR SOME FIRST ACTS AND SCENES

The Cherry Orchard: In the early hours of a cold May morning, Ranyevskaya returns home to her insolvent estate after living in France with her lover for five years.

The Three Sisters: In a town with a military base far from Moscow, on a sunny Sunday morning in May, a year after the death of General Prozorov, his four children celebrate the seventeenth birthday (saint's day) of Irina, the youngest, during which, Vershinin, the new battery commander, pays them a visit.

The Seagull: On a close summer evening on his family's country estate, Konstantin presents a play he has written and which Nina performs for his actress mother, household and guests.

A Doll's House: As the Helmer family prepares for Christmas, Krogstad, an employee of Torvald, tries to get his job at the bank reinstated with the help of Torvald's wife, Nora, while, at the same time, a former woman friend of hers also seeks Nora's help to get a job in her husband's bank.

Hedda Gabler: On the day after the Tesmans return from their honeymoon, Hedda begins life in her new home receiving visitors, during which she learns that Eilert Lövborg, a former acquaintance, has become a reformed character, but is back in town and in danger of a relapse.

Cymbeline: Cymbeline, King of Britain, having discovered his daughter Imogen's secret marriage to Posthumus, a commoner, banishes him.

Blood Wedding: Early in the morning in the Andalusian countryside, as a mother offers her son breakfast before he sets off for work in their vineyard, she expresses her ominous concern for his planned marriage to a woman connected to a family with whom her menfolk had been enmeshed in a lethal vendetta.

A Streetcar Named Desire: In the heat of summer, Blanche DuBois, having lost her job and her family mansion, Belle Rêve, arrives unannounced to stay with her sister, Stella Kowalski, who lives in the run-down Elysian Fields quarter of New Orleans with her husband, Stanley, whom Blanche has never met.

These pieces of information are comparatively easy to use as acting material. Without a huge amount of emotional digging, psychological analysis or historical research, the experience of celebrating a birthday, participating in the return home of someone after a long absence or watching some amateur theatrics should be reasonably available to most actors and directors. Before they know anything much about their characters and the specifics of their *milieux*, these facts are at least something concrete for the actors to take hold of as a starting point, something that will get the imagination working in the right direction. *And these obvious and indisputable facts will still be there when they eventually reach performance,* enriched and informed by the complex fabric of relationships, themes, and stories that will have been woven into them during rehearsals.

These titles also begin to reveal the way a play is structured (how its narrative will unwind), a sense of its stylistic WORLD, its basic tone and level of characterisation. In *Cymbeline*, Shakespeare has no concern for the details of environment, but instantly plunges into the story with the event that triggers the main plot of the play. Lorca, in *Blood Wedding*, immediately establishes an atmosphere of impending menace and intense feelings from archetypal characters living ritualised and heavily patterned lives. Chekhov develops a naturalistic, ensemble world with a very strong sense of place, time and relationships and only light intimations of plot. Ibsen and Williams also establish realistic place and time but, in the tradition of realism, set their plots going early, Ibsen's tending towards the melodramatic.

TITLES FOR THE FOUR ACTS OF 'THE SEAGULL'

ACT ONE: *On a close summer evening on his family's estate, Konstantin presents a play he has written and which Nina performs for his actress mother, household and guests.*

This, I think, is self-explanatory. The act is beautifully organised: all the events and relationships in the act are shaped and influenced by this event.

ACT TWO: *Arkadina and Trigorin get through a summer morning on the estate.*

This, typical of Chekhovian second acts, is when we observe, at a more leisurely pace, the characters making their way towards their destinies through a range of disparate scenes, framed by the apparent normality of an average day. The title is a way of pulling a seemingly shapeless act together by identifying a prevailing situation; although no one major event occurs, the presence of the two glamorous visitors from Moscow is a break in the estate's normal routine that affects the behaviour of everyone there.

ACT THREE: *Arkadina and Trigorin leave for Moscow earlier than planned.*

Again, quite self-explanatory, the action of the whole act is totally motivated by this event. Konstantin's attempt, earlier, to shoot himself hovers over the action, but it is not what happens *in* the act (it is a *given circumstance* of the act).

ACT FOUR: *Two years later, on a stormy evening towards the end of autumn, Arkadina, having returned to the estate on an emergency visit to her ailing brother, invites Trigorin to join her there; Nina revisits the estate.*

As these two visits are quite separate (in fact only Konstantin knows of Nina's), they both have to be acknowledged. Sorin's illness subtly provides the occasion for bringing the characters together again. Nina's visit is catastrophic for Konstantin (not so much because of her, but of what she inadvertently makes him realise about his life and talent), but his suicide is not what the act is about, it is an outcome of it.

Sections

To make an act or scene more manageable, I first break it down into what I call *sections*, large pieces of action somewhat equivalent to symphonic movements, and I give these titles, too. They reveal very clearly the big shapes of the act. The title of a section should apply to *all* the characters who participate in it.

SECTIONS FOR THE FIRST ACT OF 'THE CHERRY ORCHARD'
(which, you remember, is about *Ranyevskaya's return*) are:

1. Lopakhin, Dunyasha and Yepikhodov await Ranyevskaya's arrival
2. She arrives
3. Family, friends and servants all catch up on each other's news
4. They go to bed

SECTIONS FOR THE FIRST ACT OF 'THE THREE SISTERS'
(which is about *Irina's birthday* and *Vershinin's visit*) are:

1. The Prozorovs await the visit of Vershinin, the new battery commander, and Irina's saint's day lunch
2. Vershinin calls
3. They sit down to lunch

SECTIONS FOR THE FIRST ACT OF 'THE SEAGULL'
(which is about *Konstantin's play*) are:

1. Family and friends prepare/wait for the performance of Konstantin's play
2. They watch the performance
3. Konstantin stops the performance
4. They react to the aborted performance

All terribly obvious and no doubt dull for the seeker after innovation. But I find these simple facts exhilarating. They give me something concrete that I can *immediately* get my teeth into. (Think of the sensuousness of going to bed that can be explored in Section 4 of *The Cherry Orchard*.) And these can be worked on *without any other knowledge of the characters and their world*. These titles also reveal the playwright's structure of the act that starts to tell me something more about the nature of the play. (An aside: just from these examples, it's clear that Chekhov, who once had a reputation for moody inaction, is a precise and organised technician.)

Units

We can now break down the sections into even more specific pieces of text – into units. I define a unit as *the largest piece of text in which one event, pertinent to all the characters present, takes place*. It can be as broad as 'The audience arrives for the performance of Konstantin's play'; or as specific as 'Masha rejects Medvedenko's declaration of love'. It could be as short as a single line of dialogue or a single stage direction; or it could cover several pages. It may take time to develop the skill to recognise an event, to define what it is and pinpoint its start and finish. In the lengthy, diffuse second act of *The Three Sisters*, one unit could be 'Vershinin, Tusenbach and Masha philosophise'. The question a director and actors have to keep asking themselves is: 'What is the basic event, situation or activity that is holding all the characters together at this moment?' Unless it is an intimate scene between, say, two characters, it is often some sort of social activity. We're not looking for what is most dramatic, but what is the *most obvious, all-inclusive frame* that holds within it the more detailed and subtle complexities that are taking place.

A change of event creates an interesting shift of energy as the characters make a transition from one unit to the next. (A new unit almost always occurs with the entrance of a character into the scene – the 'French scene' of continental playwriting.) Units should be numbered for quick identification ('Let's work on Act Three, Units 7-10').

Some Examples

UNITS FROM SECTIONS 1-3 OF ACT 1 OF 'THE CHERRY ORCHARD'

The units of Section 1 (*They Await Ranyevskaya's Arrival*) would be:

1. Lopakhin and Dunyasha confirm that Ranyevskaya has arrived

2. Lopakhin recalls his encounter with her when he was a peasant boy

3. Yepikhodov delivers some flowers

4. Yepikhodov describes his misfortunes

5. Yepikhodov leaves

6. Dunyasha reveals Yepikhodov's love for her

7. Lopakhin puts Dunyasha in her place

The units of Section 2 (*Ranyevskaya Arrives*) would be:

8. Lopakhin and Dunyasha hear the carriages arriving
9. They go to greet the party
10. Firs crosses the nursery
11. Ranyevskaya passes through the nursery

The first units of Section 3 (*They All Catch Up on Each Other's News*) would be:

12. Dunyasha is reunited with Anya
13. Varya gets rid of Dunyasha
14. Varya is reunited with Anya
15. Lopakhin moos
16. Anya presses Varya to reveal her current situation with Lopakhin . . .
    – and so on.

The titles are very simple, devoid of any interpretation or attempt to attribute motives. The titles are how a fairly intelligent fly-on-the-wall might describe what it observed. Of course, within the unit, each character is playing his or her actions, pursuing his or her objectives, many different things are going on within and beneath the main 'event', but at the start of rehearsals these cannot be known; you can only use what is indisputably clear. For example, at the opening of *The Cherry Orchard*, Lopakhin may well be deeply preoccupied by complex feelings about his relationship with Ranyevskaya, but at this stage in the work the actor cannot possibly know what these might be. But he does know that Lopakhin was waiting to meet her train and fell asleep – *which is playable*. By concentrating on the most obvious facts, the actors can give themselves a firm grounding from which to start both excavating and building.

UNITS FROM SECTION I OF THE FIRST ACT OF 'THE SEAGULL'

Section 1
(*Family and friends prepare/wait for the performance of Konstantin's play*)

1. Masha rejects Medvedenko's declaration of love
2. Konstantin arrives to check everything is ready for the performance accompanied by his uncle, Sorin, who complains about living in the country
3. Sorin enquires about Trigorin

4. Nina arrives just in time for her performance
5. Konstantin tries to woo Nina
6. Konstantin checks the final details for the performance
7. Nina and Konstantin argue about Trigorin's talent as they go backstage
8. Polina pursues Dorn
9. The rest of the audience arrive for the performance
   (a) They discuss actors and acting
   (b) Arkadina performs Gertrude from the *Hamlet* Closet Scene

---

NOTES ON UNITS 2 AND 9

In Unit 2, a lot of small events occur, but they are all connected with Konstantin's concern that everything will be in place for the performance of his play. Getting rid of Masha and Medvedenko is part of this; so is his concern about Nina being late and spoiling the effect of the rising moon, as well as his anxiety about his mother's reception of his play. Within the unit, individual events, such as: *Konstantin gets rid of Masha and Medvedenko*, will be taken care of in the next stage of the process: breaking down the text into actions.

Also, in Unit 2, Konstantin's concerns are mingled with Sorin's continual expressions of discontent about living in the country. As these two 'events' are intermingled (a rare technical occurrence), they have to be linked together in the title.

Unit 9 is an example of a unit that can have sub-units: the discussion of actors and Arkadina's 'performance' are both part of the company's process of arrival and settling themselves to watch the play.

BECOMING THE SUBJECT OF THE UNIT

I encourage all actors who appear in a unit to give it, *whenever possible*, a title that makes their character the subject of the title; for example:

Unit 1: Medvedenko declares his love for Masha, as opposed to Masha rejects Medvedenko's declaration.

Unit 5: Nina tries to avoid Konstantin's advances, as opposed to Konstantin tries to woo Nina.

Unit 8: Dorn tries to avoid Polina, as opposed to Polina pursues Dorn.

Unit 9 (b): Konstantin plays Hamlet to his mother's Gertrude, as opposed to Arkadina performs Gertrude.

This helps to ensure that the actors remain active, even if the unit doesn't seem to involve them very strongly in the action. It also helps them to build their individual journeys through the play. For example, what might Polina be doing in Unit 9 (b), which, in terms of plot, has nothing to do with her? She *is* in the scene and she *must* relate to what is going on. At the simplest, least interpretive level, the unit, from her point of view, might be: *Polina watches Arkadina and Konstantin perform 'Hamlet'*. Gradually, as the actor comes to know the scene more fully, she may find that *watching Arkadina and Konstantin* gives her the excuse to shift onto them any focus that she self-consciously feels might have been placed on her by the untimely arrival of the others during her emotional outburst to Dorn; it also gives her time to pull herself together unobserved. In this way, the simple action, *to watch*, becomes dramatically enriched and full of possibilities for the actor.

An Example of Sub-Units: a Speech from Shakespeare

It might be worth looking at the breakdown into units and sub-units – even sub-sub-units – of Hermione's speech in the trial scene from Shakespeare's *The Winter's Tale*, in which she defends herself against her husband's accusations of adultery and treason. Units give excellent initial assistance to the actor in clarifying her way through the density and complexity – and unfamiliarity – of the language.

Sub-units are useful whenever a long unit has clear subdivisions that still pertain to the overall event of the unit. This often occurs when the unit deals with a debate or argument in which the characters make their points in clear succession, as Hermione does here. (Some sub-units, as is the case towards the end of the scene here, may be no longer than the equivalent of a single action.)

FROM ACT 3 SCENE 2 OF 'THE WINTER'S TALE'

This speech is essentially one unit: *Hermione Defends Herself Against Leontes' Accusations* (or . . . *Offers Her Defence* . . . or . . . *Argues Her Defence* . . .). But it's long and broken down into *sub-units* that are identified alphabetically, and into *sub-sub-units*, identified as ki, kii, kiii, kiv . . .

HERMIONE (a) Since what I am to say must be that
    Which contradicts my accusation and
    The testimony on my part no other
    But what comes from myself, it shall scarce boot me
    To say 'not guilty', mine integrity
    Being counted falsehood, shall, as I express it,
    Be so received. (b) But thus, if powers divine

Behold our human actions, as they do,
I doubt not then that innocence shall make
False accusation blush and tyranny
Tremble at patience. (c) You, my lord, best know,
Who least will seem to do so, my past life
Hath been as continent, as chaste, as true
As I am now unhappy, which is more
Than history can pattern, though devis'd
And play'd to take spectators. For behold me,
A fellow of the royal bed, which owe
A moiety of the throne, a great King's daughter,
The mother to a hopeful prince, here standing
To prate and talk for life and honour 'fore
Who please to come and hear. (d) For life, I prize it
As I weigh grief which I would spare; for honour,
'Tis a derivative from me to mine
And only that I stand for. (e) I appeal
To your own conscience, sir: before Polixenes
Came to your court, how I was in your grace,
How merited to be so; since he came
With what encounter so uncurrent I
Have strain'd t'appear thus; if one jot beyond
The bound of honour, or in act or will
That way inclining, harden'd be the hearts
Of all that hear me, and my near'st of kin
Cry fie upon my grave!

LEONTES   I ne'er heard yet
That any of these bolder vices wanted
Less impudence to gainsay what they did
Than to perform it first.

HERMIONE   (f) That's true enough
Though 'tis a saying, sir, not due to me.

LEONTES   You will not own it.

HERMIONE   More than mistress of
Which comes to me in name of fault, I must not
At all acknowledge. (g) For Polixenes
With whom I am accus'd, I do confess
I loved him as in honour he requir'd
With such a kind of love as might become
A lady like me; with a love, even such,

So, and no other, as you yourself commanded,
Which not to have done I think had been in me
Both disobedience and ingratitude
To you and toward our friend, whose love had spoke
Even since it could speak, from an infant, freely,
That it was yours. (h) Now, for conspiracy,
I know not how it tastes though it be dish'd
For me to try how. All I know of it
Is that Camillo was an honest man
And why he left your court, the gods themselves
Wotting no more than I, are ignorant.

LEONTES You knew of his departure as you know
What you have underta'en to do in's absence.

HERMIONE (i) Sir,
You speak a language that I understand not.
(j) My life stands in the level of your dreams
Which I'll lay down.

LEONTES   Your actions are my dreams
You had a bastard by Polixenes
And I but dream'd it! (k) As you were past all shame –
Those of your fact are so – so past all truth
Which to deny, concerns more than avails; for as
Thy brat hath been cast out, like to itself,
No father owning it – which is indeed
More criminal in thee than it – so thou
Shalt feel our justice; in whose easiest passage
Look for no less than death.

HERMIONE   Sir, spare your threats;
The bug you fright me with, I seek.
To me can life be no commodity;
(ki) The crown and comfort of my life, your favour,
I do give up for lost, for I do feel it gone
But know not how it went. (kii) My second joy,
And first-fruits of my body, from his presence
I am barr'd, like one infectious. (kiii) My third comfort,
Starr'd most unluckily, is from my breast –
The innocent milk in its most innocent mouth –
Hal'd out to murder; (kiv) myself on every post
Proclaim'd a strumpet; (kv) with immodest hatred

The child-bed privilege denied, which 'longs
To women of all fashion; (kvi) lastly,
Hurried here to this place i' th' open air, before
I have got strength of limit. (l) Now, my liege,
Tell me what blessings I have here alive
That I should fear to die? Therefore proceed.
(m) But yet hear this: mistake me not – for life,
I prize it not a straw, but for mine honour
Which I would free – (n) if I shall be condemned
Upon surmises, all proofs sleeping else
But what your jealousies awake, I tell you
'Tis rigour and not law. (o) Your honours all,
I do refer me to the Oracle.
Apollo, be my judge!

LORD   This you request
    Is altogether just; therefore bring forth,
    And in Apollo's name, his oracle.

HERMIONE (p) The Emperor of Russia was my father.
    O, that he were alive and here beholding
    His daughter's trial! That he did but see
    The flatness of my misery, yet with eyes
    Of pity, not revenge!

THE TITLES OF THE UNIT, SUB-UNITS AND SUB-SUB-UNITS

Units:

1. Hermione defends herself against Leontes' accusations.

    Sub-Units:

    (a)   She admits/acknowledges her plea of innocence is obvious.

    (b)   She expresses her hope that innocence will shame tyranny.

    (c)   She reminds Leontes that he should know her virtue and
           integrity better than anyone.

    (d)   She declares that her honour weighs more than her life.

    (e)   She beseeches Leontes to give her chapter and verse of her
           misdeeds.

           (Leontes dismisses her request as typical of sinners.)

(f)   She refuses to admit that she belongs in the category of sinners.

(g)   She points out that she showed Polixenes the degree of love her husband wished for his friend.

(h)   She vows her ignorance of any conspiracy.

        (He insists she is not ignorant.)

(i)   She declares he speaks a language she cannot understand.

(j)   She declares her life is subject to the whims of his dreams.

        (He insists his dreams are real – her child is Polixenes's bastard.)

(k)   (He threatens her with death.)

        She declares that she seeks death because:

        Sub-Sub-Units:

        (ki)   She has lost his favour;

        (kii) She is denied access to her sick son;

        (kiii) Her newborn daughter has been snatched from her breast and abandoned;

        (kiv) She is proclaimed a strumpet;

        (kv)   She has been physically maltreated and denied normal medical attention;

        (kvi) She has been dragged into an open court while still recovering from childbirth.

(l)   She queries why he should think she wishes to live.

(m)   She reiterates that her honour is worth more to her than her life.

(n)   She accuses Leontes of tyranny rather than justice.

(o)   She expresses her desire to surrender her fate to the Oracle.

        (A lord confirms the rightness of this, and calls forth the pronouncement of the Oracle.)

(p)   She expresses her longing that her Emperor-father could witness her shame – with pity not revenge.

Actions

I have already discussed the nature of actions in some detail. Now is the time to begin to put them into – well – action. If the actors are familiar with the following procedure, I ask them to prepare their actions *in advance of the first rehearsal*. If this is their first time to work with me, I explain the principle of actions and work through some of the text with them to show them how to identify and define them; then, the next day, check what they've prepared before we begin to apply them practically, moving them in the space (*see:* ACTIONING in THE TEXT STRAND of REHEARSAL).

Examples of Actioning

THE FIRST UNIT OF ACT ONE OF 'THE SEAGULL'

Part of the grounds of Sorin's estate. A broad avenue of trees leads from the audience into the depths of the estate towards a lake. A makeshift stage for family entertainments has been built across it, completely obscuring the lake. Bushes on either side.

A few chairs, a small table.

The sun has just set. Yakov and some other workmen are behind the stage curtain: sounds of coughing and banging. [1]*Masha and* [2]*Medvedenko are returning from a walk.*

MEDVEDENKO [3]Why are you always in black?

MASHA [4]It's mourning for my life. [5]I'm unhappy.

MEDVEDENKO [6]But why? (*Ponders.*) I don't understand . . . [7]You're healthy, your father's not rich, but he's comfortable. [8]My life's much harder than yours, I only get twenty-three roubles a month and from that they take something for the pension fund, [9]but I don't wear mourning.

[10, 11]*They sit down.*

MASHA [12] It isn't a question of money. Even a pauper can be happy.

MEDVEDENKO [13]In theory, yes, [14]but in practice it works out so: myself, mother, two sisters a little brother, all on a salary of twenty-three roubles. People need to eat and drink? Need tea and sugar? Need tobacco? It's hard to make ends meet.

MASHA [15](*glancing around at the stage*). [16]The play will begin soon.

MEDVEDENKO [17]Yes. Performed by Nina Zarechnaya, and composed by Konstantin Gavrilovich. They're in love and this evening their souls will merge in a mutual striving to create one artistic image. [18]But my soul and yours have no such point of contact. [19]I love you, I can't stay home because of my yearning for you, every day I walk four miles here and four miles back and meet with nothing but indifferentism on your side. [20]It's understandable. I'm without means, we're a large family . . . Who'd want to marry a man who can't feed himself?

MASHA [21]Nonsense. [22](*Takes snuff.*) [23]Your love touches me [24]but I just can't respond, and that's how it is. [25](*Offers him snuff.*) Have some.

MEDVEDENKO [26]I don't feel like any.

Pause.

MASHA [27]Stifling, there'll probably be a storm tonight. [28]All you do is philosophise and talk about money. In your opinion, there's no greater misfortune than poverty, [29]but in mine, it's a thousand times easier to go around in rags and beg than . . . [30]However, you wouldn't understand . . .

ACTIONS FOR THE FIRST UNIT OF THE FIRST SECTION OF ACT ONE OF 'THE SEAGULL'

1.	MASHA	I enter
2.	MEDVEDENKO	I enter with you
3.		I enquire of/ask you why you wear black
4.	MASHA	I explain to you that I'm mourning my life
5.		I reinforce this for you by stating I'm unhappy
6.	MEDVEDENKO	I declare my incomprehension[3]
7.		I remind you of the good situation you're in
8.		I compare my financial position unfavourably with yours
9.		I point out to you that I don't wear mourning
10.	MASHA	I sit down

11.	MEDVEDENKO	I sit down with you
12.	MASHA	I state my belief that life is not about money
13.	MEDVEDENKO	I suggest/argue that your belief is just theoretical
14.		I enumerate for you the necessities of life that require money
15.	MASHA	I glance around the stage
16.		I announce to you that the play will soon begin[2]
17.	MEDVEDENKO	I describe to you the romantic and creative union of Nina and Konstantin[4]
18.		I compare our relationship unfavourably with their creative union
19.		I declare the intensity of my unreciprocated love for you[4]
20.		I acknowledge that my lack of means would discourage you
21.	MASHA	I dismiss your remarks
22.		I take snuff
23.		I admit that your love touches me
24.		I confirm my inability to reciprocate it
25.		I offer you some snuff
26.	MEDVEDENKO	I decline your offer
27.	MASHA	I predict that the close weather threatens a storm
28.		I reject your philosophising and complaints of poverty[1]
29.		I (begin to) offer you my theory of poverty . . .
30.		I (interrupt myself to) conjecture that you wouldn't understand

SOME NOTES ON THE ACTIONS

A general note: I find it more helpful if the actors flesh out their active verbs with complete sentences. If they use the verb alone (*I dismiss, I point out, I admit . . .*) without any context, they will feel a little starved of nourishment when they rehearse with the actions physically, and are likely to lose their place in the scene.

1. In Action 28, Masha *rejects* Medvedenko's philosophising. But she might well want to *deride* Medvedenko's view of life or to *enlighten him* as to the narrowness of his ideas, or to *express her irritation* or *convey her boredom* with his constant harping on the same tune, maybe *to have a row/argue with* him or, more profoundly, to *discourage* his advances any further, all of which are entirely possible. Early in rehearsal, we can have no idea which choice might be most appropriate. If we decide in advance on any of these interpretations, we lock that moment and any budding characterisation within a choice that could eventually limit both the scene and how the character develops. But it *is* clear that she doesn't agree with his ideas. So I think *the least interpretive but accurate action at this point in rehearsal* is that she *rejects* his view of life. Eventually, whether the actor playing Masha decides to *deride*, or *argue* or *express irritation* or *convey boredom* or any combination of these, *she will always be rejecting him*. The *what* (*rejecting*) is capable of containing many possible *hows* (*deriding, arguing, enlightening, discouraging . . .*). So we can say with some certainty that this action, *reject*, is an indisputable fact. The point of this work is to support the actor with *the barest interpretive bones of a scene* so that she has something specific to hold on to (*reject*), while exploring the many possibilities that the scene may offer her and her partner as they progress through rehearsals. In so doing, she learns more – and more deeply – about her role. Then, in any performance, she can play whatever instinctive *how* is available to her in that moment – and there may well be many more than those I've listed here. Working in this way, the actor has both *discipline* (the security of the *what: reject*) and *freedom* (*how* she *rejects* him).

2. Similarly, Action 16 could have many options. It may well be that she says '*The play will begin soon*' to *remind him of what they're there for, to share her anticipation, to encourage his enthusiasm, to convey her artistic sensibility to him* – all of which are interpretive. One might think it could be to *change the subject*, but that would be an intention and not the *actual* action she is playing. In this case, her objective would be *to stop him enumerating his hardships* and therefore her action would be *to draw his attention to the play*. Besides, the fact that she plays an action that doesn't respond to Medvedenko's previous action *automatically* implies that she's changed the subject. Whether this is deliberate or not will be the decision of the actor playing Masha.

3. In Action 6, Medvedenko's action (to *declare* his incomprehension) has three separate beats: (a) to query her unhappiness (*'But why?'*); (b) to ponder its mystery (*'Ponders'*); (c) to declare his incomprehension (*'I don't understand . . .'*). It would be perfectly correct to name those beats as separate actions (which, of course, technically they are). But as they all add up to the one overall action, it seems sensible to treat them as such. If you get pedantically overdetailed about actioning in this early stage of the work, the process can become laborious.

4. The above point applies to Actions 17 and 19, which, to my count, have five beats each.

ACTIONING A SPEECH FROM SHAKESPEARE
ACT 3 SCENE 2 OF 'ROMEO AND JULIET'

Juliet learns that Romeo, to whom she has just been secretly married, has killed her cousin, Tybalt, and has been banished from Verona. Her speech is directed to her Nurse, except when she addresses her own tears – even then, it's really for the benefit of the Nurse's understanding:

¹Shall I speak ill of him that is my husband
²Ah, poor my lord, what tongue shall smooth thy name
When I, thy three-hours wife, have mangled it?
³But wherefore, villain, dids't thou kill my cousin?
⁴That villain cousin would have killed my husband.
⁵Back, foolish tears, back to your native spring!
⁶You tributary drops belong to woe
Which you, mistaking, offer up to joy.
⁷My husband lives that Tybalt would have slain
And Tybalt's dead that would have slain my husband.
⁸All this is comfort – wherefore weep I then?
⁹Some word there was worser than Tybalt's death
That murd'red me. ¹⁰I would forget it fain.
¹¹But, O, it presses to my memory
Like damnèd guilty deeds to sinner's minds.
¹²Tybalt is dead and Romeo banishèd.
¹³That banishèd, that one word banishèd
Hath slain ten thousand Tybalts. ¹⁴Tybalt's death
Was woe enough if it had ended there
¹⁵Or if sour woe delights in fellowship

And needly will be ranked with other griefs
Why followed not when she said 'Tybalt's dead'
Thy father or thy mother, nay, or both
Which modern lamentation might have moved?
[16]But with a rearward following Tybalt's death
'Romeo is banishèd' – to speak that word
Is father, mother, Tybalt, Romeo, Juliet
All slain, all dead. 'Romeo is banishèd' –
There is no end, no limit, measure, bound
In that word's death; no words can that woe sound.
[17]Where is my father and my mother, nurse?

ACTIONS FOR JULIET'S SPEECH

1. I question/challenge your idea that I should condemn my husband
2. I stress/stipulate/state to you that if a wife doesn't support her husband, who else could
3. I demand to know why Romeo killed Tybalt
4. I myself offer you his reason as self-defence
5. I order my tears to go back to their source
6. I point out to my tears that they're confusing woe and joy
7. I clarify for you the reason that I'm happy is because my husband is still alive and safe
8. I question you as to why I am crying, then, if I am happy
9. I explain to you that the memory of a word far worse than 'murd'red' has murdered me
10. I share with you my longing to forget it
11. I admit to you that I can't get it out of my mind
12. I reveal to you that the word is 'banishèd'
13. I emphasise for you that Romeo's banishment is worse than the death of 10,000 Tybalts*
14. I declare that Tybalt's death would have been enough to cope with*
15. I declare further that if my parents had also been killed, I could have coped with that, too*
16. I state to you that Romeo banishèd is inexpressibly greater than any other conceivable griefs*
17. I ask you where my parents are?

SOME NOTES ON THE ACTIONS

* Actions 13-16 inclusive could be played as one action and stated exactly as 16.

Important: It's often a source of disappointment or dissatisfaction to an actor that the actions don't deal with the emotions implicit in the speech. But that is not what they're there for. We are not concerned (yet) with what Juliet is *feeling*, but with what she is *doing*. Despite the obvious intensity of what she's expressing, Juliet is nonetheless executing very ordinary and available actions: *explaining, questioning, declaring* and so on. This is a helpful way into an intense speech so early in rehearsals, when the actor can be in no state to fulfil the emotional heights the scene will eventually demand of her (nor should she be). But she *can* fulfil – play – her actions fully and strongly. Of course, she can imbue them with as much feeling and power as she currently feels able *truthfully* to employ. As with the unit-ing, this process also helps to clarify the language.

A Pyramid of Titles

Now, returning to *The Seagull*, we can put all these layers of titles together and see what they actually offer the actor. Let us take a beat from Medvedenko's text, *'But my soul and yours have no such point of contact'* and put it at the base of an inverted pyramid of all the titles (act, section, unit and action) that are its context, in order to see how many layers of meaning it has already accrued.

ACT ONE: On a close summer evening on his family's estate, Konstantin presents a play he has written and which Nina performs for his actress mother, household and guests.

SECTION ONE: They all prepare/wait for the performance of Konstantin's play.

UNIT ONE: Masha rejects Medvedenko's declaration of love.

ACTION: Medvedenko compares their relationship with Nina and Konstantin's.

BEAT: *'But my soul and yours have no such point of contact.'*

Or you might visualise the pyramid the right way up.

BEAT: *'But my soul and yours have no such point of contact.'*

ACTION: Medvedenko compares their relationship with Nina and Konstantin's.

UNIT ONE: Masha rejects Medvedenko's declaration of love.

SECTION ONE: They all prepare/wait for the performance of Konstantin's play.

ACT ONE: On a close summer evening on his family's estate, Konstantin presents a play he has written and which Nina performs for his actress mother, household and guests.

The beat contains all these titles within itself. It's worth pointing out that all the titles contain each other. They interrelate in both directions, up and down the pyramid. They are all contexts for each other.

Already, without any deep analysis of the text, purely taking the information in these titles, the actor playing Medvedenko has the following facts available to work with (to get his imagination going).

It is a summer evening

He is on a country estate (belonging to Konstantin's family)

He's waiting with Masha for a play to be performed

The play has been written by Konstantin and will be performed by Nina

Medvedenko thinks they are in love with one another and have an artistic union, too

He is in love with Masha

She doesn't reciprocate

He compares their relationship unfavourably to Nina and Konstantin's

---

So already, when he plays this beat *'But my soul and yours have no such point of contact'*, he has that pyramid of facts to inform it with. He also has a lot of other factual information from within the whole unit itself.*

---

* This opening scene is a masterly example of subtly delivered exposition. Within less than a page, Chekhov absorbs us in a relationship and, with the utmost naturalness, gives us a lot

PREPARING THE REHEARSALS

Reminder: What It's All For

The purpose of this rehearsal process is to immerse the actors so thoroughly in the WORLD OF THE PLAY that they'll have the complete confidence and ability to play freshly, with freedom and spontaneity, at every performance, living in the moment, in a continuous creative flow, able to adapt to – and absorb – change, variation and discovery.

Two Analogies

1. *A Freshly Cooked Meal*

I like to think the actors are giving each audience a freshly cooked meal rather than one reheated in a microwave oven; food that's continuously reheated, though it might improve for a day or two, eventually loses all flavour and nutriment. Yesterday, a dish might have been made with parmesan, but tonight with pecorino; today we may have found something in the market that wasn't in season last week. But essentially the ingredients are the same, gathered daily, fresh and cooked to order.

2. *A Soccer Match*

Theatre is like a game of soccer (or any team sport). The players know their positions (*roles*), their *relationships* to the rest of the team and to their opponents. They practise rigorously and develop their skills (their *actions* – dribbling, passing, heading, tackling . . .) to the peak of their abilities. They know the rules of the game, *the conventions of the world the game inhabits*. They have clear *objectives*: to score and to prevent their opponents from scoring. They have a *super-objective*: to be the winning team in their division or in the world. They have *given circumstances*: the opposition's form and morale; their own team's form and morale; their

---

of information about these two characters, some other characters and the main action of the first act, as follows: Masha wears black, takes snuff, looks healthy and has a comfortably-off father; Medvedenko has a family of four to feed (mother, two sisters and little brother), only earns 23 roubles, pays into a pension fund, smokes, 'philosophises', walks four miles both ways to see Masha and is in love with her; she doesn't love him; they have divergent attitudes to the value of money; they are going to watch a play written by Konstantin and performed by Nina; he thinks that Nina and Konstantin are in love and have a creative union; the weather is close; there might be a storm . . . All this within ten short, naturalistic speeches. Awesome!

standing thus far in the season; whether they're playing at home or away; environmental conditions such as the weather, altitude, state of the pitch, mood of the crowd; and so forth. They then go onto the pitch with all their rules, roles, given circumstances, objectives and possible actions – and *improvise*. They can't anticipate where the ball will go, but must deal with it appropriately, however and wherever it arrives. And their appropriate and necessary spontaneity comes from the rigour and discipline of their preparation and training. Actors, too, since they can't know exactly *how* things will happen, must adapt to circumstances – and *improvise. Both groups are, appropriately, players.*

Two Approaches

There are two basic philosophies of rehearsal, two approaches which reflect very different visions of theatre. One of them is what this book proposes: an immersion in the material, with time for discovery and natural evolution. The principle is to stay open to possibilities and to delay for as long as possible any decisions that might close off further search. It means using whatever techniques – games, improvisations, exercises – you believe will facilitate your exploration. This way inevitably takes longer but reaches deeper than the second and more traditional journey.

That journey is, mainly, to work your way through the script scene by scene, discussing and trying things out, usually with the script in hand, making decisions as soon as is reasonable, that are then fixed. In this sort of procedure, there is little use of improvisational techniques; in fact, there is little use *for* improvisation. This is about expediency, using common sense and past experience (what you already know) to aim for decisions (results), often without attempting to look too far beyond the first good idea. At times, this can be exhilarating, as my experience with weekly musicals in New England proved to be. Eventually, it becomes creatively eroding. Actors who have continuously to produce (quick) results may pride themselves on their professionalism, but they'll be thrown back more and more on old patterns, habits and tricks to survive. Working like this ultimately atrophies an actor's creative muscle.

Two Processes

In rehearsal, the director and actors have to go through two essential processes: *the understanding* of the play and *the embodiment* of the play. This, in fact, is the purpose of rehearsal: to discover and embody the particular *world* hidden in the mysterious text. By *embodiment* I mean that the actors and the text take total possession of each other and become one. Think of it like this: at the start of rehearsal you have the text; at the end of rehearsal you have the text *embodied*.

Two Understandings

These processes of *understanding* and *embodying* are, inconveniently, not consecutive – that is, first the understanding, then the embodying. They can happen simultaneously, erratically, out of sequence, back-to-front. Most acting is understanding by *doing*. The good actor works with a blend of sense and sensibility – *la raison* and *le sentiment*, that particularly eighteenth-century French ideal of a balanced head and heart. *This combination forms what I'd call a natural actor's particular intelligence.* If, however, actors are encouraged to understand the play by too much talk, too much *raison*, they get locked inside their heads. The wrong sort of thinking prevents embodiment. (Some actors are quite happy about this! We're all familiar with actors who work from the neck up – a young director described them to me as 'actors who have trouble with their legs'.) It's one thing to understand something intellectually, it is quite another to understand it cognitively. When the latter occurs, a flush of recognition seems to sweep through your whole body, you literally *feel* the realisation falling into place. There are two levels of understanding – reason and experience – and we need them both. But the latter is where the 'heart' takes over from the head – and from where imagination takes flight.

This is frustrating for a director. You can explain things to actors with clarity, accuracy and specificity, and the actors can understand the words you're saying perfectly well. But it won't really *mean* anything until they've 'experienced' it, understood it in their bodies, their senses, their instinct, with that hot flush of recognition I've described. I've sat in rehearsals, saying things that I believed to be revelatory, insightful, problem-solving, stimulating – very pleased with myself indeed – only to be met with blank stares and polite smiles. And this process, getting from head to gut and back again, happens, alas, in its own time. You cannot speed it up, you cannot force it, because it is a process through which the unconscious is made conscious. There are no guaranteed methods of unlocking the unconscious on demand. The director's work is to find any way possible to help the actors towards their instinctive, experiential understanding of the play. I'm not saying that actors shouldn't be spoken to, but you can better coax a realisation by non-verbal means, setting up the right sort of processes, exercises and improvisations by which actors will *find things out for themselves*. What you discover for yourself is infinitely more meaningful than what you are told; it goes deeper and lasts longer. (Maybe that's why history repeats itself.) The most productive rehearsals are those in which the least is said. If I find us talking, talking, talking, talking, talking . . . , I know I'm stuck and work isn't going well. If you've done your (director's) work properly, the actors are likely to make discoveries similar to yours, but in the best cases they will each bring back to you not only what you've discovered, but that extra 'something' that makes their talents so individually their own. (You could give ten actors the same instructions about the same character in the same scene and they would create ten totally different performances.)

Two Creativities

There are, similarly, two types of creativity (everything seems to be binary), which mirror the two types of understandings: *invention* – let's use that word to designate the cleverness that comes from the head; and *imagination* – that comes from the 'gut'. Nothing wrong with a clever head, but the 'gut' is where actors function most creatively. From there, what emerges is spontaneous, unexpected, therefore unconstrained by that tiresome, judgemental self-censor in the actor's head that worries about whether a choice might be good or bad, right or wrong, clever or dull, might or might not get a laugh, please or displease the director. Such momentary calculation – even the briefest of nano-seconds taken to decide – often means that the moment has passed and the potential choice has been over-taken by the continuing action. *The inventive actor makes choices happen; the imaginative actor allows choices to happen.* The actor making the conscious choice is always somewhat in control, standing a little outside the action; the imaginative choice can only come to the actor who is somewhat *out* of control, that is to say, has let go of that controlling head and allowed action its autonomy. When actors perform through reason, they create by conscious invention; when they perform through action, their imagination comes straight from the unconscious. If we assume that both are played with honest intention, the latter must be the more truthful, the more revealing, because it isn't mediated through any filter of evaluation or calculation. Spontaneous choices (are allowed to) happen. The director's job must always be to help the actors find their way into such a creative state.

————

What the Director Brings to the Start of Rehearsals

I became a much happier (and better) director when I stopped coming to the start of rehearsals with a very precise series of results already in my head and allowed myself to discover the play along with the actors. This does *not* mean that a director doesn't prepare. On the contrary, you come to rehearsal with some *preliminary and reasonable conjectures.* These are derived from the indisputable facts you've extracted from a careful deconstruction of the text and act as a series of *starting points* for the actors – images with which they can run, paths down which they can travel. *How* they go down those paths is up to them. Some may rush straight ahead, others may loiter to survey the scenery on either side. All you can ask is that they go down the same paths and not down others on some personal agendas of their own. (We all have to play by the same rules!) Rewardingly, actors will almost certainly return with insights unique to them, that you, the director, could never have realised. They'll reveal new aspects of the play to you. Actors and directors are different creatures. You, the director, can detect possible avenues worth exploring, but it's the actors who have to do the exploring. Because they're active, they'll reach into areas where a director can't really follow. Whatever you give to creative actors, they'll give you back in spades.

At this stage in the proceedings, travelling is more important than arriving. In fact, results would be detrimental, because, inevitably, they'd be shallow. *Work on processes, not results.* The results will be whatever they'll be. If the work has been honest and specific, the results will be the right ones for this particular group of people at this particular moment in the process; you cannot say they're wrong. This is even truer by the time we arrive at performance, by when the actors will deeply know the WORLD they're inhabiting. What gets played on a particular night is the reality of that performance – neither right nor wrong, better nor worse, but *true to the moment.*

So, directors, prepare appropriately and start as you mean to continue. Set the tone and terms of the work clearly, not necessarily by talking about them, but by the way you set up each step on the journey, the way you define exercises, the sequence in which you structure the events of each rehearsal, your response to what the actors do, your choice of words . . .

Rethinking Rehearsal Structures

Once you've done all your preparatory work on the text, you must consider what sort of rehearsal process will most effectively put the company in touch with those elements you believe might open up the unique WORLD that your preparation has suggested to you. Does it suggest, for instance, that more time than usual should be devoted to physical skills; to the acquisition of particular patterns of social behaviour; to the release of heightened levels of passion; to the development of complex psychology? Will the actors' relationship to their space need consideration; will the handling of objects need special treatment; might there be some form of mime; will the language require a particular delivery; will the text itself need more than usual time for study . . . ? And what takes precedence? In what order should these areas of work be presented to the actors? What might be the best rhythm for each day's rehearsal? What sort of energy and images would you like to be uppermost at the beginning of the work? What associates – trainers, coaches – would you like to include as part of the rehearsal process, and how are you going to adjust your ideal schedule to their practical ones?

All directors should think imaginatively about how they want to structure their rehearsals. You should not automatically accept what is conventionally offered. First of all, how much time do you believe this particular text requires to be brought to embodied fruition? Traditionally, a rehearsal lasts an average of four weeks. This has nothing to do with artistic necessity, only with financial considerations. But how, in a month, can a group of people, without common language or shared vision, make creative sense of a play that most likely took the playwright a year or more to write, longer to conceive? Short rehearsals work (at a certain low level of achievement) as long as everyone involved implicitly agrees to take short cuts, makes reasonably quick choices and relies on adrenaline to get them through the first few performances at least!

It's not a question of talent whether or not you are able to produce something quickly. It's a question of sufficient absorption time. Actors absorb at different rates and respond differently to particular material. If you're dealing with a realistic, contemporary play with recognisable characters in familiar locations, then it's just possible to do good work within a month; such material is clearly more available to you. But for a company reaching out towards a WORLD that's alien in time, place and form, four weeks are totally inadequate to absorb a whole new culture of thinking and being.

My time in Israel habituated me to long rehearsals – often as much as four months. Occasionally longer! At last I was able to do all those things that, as a beginner, I used recklessly to announce we'd be doing during rehearsals, but actually never got round to. Far too often, I'd get to the dress rehearsal and realise with an unpleasant jolt that many of the things that, on the first day, I'd promised the company we'd be working on had never been touched! Longer rehearsals meant that at last there was no excuse not to do all I intended. Longer rehearsals meant that we could be rigorous, thorough and detailed. Without the pressure of insufficient time, the actors could breathe more creatively, investigate more complex acting challenges and learn new skills. It meant that we could *really* explore, could take the risk of ending up down the occasional cul-de-sac; if rehearsals are genuinely heuristic, there can be no guarantee that everything you mine will be gold. But by the gradual elimination of what doesn't work, you end up with what *does* work – a version of Grotowski's *via negativa.** Continual trial and error removes the dross from your excavations and reveals the essential gold.

If trial and error sounds like a recipe for irresponsibility and indulgence, I stress that you can only base your explorations on what, factually and specifically, you've gleaned from a meticulous analysis of the text. Freedom comes from discipline. Many books have been written on the subject of improvisation and actors' exercises, but any sort of enquiry, exploration, research, investigation, laboratory work – call it what you will – must be set up in a spirit of scientific enquiry.

You don't do any old thing that uncritically takes your fancy because you think it might be amusing to see what happens. For example, don't just play games because it's a fun way of getting the day started, or will make you popular with the company (to start with, at any rate). Your games may work well for a while; actors who are willing to improvise are essentially trusting (if they weren't, how could they ever work – I think actors often exemplify the embodiment of hope over experience). But as rehearsals develop, they'll begin to grow fractious and suspicious of

---

* The *via negativa* is the elimination of blocks to potential creativity. Acting problems for most actors are indeed caused by the barriers they've imposed on themselves, usually as protection against imagined threats. The solution is not always by addition, but by subtraction; you cannot give actors talent, but you *can* (try to) remove the obstacles that prevent the release of their talent.

your ability if they can't see any connection between such games and the actual work in hand. I've watched directors spend a couple of weeks setting up games and exercises which the actors enjoyed, assuming they were leading somewhere. And then, all of a sudden, they ceased, to be abruptly replaced by an utterly conventional rehearsal process ('Move here', 'Do this') which left the actors in a state of perplexity, then irritation, then distrust of someone who had wasted good rehearsal time to little benefit. If you do use improvisation, *it must be woven into the fabric of the whole rehearsal*. Nor is it a good idea to bring random teachers into rehearsals to give the odd class, unless you've thought through their purpose *vis-à-vis* the production. Their occasional appearance is no more than an annoying interruption to the flow of the actors' work, and little more than paying lip service to something you feel should be seen to be done (it looks good on applications for funding). By all means use teachers, but, as with improvisatory techniques, integrate them into the production. They can be invaluable colleagues if treated as such. Voice and movement teachers often feel they are called in merely to stick plasters over gaps in directors' abilities.

Getting back to scientific enquiry: your improvisatory work must be devised with a combination of knowledge, insight and experience: you put A and B together in the anticipation – with the *informed* hunch – that they might yield something like C. They might not, but if set up well, they usually get somewhere close. Sometimes, they can exceed expectations and yield you not only C but D also – and even E. I've found that once you've discovered the language of a rehearsal, and you're on the right track, your instinct has a gratifying way of taking you into territory you never had any idea of visiting, but which rewards you with unexpected bonuses when you find yourself there. You develop a subliminal awareness of what specifically stimulates your current company of actors. A cast's collective demeanour will open up or close down different avenues of exploration for you. You must not expect a particular process to succeed whatever the circumstances. I've come to learn, from unhappy experience, that if, in new circumstances, you unthinkingly repeat past techniques that were successful with another group of people, there's no guarantee that they won't go dead on you this time around. You have constantly to re-evaluate what you're doing.

Never assume. I did, when I was teaching at LAMDA. I taught first-year acting for five years, and each summer I would rethink what I'd done throughout the year, reinvent, refresh and reshape the class with additions and deletions for the forthcoming year. In my fourth year, the students' response to what I offered them was so triumphantly exhilarating that I thought I'd got the whole thing sorted. So the following summer, I didn't bother to examine my work further. When I started teaching the same process to a new intake of students in the fifth year, it went down like a cup of cold sick. After the initial slap in the face, I was forced to think about what had gone wrong. I came to the conclusion that because what I was teaching had already worked so well, I (unconsciously) didn't feel the need to sell it, to present it with that mixture of apprehension, excitement and determination with which you offer new ideas to a group of actors. No doubt I transmitted a sort of complacency, even (unintentionally) an air of patronising authority ('I know how this works and you're going to be knocked out by it!'), all of which may have got up that class's collective subliminal nose. Techniques not re-examined or refreshed have an unpleasant habit of backfiring. Now I *do* use certain procedures as a definite part of my rehearsals – the strands of work connected with text and character that I'll describe in due course – but each time I establish them with a new company, I try to ensure they're freshly presented and that, possibly, the parameters and some details are slightly altered; not changed for the sake of change, but refined and tilted towards the new material.

Short rehearsals, for me, seem meaningless. Getting a show on at all costs is very low on my list of priorities. I'm interested in creating a WORLD. And for that I need time. So for most of my career I've begged, bargained and clamoured – or created my own circumstances – to get the conditions I wanted. I wanted long rehearsals and I got them. I had, of course, to compromise in other areas: a smaller production budget, maybe, or fewer actors. But that was my choice. It is no mystery that if you have time and you know how to use it, your work *de facto* must be richer. The directors I admire – Mnouchkine, Stein, Brook, Lepage – demand long periods, imaginatively structured and supported with the appropriate physical conditions, in order to achieve their aims, the evidence of which is in their productions, rich and complex, skilful and rigorous, beautiful and innovative; everything that is placed before us seems deeply considered, *meant*.

I'm still deeply influenced by memories of my first enthralling encounters with the accounts of the highly creative rehearsals, conducted over long months, by Vakhtangov, Meyerhold, Tairov, Stanislavsky and their contemporaries in a period when theatre seemed so vivid, so vital and so wanted.

Time Out

When I described the start of my work at LAMDA, I mentioned the surprising fact (as it was then to me) that, as soon as I began to teach, a lot of things I hadn't really understood when I myself had been studying suddenly made sense (that flush of recognition, I described earlier). It was as if the three fallow years I'd just experienced had been necessary for this to happen. The unconscious had been given time to breathe, as it were, without the conscious mind stifling it with the constant demand for solutions to problems. That revelation stayed with me and eventually I began to see that so much theatre practice was unsatisfactory, not only for lack of time, but also for lack of time *away* from the work.

The traditional structure of rehearsing a production in which, once you've started, you don't stop until the first performance, works against full creativity. The actors and director are under constant pressure to achieve, to produce results, to 'get it right', so much so that the head takes over and the experiential side of things gets neglected. The closer to the first performance, the greater the pressure. Problems that can't be solved by intelligence alone don't get solved. The tendency is to keep digging the same hole and get nowhere – except deeper into the same impasse. The increasing limitation of time means that there's no space for lateral thinking. I believe that, for a really creative process, there has to be a period when those involved can get away from the work in hand and occupy themselves with something totally different. It seems that only when the mind is freed from the *conscious* pressure to solve problems can it get on with its work of actually doing so.

When I ran Shared Experience, circumstances found us working on two *Arabian Nights* shows at the same time, rehearsing them on alternate weeks. Whenever we returned to Show A, it seemed to have leapt forward in the period we'd been totally involved in Show B. And vice versa. While we were consciously occupied with one set of problems, the unconscious, it seems, was dealing with the other set. I later put this process into deliberate practice while simultaneously working with a group of actors on two Marivaux plays. Both productions, by alternating rehearsals, progressed faster and more productively than if they'd been worked on one at a time. Similarly – and not an uncommon experience – whenever we returned to a show after leaving it for a reasonable length of time, we found that it always started from a more advanced place than where we'd left it. Experiential understanding takes its own time. Neither the actors nor the director can speed it up or force its birth. All they can do is to provide the conditions they believe most conducive to its eventual arrival. I'm prescribing sufficiently long rehearsals that contain a period in which the actors can get away from the current work and put their minds elsewhere.

Make Demands

If you have a strong belief in the way you want to conduct your rehearsal and what you need for it (a decent floor, for example, special lighting) you must pursue its realisation. *Part of our job as directors is to demand the conditions that we believe will nurture the creative process we envisage, rather than uncritically accepting prevailing circumstances.* I believe that if you sincerely want something and keep pushing for it, you'll eventually get it. Otherwise, nothing changes. The *status quo* reigns supreme. And the *status quo* doesn't remain *what is* for long; *what is* very quickly becomes *what was*, and never *what might be*. If you don't go forwards, you go backwards.

CASTING

Casting the Role

As with much else, you have a basic binary choice for the way you go about casting. One way, probably the most common, is to cast someone as close as possible to your vision (or the received idea) of the role. This means that you've more or less decided how the role should be played and you're probably requiring actors to give you something close to what they've done before that more or less matches that decision. You're taking no risks, trusting them to come up with the required goods – which they *will* oblige you with. You're certainly not looking for any discoveries or surprises. This probably means that you're not too concerned about their approach or attitude to acting, just so long as you can be reasonably reassured that they're sociable and professional. You're looking for a commodity rather than a creation. In this way, you end up with a cast of a certain competence, but probably with little artistry. They will sort out their blocking ('Look, if I sit down on this line, that allows you to get up and go to the door more easily, what d'you think?') and generally accommodate each other. You can end up with a show that's undoubtedly slick and smooth, but almost guaranteed to have none of the life that I've been advocating throughout these pages.

Casting the Actor

The other way is to cast the actor, rather than the role; an actor with whom you have a mutual sympathy, with whom you can speak a similar language. Often, when I get good 'vibes' from actors I'm meeting for the first time, who on the face of it aren't right for the roles I'm trying to fill, my imagination begins to see ways in which they *could* play them. Given the opportunity and the encouragement, actors can surprise even themselves with their versatility. Selfishly, I'm looking for actors who share my ethos, stimulate my imagination and give me energy.

Recognising Actors

There are many sorts of actors and your job is to distinguish between those who, talented as they may be, are not for you and those who are. Actors are individuals, but, alas, they can fall into categories and you need to recognise them. There are, for example, some (usually men) who've become disillusioned by the failure of their career to take off as they were led to expect it would. Around mid-life they have been forced to confront the reality of a career unrewarding from any standpoint. They may well wonder what they're still doing in a profession that looks less and less suitable for a grown man with a family and a mortgage. But they've been in it too long to extricate themselves and haven't the courage to embark on a new career, so they cling on, often, as they get older, becoming useful 'character types', getting small roles in film, a few days here, a few days there, being paid reasonably well for not too much effort. They may tend to have become cynical and lazy. These are probably not the best actors for an improvising ensemble. But, to be fair, *you never know*. It's possible you might meet such an actor at a moment when his former aspirations have begun to reassert themselves. You may be instrumental in encouraging them back to their full expression – a rewarding thing to be able to do. You have to weigh up the pros and cons carefully,

There are actors of middling reputations – they haven't made it as 'stars' but feel they should be treated as such – who often create a lot of fuss around themselves to assert their unfulfilled self-image. They can waste a lot of time and energy and are usually not good team players. The danger when you first meet such actors is that their reputation can impress you – and their charm flatter you – into letting them persuade you they're just who you want.

You may meet actors insistent that they *must* work with you, *need* to work with you, and, indeed, *are* going to work with you, insistent on *how* important for their careers, their development, their souls it would be, if they were so fortunate as to spend a period of time in your more-than-talented hands, and insistent that, to achieve such an honour, they're ready to do *anything* you want. Beware! They say exactly what directors, especially those with a fragile sense of self, want to hear (actually, we all like flattery, even when we recognise it as such). They may well be sincere in what they're saying at the time. They may be desperate to work and consequently don't really take in the nature of the job. But what they present during such a meeting may be very different from what you get in rehearsal, once the reality of the way you work throws them into alarm. Then they can become very far from the open and malleable creature they initially offered you.

When you first meet actors, describe precisely how you work. And make sure they listen carefully to what you're telling them. To be certain that the conduct of rehearsals and the nature of the production is absolutely clear to them in advance of any offer that may come their way, it's probably necessary to repeat such information – twice, at the very least! Like most people, actors take in only so much, usually what they want to hear. They can be far too busy trying to create an impression of enthusiasm (after all, they do want to work) to be able, calmly, to absorb what you're telling them. I often invite a response from actors along the lines of 'Would that worry you?' or 'That is clear to you, isn't it?' just to ensure that they *have* heard what I said. This double-checking has two uses: any actor who *is* only per- forming a show of enthusiasm for this sort of work will, if made an offer, swiftly turn it down; and if the way of working does create problems later in rehearsal, you're at least in the position of reminding a resistant actor that you did lay your cards on the table when first you met.

Gut Feelings

And you, listen carefully to your gut feelings about actors, not your head! Your instinct will stand you in better stead than an intellectual calculation about actors who, on paper and by general report, have excellent reputations. They may well be excellent, but they may not be excellent for you. Instinct is, as I say, no more than the combination of your natural talent and taste welded to your experience. Listen to it! I've learnt from myself that every time I let my calculating head overrule my gut instinct, I've come to rue my choice.

There was an actor whose performances I had frequently admired, and my admiration was reinforced by other people's opinions. This actor became a sort of *idée fixe* in my mind, someone I really had to work with. At some point, we met socially and agreed a mutual interest in working together when an opportunity presented itself. When we eventually discussed a specific production, the longer we talked, the more my 'gut' had negative vibrations. But my head didn't want to listen, didn't want to let go of the decision it had already made; I'd wanted this actor for so long that I wasn't about to give up that possibility now. Well, I offered the role, the role was accepted – and from then on, it was all downhill. The actor challenged every step of the work, and tried hard, but in vain, to get me to block scenes; then, perversely, or in retaliation, treated the open structure of the performance as an invitation to waywardness. It wasn't a happy collaboration – indeed, it wasn't a collaboration. Now, what had probably gone wrong was that both of us, from hearsay, had conceived a very misguided idea about each other's working methods and had in mind totally different sorts of journeys, so that when we finally met, neither of us really heard what the other was saying. Subsequently, I've seen this actor give wonderful performances! Regretfully, I now see we could neither of us give each other what we each needed.

Casting Processes

In terms of how I actually cast, the process varies from production to production, from casting exclusively from actors I've already worked with to holding elaborate workshops over several days. I find that the material and circumstances of a new production often inform how I go about recruitment. Sometimes I find it sufficient just to have a chat. But however I proceed, I always have a thirty-minute meeting with each actor, in which I make very clear what the project involves, find out as much as I can about them, especially their beliefs and attitudes to acting, and encourage them to interview me. (I suggest to them that such meetings are a two-way process.) If someone comes with good energy, sits up and looks me in the eye, asks intelligent questions and shows me they've thought seriously about the material (they'll have always been sent a script in advance), I'm instantly predisposed in their favour. My gut has learnt to pick out the distrustful, the defensive, the deferential, the resentful, the bluffers who say what they think you want to hear . . . And still I make mistakes!

I usually enquire of actors whether, should I invite them, they'd be prepared to come back for a workshop with some other actors (nobody's ever said no). What I never do is hold conventional auditions where the actors are given ten minutes to recite a couple of speeches or read the script cold. From that process, I can tell nothing of much value or interest. In a workshop, you can see how attentive actors are to instructions, how imaginative, how cooperative with their colleagues, how physically and vocally skilful, how flexible, how laterally they think, whether they can 'take direction' and what sort of atmosphere they contribute to the session. As such a large part of my life is spent in a rehearsal room, I want to spend it with congenial colleagues.

Never Assume

Earlier, I gave an example from my time at LAMDA, when complacency encouraged me not to rethink one of my classes – and how badly that backfired. I once let the same thing happen while casting, when – either through complacency, tiredness or laziness – I assumed that the same group of actors in a new production would behave in exactly the positive, creative way they had previously, and discovered to my cost it wasn't so. With a little forethought, it should have been obvious that the relationship between us was different from when we'd first worked together. This time around, the actors already knew each other and they all knew me; they were now in different personal and professional circumstances, the play was different, their roles were different, their relationships within the roles were different . . . In fact, things couldn't have been much more different! But I didn't anticipate anything but a rerun of the wonderful rehearsal we'd all experienced before. And it didn't happen! And it was my fault for not re-evaluating the situation. I say again: *never assume; never take anything for granted*. It can feel relentless always to be reconsidering what you're doing, never allowing yourself the ease of routine. But you have to think afresh through all aspects of the work with each and every production.

4

THE WORK: REHEARSAL, PRODUCTION, PERFORMANCE

REHEARSAL:
SOME BASIC PRINCIPLES

I don't apologise that it's taken almost half the book to get to the start of rehearsals. It indicates the amount of thought and preparation that's necessary before you can embark on any serious work with the actors.

Working Together: the Real Meaning of Ensemble

The actors are all continuously in rehearsal. Moving forward together ensures greater likelihood of the actors moulding themselves into an ensemble – that is, actors playing together by the same rules of the same game. (Some critics seem happy to identify an ensemble as a rather large cast not bumping into each other.) The actors develop a shared vision of what they're creating and *in performance do look as though they all inhabit the same world*. This rehearsal process ensures that the actors are up on their feet, active and in contact with one another from day one. They work on the text regularly, but only have the scripts in their hands for one stage of the process. Depending on the nature of the language, they might also do some seated script work (*see*: LOGIC TEXT). They realise, early on, that most of their creativity and stimulation comes from what they give to and take from each other. Life on stage can only be created by the actors and between the actors. Let me repeat that: *Life on stage can only be created by the actors and between the actors.*

Common practice has actors being called just for the scenes they're in. The concept of an actor only turning up to rehearse 'my scenes' is anathema to me. They aren't 'your' scenes. The whole play belongs to the whole company; how it's being brought alive should be of the utmost importance to everyone involved in its creation. The very nature of theatre is collaborative. It is, of necessity, about working together and playing together. Actors have to work in the greatest intimacy with one another. They have to be vulnerable enough to let their partners affect them and daring enough to affect them in return. The more they work together at all stages of the work (physically, emotionally, intellectually), the more easily that intimacy will develop and, with it, trust. Then they'll dare to move into more sensitive areas of experience together. In fact, this will happen quite naturally, without any pressure, comment or reserve.

A caveat. When I started out as a director, I used to insist that the whole company was present at all rehearsals. Instinctively, I felt this to be artistically right. Unfortunately, I hadn't yet developed any processes for incorporating them creatively.

Years later, an actress who'd been in that company, sharing what turned out to be some revelatory reminiscences with me, admitted how they used to dread having to sit around, watching me and the particular actors in a scene have endless discussions (arguments) about moves and line-readings and how uneasy they felt, when their turn came, to have the other actors, filled with resentment and drained of energy, watching them going through the same paces. I think I blushed. Well, that was a while ago and I hope that, long since, I've learned how to achieve what I then instinctively understood, but hadn't the knowledge to put into practice.

Directors, ensure that if you do have the whole company present, you keep them reasonably occupied. Actors sitting around for any length of time, unused and un-engaged, will – even with the best of intentions – become restless and unfocused. There are generous and curious actors naturally predisposed to watch their part-ners at work, but they're probably in the minority. You have to create a stimulating environment in which actors feel they'll miss something if they're not present. Set up the rehearsals appropriately and you'll find everyone *wants* to be there. Of course, we're not there to entertain each other, and inevitably there are times when actors have to wait their turn. But it's the director's job to maintain good energy and a sense of purpose in their presence.

Isolating the Components

I divide the work into three strands that travel in parallel throughout the rehear-sals, gradually blending together as we get closer to performance:

> Strand One is work on the TEXT.[*]
>
> Strand Two is work on CHARACTER.
>
> Strand Three is work on the WORLD OF THE PLAY.

The principle here is to separate out all the components that go into the creation of the actors' performances and to deal with them one at a time. It's important that the actors know what to focus on at any particular moment and that the whole cast is investigating the same material and practising the same set of skills *together*. Actors, consciously or not, have their own agendas. This can result in members of a company, by no means deliberately, pulling in different directions. One is absorbed by character, another by language, one with social relevance, another with emotion, one is questioning while another is deciding, one wants to please you, one is frightened of taking risks . . . This is inevitable, unless you, the director, firmly establish what is to be worked on. This is a vital part of the director's job: to provide a clear starting point from which the actors can create.

---

[*] I am describing work on an existing text (play), but most of these processes can be applied to devised, improvised or text-created collaborations.

Some actors (and directors) work on everything at once in a sort of clutter! Pre-occupations about psychology, style, business, language, intention and so forth are brought up as they come into an actor's (or director's) mind. Within one rehearsal session, participants can be trying to solve mutually exclusive problems, the focus leaping from one actor's concern about her characterisation, to another's good idea for some props, to another's need to know what he's going to wear . . . While one actor's worries are dealt with, the rest, who are not concerned with this, have to put their work on hold and, with nothing better to do, may start contributing their ten-cents' worth to the problem. A lot of unstructured discussion then drains swiftly into the void created by these intrusions into the flow of the work. By the end of such rehearsals, the experience for most participants will be one that's decidedly 'bitty', messy, vaguely unsatisfactory . . . I have a suspicion that this is what happens in many rehearsals – so that, though everyone appears to be working together, there are, in fact, different productions evolving simultaneously in several different heads. You can see the outcome of all this very clearly in per-formances where the members of a cast appear to be inhabiting totally different WORLDS, existing in separate realities.

Isolating areas of work has many advantages. The company begins to learn a com-mon language and common frames of reference. They share in each other's obser-vations within a structured framework. This enriches the group's understanding of the work as well as helping them to get to know each other's creativity. They're not distracted by concerns that, though legitimate, aren't relevant at that particular moment and can be dealt with elsewhere in the proceedings. (Always reassure concerned actors that their preoccupations *will be dealt with* in due course. And make sure they are; never make unfulfilled promises.) The actors all contribute to the matter at hand, and come away from a rehearsal feeling that they've moved forward together and that they've been stretched and exercised by the focused intensity that comes from a group's concentration on one issue at a time.

Structuring the Strands

As I've explained, I divide the rehearsal process into three strands – work on THE WORLD OF THE PLAY, on CHARACTER and on TEXT – which all proceed in parallel through a large portion of the rehearsal period. I usually work on them in that sequence, starting with the more open, rather broad work (at least, to start with) of WORLDS, moving to the greater specificity of CHARACTER and ending with TEXT. I divide the day into six sections roughly of an hour each and rotate the strands.

	(am)			(pm)		
Monday	I hour	I hour	I hour	I hour	I hour	I hour
	World of Play (Work on Culture, Reality, Behaviour, Skills, Space, etc.)	Character Work (Lists, Improvis- ations, etc.)	Text Work (Actions, T-N-T, Reading-In, POCs, Runs, etc.)	World of play	Character Work	Text Work
Tuesday	World	Character	Text	World	Character	Text
Wednesday	World	Character	Text	World	Character	Text
Thursday	World	Character	Text	World	Character	Text
Friday	World	Character	Text	World	Character	Text
Saturday	World	Character	Text	World	Character	Text

This is a useful basic structure with an inbuilt flexibility. If you need to do some work that doesn't seem to fit into any of the strands, you can make easy adjustment; for example, a warm-up might become part of the morning world strand or could take some time away from it:

Monday	Warm-up World	Character	Text	World	Character	Text

The Hour

An hour is a good average unit of time to devote to any one particular process or exercise. If a director merely snatches at different processes, hurrying from one to another, the actors only experience the frustration of insufficient absorption time. Remember, the work has to travel through their whole being. If, on the other hand, the director insists on labouring something beyond the point of productive absorption, the actors lose focus and energy. Ideally, you want to finish each session on a high that will carry through to the next process. On occasions, if you want to develop a smooth progression – an accumulative experience throughout a morning, say – it's productive to create seamless transitions from one session directly into the next. Good energy is created as one piece of work informs the next. Directors should be constantly alert to the appropriateness of their use of the time. There will be days when certain work simply doesn't penetrate. No use flogging a dead horse. Avoid leaving the actors with a sense of failure. Move on, positively, to something else and come back to what you abandoned on a more suitable occasion. On the other hand, if the company is flying with a particular piece of work, stay with it until you feel it's run its course.

The hour length is adjustable. On a particular day you might want to devote more time to one of the strands. For example, you may find you need twice the time to complete an analysis of a character who commands a lot of material, in which case, you can put two CHARACTER sessions together:

Wednesday	World	Character▶	Character	World	Text▶	Text
			or	Text	World	Text, etc.

Like much that I'm recommending, this may seem glaringly obvious. But actors feel more secure if they know they're working within a structure that gives them some idea of where they're going, of what they can anticipate and therefore of what to prepare. On the other hand, if the structure becomes relentlessly predictable, it risks damping down any creative excitement. So, from time to time, it's important to throw them a few curves – altering the order of the strands; setting up an existing process in a totally different way; introducing a new 'one-off'. It refreshes the actors without destroying their confidence that they're still working within an overall plan.

Structure supports a director's work. You're able to act on fresh insights while those insights are still warm, to find space to explore them within the structure. You can always return to the regular pattern when such muses depart. Structure ensures that your work is detailed and thorough. This scheme reinforces the principle of freedom through discipline, innate to this whole way of working.

Thoughts about the First Day

I would earnestly recommend directors not to waste the first day of rehearsal or their breath by giving a big speech about their interpretation of the play and concept for the production. I'm sure, that like me – or as I used to be – you will be eager to share your exciting ideas with the actors. But they will be too nervous, too unconcentrated, to absorb much of what you have to say. Get them on their feet as soon as possible and make them sweat a little. There's nothing like physical work to reduce anxiety and focus attention. Then, at some point later in the day, by all means give them a *brief* and *simple* outline of the direction you'd like the production to go in, so that they can take some image of it away with them. Far better to have the patience (and modesty) to portion out your ideas bit by bit. In this way, the actors, who'll be gradually getting on your wavelength, will grow more relaxed and able to appreciate what you have to offer. Too many times I've heard the refrain 'I never heard you say that!' when I complained to an actor 'I told you that on the first day of rehearsal!'

Nor have them read the play together. It's another waste of time. They won't hear it. They'll be too concerned with the impression they're making and with evaluating their colleagues. Some will give you the reading they are more or less planning to give in performance; some will refuse to give any meaningful reading at all, mumbling the text with their cards very close to their chests; some are impressive sight-readers, some no good at reading at all. It's quite definitely not a useful or exciting way to meet the play together for the first time. If it's a new play, it's not going to help the writer to hear it read badly. But, at some later stage in rehearsal, when the cast has advanced quite far with the material and know each other, it might then be a very useful exercise to sit down and read it. Some directors read the play or have someone else read it to the cast. Inevitably, this involves the actors in hearing choices and interpretations that they may unwittingly absorb without questioning them; already something will have been imposed on the text. What's most dangerous: a reading takes place with everyone seated and inevitably leads to a discussion, which means that the actors will start rehearsals, seat-bound and head-bound, en route to *deadliness*. Reading the play is the soft option for the first day of rehearsal.

One assumes that the actors will have read the play at least once before they come to rehearsals, though, of course, there's no guarantee that they'll have consciously paid much attention to much of the text other than their own. To counteract this tendency, I always ask the actors to prepare some lists. This ensures that they've been through the text with a fine-tooth comb at least four times before they arrive for the start of rehearsals (*see*: ACTIONS in PREPARATION; and CHARACTER in REHEARSAL). Having the actors already primed with some accurate and basic knowledge of the play, we can all begin work at a more advanced level than might otherwise be the case.

As I say, far better to get them up on their feet with physical work, games, improvisations, all of which should be seen to have some connection with the material, so that they get a sense that you know what you're doing. Physical work breaks down inhibitions between actors and gets rid of those somewhat false personae that some actors assume to get them through the first gathering. They'll go home feeling that they've actually done a good day's work.

STRAND ONE: THE TEXT

Approaching the Text with the Actors

The wrong sort of work on the text, result-orientated, decision-making, prescriptive, static, will kill off any imagination on the part of the actor. If, on the other hand, the director and actors ignore the specificity of the text so that it becomes about what everyone *feels* (unproved assumptions) rather than *knows* (proven facts), you'll end up with indulgence and incoherence. There is often a desire for the play and the roles to be what directors and actors want them to be, despite little or no supportive evidence from the text. An actor, because of self-image and fear of the unknown, may well decide, no doubt unconsciously, that a role should be played in a way that supports the former and avoids the latter. As for directors, lack of rigour, overconfidence and, most corrupting, the dictates of fashion are some of the stumbling blocks that lie in their path to a disciplined appraisal of what the text is offering.

Actors often want to leap into the depths and complexities of a play right from the start, to run before they can walk, which, early in rehearsal, results in far too much uninformed chat. (No writer lures them down this path more so than Chekhov with his promise of rich characterisation, profound psychology, intense feeling and plenty of stage time.) However, patience! You need to work from the simple to the complex, from the surface to the depths. If you leap before you look, you'll hurt yourself. You'll be guessing wildly, relying on hearsay or falling back on old habits. Because acting is not an exact science and actors are working in a somewhat chaotic mélange of intelligence, imagination, imitation, instinct, habit, experience, emotion, body, voice, ambitions and fears, it's easy for the work to detach itself from the demands of the text. Generalisation is death to creativity.

The challenge is to find *ways of working on text that are both disciplined and open-ended*, allowing the actors' imaginations to flower in conjunction with absolute specificity towards the material – to find a method by which the actors meet the play organically, in action rather than in their heads. You discover far more by doing. *Things learnt in the sweat of doing go deeper and last longer.*

The only way you can start work is from the outside of the text. The outside is, of course, the words of the script. This would seem obvious. But actors and directors can be easily seduced by tangential material, which might include research, other people's writings on the play and received ideas which seem to float to us on the breeze. The rehearsal process ahead will describe ways of *bringing the actors together with the script in an active and organic way.*

Stage One: Actioning
Applying the Actions

Purpose

I've described the text as a mystery that offers only the surface of its hidden world as a clue to its deeper reality. We have to deconstruct that surface – practise reverse engineering – to discover that deeper world. The surface offers us dialogue and, usually, limited descriptions of behaviour (stage directions). What we first need are facts from which we can start to put together an idea of the play's inner life. What the characters do and say constitute those facts. What the characters do cannot be questioned. The playwright says the characters do these things, therefore they *do* do them. It's also true that the characters do say what they say, but here we have a problem: we have no idea whether what they say is true or false, we have no idea why or how they say what they say, we only know that they say it. The content of what they say will need eventual interpretation. As yet, we haven't enough information to be able to do this with any accuracy; we can only use guesswork or go by hunches, which is clearly unreliable. So for the moment we're left with the fact that *they say what they say*. Therefore, we must try to understand *with a minimum of interpretation* (that is, as factually as possible) *what action has caused a particular piece of dialogue*. We must take the dialogue at more or less face value and decide what are the least indisputable *actions* it implies, that is, what the characters are *doing* when they speak. To reprise: we know what they're doing when they *do* something (entering, sitting, humming, laughing . . .); we need to know what they're *doing* when they're *talking*.

If we take the first line of *The Seagull*, Medvedenko's '*Why are you always in black?*', we can say without a doubt that, at its first level of understanding, *he is asking Masha a question*. Now, it is possible that it might be merely rhetorical, a form of criticism or disapproval, or it might be a genuine expression of surprise or curiosity; it might be a joke between them about something we don't yet know. (I've given other examples of interpretive ambiguity in the ACTION section of PREPARING THE TEXT.) But it's there in the form of a question to Masha from whom we can reasonably assume that he wants an answer – and she does in fact give him one. So as a way of entering the play at *a really simple surface level*, we can say, *without any argument*, that Medvedenko *asks Masha why she's in black*. And in this way, we proceed through the text, action by action.

Now, remember, we are wanting the actors to meet the text in the most organic way possible, which means meeting the play holistically, not just with their intellects and their tongues, but also with their *bodies*, which contain their emotional and sensory life, their memories and experience. Getting the actors on their feet and *moving* through the play at this simplest of levels, *literally enacting their actions*, is the first step in this process. As I've already indicated, there are many ways of playing any one action, many *hows*. This means that the actors, in the absence of more information, have the freedom to express those actions in the manner most natural to their experience and imagination *at that moment*. *How* Medvedenko asks his question is completely up to the actor playing him. *In this way, the actors are already starting gently to experience creative freedom and to make the play their own.*

AN OUTLINE OF THE PROCESS

The actors work their way through a scene or act on their feet, with the scripts in their hands for reference, stating-and-playing their actions. ('*I ask you why you're in black*', etc.).

Note: For this process, refer to the example of actioning from the opening scene of *The Seagull* in the ACTION section of PREPARING THE TEXT.

PROCESS

This process starts on the first day of rehearsal. Let's assume that the actors have done their preparatory work on the actions (*see*: ACTIONS in PREPARING THE TEXT). The ground plan should already have been explained to the company, exits and entrances marked out and any furniture or scenic elements in position.* If I haven't already given the actors the unit divisions and titles for the act or scenes we're about to work on, I will do so now. Assuming you're using about two hours each day to work on the text strand, divide the text up so that you give yourself three or four days to action the entire text. I usually try to get through an act a day.

1. The actors, scripts in hand for reference, go into the acting space.

2. They state-and-play (act out) their actions *as if* the words defining the actions were the text itself, i.e. *literally using the words defining the action. They do not use the actual dialogue* (though, of course, at times, some words from the text will inevitably be incorporated into the statement of the action). They must play fully, exactly as if they were playing the scene. Make sure

---

* If the space has not yet been designed, then you need to give the actors a few directional ideas, even if they're provisional, so they're not left wandering vaguely in a void: the forest is upstage, the war is taking place offstage right . . .

that the actors use the words 'I' and 'You' and don't, as sometimes happens, drift into the third person ('He' and 'Her' or 'She' and 'Him').

3. They play the actions just as they would play the text, but it must be clearly established that they are *not* giving line-readings, *not* just saying the actions reasonably intelligently *at* one another. They must play *to* and *with* each other, *using each phrase to further their action*.

4. They should be encouraged to heighten the physicality of each action they play, so that while the playing is utterly truthful, *it is not necessarily naturalistic*. They should be seeking to play what is for them the absolute epitome of each action. If '*I enquire*', my whole body, energy and focus on my partner must be totally committed to and expressive of the *act of enquiring*. The increased muscular commitment will help actors to remember the structure of the scene. Urge the actors to be daring in their physicality and not to be limited by *how they think* the scene ought to be played (preconceived results).

5. The actors must be open and courageous, genuinely trying to effect each other, *really doing something to move or change their partners*. They must deal with their partners IN THE MOMENT. If '*I enquire*', I really want an answer from you. If '*I dismiss*' your remarks, I want to make sure you don't continue them.

6. Encourage the actors to use the space expressively to enhance their actions.

7. Ensure that all actors react specifically to every action played by their partners. *Reaction is as important as action*.

8. If they ever resort to '*I say . . .*' or '*I tell you . . .*', let them know these choices of action (verbs) are *not* acceptable. They are too unspecific and could apply to any piece of dialogue.

THEN

9. When the actors have completed playing the actions of the scene or act, instruct them to do so again, this time *without* their scripts in their hands. There are two reasons for this: to give them greater physical freedom released from holding their texts; to see how much of the scene they understand – *understand, but not necessarily remember*. This is *not* a test of their memory.

10. You may need to coach them gently through this. If they don't remember what the next action is, *insist that they nevertheless keep going* by inventing what seem to them likely logical actions until they get back on

track. It doesn't matter if they go round in circles. If absolutely necessary, throw them the occasional clue, but never state the actual action. Encourage partners in the scene, should they know what comes next, to state-and-play an action that might provide a hint.

11. *This is an improvisation.* Make it clear that only you, the director, can stop an improvisation. The actors *must* keep going. The pressure forces them to focus on what they understand of the situation. If they stop to ask for help or to tell you they don't know what comes next, they're avoiding the exercise and its benefits. Make it clear that they're not necessarily expected to remember everything; I reiterate, this is *not* a memory exercise, but one in which they explore what they so far know about the scene in terms of simple actions. Stress that if they don't remember everything, they have *not* failed. You should encourage them to support each other. Keep reminding them: *though the work is serious, it should be conducted in a spirit of play; they have nothing to lose and a lot to gain.*

12. If they've really remembered very little, you can, later, make the point that they didn't recall much of the scene because they had stayed 'in their heads' and hadn't played their actions with sufficient physical commitment (therefore no muscle memory). They had probably just been giving line-readings.

13. If you think it would be more manageable for the actors, you can do this second, script-free sequence in blocks of several units at a time, rather than straight through the whole act or scene.

14. This process continues for the number of days it takes to work your way through the text. Try to avoid stretching it out much beyond four days. For *The Seagull*, you would probably allot one act a day.

FINALLY

15. On the day after completing *all* the actioning, I recommend doing a run – *in actions, of course, and without scripts* – of the entire play. It will no doubt become chaotic at times, but at the end of it, the actors will have a great sense of achievement; by day four or five, they will have actually done their first full run of the play! You – and they – will be gratifyingly surprised by how much they *do* remember.

16. What will be clear is the overall shape and structure of the play, its bare, active bones – the vertebrae, which you will now proceed to enrich with muscles, tendons, joints, veins, arteries, fat, skin . . . The actors will have experienced their characters' rough journey through the play and the journey of the play itself.

WARNINGS

1. Don't get hung up on semantics. One of the dangers of this work is
that you and the actors will get locked into endless discussions and
disagreements about verbs. That can cause the work to get heavy. The
actors will start to worry so that when they're on their feet they will still
be in their heads, having lost all spontaneity and with it, their imaginations.
If you, the director, feel that some of the actors' choices are not as accurate
as you'd prefer, fight your inclination to correct them. Let them go. After
all, this is just the start of a long process of work, and later on, other
procedures will rectify any less-than-accurate choices. The only exception
is if you think a choice is so wildly inaccurate that it will create a problem
for the actor; then you might, *afterwards*, gently suggest an alternative.
Note: *there are some actions that the actors will eventually choose to play of
such nuance and subtlety that they are almost impossible to label with
a convenient verb.*

2. Don't get overanxious if the first day's work on actions doesn't flow as
smoothly as you anticipated. As the days proceed, you will see the actors'
skills progress. This is a good reason for spreading the actioning over a
few days. Being able to sleep on an exercise can be productive.

3. *Important*: There must be *no discussions* during this process (about
motivation, character and so on). Keep the actors' focus firmly on dealing
with the actions and the technique of accurately playing them. It's about
doing. If necessary, deal only with very practical matters, such as where
they enter and exit. Keep them active and on their feet. And I repeat:
no discussions!

ACTIONS — AN OPTION: PHYSICALISING RATHER THAN VERBALISING

Some actors have difficulty in coming up with suitable verbs for their
actions. This often makes them feel inadequate, 'intellectually' inferior to
those who have a natural flair for language. In this case, it's perfectly
acceptable for an actor to use signifiers such as sounds/noises/gestures in
place of words, e.g. *I grrrr you, I m'mmmm you, I shhhhh you, I ahhhhhh
you, I (tut) you, I (wrinkle up my nose at) you; I (spit at) you.* These can be
just as specific as words. It's the *doing* that matters, the putting the whole
of themselves into *action*. Again, I stress that choosing and playing actions
should not be thought of as purely intellectual activity. *It's holistic.*

BENEFITS OF ACTIONING

1. You are introducing the actors to the play in the lightest terms possible, avoiding their need to deal with the dialogue itself. If they have to start using the text cold, there will be the same problems that arise at first readings: either they feel the responsibility to try to *'get it right for you'* with head-bound line-readings, or they simply refuse to make any commitment to anything.

2. You are making them concentrate on the essential concept of *being in action*. You are establishing some ground rules for how they're to proceed from the first day of rehearsal to the final performance.

3. You are stressing the need for them to play with and off each other from the word 'go', demanding and developing an interdependence between themselves to *make things happen*, to be genuine partners, supporting, trusting and stimulating one another.

4. You are getting them on their feet and into a physicality which will stimulate their imaginations far more fully than sitting round a table, talking. You are stressing the holistic nature of acting.

5. You are getting them used to the idea of being permanently in some state of improvisation, always in process, in seeing possibilities but *not* looking for results, never fixing.

6. You are getting them to move naturally and spontaneously in the space.

7. Because they're free of the text, there's an implicit sense of 'fun', 'freedom', 'playfulness', not having to come up with results, working with playful seriousness – or serious playfulness!

8. They are learning the story of the play organically, starting with the simplest, least interpretative, surface level of plot and situation.

9. Because at this point, there will have been very little or no discussion of the play, its meaning, themes and purposes, they will be working with an uncluttered mind. While on their feet – if they're serious actors – they'll be instinctively (silently) questioning, observing, noting things for themselves for further (private) exploration.

10. You are beginning the process of layering in the WORLD OF THE PLAY with them.

11. They are starting to accumulate some basic facts.

12. When they come to work with the language of the text itself, they will already have some physical, intellectual and imaginative experience of the scene to bring to it.

13. From what the actors do, you, the director, are almost sure to come out of this process with greater knowledge of the play – and of how the actors individually go about their work.

Some Exercises for Actions

It may be necessary to get the actors used to the concept of actions. So there are a few simple exercises which may help their understanding before they embark on the actual playing of the actions in the text.

SIMPLE ACTIONS

Have all the actors moving freely – and individually – about the room.

Instruct them *to run*, stressing that they should totally absorb themselves in that *action*. They should be completely committed to the experience and sensation of running – in terms of thought and feeling as well as body. They should be executing what is for them the epitome of running. It sometimes helps to strengthen involvement in an action if the participants repeat under their breath the words of the action: '*I am running.*'

The actors should *not* give themselves a motivation for the action. The reason for this is to prevent the actors diffusing the purity of the action into an imaginary situation.

Continue to give them different actions to execute: e.g. *walk, stroll, tip-toe, prowl, crawl . . .*

Then open the exercise up to actions concerned with observing their environment, such as *finding as many blue items as possible in the space*. Again, tell them to absorb themselves in this action, to commit themselves totally to this. Then continue to invent other simple actions like *counting the chairs in the room, visualising how to arrange the room for a meeting, memorising what they can see from a window*. Where you've asked them to look for specific things, get them to tell you what they found.

Then extend the actions to involve observation of the other people: *check out carefully who is wearing green, study other people's profiles, identify the people with blue eyes*.

Then start them exploring active attitudes towards each other *without talking*, such as *letting them know you admire them* or *feel sorry for them* or *despise them*. The action is *letting them know* (not admiring or despising which, if you remember, are verbs expressing states of being). It should involve all the means *except speech* that are at the actors' disposal to communicate to the individuals concerned their attitudes towards them. They should be encouraged to fulfil their actions – that is, to ensure that their partners *do* know how they feel about them.

Then try some actions which involve getting a clear collaborative response from their partners (*again without speech*), such as *getting them into a corner to protect them* or *inviting them to look out of the window with you*.

The reason for not using language at this stage is that it has the tendency to weaken the intensity and strength of the actual playing of the action. If you can simply tell someone what you think, feel or want, *there's an implicit assumption that the words will do all the work for you.* This frequently occurs in performance, where actors automatically assume that by saying the words intelligently, their partners will hear and react. *Speaking text without specific intention is a cause of dead performance.*

ACTIONS IN PAIRS

Pair the actors off.

Give them a sequence of actions – one at a time – to state-and-play, such as *I reject you, I comfort you, I warn you.*

Each pair takes it in turns to execute each action to their partner. As soon as one actor has played the action *to both their satisfactions,* they reverse roles. If the actors to whom the actions are played don't believe their partners – are not convinced by them – they should insist on them doing it again.

They are now using words – but *only* the three or four words of the action (*I reject you,* etc.). Their total energy and focus should be on executing this action and really affecting their partner. Their body, their entire physical being should be totally expressive of *rejecting* or *comforting* or *warning* . . . They should explore how they can utilise the space to reinforce their action.

Practically the sequence goes like this:

A to B: (states-and-plays): *I reject you.* B reacts.

(Repeat if B doesn't believe A or finds the playing of the action in any way unsatisfactory.)

B to A: (states-and-plays): *I reject you.* A reacts.

(Repeat if A doesn't believe B . . .)

Then move on to the next action:

A to B: (states-and-plays): *I comfort you.* B reacts.

(Repeat, if necessary.)

B to A: (states and plays): *I comfort you.* A reacts.

(Repeat, if necessary.)

Then on to the next action which, you, the director, are suggesting and calling out . . .

Note: Reactions must be played as fully as the actions. Sufficiently committed and followed through with full imaginative involvement, the actors will find they can sustain an action for longer than they might have expected: A reacting to B's reaction and B, in turn, reacting to A's reaction – and onwards – is the way in which the action (that has now developed into a situation or small scene) can be extended. This should never be forced and will depend entirely on the energy and conviction with which A (in this case) has played the initial action.

PLAYING THE SAME TEXT WITH DIFFERENT ACTIONS

This exercise begins to weld action to text. One of the points it implicitly makes is that a line of text can be played in innumerable ways (*hows*).

The whole company works together in this. Offer the actors a line or phrase of text or ask them to chose one (e.g. '*Why are you always in black?*').

All the actors, in turn, must use *exactly the same line* to play an action to one of the others, but playing *a completely different action* from their predecessors. Either the director can suggest the action, or let the actors choose for themselves.

With a large company, you might need to choose another line halfway through the exercise – the first one may exhaust its possibilities.

Some examples of different possible actions (and meanings) for '*Why are you always in black?*':

I express my desire to understand you better

I make fun of you

I declare my impatience with you

I sympathise with you

I advise you to think about how you come across to other people

I confront you

I flirt with you . . .

PLAYING THE SAME TEXT AND THE SAME ACTION DIFFERENTLY

If we were to fix *how* an action should be played, this would be the equivalent of setting a line-reading or blocking a move, and would totally deny the very principle and possibility of spontaneity. The point of this exercise is to reassure the actors that even if their choice of action becomes more or less decided, they can still play the same action in *an infinity of ways*. It extends the principle of flexibility from the previous exercise. The *what* may be reasonably consistent (e.g. Medvedenko's first line to Masha will always have the basic action of asking a question), but the *how* ensures spontaneity.

Offer each of the actors a small phrase from the text or ask them to choose one of their own. This time, instead of all working on the same sentence, they each have a line of their own.

Give each actor an action, then instruct them to play that action to a partner of their choice using the selected sentence.

Now ask the same actor to play the same line to the same partner – *and with the same action*. But this time *in a completely different way*. Then a third time . . . and a fourth time . . .

Keep doing this with each actor until you feel you have exhausted the potential of the line and action – or of the actor!

Constantly check that *this does not become an exercise in line-readings*. Make sure the actors really use the piece of text to fulfil their action. *Encourage them to understand that playing an action includes spatial relationships, physical relationships, physical expressiveness, and is not just about 'how they say the line'!*

As a possible example of varying the *how* of an action, let's say the chosen action for *'Why are you always in black?'* is *'to advise you to think about how you look to other people'*. I can play it:

Expressing varying degrees of solicitude for you
Encouraging you to think more objectively about yourself
Genuinely offering you help
Reminding you I have asked this several times before
Controlling my growing impatience with you
Demanding to know how your idea of yourself has become so deluded
Enquiring why you wish to make yourself different from other people
Laughing at your self-delusions . . .

REVERSE ENGINEERING

I offer this next exercise with the proviso that it is not an encouragement to indulge in line-readings. It is merely a simplistic experiment in reverse engineering.

Repeat the line, each time stressing a different word:

Why are you always in black?

Why *are* you always in black?

Why are *you* always in black?

Why are you *always* in black?

Why are you always *in* black?

Why are you always in *black*?

Then try to define what action or actions is implied by each new emphasis.

But I reiterate: this exercise – in fact, all of them – *must never, never, decline into mere line-reading*; the words must be used to *support* the purpose and execution of the action.

Reminder

Actions are not all that you'll be working on during the first few days of rehearsal. You'll have also started to investigate, in parallel, both the CHARACTER *and* WORLD OF THE PLAY strands of the process. Already some sort of cross-fertilisation will be taking place (and will continue to do so increasingly throughout the rehearsal): a gradual growth of knowledge about other aspects of the play will be infiltrating the work on actions.

Stage Two:
Text – No Text – Text (T–N–T)
Applying the Scene Objectives

This process starts towards the end of the first week, or at latest, the beginning of the second week, after you've finished the previous stage on actions. For the first and only time, the actors will work with the scripts in their hands, *actually using the text of the play*.

Purpose

Having experienced the rough shape of each scene and the play as a whole through actions, the actors now start to look in greater detail at each scene and start to consider what their SCENE OBJECTIVES might be.

AN OUTLINE OF THE PROCESS

The actors work through a scene or act unit by unit or in small blocks of units, each played three times, first with the text, then without the text, then with the text again.

PROCESS

1. Each day, you cover the same amount of text as with the actioning; usually an act or one or two scenes, dependent on how the play is constructed.

2. You work unit by unit. If the units are very short, you can work on a group of units that cover a couple of pages at a time. If this is the first time the actors have done the exercise, it might be good to start unit by unit until they're comfortable with the process; then you can extend the amount of material. (The actors working on the opening Masha and Medvedenko scene in *The Seagull*, for example, should have no problems coping with it in its entirety. That scene has only one unit.)

3. The actors in the unit(s) go into the acting space with their texts.

4. They are going to play the same unit(s) three times. Do *not* tell them this.

i. The first time: you instruct them to play the scene, reading from the text, but *concentrating on contacting each other* and, between them, beginning to carve out the situation contained in the unit(s). I often suggest that 'This is more for you than for me'. You urge them not to force anything or try to reach for an emotional level that they don't feel ready to deal with, but to play the text truthfully at a level which is available to them at this moment, even if they know it's a long way from where they sense the scene should reach. Keep encouraging them to listen and talk to one another. And to use the space.

ii. The second time: you now instruct them to put down their scripts and play the same unit(s) again to the best of their understanding. This is *not* a memory exercise (i.e. to test how much they remember); rather, it's for the actors to see how much they understand about the situation contained in the unit(s). It's an improvisation and, just as when playing the actions without their scripts, they must keep the improvisation going and only you, the director, can stop it. If they do remember text, they should use it and only paraphrase where they don't. (Note, however, that paraphrasing is *not* the purpose of this exercise.)

When they have gone through the unit(s) a second time, ask them to state what they think their scene objective(s) might be in this unit/ these units. Make sure they make a note of their conjectures. *Do not let this develop into a discussion!* The purpose is to keep the actors working on the units while they're still warm.

iii. The third time: you ask them to play the same units again, once more with their scripts in their hands. This gives them the opportunity to see what they might have missed or misunderstood the second time through (a transition, perhaps). They can also start consciously to apply the objective(s) they've just identified.

5. When you ask them to play the text for the third time, you *also* instruct them to continue straight into the next block of units for their first 'go-through'. The sequence goes like this:

i.   Play units (say) 1,2,3 with text
ii.   Play units 1,2,3 without text; then state objectives
iii & i.   Play units 1,2,3 with text again, *plus* (say) 4,5,6 with text
ii.   Play units 4,5,6 without text; then state objectives
iii & i.   Play units 4,5,6 with text again, *plus* 7,8,9 with text
ii.   Play units 7,8,9 without text; then state objectives
             . . . to the end of the act or scene.

6. Then get the actors, scripts in hand, to work straight through the whole act or all the material they've worked on in the session. Having explored it in manageable sizes, you want them now to have the chance to get a sense of the whole.

7. At the end of this session, tell the actors they can start learning the text they've just worked through.

WARNINGS

1. Make sure that when the actors *are* working with their scripts, that they *use* them and read accurately. If they start approximating the text, they're likely to learn it approximately. Then it becomes difficult ever to relearn it accurately. Be rigorous about this.

2. In the second phase (without scripts), encourage the actors to keep the improvisation going, even if they find they're moving away from the actual situations in the unit. Sometimes when this happens, they stumble on useful insights. Also you're encouraging the actors' improvisatory skills: being spontaneous, responsive to impulses without censorship, open and vulnerable to what their partners are giving them and, in turn, unafraid to affect their partners. Again, keep reminding them to 'play', have fun; they have nothing to lose and everything to gain. There can be no concept of 'getting it right'. There is no one right way in any of these processes.

3. To reiterate: at the end of the second phase, when you ask the actors to state what they think are their objectives, *don't let this become a long discussion session.* If you do, the third phase will lose much of its value. If an actor's choice of objective seems too wide of the mark, you can suggest an alternative. The point is to keep the actors moving through the text, playing the same section of text three times in succession with as little distraction as possible, making sure they stay warm, rather than cooling off with chat.

Reminder

You will be working on CHARACTER and the WORLD OF THE PLAY parallel to this T-N-T process.

By the end of this second stage, the company, in under two weeks, will have worked through the entire play in sequence at least seven times!

Stage Three:
Feeding-In: Applying the Beats

Purpose

You are now at the end of week two or the start of week three. The actors are at that awkward period when they are still learning the text. This next process gets them up on their feet without the script, but with the security of the text being fed to them, beat by beat, by other members of the cast.

They're now familiar with the larger movements of their scenes, their actions and objectives. This new process focuses them on the text at the detailed level of beats, so that there's no possibility that any part of the text can be overlooked or left unconsidered. It's not uncommon for actors to become so absorbed by those parts of the text that seem to demand their focus that they unwittingly take for granted those elsewhere they find unproblematic. However, if these remain unexamined, they may possibly miss key moments.

As well as exploring their own beats in specific detail, the actors are forced to listen and respond to their partners' beats with equal specificity. *Actors should not make any distinction in value or importance between those beats they activate and those they react to.* All beats are of equal necessity and make up the melodic line of their score; missing or ignoring beats will distort the tune.

This process also demands that the actors explore the greatest expressive potential of each beat. It challenges the actors' imaginations and resourcefulness. It encourages them to discover what unexpected possibilities a scene might contain by pushing out its perceived boundaries as far as they can.

A by-product of the cast feeding each other text is an increase in the spirit of ensemble.

AN OUTLINE OF THE PROCESS

The actors, without scripts, play straight through an act or scene, beat by beat. Other actors feed them their lines, beat by beat.

PROCESS

1. You work each day on the same overall amount of text (act or scene) as you've been using in the previous two stages of the text work. Now, you work straight through an act or scene; but, if you feel it would be more manageable, you could do it by sections. Preferably, you should work on fairly extended sequences, as in this exercise it's possible to build up a strong head of emotional steam.

2. The actors involved within the scene go into the acting space *without* their scripts.

3. The actors in the scene each have another actor assigned to feed them their lines. If you're short of actors, you can use stage managers, assistants or anyone else in the rehearsal room, yourself if necessary, though it's preferable for a director to be free to observe what's going on.

INSTRUCTIONS FOR ACTORS WHO ARE FEEDING-IN THE TEXT

1. The actors who are assigned as feeders-in (or readers-in) will work from the script, feeding the text, beat by beat, to the actors to whom they've been assigned. (Refer back to the section on BEATS in PREPARATION for examples of how the script is broken up into beats.)

2. The feeders-in must make sure that each beat is a *complete thought or idea*. The thought can be as short as an 'Oh!' or a long complex sentence. They may at times have to break up what is essentially one thought if they believe it may be too long or too complicated for the actor receiving it to remember. (This can be the case with Shakespeare, for example, when there are clauses within clauses within a clause – thoughts within thoughts within an thought). On such occasions, the feeders-in must make a decision as to what will be most helpful to the actors they're feeding. To help them decide, I always recommend that feeders-in ask themselves what they would find most helpful, were they receiving a particular piece of text.

3. The feeders-in stand at the perimeter of the acting area and never intrude into it.

4. They do not make eye contact with the actors receiving the text. They feed it to the back of their heads. They may need to move around the perimeter to do so.

5. They must stand to deliver the text, never sit, lean, crouch or slouch. They have to give those receiving the text an alert, focused energy and the reassuring sense that someone behind them is there to support them.

6. They must deliver the text without any interpretation or undue emphasis (often difficult for actors who instinctively want to give a line some sort of expressive inflection). They must deliver it logically, but as a piece of information, without suggestive inflections.

7. The feeders-in should *never assume* that beats are defined by punctuation. Sometimes they do coincide, but it *must not* be a foregone conclusion.

8. To a certain degree, the feeders-in control the playing of the scene. If they feel that an actor is on automatic, rushing to repeat the piece of text that's being fed without really exploring it – more or less treading on the heels of its delivery – the feeders-in should slow matters down, making the actor wait, as an implicit instruction to take the necessary time to explore. If, on the other hand, they feel the actor is being indulgent and taking unnecessary time, they can deliver the text more briskly. They should be watching the scene very carefully, so that if something interesting is happening between the actors in the scene, they themselves don't rush to intrude the next beat into it. Feeders-in need a great deal of sensitivity. They share equal responsibility with the receivers for the success of the exercise.

INSTRUCTIONS FOR THE ACTORS RECEIVING TEXT

1. The actors within the scene have only to be concerned with two things: sustaining their scene objectives; and playing each beat fully and imaginatively. Their objectives will ensure that they stay *in* the scene, which will, of course, be played far more slowly than normal. They should not concern themselves with anything else. As with all these processes, they must put aside any agendas or preoccupations of their own, otherwise they will blur and dilute the current exploration. *One thing at a time!*

2. The actors receiving their beat of text take *as long as they need* before they play it. Before they do play, they must really search for an exciting and interesting choice, but always influenced by their objectives and how their partner has just reacted to them. They have to act as they would do when playing normally, in an open and creative manner, but slowed down sufficiently to give them room to explore and search. An image I often suggest is that they are like boxers sparring (trying, testing, probing), rather than engaging in the actual fight. It is vital that the actors do *not* play the text they've been fed *until they feel one hundred per cent ready to play a choice that is full and totally centred.*

3. The actors receiving text should *not* treat this as an exercise in line-readings, but in *playing meticulously detailed actions* for which the text is just one of their tools. As usual, they must use their physicality and the space as part of their actions.

4. The actors' purpose is to extend the preconceived contours of the scene as much as possible, expanding its parameters, pushing out the perceived envelope of a piece of text, giving even a seemingly unimportant beat a fullness and dimension in order *to discover what unexpected range of expression and meaning it might contain.*

5. *Critical:* the actors should ensure their focus is *never on themselves* (how they're feeling, what they're doing) *but always on their partners* in the scene, watching their reactions and considering what effect they want to have on them, what they're doing to them.

6. Actors *must react* tangibly to every beat that is played to them.

7. The actors need huge reserves of energy and concentration. The exercise is very demanding of both.

8. The actors receiving text must, between them, keep the space and moments alive in the 'gaps' between their playing of a beat and their being fed the next one. How they effect this is to make sure that they are not just giving intelligent line-readings, but – I repeat – *are using the text to play actions. The action continues to be played after the words have been said* and must continue to be kept alive between them until the next beat is played. All the actors in a scene are responsible for keeping such an extended beat alive. In these moments, the actor receiving text is doing two things at once (rather like patting one's head while rubbing one's stomach): extending the current action and keeping it alive, while exploring how to play the next beat. The actors should always be fully in action, never allowing gaps in which they stop acting to 'think about' the next beat. (The following note builds this process.)

9. The actors receiving text must accumulate the experience of each beat they play and never go back, emotionally, to square one after playing a beat. (That is, they mustn't drop from top gear down into neutral after they've played their beat, but must keep their energy and intentions consistently engaged in fifth!) In this way, the actors can often build up between them a strikingly imaginative and emotionally driven sequence.

10. If the actors receiving text don't quite hear the beat being fed to them, they should sustain their acting state while asking for it to be repeated. They should not for an instant drop out of the scene to do so.

11. If the feeder-in happens to feed more than one beat at a time, the actor in the scene is perfectly capable of making the decision to separate them and play them one at a time.

12. The actors receiving beats will already be pretty familiar with much of the text by now. In the heat of working, they must resist the impulse to anticipate a line before it's fed to them, or to deliver more text than they've been fed.

13. When the technique is working well, the actors can really make discoveries. Within the pressure and intense concentration of their work, they are getting in touch with their more visceral, deeper imagination.

WARNINGS

As you see, there are a lot of technical details connected with this process. You, the director, should avoid trying to tell the actors all of the above in one go. The actors will only become clogged with instructions and unable to function. So introduce the exercise judiciously, adding details as you observe the actors getting more comfortable with the process. *This is true for all the work. You must decide carefully how you are going to set up any exercise or process – what you think is the minimum information sufficient to start the actors off.*

Some actors will immediately understand the exercise and rise to amazing heights. Others will find it difficult. It requires a lot of patience on your part. Always encourage the actors to treat all of these processes as a sort of adventure in which they may make some discoveries – and that there's no such concept as 'getting it right'. Only the technique has to become accurately executed. As with the actioning, you will see day-by-day improvements as the actors learn to develop the skills required by the process.

Once more, remember, while working through any of these procedures, that the actors must *not* be allowed to stop and get into discussions. They have to learn *on the job*. There will always be time for discussion and analysis after you've actually done the work.

Reminder

You are continuing with your work on CHARACTER and the WORLD OF THE PLAY parallel to this strand on the text. The actors are acquiring more and more knowledge of the play. The texture of what they're doing is becoming increasingly enriched.

Stage Four:
Points of Concentration (POC)
Applying the Given Circumstances

Purpose

Applying points of concentration is the final major stage in working on the text. You are somewhere around the fourth week of rehearsal. By now, the actors should be off-book. I'll have given the actors deadlines, act by act or scene by scene (depending on the structure of the play), by which to have learnt their lines. The actors have to know the text securely for this next stage in the process. So the deadlines are coordinated accordingly.

Using points of concentration is the process of applying the given circumstances to the action. Now that the actions, objectives and beats have been fully established, it's time to expand them so that the performance not only moves forward *horizontally*, shall we say, but also acquires *a layered verticality*, something akin to an orchestral score. Points of concentration give the performance richness of texture, complexity and resonance. They add colour and juice to the relatively spare linearity of actions and objectives. Working on given circumstances, one at a time, is a process of layering experience into the actors' psyches so they can eventually function on several levels simultaneously.

Technically, the point of concentration functions as a preoccupation with a given circumstance. Its purpose is achieved by the actors *simultaneously* pursuing the objectives and playing the actions of a scene *while* fully preoccupied by a POC.

Conventionally no doubt, actors take their given circumstances into account, but usually only relate them to the moments in the text in which they're mentioned. Without imputing negligence, I would claim that most actors are very selective and not very thorough in their use of them. But given circumstances preoccupy and affect us even when we're not discussing them. For example, in the first act of *The Cherry Orchard*, although Ranyevskaya has just returned home after a five-year absence in Paris, her lover, the partial cause of her flight and with whom she has lived for most of that period, is not mentioned at all except, implicitly, by the appearance of some telegrams whose provenance is not spelled out. But the fact of her five-year absence with her lover must be strongly present in her thoughts and in those of most of the other characters, influencing their attitude towards her, even though nothing is said. This is an often unexplored sort of theme that a POC could help to bring alive.

This process ensures that all the actors explore each given circumstance, not just as private work, but together in action, on their feet – in the heat of actually playing. Working this way, without being able to anticipate how the given circumstance will affect their actions, they produce moments of true spontaneity, unexpected and unique to them. The pressure of playing a scene while dealing with a strong preoccupation awakens their imagination, not just their invention. *In the sweat and heat of playing, the actors' creativity can release profound areas of experience.*

Points of concentration function in our actual lives in this way: we are complex organisms whose psychology and conduct have evolved from the infinite number of experiences we've absorbed throughout our lives. (Here we're discussing nurture, rather than nature or genetic predisposition.) Accordingly, we will have learnt to behave very differently with our parents from the way we behave with our lovers, differently with current partners than with exes – or with professional colleagues or old schoolmates or holiday acquaintances or people who have higher or lower status than us . . . and so on. Throughout our lives, as we come in contact with individuals, they activate certain triggers within us that elicit specific behaviour that we instinctively feel is appropriate towards them. This is also true of different locations or circumstances in which we might find ourselves – places with happy memories, situations with painful ones . . . The process of applying given circumstances as points of concentration is a condensed version of this sort of experiential life-programming, equipping the actor-characters with material that will encourage in them a similarly wide range of responses and behaviour, depending upon where, when and with whom they find themselves. We're trying to fill the actors with all the 'ingredients' that the text suggests the characters would have acquired in their lives, relevant to the play's action.

To give the actors some idea of how a POC works, you could give them the example of a very common situation, say, having an interview for a job. Ask them to imagine the difference between the circumstance of being interviewed when they're preoccupied with the fact that they've just been offered an equally desirable job elsewhere and that of being interviewed when they're preoccupied with having been continuously turned down for jobs during the past month. They should easily be able to understand how differently those two preoccupations might affect their behaviour in the same situation.

I've found the POC to be the most liberating of all the processes, both for the actors and for myself. The actors, for their part, become so filled with information, knowledge and experience of the WORLD OF THE PLAY they inhabit, that they carry within them the utmost sense of security and are rarely, if ever, thrown. POCs encourage them to be creatively daring. For myself, it means that the freedom and spontaneity that I've been seeking becomes an absolutely natural part of the actors' performances, and I can have total trust in what they do.

When the process is working well, there's a noticeable fluency and naturalness in the playing. One of the useful by-products of this technique is the wiping of that destructive tape that constantly runs in actors' heads, judging and censoring what they and their partners are doing ('Am I pleasing the audience?' 'Did I remember that note?' . . .) and detaching them from total involvement in the scene. POCs replace such self-conscious thoughts with the necessary thoughts genuinely engendered by the circumstances *within* the scene. *POCs allow the actors to think in and as the character.*

AN OUTLINE OF THE PROCESS

The actors, now off-book, play a whole act or scene through the filter of a specific given circumstance with which they are totally preoccupied for its entire duration. They should play the same act or scene several times in succession, each time preoccupied with a new given circumstance. (Preoccupation with a Given Circumstance = A Point of Concentration.)

PROCESS

PRE-SEQUENCE

1. The actors should know their text deeply and accurately. If the points of concentration are to work fully, the actors' minds cannot be even partially preoccupied with remembering lines. Otherwise that becomes their POC! So it's advisable to make sure that their text is firmly lodged in their memories before embarking on the POC process proper.

2. Have the actors seated in a circle, not too close together. If possible, have a stage manager, assistant or actor not in the current act or scene seated behind each of them, holding a script and ready to prompt.

3. Instruct the actors, although seated, to play the act or scene fully, to pursue their objectives, talk and connect with each other as if they were running the act on their feet.

4. Do *not* imply this run is merely to check lines. Ensure they play with total commitment.

5. If the actors forget text, they should, *without* breaking concentration on their partners in the scene, ask simply for 'Line!' from their personal prompter seated behind them.

6. If the actors make errors, the prompters should *not* interrupt to correct them, but make notes to give the actors *after* the run of the act has finished.

(This procedure for prompting should be conducted on all occasions from now on, the intention being to keep the action flowing. If you keep stopping the actors to correct lines, the run ends up being about remembering lines – a waste of rehearsal time.)

NEXT

7. If this run has worked smoothly, get the actors up and have them repeat it in the proper space, this time on their feet.

8. If you then feel their lines are sufficiently secure, you can proceed to the points of concentration. *If not, wait another day before you do so.*

SEQUENCE PROPER

1. You choose the given circumstance that is to be worked on by all the actor-characters in the act.

2. You instruct the actors that they are to preoccupy themselves with this given circumstance *throughout the entire length of the act* they are playing. They should not attempt to edit its use, that is, to decide when it's appropriate or inappropriate to activate it. *They should deal with it all the time, no matter what else is happening in the act.* They must neither anticipate the outcome of how it might work (i.e. think in results), nor censor anything unexpected that it arouses in them. They should treat their journey through the text with the point of concentration as an adventure to see what comes out of it. *Make sure that they allow whatever happens to happen.*

3. You give them a short period before they start playing the text to absorb the POC. Just as with the playing of objectives, you should urge them to think about it in a lateral manner, allowing all sorts of associations and corollaries to arise – to treat the material imaginatively, not to limit it to one idea or attitude. *This is extremely important.* If they think about the POC one-dimensionally – in a block or having only one attribute – they will limit its use and what it might deliver. There are many ways of approaching a POC. If, for example, in *The Cherry Orchard*, the POC was *the Nursery* the actor-characters could think about:

   The physical room itself
   The sorts of objects that might be in it (Is the washstand that Lopakhin remembers still there?)
   The view of the orchard from its windows
   Themselves as children

Other characters as children
Their own age now and how far away they are from their childhoods
The nature of childhood itself
Growing up
Their parents
The nature of parenthood
The old nurse who has died in Ranyevskaya's absence . . . and so on

Actors can use the direct opposite of the POC. If, for instance, in the same play, the POC is *the family's debts*, they could think of the time when money was abundant and taken for granted. I'm stressing the point, that the actors should allow their thoughts and imagination to explore the POC from many directions.

4. Once they have had the time to absorb the POC, you instruct them to hold on to it while they focus on their initial objective in the act. You then run the act, exploring the POC.

5. You remind them that *they must always pursue their objectives*. One of the challenges of the process is for the actors to maintain a balance between their POC and their objective. This will sometimes create an inner conflict, the objective pulling in one direction, the POC in another. *That's exactly as it should be.* The pressure of that conflict can create an emotionally imaginative release. If, however, the actors indulge in the POC to the neglect of their objective, they will have a tendency, while no doubt appearing very absorbed, to *float* out of the scene. *Objectives, after all, are what hold actors in scenes.* If, on the other hand, they favour the objective and neglect the POC, they're simply not fulfilling the exercise!

6. *Of course, the dominant purpose of the exercise is to discover how the POC affects the playing of actions and objectives. But, correspondingly, the subject-matter of the scene, its actions and objectives can affect the POC. The two – preoccupation and occupation – should be continuously cross-fertilising.*

7. The actors should not try to produce feelings, but to encourage and allow thoughts and images to arise. Feelings will take care of themselves; thoughts and images will naturally evoke feelings.

8. You keep repeating this process, running the whole act or scene with a fresh POC. Each time, the texture and quality of the act should be considerably different; often two run-throughs can seem to be of totally different plays! Do it for as many times as you sense the actors have sufficient energy and focus. For example, you could ask the actors in *The Cherry Orchard* to play the whole of Act One, concentrating on the fact

that it is *the small hours of the morning after a sleepless night*. Then you might ask them to play the act again, this time concentrating on the fact that *Ranyevskaya has returned home after five years*. Then, concentrating on the fact that *the cherry orchard is in bloom*; then on *the estate's debts . . .* and so on. In *The Seagull*, the first time through Act One could be played with the POC on *the environment* (moon, lake, evening, humidity . . .), and then on the fact that they are in *the presence of the famous novelist, Trigorin*. In both cases, very different choices, tones, attitudes, values and shifts of relationships should come to the surface. You should stress that the different choices that come up are *all equally valid*.

9. You make clear to them that they can only concentrate on one POC at a time and that when they embark on a run with a fresh POC, they should let go of previous ones. However, should an earlier POC surface of its own accord, they should not censor it, but, rather, *let it happen*.

10. At some stage, you can point out (if they haven't already noticed) that not only do they have the fresh stimulation of their POC affecting how they play, they will also have the additional stimulation of very fresh responses from their partners, who are also being influenced by a new POC and therefore more than likely to offer very different PROVOCATIONS (*see*: GLOSSARY).

11. When the actors have explored an act through the filter of a POC, it is useful to observe what they have found. *But do not encourage them, or even intimate, that they should hold on to certain moments (results/choices) to play again*. On the contrary: tell them to trust that the experience of that POC is now lodged somewhere inside them and may assert itself at any time. Some POCs may be extremely vivid for the actor and remain available, others may have had less impact and could eventually fade. However, many POCs will be used for more than one act or scene, so that there's a natural opportunity to reinforce them. If you feel it necessary – should you think that something important has been lost – you can, at a later date, explore such POCs again. But if you do so, you must urge the actors to treat the exercise as though it's being done for the first time. They should never deliberately try to recapture the previous experience, otherwise they will be aiming for a result, rather than making a discovery.

12. Remind the actors that each time they explore a POC, they should treat it as an adventure, something to approach in a spirit of excitement and curiosity to see what fresh discoveries they can make. Never let them feel they have to 'get it right'. There can be no 'right'. The excitement is discovering how each individual actor's imagination responds. No two

actors are likely to respond in the same way. It's another way of actors making their roles their own. Once they have understood the technical demands of the exercise and mastered them, whatever happens in a run is the truth of that particular run.

13. Gradually, you are layering in all – or as many as possible – of the given circumstances that go to make up the characters' world, the WORLD OF THE PLAY.

WARNINGS

To reiterate: if the actors indulge the POC to the neglect of their objectives, they can drift out of the action. POC and objective must be maintained in equal balance. When the POC supports the objective, this is not a problem. But, often, the two are working in opposition, pulling in different directions – there is an emotional conflict between the POC and the objective. Then some actors let go of the POC. They find it too confusing or disturbing or exhausting. They are missing the point! The conflict between the two is actually what will put them into a creative state from which exciting and surprising revelations of character and situation can be released. I repeat: *in the sweat and heat of playing, the actors' creativity can release profound areas of experience.*

It's unwise ever to attempt to repeat the same POC twice in succession. All you'll get is a tired replay of what's just happened. This is true whether it has just worked wonderfully or weakly. In both cases, the actors will almost instinctively focus on results rather than exploration, either trying to re-experience the excitement of what, in the former case, they've just found or, in the latter, judging whether this time around they're doing it better!

Points of Concentration for Technical Concerns

As well as absorbing given circumstances into the fabric of the actors' perform-ances, POCs can also be applied to technical matters. They can reinforce external techniques. You can instruct the actors to play an act or scene with their POC on exploring the tempo, the space, the set, their clothes, their physicality, speech or language. For example, you could give the cast the POC of finding a justifiable use for every single piece of furniture and prop on the set during the course of the act or scene. Of course, they play their objectives with their usual commitment. Actors eagerly respond to this sort of challenge to their ingenuity and imagination. You'll observe how the space comes vividly alive as they seek reasons to sit in a chair or pick up a cup . . . The rewarding outcome of this is that the actors take possession of their environment and make it a part of their world.

This is a very useful way of incorporating into the performance some aspects of your work on the WORLD OF THE PLAY that haven't organically found their way into the production. If, for example, you're dealing with a play in which etiquette – manners and protocol – is important and you've already spent considerable rehearsal time on this without much evidence of it entering the fabric of the playing, you can make this a POC. As you near the end of the rehearsal period (*see*: BRINGING THE STRANDS TOGETHER), POCs are a way of pulling many of the strands of your work together. Instead of having to change artistic gears by the more conventional method of demanding results for technical matters ('Do this!', 'Go there!', 'Play faster!'), you can, by means of points of concentration, achieve what you need by continuing in the creative, organic, process-led approach you've been pursuing up to this point.

When Shared Experience produced its adaptation of Evelyn Waugh's *A Handful of Dust*, we had, by some quirk of scheduling, the opportunity to do a dress rehearsal in front of an audience a week before we actually opened. It went encouragingly well. The actors of course felt tremendously reassured. We took advantage of the following week to hone the form of what was a sophisticated and heightened production (*see*: PRACTICE in WORLD OF THE PLAY). Each day we would run a section of the show with the POC on speed and attack, then on the characters' use of language, then on the way they wore their clothes . . . and so forth. Of course, the actors would always be pursuing their objectives and playing their actions with freshness and spontaneity, but the form of the WORLD was being continuously reinforced and the execution perfected in a playful and creative way. By the time we opened officially, the WORLD OF THE PLAY was defined to an impressively skilful level. These 'technical' aspects of their performance were not a burden or limitation or inhibition to the actors (as technical demands sometimes can be), but had become for them a necessary and natural expression of the world they inhabited.

The Interchangeability of Objectives and Given Circumstances

A technical acting note: sometimes, *objectives* can become *given circumstances* and *given circumstances* become *objectives*. It's possible for them to switch functions. For example, in the first act of *The Cherry Orchard*, Lopakhin comes on a quick visit *to persuade Ranyevskaya to sell part of her land*. For most of the scene, that's his *scene objective*. One of his *given circumstances* is that *he has to catch a train back to Kharkov*. As time presses on, these could switch so that his *objective* would become *to make sure he catches his train* – and his attempt to persuade her would then become a *given circumstance* that impinges on his need to catch his train. This is a sophisticated technique that can help to vary the energy and tone of a scene.

Some Exercises for Points of Concentration

Here are some exercises to introduce the concept of points of concentration to the actors.

AN ACTIVITY FOR ACTORS INDIVIDUALLY

Instruct half of the cast to deploy themselves around the room where they won't be in each other's way. The other half will watch them. It's useful to split the company in two for this exercise, so that they can observe how it works as well as experience it. The sequence should be given a lot of space and last about half-an-hour.

Ask each actor to choose a simple activity to mime for the next twenty to thirty minutes. It should be an activity that has a certain amount of routine, rhythm and regularity. There should be nothing dramatic connected with it. The actors are simply to execute the activity (without props), such as *washing (a mountain of) dishes, giving oneself a manicure, cleaning and polishing (Imelda Marcos's) shoe collection, ironing (a hill of) shirts* and so forth. Make it clear that this activity is their *action*.

Give them time to sort out what they are doing. Though this is not an exercise in mime, coach them to create for themselves the accurate shape, dimensions, weight, texture and overall feel of all the objects they are 'handling' and the space that those objects take up.

Once this is achieved, ask them to choose an objective for this activity (action). It must be for an imagined person and there must be a reason, such as *to give them a pleasant surprise, to prove they can keep a promise, to get their own back* . . . Coach them to remain meticulous about their mime and to *allow* the objective to influence *how* they execute their activity.

Once this is secure, give them an environmental point of concentration, for example, *indoors on an excessively hot and humid day; out of doors on a bitterly cold day; indoors on a summer morning just as dawn is breaking* . . . The actors need to justify for themselves why they are doing their chosen activity at such a time and place. They must maintain the objective. Coach them not to jump to results or demonstrations, for instance, of being hot or cold. They must be totally preoccupied with the environmental POC, *constantly maintaining their activities and their objectives* as they explore it – and, most important, allowing it to affect them. They must not stop the activity. If they do stop, coach them to keep working. Allow time for the POC to take effect.

Next, give them each an *individual* point of concentration which has no overt connection with what they are doing. You give these to them privately, whispering to each actor in turn; you do not break the flow of their activity. These should be intense preoccupations, either with something that will happen or something that has already happened. For example, *A has lost a wallet with money, credit cards and items of personal value,* or *B has to go for a medical check-up tomorrow which will include some serious X-rays,* or *an acquaintance of C's is coming to town to settle an old score* (the actors decide on the specific details for themselves). Instruct them to think around these POCs as fully, as laterally and as imaginatively as they can, allowing their thoughts to take them wherever they want to go. Keep coaching them to allow the POC to influence their activities (actions), which they must continue to keep fully alive, as well as their objectives. They should let go of the environmental POC, but they should not reject it if it spontaneously reasserts itself. *You can only explore one POC at a time.* Coach them to ensure their thoughts do not become static. They should allow the POC to keep moving, naturally, through different thoughts, feelings and attitudes.

Warn them not to let the initial impact fade, but to develop and intensify all the elements (objective, activity, POC), to raise the stakes, up the ante . . .

Leave most time for this final stage of the exercise. Periodically, as you think appropriate, coach them to intensify or strengthen their POC, or their objective, or their activity, *so that they keep all three elements alive.*

Remind them that *as they are on their own, they can express anything they feel and in any way an impulse suggests to them.* They can talk to themselves, make sounds . . .

This whole sequence should flow without any breaks.

What will or should happen is that the POCs clearly influence how they execute their activities. The mime will no longer be as self-conscious as it was likely to have been when they started. It will become more and more natural. And the way they carry out their activities should grow increasingly revealing and expressive.

At the end, discuss the exercise. Could they sustain the POC all the way through? Could they keep their objectives alive? Was there a conflict between the objective and the POC? Did the POC support and enhance the objective? What did the observers notice?

The POC should have changed the actors, how they executed their activities and how they behaved within the context of the exercise.

AN ACTIVITY FOR ACTORS IN PAIRS

Set up the exercise with one pair at a time.

Instruct them to choose a simple activity to share. It should also have a basic routine, like *peeling a pile of potatoes, washing up, painting a room* . . .

They should not characterise, but use themselves.

They should not talk, except for very elementary reasons, such as 'Pass me the cloth' . . .

The activity should be devoid of story or drama.

Before they start, they should decide what objects they are using and where they are.

They should also decide on a *shared* objective for working together.

Coach them to ensure their handling of the imaginary objects is accurate (dimension, weight, shape, texture . . .).

Coach them to focus on their objective.

Next, give them a *shared* environmental POC.

Next, give them a *shared* personal POC, for example, that *they've just had a row* . . .

Next, privately (without breaking the flow of the exercise), whisper to them their individual POCs, so neither knows what their partner is thinking about. These could be connected along the lines of: *A thinks that B is really stupid, while B fancies A*; or without any connection, such as: *A hit someone while driving and is waiting for the hospital reports to know how serious the injury is; B is anticipating a wonderful career move to Hollywood.* It's good if you can set up contrasting POCs. Remind them not to hold on to their previous POC; but by all means allow it to come into the exercise if it surfaces of its own accord. Remind them not to get into conversation and on no account to discuss their POCs with each other. They should *justify* to themselves why they don't want to discuss their POC.

Coach as above, ensuring they keep equally engaged with the activity (action), objective and POC.

Everyone else observes.

Discuss as above. first, ask the two participants if they could figure out what their partner's POC was, and then ask the observers whether they could work out what they might have been.

Note: often, in these pairs, potentially interesting scenes emerge that could be the basis for devised work.

AN IMPROVISED SCENE IN PAIRS

Set up an improvised scene in pairs.

The actors must choose a situation with a strong, clear action of two people meeting to sort out some problem: *to plan a holiday; to choose a flatmate; to come to an agreement about the custody of their child; to deal with aging parents.* Both should have an *equal* need to solve the problem so that the improvisation can start with the strength of need evenly balanced between them.

The actors should *privately* choose an objective which they do not reveal to their partner.

They should settle, in advance, as many facts about themselves necessary for their choice of situation. They should work as closely as they can from themselves. They should not play characters, and they should not make their backstory overly complicated.

They must choose a neutral meeting place: a café, a park bench.

Now, of course, they can talk.

Once they have begun the improvisation and established themselves and their conflict, you, the director, without stopping them, whisper in their ears their private POCs, as in the previous exercises. Remind them never to discuss or let their partner know what their POC is. They must justify for themselves why they don't wish to discuss or refer to their POCs.

Keep coaching them to intensify their objectives, then to intensify their POCs, then to intensify their action (the discussion/argument), as you see necessary. They have to keep all three 'balls' (action, objective, POC) in the air. Keep pushing them to strengthen whatever they're playing.

Everyone observes.

Discuss. Ask the two actors whether they had any idea what their partner's POC or objective was. Usually, they are so preoccupied with their own problems that they only approximately register any change in their partner. The observing group, however, will clearly see changes and will frequently be able to pinpoint what the POCs were from the actors' changed behaviour.

Often these scenes become quite complex and technically sophisticated, with the actors having to balance their POCs against their objectives, to allow themselves to be affected by their POCs but to try not to let their partner know what they are.

Note: these improvisations, too, can be a rich source of material for devised work.

A VARIATION

If you have a large cast, working in pairs may take up too much rehearsal time. Accordingly, you set up, say, a café in which a maximum of three pairs meet simultaneously, *all quite independent of each other*.

The rules and structures of the improvisations are as in the previous exercise.

However, in order to gain clarity, you will have to introduce a new feature into the improvisation. You label the pairs, A, B and C. You instruct them that, when you call A, pairs B and C have to justify not talking, while A continues with their situation. When you call B, A and C stop talking . . . and so on.

The silent pairs *do not* freeze. They must remain *active*. As they are in a café, they should be able to find activities and reasons to justify their silence. Sometimes, they reach an emotional level where it seems quite natural for them not to want to talk for a while.

Calling one pair at a time allows those watching to be able to concentrate on each individual improvisation.

You will have to judge how much time to give each pair on their own and how long you can keep the other pairs silent.

You start the improvisation allowing all three pairs to talk at the same time. Once they have all established their situations sufficiently, you then start to call on them individually.

Periodically – to give them all more playing 'space' – you can again let them all talk at the same time, calling out '*A, B and C together*'.

You should let them play the last few moments this way, too, then complete the exercise by calling each pair in succession to silence.

Then, as with the previous exercises, discuss. In what way, if any, did the actors change? Could the observers guess what the POCs were? What changes did partners observe in each other? And so forth.

These exercises should give the actors a reasonably good understanding of how POCs work. Observe very carefully whether they are really allowing themselves to explore their POCs and whether they're really allowing their POCs to influence their behaviour. Often there is a vivid change of body language. For example, the person who began an improvisation confidently sitting upright and forward may end up slumped and withdrawn in their seat.

Directors should try to make choices of POCs that imaginatively anticipate possibilities of contrast, conflict and technical challenge to the actors.

Logic Text

Logic Text, as its name implies, is an exercise to make sense of the text at its simplest, logical, grammatically structured level. It can be applied anywhere in the rehearsal process, parallel to other text work. The only proviso is that it shouldn't be used *too early* or it might seem like – or unintentionally become – an exercise in imposed line-readings, which it most definitely is *not*.

Purpose

Its purpose is to ensure that the actors understand the basic, bottom-line common sense of their texts: if there is a statement, they *make* a statement; if there is a question, they *ask* a question; if there is a reply, they *give* a reply; if there is a command, they *issue* one; and in a sequence of thoughts, one thought *leads* to the next.

It's embarrassing to state the obvious, but characters, most of the time, say things in response to what has just been said to them. This is the nature of dialogue. Nonetheless, many actors become so absorbed by the psychology of their character that they neglect any spontaneous give-and-take with their partners. They treat each speech as a self-contained, sealed unit for the investigation of their own feelings, not as part of a conversation. This is particularly prevalent when heightened texts are involved, especially those of Shakespeare. I can't stress enough that, however heightened or poetic the language of a play may be, *the characters are always engaged in conversation and the dialogue must be heard as conversation*. The dialogue, whatever its eventual implications, is, for an audience, their first level of entry into the basic situation of a scene, their initial means of grasping what's going on.

Look v. Listen

Language of the past is receding rapidly from our comprehension. Anything written earlier than, say, twenty-five years ago can begin to seem like a foreign language. We've also grown suspicious of language. We distrust much of what we read or are told. We're cynical about the slipperiness of words.* On news items, public figures state irrefutable facts and figures, only to be challenged by others

---

* *Unspeak* by Stephen Poole deals in great detail with the cynical use of language in politics to prejudice the public's attitude to a subject. For example, those groups and organisations that seek to minimise the threat of increasing temperature identify the phenomenon by the phrase *climate change*. After all, the climate has always been prone to change. This they feel is less ominous than the more specific *global warming*.

claiming equal irrefutability for contradictory information. Politicians, especially, have grown adroit at avoiding interviewers' questions with blatant *non-sequiturs*. At the same time, technology has given us more and more means of looking at things, so that we've grown visually literate, increasingly sophisticated at interpreting the images that engulf us (some commercials are challengingly hermetic). People brought up on a diet of television relate to language very differently from those brought up on radio. We trust what we see far more than what we hear. (Aiding and abetting this tendency is the fact that light travels faster than sound!) In film, dialogue is frequently smothered by numerous other soundtracks; it's presumed less important, because what we see will tell us what we need to know. In the Elizabethan period, we would have gone to *hear* a play; now we go to *see* one. Language, however, expresses complex ideas far more precisely than imagery.

Unreceived Pronunciation

During the 1960s, actors began to react against the drama-school practice of automatically training them all to speak in the same way. Up to then, they had been taught to replace their natural, regional accents, with received pronunciation (once the King's – now the Queen's – English), exemplified at the time by BBC announcers with accents and voice placements that to our ears can now sound 'posh' or effete. Their reaction against this had considerable virtues. It did a lot to break down the perceived artificiality of theatre and affectation of actors, as well as the clichés of class structure, embalmed in the way actors then played. (Take a look at some English movies from the '30s and you're sure to come upon examples of actors attempting their excruciating ideas of a Cockney accent.) The new generation of actors was, of course, responding to social change and to a new generation of playwrights for whom middle-class life was no longer the main source of subject matter. However, a lot of babies were thrown out with the bath water: specifically, those dealing with the expressiveness and accuracy of speech. Actors in the past, whatever their failings in other departments, were skilful in handling language.

Elitism

Literate and articulate speech for many is tainted by its perceived connection with the educationally privileged, with class and the elite. A vivid, oppositional street counter-language now flourishes, but one that keeps reinventing itself – a fine example of permanent change and, in fact, another form of elitism, its main purpose being to remain exclusively the property of its creators. By the time the rest of us, with much huffing and puffing, think we've caught up with it, it's already moved on! It has virtually no roots in what's gone before (a knowledge of Latin won't help you here), so that now there are sections of society that have difficulty understanding each other, both in sound and meaning.

Distrustful Inarticulacy

If you distrust words, you're likely to be wary of how you use them. So a lot of speech is slurred, mumbled and remains safely non-committal at the back of throat. Some people hardly bother to open their mouths. Volume comes in two levels: inaudible and screamed. This encourages two other particularly unhelpful vocal tendencies: to speak with very little inflection, in something close to a monotone, so that what is said loses almost all meaning (a Canadian actor once told me that it was un-Canadian to inflect!); and to let words die before the completion of a thought. Both are liabilities in the theatre. In the latter case, audiences get the wrong signal and, assuming the thought is complete, stop listening before the idea has actually come to an end. This often happens in performances of Shakespeare, when the actors run out of steam before they complete a lengthy and elaborately structured idea. In fact, the point of most thoughts is made at the end of a sentence, often on the last word. Verbal skills apart, if you're truly playing your action, that should carry the thought well beyond the last word.

Sustained Thought v. Sound Bite

All this is critical for audiences, especially when coping with classical texts, where the language is already sufficiently challenging. The difficulties are intensified by the fact that in our sound-bite culture, we're losing the ability to speak, listen or even think in extended thoughts composed of multiple clauses. This was clearly not so in the past. We have only to look at a page of Shakespeare to see elaborate and sophisticated thoughts that sustain themselves through several clauses, often over many lines of verse.[*] In order for us, the audience, to understand them, actors have to sustain such thoughts with fluency, rather than making them hard to follow by the current fashion of breaking them up into jerky, bite-sized phrases. I suggest to actors that they imagine a sequence of clauses in a complex speech as the equivalent of juggling balls that have to be kept buoyantly aloft until the entire thought-sentence has been completed, only then to be caught and brought to rest.

---

[*] In *Amusing Ourselves To Death*, Neil Postman describes the Lincoln-Douglas presidential debates of 1858, when people would come to hear the two political adversaries share anything from three to seven hours of debate in which they used the most elaborate and complex language, often extemporised, to pursue their arguments. Douglas once appealed to his audience, after they had lengthily applauded a statement of his: 'My friends, silence will be more acceptable to me . . . than applause. *I desire to address myself to your judgement, your understanding and your consciences and not to your passions or your enthusiasms. (My emphasis.)*' Their audiences, far from being comprised only of the well-educated, consisted of a healthy social cross section of the community who clearly understood what they had come to listen to. They were not talked down to, but treated with respect by the two politicians.

Logic Text in Action

The fact that we're no longer taught grammatical structure is yet one more barrier to clear thinking.

Logic text is helpful in sorting out many of these problems. I found logic text unexpectedly useful when working on an adaptation of Jane Austen's *Emma*. I'd assumed the actors would find the text totally comprehensible; Austen's novels are popular and relatively recent. So I hadn't put any time aside in the rehearsal schedule to deal specifically with her way of saying things. But in the event, I had to find some. The cast, despite an age range spanning several decades, needed some logic text sessions in order to decode her wit and her characters' thought-patterns.

Logic text is not only of benefit for clotted classic texts. It also proves useful for contemporary material. Actors can feel so *au fait* with the language that they take for granted what needs closer examination. Logic text can solve acting problems. If actors don't understand what they're saying or don't recognise the connection between a sequence of speeches, they can't play the situation or enact the story.

Logic text needs careful handling. It can become a frustrating and irritating exercise for the actors, especially when you insist that a sequence of lines is repeated until you hear the basic logic to your satisfaction. If the actors begin to lose any sense of what they're saying or how to say it, it's probably wise to relinquish the session and return to the process at a later date.

AN OUTLINE OF THE PROCESS

The actors, seated with their scripts, work their way through a scene or act, speech by speech, thought by thought, ensuring that they are making basic, logical sense of the text, free from interpretation or emotional colouring.

PROCESS

1. You want the text delivered more or less free of emotion or interpretation beyond what is its *basic, bottom-line, common-sense logic*. Take as an example, Arkadina's line from Act 3 of *The Seagull*: '*If you abandon me, even for an hour, I'll not survive, I'll go mad, my marvel, my magnificence, my sovereign . . .* ' This is clearly a piece of text that needs eventually to be delivered with a lot of emotional colour and intensity. Nevertheless, it still contains a semantic, grammatical and structural logic – and it's this level that you want to hear from the actors. You're ensuring that the actors find

the logical truth of the text at a stage which *precedes* interpretation. You must emphasise yet again that this is absolutely *not* an exercise in line-readings, but one to ensure that the actors are quite clear about the common-sense progression of their dialogue. Reassure them that once they understand the basic logic, they're free to play the line in any way they choose. Once you know a rule, you're in a position to break it.[*]

2. When you decide it's the appropriate time in rehearsal to embark on this process, do it over several sessions. It's usually slow work; concentration and patience survive for only a limited time. Never do more than an hour at a time.

3. The actors should be seated, with their texts available.

4. It's a totally technical exercise and, unlike the other rehearsal processes, will probably need a lot of intervention and explanation, encouragement and insistence from you, the director.

Every text throws up totally individual structures and presents different problems for the actor, but here is a sample of the sort of thing you might need to look out for.

BEATRICE AND BENEDICK
FROM ACT I SCENE I OF 'MUCH ADO ABOUT NOTHING'

BEATRICE I wonder that you will *still*[1] be talking, Signor Benedick, nobody marks you.

BENEDICK What, my dear Lady *Disdain*![2] Are you *yet*[3] living?

BEATRICE Is it possible *disdain* should die while she hath such meet food to feed it as Signor Benedick? *Courtesy*[4] itself must convert to *disdain*, if you come in her presence.

---

[*] During my training at Carnegie Mellon, an energetic eighty-year-old authority on speech, called Margaret Prendergast McClain, came out of retirement to deputise for our indisposed regular voice teacher (well-known for taking a nip too many). Guiding us through some speeches from *Romeo and Juliet*, she claimed that Shakespeare's texts were written in a form that allowed only one way of speaking them. She demonstrated this through a careful analysis of the language's structure. At the time, I baulked at this seemingly rigid imposition, but over the years, I've come to accept that, in terms of sheer logic, she was absolutely correct. However, the intention behind a line and the emotional state in which it is delivered still opens it up to endless variation. But: *the logic must always be there as a ground bass*.

BENEDICK Then is *courtesy* a *turncoat*.[5] But it is certain I am loved of all ladies, only you excepted, and I would I could find it in my heart that I had not a hard heart, for truly I love none.

BEATRICE A dear happiness to women, they would else have been troubled with a pernicious suitor. I thank God and my cold blood I am of your humour for that. I would rather hear my dog bark at a crow than a man swear he love me.

BENEDICK God keep your ladyship still in that mind. So some gentleman or other shall 'scape a predestinate scratched face.

BEATRICE Scratching could not make it worse and 'twere such a face as yours were.

BENEDICK Well, you are a rare *parrot*-teacher.

BEATRICE A *bird* of my tongue is better than a *beast of yours*.[6]

BENEDICK I would *my horse*[7] had the speed of your tongue – and so good a continuer. But keep your way, a' God's name. I have done.

BEATRICE You always end with a *jade's*[8] trick. I know you of old.

SOME NOTES ON THE LOGIC

The logic of this exchange of dialogue depends on both characters scoring points off each other by playing off the words the other has used. It's based on the inference that in the past they've had some sort of relationship that's turned sour. So the comments are *specific* and *personal*. They aim to hurt. Much of the *repartee* is clear, but here are three exchanges that are possibly less obvious:

1 and 3: *Still* and *yet* are synonymous. So the logic of the two speeches must be based on Benedick picking up on Beatrice's use of the word *still* and throwing it back to her as *yet*:

BEATRICE: I wonder that you will *still* be talking, Signor Benedick . . .

BENEDICK: What, my dear Lady Disdain! Are you *yet* (still) living?

Many Benedicks I've seen play this line without any reference to what Beatrice has said.

2, 4 and 5: He has characterised her as *Disdain*. To reclaim her self-image, she characterises herself as its opposite, *Courtesy*. ('You refer to me as

Disdain, I am actually Courtesy. If I appear to be Disdain, that's your fault. Even Courtesy could not help but become Disdain near someone as unpleasant as you!') His reply, 'Courtesy is a turncoat', implies that she's not very secure then, in her role of Courtesy.

6, 7 and 8: She uses *beast* as a pun: both as an animal in opposition to the bird he has mentioned *and* to identify Benedick with his 'beastly' nature and tongue ('If I'm a bird, you're a beast'). He deliberately chooses to misunderstand her, so that '*a beast of yours*', instead of meaning him and his coarse tongue, he pretends to understand in its literal sense as a horse of his ('I agree with you. I wish, my horse – a beast of mine – did have the speed of a tongue like yours'). She retaliates that, unable to keep up with her, he is, as ever, backing off ('You always end with a jade's trick'), a *jade* being a worn-out horse.

These examples may seem quite obvious . . . or not! (Explaining wit and wordplay is not a grateful job!) But they must be *heard* in the playing of the line. Otherwise the audience only gets a generalised idea of what is said and loses the very focused wit of the text and the personal attack it carries.

STRAND TWO: CHARACTER
The Starting Point

How Not To . . .

I've often heard actors talk about hiding behind – or putting on – a character. I suppose they meant that they had created a façade of wigs, facial hair, spectacles, make-up, accent, the 'right' shoes, 'funny walks', a couple of well-chosen physical mannerisms – in short, a selection of externally applied bits of business and artificial aids – to mask themselves from the audience. Behind this they felt safely unseen, as if there were absolutely no connection between themselves and the character they were playing.

At the other extreme – a more contemporary tendency – there are actors who seem to make no effort whatsoever to characterise. They give the same performance whatever the role, playing 'themselves' or, more accurately, the stage persona they've constructed to see them through their careers without too much exertion or self-exposure. All their performances are made from the same bolt of material from which they periodically cut another length.

These two apparently opposing ways of working are different manifestations of the same syndrome: fear disguised as a sort of arrogance. The former (old school) pride themselves on their professionalism by doing everything – except acting truthfully; the latter (new school), on their naturalness by doing nothing. Both their choices deny the creation of either serious inner life or accurately observed outer life – in other words, the commitment of themselves. Creating a role does demand that actors shake themselves up a bit.

The theatre is not the place to work if you want to hide – whether behind a disguise, or a thick skin.* The fact is, *it's you up there*. You never stop being you. You cannot be any other than yourself. You can only play aspects of yourself. Whatever you choose to play and however you choose to play it, you cannot avoid revealing yourself to the audience – even if it's no more than your evasions and

---

* When I was working in Germany on a storytelling project based on an epic from *The Arabian Nights*, an actress, required to play a princess who, in the convention of the narrative, had to describe herself in typically hyperbolic terms as radiantly beautiful, found this unbearably painful. She was, in fact, a very attractive woman who chose to hide her body in sack-like dresses and her face behind uncombed hair. 'You want me to expose myself to the audience,' she cried, 'when I came into the theatre to hide!' I gently suggested she might have given herself a better chance of achieving that ambition in a library than on a stage. Interestingly, she eventually fractured her leg and was out of the show.

dishonesty. David Mamet makes this point in his book, *True and False*, but in doing so, entirely refutes the concept of characterisation, claiming that it only occurs in the eyes of the beholders. I disagree. We *can* transform ourselves; in fact I believe the impulse and the potential ability to imagine and experience ourselves as someone else lies deep within all human beings.

Though it's true that we have only ourselves, the encouraging fact is that we're all equipped with the capacity for every possible experience. We're all made from the same physicality – nerves, muscles, bones, veins . . . We have the same potential range of emotions. Obviously the expression of emotion is qualified by variations in cultural conditioning, but, given time and study, we can learn to bridge those differences (*see*: EMOTION and WORLD OF THE PLAY). We can find those qualities, energies and impulses within us that conform to those of someone else. Clearly, there are physical limitations as to how much we can transform our bodies without resorting to the cumbersome and unconvincing aids I mentioned in the first paragraph. (It's hard to make such dead elements as wigs or padding into an organic part of ourselves.) But the mind – the will – is able to exert extraordinary control over the body.* We can, with determined concentration, convincingly create the illusion that we are physically other than we actually are.** *Actors must reach out from their habitual selves towards a character, rather than imposing themselves on a character.* We all contain within us something of each other; we share a universal humanity.

How To . . . Instinct and Analysis

Once again – but this time I address the actor – you have a two-pronged start to your work on a role: instinct and analysis, the subjective and the objective.

---

* There are astonishing instances of mind over matter. We hear cases of mothers single-handedly lifting cars to release their trapped child. And there are less dramatic but equally surprising examples. If I, seated on the ground, decide that I want to make myself heavier, I can do so *by believing – imagining, visualising –* that I have roots from my coccyx burrowing deep into the earth. Someone who has previously lifted me with comparative ease, will now have great difficulty getting me off the floor. Similarly, if I stretch out my arm and *imagine* that there is a metal rod running along the top of it from shoulder to wrist, someone who has previously been able to bend my elbow, will now struggle to do so. If I press a thumb and first finger together, no one would have much difficulty in prising them apart. However, if I imagine that where the thumb and finger meet, they are actually fused together, and that the separation lies in the curve between the base of thumb and the finger, it will be difficult for anyone to pull thumb and finger apart.

** Helen Hayes, a diminutive Broadway actress who had great prestige and popularity in the mid-decades of the last century, was reputed to be able to create the illusion of great stature. Edith Evans, despite rather undistinguished looks, created an impression of great beauty and allure that went way beyond the application of make-up. Elsewhere in the book, I quote G.B. Shaw, similarly, on Eleonora Duse.

If instinct means experience wedded to natural talent, we can assume that your spontaneous response to a first reading of a play would be a healthy and useful point of departure. And if course it is. But it does have one or two drawbacks, especially if the play and the role are familiar. You will probably have seen umpteen productions of *Twelfth Night* or *The Three Sisters*. Whether or not you liked the performances of the actors playing Viola and Masha, you'll be left with the residue of images that cannot help but influence your own reading. You may be so determined not to repeat what you've seen, to be original at all costs, that you force yourself down paths that take you far away from what the text is telling you. You may be so swayed by a performance that you cannot help but copy it. Often, these decisions are not made consciously. What's more, such roles come with a weighty accumulation of received interpretation which in fact has more to do with tradition, hearsay and academic gloss rather than what is necessarily in the play. Years of accreted false interpretation often need scraping off a text. When I was preparing the adaptation of Dickens's *Bleak House*, I read a lot of literary criticism on the novel, most of which described the heroine-narrator, Esther Summerson, as just one more of the writer's unconvincing, anodyne, sentimentally idealised virgins. In fact, working with the character in rehearsal, we discovered that she made perfect psychological sense and was considerably more complicated than these dismissive clichés about her might have led us to believe.[*] This experience alerted me to the fact that authorities aren't always authoritative. I've come up against glosses of Shakespeare texts in which the editor agonises about the possible meaning of a phrase and offers convoluted, totally unplayable options, whereas an actor, in the process of playing, makes instant sense of it.

And there are other, more insidious traps lurking within many actors – their personal needs. They may be attracted to certain aspects of a role because that is how they see themselves or wish to be seen, or because the role contains certain types of scenes they want to play. They may equally avoid or deny aspects of a role because, for largely unconscious reasons, they don't wish to display themselves in the psychological or behavioural lights that these demand.

The good actor has to steer carefully between such impositions and avoidances. So if the play is well known, try to read it as if it were brand new, one you've never seen or heard of before. Try to avoid jumping to instant decisions as to how you're going to play the role. Leave your imagination open for as long as possible to allow the play to become absorbed into your psyche (*see*: PREPARATION OF TEXT). Make notes of your initial responses. Then check your instinct against your analysis.

---

[*] She is, in fact, an orphan, born under mysterious circumstances, brought up by an aunt who tells her it would have been better had she never been born. She is, in every way, made to feel that she's not wanted anywhere. Consequently, she spends her life trying to justify her existence by making herself useful and amenable to those around her, trying to create a safe haven for herself where she will be needed and can belong.

As I've said, you can only find out what's in a play from the words of the play. In the same way that you broke down scenes into sections, units and actions, you now need to perform a comparable deconstruction on the text to extract information about the characters. Again, you are trying to ascertain the facts. By doing so, you'll inevitably scrape away some of those accumulated layers of misinformation.

The Character Lists

Sifting the Text for Accurate Information

The director should ask the actors to prepare this work *before* the start of rehearsals so that they arrive on the first day fully primed and ready to use what they've gathered. This is the director's work, too. The director should make lists for the entire *dramatis personae. This is certainly the way in which I find out about a play.*

To discover what information the play actually gives us about a character, make the following lists:

1. Facts about the character

2. What the character says about him- or herself

3. What the character says about other people – including those mentioned but not seen in the play

4. What other people say about the character

5. Imagery used by the character or by others to describe the character (optional)

Work through the text separately for each list. (If nothing else, this ensures that an actor has read the *whole* play four times at least before the start of rehearsal.)

List 1: Facts means no suppositions, only what is incontrovertible, unarguable, such as physical description, biographical details, behaviour patterns. Include what you *do* in the play: the major actions (shoots a seagull, commits suicide, etc.). Pay great attention to stage directions of physical behaviour and actions such as 'coughs a lot', 'rubs hands together', 'paces the room', but ignore those that are adverbial and adjectival. (Adverbs and adjectives encourage generalisation.) Don't be alarmed if you find very few facts. Accuracy, not quantity, is the criterion.

Lists 2-4: Write these three lists *verbatim*. Do *not* paraphrase. If there are only one or two pertinent phrases in a speech, it's not necessary to write it out in its entirety. We need the relevant words and phrases to stand out sharply. List what characters say about each other both behind their backs and to their faces. Sometimes the same piece of text needs to appear in two lists – both what you say about yourself and what you say about another character, for example, 'I love her'. When in doubt about a piece of text, include it. If a character frequently uses phrases such as 'I feel that . . . ', 'In my opinion . . . ', 'To my way of thinking . . . ', 'I believe . . . ', it's worth including them in the list of what you say about yourself. You can never tell when the most seemingly routine phrase may yield useful information.

Lists 3-4: For these two lists, you can gather the information either by moving through the play chronologically or moving around it in character blocks, dealing with one character at a time (e.g. if you were playing Konstantin in *The Seagull*, you would include in the third list all that you say about Nina, then all that you say about Arkadina and so on; in the fourth, all that Nina says about you, then all that Arkadina says about you and so on). Each method has its advantage: chronologically, you keep the shape and flow of the play; in character blocks, you have a more immediately concentrated picture of each relationship. Note that questions about someone (e.g. '*Why are you always in black?*') should be included as they imply an impression that the character has made on the questioner.

(*List 5:* If you are working on Shakespeare, Lorca or any writer who uses heightened language, you can include the optional fifth list dealing with imagery. This clearly does not give you facts, but it might reinforce some ideas you're beginning to gather about the character. In *Cymbeline*, Imogen uses recurring images concerned with sight and birds. Put together with other information about her, you might decide that the first implies that she is clear-eyed, looking, searching, a seeker after truth; the second that she longs to be free, liberated from the earth. Of course both instances are highly interpretive but they might support other, more factual conclusions you are coming to about her character; Shakespeare has chosen those images for a reason.)

Applying the Lists in Rehearsal

The lists having been made, they now have to be applied practically. They are in fact the means of embarking on the second strand of the rehearsal process, parallel to the work on the text.

The actors bring their lists to rehearsal and, starting on the first day and moving on till all the characters have been dealt with, the company analyses the information they have gleaned. Depending on the length of text involved, you work on one or two characters a day. You need anything from one to two hours for each character.

PROCESS

First of all, the actor playing, say, Masha in *The Seagull* reads out her list of facts about her character for the rest of the company:

I. FACTS ABOUT MASHA

Her name is Marya Ilyinichna Shamraeva

She is a woman of 22; in Act 4, she's 24

She is the daughter of Polina and Shamraev, a former military officer

She lives with them on Arkadina's estate where her father is the steward or manager

She wears black

She takes snuff

She drinks vodka

Her foot goes to sleep

She is in love with Konstantin

Konstantin expresses his irritation with her

She reveals her feelings to Dr Dorn[*]

Dorn has had an affair with her mother, Polina

Medvedenko, the schoolmaster, is in love with her and wants to marry her

---

[*] Some people assume that, because Dorn has had an affair with her mother, Polina, that he is her real father. However, this is an unsubstantiated conjecture. There's not one word of text that gives evidence for this. Because Dorn is a doctor, Masha, like some other characters in the play (Sorin, Konstantin, Polina), treats him as a counsellor from whom she erroneously expects to receive sympathetic advice.

She rejects his advances

She offers her 'story' to Trigorin to use in a novel

She announces to Trigorin that she is going to marry Medvedenko

By Act Four (two years after the preceding acts) she has married Medvedenko, lives with him, his mother, two sisters and little brother, four miles away from Arkadina's estate

She has a baby son

She leaves the baby at home and spends a lot of time at the estate where Konstantin still lives

Currently she has stayed there three nights running

She refuses to return home, when besought to do so by Medvedenko

She openly expresses her contempt for her husband and her animosity towards him

She helps her mother make up a bed for Sorin in Konstantin's study

Embracing a cushion, she waltzes to the piano music Konstantin is playing offstage

She often says 'Nonsense'

She plays lotto

After these facts have been read out, ask the actress playing Masha to say what impression of the character she gleans just from them. Once she has given her thoughts, the question gets thrown open to the whole company. The actor in question writes down whatever strikes her from the opinions and images suggested by the others. The director, of course, monitors this.

Then you proceed to the other lists, stopping after each one to ask the same question, first of the actor, then the company: what impression have they gathered of the character from each list? What are the dominant facts that surface? Does anything get stated several times? Does she talk about herself in a particular manner and tone? Who talks about her and who doesn't? Whom does she talk about a lot and whom not at all? *The omissions can be as revealing as the statements.*

2. WHAT MASHA SAYS ABOUT HERSELF

Act One

I'm in mourning for my life. I'm unhappy.

Your love touches me, but I just can't respond.

In mine (opinion), it's a thousand times easier to go about in rags than . . .

I'm not going to (ask my father). Leave me out of it.

I'll fetch him (Konstantin).

I want to talk to you (Dorn) some more. I must talk to you . . . (*Agitated.*)
I don't love my father . . . but I feel close to you . . . Somehow I feel with
all my soul that I can confide in you. Please help me . . . Help me or I'll do
something silly, I'll make a mess of my whole life, I'll ruin it . . . I can't go
on (like this).

I'm suffering. Nobody knows how much I'm suffering! I love Konstantin.

Act Two

Mother brought me up like the princess who lived in a flower. I don't
know how to do anything.*

I feel as if I'd been born long, long ago; I drag my life behind me like an
endless train . . . Often I lack the impulse to go on living. Of course, all this
is nonsense. I should give myself a good shake and pull myself out of it.

My foot's gone to sleep.

Act Three

I'm telling you (Trigorin) all this as a writer. You can use it. I tell you the
truth, if he'd seriously wounded himself (Konstantin), I wouldn't have
gone on living another day. But all the same, I've got courage. I've decided
once and for all to tear this love out of my heart, roots and all.

I'm getting married to Medvedenko.

To be hopelessly in love, to wait (for something) years on end . . . When
I'm married, there'll be no time to think about love, new cares will grow
over the old. Anyway, it'll be a change.

Women drink more often than you think, a minority drink openly like me . . .
Yes, and they drink vodka and cognac . . . I'm sorry to see you (Trigorin) go.

. . . However, it's none of my business (Konstantin's jealousy concerning
Nina – and his mother).

My schoolmaster . . . loves me terribly, I feel sorry for him. And for his
old mother.

---

* This line is from an earlier draft of the play, which I thought revealing enough to insert in
the accepted text.

I'm very grateful to you for your friendly interest . . . (Inscribe your book) 'To Marya, who doesn't remember where she comes from or why she is living on this earth.'

Act Four

I'm staying here for the night.

Who needs it! (Medvedenko's pity)

One only needs to get hold of oneself and not always be waiting, waiting by the sea for the weather to change . . . If love stirs in one's heart, it has to be removed . . . My husband's been promised a transfer to another district, as soon as we get there, I'll forget it all . . . I'll tear it out of my heart, roots and all.

The most important thing is not to have him always before my eyes. If only my Semyon gets his transfer, believe me, within a month, I'll forget it all. It's all nonsense.

I wish I'd never set eyes on you (Medvedenko).

A long time (I've been married).

3. WHAT SHE SAYS ABOUT OTHERS

Act One

(*Medvedenko*) Your love touches me but I just can't respond. All you do is philosophise and talk about money. In your opinion, there's no greater misfortune than poverty . . . however, you wouldn't understand.

(*To Sorin about Shamraev*) Talk to my father yourself.

(*To Konstantin about Arkadina*) Go inside, Konstantin Gavrilovich, your mother's waiting for you.

(*Dorn*) When people have nothing better to say, they say 'Youth, youth!'

(*Konstantin*) I love Konstantin.

(*Shamraev*) I don't love my father. (*Dorn*) But I feel close to you . . . Somehow I feel with my very soul that I can confide in you. Please help me.

Act Two

(*Polina*) Mother brought me up like the princess who lived in a flower.

(*Konstantin*) His soul is troubled.

(*Konstantin*) When he recites, his eyes glow and his face turns pale. He has a beautiful, sad voice and he looks like a poet.

Act Three

(*Konstantin*) If he'd seriously wounded himself . . .

(*Medvedenko*) I'm getting married. To Medvedenko.

(*Women*) Women think more than you think, a minority of them drink openly like me, most drink in secret. And they drink vodka and cognac.

(*Trigorin*) You're a straightforward man, I'm sorry to see you go.

(*Trigorin, Konstantin, Nina*) There's jealousy, too. However, it's none of my business.

(*Medvedenko and her future mother-in-law*) My schoolmaster's none too bright, but he's kind and he's poor and he loves me terribly. I feel sorry for him. And for his old mother.

(*Trigorin*) I'm very grateful to you for your friendly interest. Do send me your books, autographed, of course.

Act Four

(*Konstantin*) Konstantin Gavrilovich! Konstantin Gavrilovich! No one's here!

(*Sorin, Konstantin*) Every other minute, the old man keeps asking 'Where's Kostya? Where's Kostya?' . . . he can't live without him.

(*Her baby and one of her sisters-in-law*) Matryona will feed it.

(*Medvedenko*) You've become so boring. In the old days, you at least used to do a lot of philosophising, now all you can say is 'baby, home, baby, home . . . ' – one gets nothing else out of you.

(*To Medvedenko about Shamraev*) He will if you ask him (give you a horse to get home).

(*Medvedenko*) Stop pestering me!

(*To Polina about Konstantin*) Leave him alone, Mama . . . Now you've made him angry. Did you have to pester him?

(*Polina*) Who needs it (her pity).

(*Medvedenko*) My husband's been promised a transfer to another district.

(*Medvedenko*) If only my Semyon gets his transfer . . .

(*Konstantin*) The important thing is not always to have him before your eyes.

(*Medvedenko*) Haven't you gone yet?

(*Medvedenko*) I wish I'd never set eyes on you.

(*Konstantin*) It's more convenient for Konstantin to work here. He can go out into the garden when he pleases and think there.

(*Trigorin*) You recognise me.

(*To Shamraev about Medvedenko*) Papa, let my husband have a horse, he has to get home.

(*Shamraev*) Who can deal with you! . . .

4. WHAT OTHERS SAY ABOUT HER

Act One

Medvedenko: Why are you always in black?

You're healthy, your father's not rich but he's comfortable.

My soul and yours have no such point of contact (as Nina's and Konstantin's). I love you, I can't stay at home because of my yearning (for you) . . . I meet with nothing but 'indifferentism' on your side.

Arkadina: Do (fetch him) my dear.

Konstantin: Masha's hunting for me all over the park. Unbearable creature. Leave me alone! Leave me!

Dorn: That's revolting! (*Taking her snuffbox from her and throwing it into the bushes.*) How overwrought they all are . . . How overwrought! . . . But what can I do, my dear child? . . .

Act Two

Arkadina: You are 22.

. . . you sit in one spot all the time, you're not living . . . Would I allow myself to go out of the house, even into the garden, in a house-coat (loose blouse) or with my hair not done? . . . I've never been slovenly, never let myself go like some people . . .

Dorn: She'll go and have a couple of drinks before dinner.

Sorin: The poor thing has no personal happiness.

Dorn: Nonsense, Your Excellency.

Trigorin: Takes snuff and drinks vodka . . . Always wears black, the schoolmaster in love with her . . .

Act Three

Trigorin: I don't see the necessity for that (getting married)?

Haven't we had enough (to drink)?

Act Four

Medvedenko: Let's go home, Masha.

Let's go, Masha. It's pitiful. The baby might be hungry.

It's pitiful. Three nights now he's been without his mother.

Let's go, Masha!

So, you'll come tomorrow?

Polina (*to Konstantin*): Be a little nicer to my Mashenka . . .

She's a nice little thing.

A woman doesn't ask for much, just a kind look now and then.

I feel sorry for you, Mashenka.

My heart bleeds (for you). After all, I see everything, I understand everything.

Medvedenko: There are six in our family now and flour costs seventy roubles.

Trigorin: Marya Ilyinichna!

Married?

PROCEDURAL NOTES

The director and actors need to develop a skill for seeing connections within this information. Each time the actor makes and reads a list, she is shaking the text through a differently perforated sieve to release patterns that are not always noticeable when reading the play linearly.

The actor must read her lists clearly and fluently so that the listeners receive the information vividly. If the lists are long and badly read, the information can become blurred and the exercise dangerously soporific.

When all the lists have been read out and analysed collectively, *you can now start to make reasonable conjectures* about the character. If she says such-and-such about herself and a couple of her facts are such-and-such and other people say such-and-such about her, it is *reasonable to conjecture* that she has such-and-such a tendency or behaves in such-and-such a way. You must eschew adjectives and value judgements. Your conjectures should be in factual sentences and actions, such as 'She argues with her parents', 'She tends to indulge her image of herself'. They are more concrete and more specific than 'She's argumentative and self-indulgent'.

Now you can start to ask more specific questions. What might her super-objective be? What might be her through-line? What, her main Laban effort? What, her inner pulse? Where might her physical centre be? (*see*: LABAN EFFORTS *and* PHYSICAL CENTRES *in the section on* TECHNIQUES

TOWARDS CHARACTERISATION.) You can add as many items here as you find useful, such as: What might her animal be? But when it gets to 'What is her colour' or 'What is her music?', I find these far too subjectively generalised for group discussion. These sorts of images are a private matter for the actor – if they're of any help at all. (I heard of a cast who were asked what vegetables they were!)

Throughout these discussions, the director should keep firm control of proceedings. Some people are not used to discussing things logically or pertinently. If actors give generalised opinions totally unconnected to the facts they've heard – or if their arguments are wildly specious – that should be pointed out, but always with clear reasons. *You want to keep the actors engaged in, not discouraged from, sharing in the process of finding out about each other's characters.*

ANALYSING THE INFORMATION ON MASHA

One of the dangers in dealing with a character is to take her at her own self-evaluation. I've seen many Masha's sentimentalised and indulged, the actor having given her credit for being sensitive and poetic. But this is not true to the facts we have.

The fact that she wears black (an unusual practice for a young woman – Medvedenko's first line bears some evidence of this) suggests that she wishes to draw attention to her premature sense of life being over for her. This implies that she wants to make an impression on others by dramatising herself and her unhappiness. Her offer to Trigorin to use her 'life story' for a book seems to reinforce this and to suggest that she has an over-developed sense of how interesting she is. That she drinks and takes snuff suggests she does so both to ease her pain by numbing herself, and to intensify her dramatised self-image. Snuff-taking, even in fin-de-siècle Russia, was not common practice for young women (Dorn calls it 'Revolting!'). Her neglect of her appearance (note Arkadina's comments on her) implies that she doesn't dare to compete sexually, and that she wants to show her indifference to conventional conduct. So we can reasonably conjecture that she is trying hard to make a strong impression on others of how special she is, how tragic her life is, and that she is, metaphorically, already dead. This is further compounded by her request to Trigorin to inscribe one of his books to her with what sounds like an epitaph, something more suitable for a gravestone.

She twice tries to prove that she can exhibit practical common sense and self-knowledge. The first time, she tells Trigorin that her love for Konstantin is all nonsense and that she must pull herself together and uproot it from her heart by marrying Medvedenko. The second time, after marrying Medvedenko, she tells her mother the same thing. The validity of her statements are undercut by the fact that, two years into the marriage, she is still trying to be near Konstantin as often as possible, even to the neglect of her baby. Her self-delusion is stressed by the telling image that Chekhov has created in Act Four of her still repeating that she must uproot her love, while hugging a pillow and dancing to the waltz Konstantin is playing on the piano in an adjoining room. That her foot goes to sleep is a Chekhovian indication of indulgence, lethargy, even of a self-induced living death.

So from the factual evidence of the text, one can make a very strong case for the likelihood not only that Masha is undoubtedly unhappy but also that she is conducting herself in a ridiculous, self-deluded manner – which is essentially comic.* And she is in no way sensitive, except to her own feelings. Her treatment of Medvedenko is merciless. She clearly hasn't accepted the reality of her decision to marry him. She tries to appear what she is not: tragic, interesting and honest about herself.

From all this, we can now make *an initial and conjectural evaluation* of her character.

CONJECTURES ABOUT MASHA

She is unrealistically fixated on Konstantin. She never gives up her pursuit of him. She might almost be accused of harassment, of stalking him!

She possibly finds some sort of satisfaction from Konstantin's continuous rejection of her; it enhances both the suffering and the tragic self-image. It's possible that she wants to sustain her state of unrequited love!

She sees her life – or wants it to be seen – as already over.

---

* This is an example of a very particular Chekhovian vision that helps to create the richness and complexity of his characters: they are at one and the same time unhappy (tragic) and foolish (comic). That is, they do genuinely suffer emotional pain, but their behaviour in attempting to solve their problems is totally inappropriate, self-indulgent, imperceptive and ultimately ludicrous. This presents a technical challenge for the actor who has both genuinely to identify subjectively with the character's pain while objectively revealing for us the foolishness of her behaviour. Its achievement creates a richly three-dimensional characterisation. Too often, actors stop at the subjectivity and give us a sentimentally self-indulgent, soft reading of the character and none of the edge. Chekhov was both an artist and a doctor!

She uses images of already being dead.

She has assumed an image to draw attention to herself as someone both tragically unhappy and defiant of social conventions.

She tries to show herself as someone who is ultimately realistic about her situation. She assumes a sort of self-irony.

She has given up trying to function or compete on the same terms as most other young women might, by neglecting her appearance.

She is self-indulgent and lethargic.

She has no occupation, so does nothing all day and presumably lies around, drinking, taking snuff and feeling sorry for herself.

She insists that she has a special sensitivity (Konstantin reads and looks like a 'poet', 'it's a thousand times better to go around in rags . . . '), but she is insensitive to others.

She despises her parents, even her mother, whom, ironically, she takes after (Polina displays similar tendencies in a less demonstrative way).

She is clearly unsatisfied with her life.

Her drinking and snuff-taking can give her a momentary sharp sense of being alive. She might at times be drunk.

Her physicality is possibly rather sluggish (drink, inaction, foot going to sleep), a sort of distorted, bloated, warped sensuousness.

We can now translate these conjecture and facts into *more specific acting processes*.

TECHNIQUES TOWARDS CREATING MASHA

Her Super-Objective: to be appreciated as a sensitive, special and suffering figure

Her Through-Line: to pursue Konstantin or, rather, to sustain/keep alive her unreciprocated love for Konstantin

Her Dominant Laban Effort: Wringing (Strong – Flexible – Sustained). This effort's dominant characteristic is self-indulgence, both giving into sensuality and suffering (*see*: LABAN EFFORTS in TECHNIQUES TOWARDS CHARACTERISATION).

*Her Physical Centre:** her stomach

*Her Animal:** a sloth; some marine creature that lies on the seabed; a sea cow; a hippopotamus . . .

Her Inner Pulse: slow, writhing, legato

Some Possible Traits: sighing a lot; heavy, ironical smirking; snorting snuff and brushing away any residual grains; movement redolent of always being slightly under the influence of vodka

It is important to stress that all the above are *reasonable suggestions*. They are, at very least, helpful and practical points of departure to get the actor started on her journey towards the character, and as the work develops, these possibilities can be adjusted and refined, depending on what the actor discovers during subsequent rehearsals.

* The categories of physical centres and animals are subject to the imagination of the actor who has to find out what works for her. The other categories do have a more objective element, though they are by no means irretrievably fixed.

CONTINUING THE PROCESS: THE COMPANY WORK ON THE CHARACTER

When the discussion is over and this list compiled, *the entire cast* work physically on the character for about half an hour. We're now moving from head-work to holistic work. The actors find a space in the room and explore, alone, some aspect of the character that is most available to them from what has been said, whatever has most struck their imaginations. It could be a physical attribute of the character, e.g. how she walks or how she uses her hands. Some might imagine her in a particular situation, either invented or from the text. Some might pursue ideas based on the suggested super-objective or the through-line. Someone else might work on her animal or Laban effort. It's possible to heighten or exaggerate a tendency if that seems relevant. The actors participating in this exercise must remember its purpose (POC) – and therefore theirs – is to share their discoveries with the actor whose role it actually is. It is of no use for actors to curl up in a corner for half an hour, trying to feel or 'think' themselves into the character, whilst expressing absolutely nothing. *The actors' thoughts and feelings must be translated in behaviour.* That behaviour should never be demonstrated but arrived at through a committed and truthful process. The actors should not work towards a preconceived idea (result), but explore a possibility. If an actor's initial choice takes them down a cul-de-sac, they should turn around and try another avenue. An actor must not feel under any obligation to come up with something, no matter what. If nothing comes, nothing comes. And there's no disgrace in that. However, I've never known this to be the case. Usually, actors love having the chance to play other actors' characters. They can have the creative 'fun' without any of the responsibility!

The actor whose role it is should start working like the rest, then gradually shift into a watching mode and make notes of anything that strikes her from what the others are exploring.

At the end of this session, the rest of the actors can report on any realisations or possible insights they've just experienced that have not so far been mentioned. Someone might say they found Masha very lonely. Or describe how her drinking sends her into an absolute torpor, or – the opposite – makes her feel optimistic about her chances with Konstantin.

The actor in question makes a note of what the others say. She is not obliged to use any of these suggestions, but the possible insights are there if she wants them. She is acquiring a rich dossier on her character, to which not just one, but several people's imaginations have contributed. Nothing has been set in stone. Even the choice of super-objective is open to change and adjustment as the work proceeds. What it *does* mean is that, even from the first day of rehearsal, the actor has a collection of reasonable starting points on which to begin specific and concrete work. Otherwise, actors can drift through rehearsals, unwilling or unable to commit themselves to any choice concerning their character. (Actors often find it easier to identify with characters other than their own!) What is important: all the material stems from a thorough distillation of the text and a sharp evaluation of it. So we have moved from fact to reasonable conjecture, and from reasonable conjecture to imaginative suggestion. It is important that the director delicately checks any suggestions that seem to fly wildly in the face of the facts and have no basis in the text.

ADDITIONAL BENEFITS

There are valuable bonuses to this work. For however many days it takes, the company is hearing the text over and over again, hearing their own characters' dialogue repeated to them in different selections and within different frames. As we move through the *dramatis personae*, they will start to see thematic connections between the characters, the similarities or counterpoint of their collective super-objectives and through-lines. An actor once told me, after just four days rehearsing in this way, that he already knew so much, he felt he'd been working on the play for a month.

So not only are the actors learning about their characters, they're also learning about the play in its entirety. And they're learning this in an organic fashion, without great pronouncements and dissertations. *What's more, they are also being welded as an ensemble, sharing in every step of each other's work.*

CHARACTER SEQUENCE

The initial work on all the characters will take one or two weeks depending on the number of roles and the amount of daily time allotted to character work. Directors, don't get too anxious about those actors whose characters get dealt with last. The work on the other actors' roles will be spilling over and feeding into their preliminary thoughts about their own roles. How you select the sequence in which the characters are dealt with will depend on different factors. If you're working with actors who know the process and have large parts, they can probably wait until quite far along in the sequence, as they'll already be able to do some of the work ahead of time, at least in their heads. Actors with small roles shouldn't be left until last as that will only heighten their sense of having less to do than the others. Give them a little bit of status by placing them strategically in the sequence. If you feel that certain roles will reveal most effectively to the company how enlightening this work can be, place them first. There are no rules for this matter, only your judgement. Evaluate each situation afresh.

FROM CHARACTER TO THEME

When you've completed this initial work on all the characters, you are ready to discuss the play and its themes in more detail. You can start to talk more concretely about your ideas for the production. By now, the actors will know enough about the play to be able to take those ideas on board. They are equipped with a lot of evidence to support and make sense of what you have to say. One of the firmest ways into an analysis of the play is to see what thematic links there are between the characters. In a well-written play, the accumulated super-objectives of the characters should point to the super-objective of the play, its overall thematic movement. What all the characters in *The Seagull* have in common (except Polina) is their relationship to art, that is to say, the way they manipulate art to support their sense of themselves. Another aspect of this is that the characters try to transform their failed lives into dramatised self-portraits. They present their failures as interesting autobiographies that beg for understanding, sympathy and, best of all, refutation. Sorin, Trigorin, Medvedenko, Dorn – and Konstantin for the first three acts – give performances of themselves as 'characters'. Arkadina, Masha, Shamraev and Polina do the same, but without any acknowledgement of failure, rather giving performances of themselves as misunderstood and under-appreciated. You could say that the theme of the play is how people use art for their own needs – to give themselves identity or status and to compensate for their sense of failure in life. Only Nina, at the end of the play, has come to live with art on its own terms rather than manipulating it for her own aggrandisement.

THE CHARACTERS' RELATIONSHIP TO ART

Arkadina is an actress.

Nina becomes an actress.

Trigorin is a novelist.

Konstantin writes plays and becomes a published short-story writer.

Sorin talks about his inactivated ambition to become a writer.

Dorn talks of the imagined satisfaction of being an artist – and sympathises with Konstantin's artistic efforts.

Medvedenko tries to impress people by dropping the names of philosophers.

Masha aligns herself with poetic sensitivity, i.e. with Konstantin.

Shamraev refers to cheap, melodramatic performers from the past and plays the role of Arkadina's devoted admirer.

Polina doesn't relate to art except in a sentimental reference to Konstantin's piano-playing.

THE CHARACTERS' CREATION OF SELF-IMAGE

Trigorin presents himself as an essentially simple man, longing to do nothing more than go fishing, exhausted by the tyrannous need to keep writing, while acknowledging he'll never be ranked with Tolstoy, Turgenev or Zola.

Sorin presents himself as a figure of fun to soften his failed ambitions in life.

Medvedenko presents himself as a victim of circumstances by advertising all his lacks and failures in life.

Dorn presents himself as a man without any illusions about the failure of his life, whose professional function is to strip them away from any of the others foolish enough to cling to theirs.

Konstantin presents himself as a misunderstood talent, if not genius, for the first three acts of the play. In the last act he slowly comes to accept the truth.

These five either want to be assured their lives were not wasted or that they were not to blame for their failures; even better, they want a total refutation of their performed self-image. They operate on what I call the '*dressing-room*' principle: after a performance, before visitors backstage have a chance to open their mouths and tell the actors what they thought of their performances, the actors get in first with 'Why did you come tonight? I was terrible!' Then their guests are almost obliged to insist, 'No, no, on the contrary, you were wonderful!' ('No, no, you *are* a great writer' – that's one of the reasons why Trigorin is attracted to Nina: she's a fan, she boosts his ego.)

Arkadina presents herself as a popular, successful and eternally youthful actress, always a slave to the demands of her career, but frequently under-appreciated and misjudged.

Masha presents herself as one of the walking dead, as someone whose sensitivity has been cruelly punished by being born to coarse and stupid parents and doomed to suffer an unreciprocated love.

Shamraev presents himself as the sole saviour of the estate, using a lot of bluster to cover up both his possible incompetence and fiddling of the books.

Polina presents herself as a suffering woman who has led an unhappy life.

These four want their self-images reinforced and to be accepted on these terms.

Nina: Initially, she doesn't so much present herself as exploit her charm and youthful eagerness to be accepted as a future actress.

Ultimately, she no longer presents any image but honestly reveals herself as someone who has come to terms with the harshness of life and her struggle to become an actress. *She is the only adult in the play, the only one who grows up and faces life directly.* In the first three acts, she is as deluded as all the other characters, blinded by the idea of celebrity. She almost passes out with the excitement at the thought of one day being famous. In the subsequent two years, she learns what life is really like: she survives running away to Moscow, having an affair and a child with Trigorin, being abandoned by him, the death of the child, her family's rejection, the coarseness of some men in the theatres she tours to, her initial incompetence as an actress and, finally, a breakdown from which she emerges stripped of all illusion – and finds a sort of redemption in beginning to be a true actress. She succeeds in learning to cope with life. *This, in part, is why the play is a comedy.*

A Note on Avoiding Actor-Avoidance

This approach to character from the lists solves several problems of actor-avoidance. first, it gets rid of those tiresomely unproductive conversations in which the actor declares, 'My character would never say that' (well, the playwright thinks differently), 'My character would never lose her temper', 'My character would never feel that.' There is no such thing as never. Any character has the potential to express the entire range of human emotion. It is only an actor's fear of moving into possible areas of emotional discomfort that denies this.

This approach also defuses the avoidance strategy of an actor who informs you, 'I can't play with my partner till I have my character.' When will *that* be? When *will* you have your character? Tomorrow? Next week sometime? When you get your costume? On the first night? Actors never 'have' their character. They're always working towards it. But you discover much about your character *through* interaction with your partners. Those actors who don't trust working on the floor with their colleagues are inclined to construct their roles secretly at home until that day – usually late in rehearsal, often not till they *do* have their costume – when they produce their character fully grown as well as fully clad, but without any of the nourishment and natural growth that comes through organic interplay with the rest of the company. Their character is usually one-dimensional and inflexible.

Finally, this way of working eliminates any actor-fantasies about *how they would like to play the character* or *what they would like to think the character is*, when such wishes clearly bear no relation to the text. Once the initial session with the lists has taken place, you'll find little need for further discussion of characterisation. The actors have all the information necessary at their disposal, and where they take it is up to their particular talents and insights.

Character Development

SOLO ÉTUDES IN CHARACTER

Once all the character lists have been dealt with, you can proceed to the next stage of work. This is to give the actors space and time to absorb and shape the mass of information they've gleaned from the preceding process. I try, daily, for at least the following three or four weeks, to give the actors up to an hour each day to concentrate on the gradual embodiment of their roles through a series of études, that is, small character studies or exercises. For some sessions, I might specify what they should work on, for example, their LABAN, their super-objectives or some other aspect of their physical life. If the characters in the play are involved in physical work, I might have them spend time doing that work, either with props, or in mime. At a later stage, I might ask them to work on that aspect of the character that seems furthest from them or of which they're most 'afraid'. I might ask them, also much later along the road, to imagine their characters in the most painful situation they can. Other sessions I leave open for the actors to work on whatever seems important to them at that moment. All this work is separate from work on the text. (If you think actors are working on a scene from the play in this session, mouthing the text, stop them from doing so; they're in danger of shaping results. The point of separating out the work is to explore the character, emancipated from the constraints of the text.) The actors work *on their own* in their own space.

Throughout these sessions, the director is a silent observer. You're getting to know how the actors work, in which direction they're taking the character, how their imaginations function, and so forth. This is a huge learning time for you. If you see choices being made in these sessions that make you uneasy, or you feel are just plain wrong, I advise you not to leap in too quickly to interfere. The actors are on a journey, and where they are now may be far from where they're headed. Checking too soon the actors' work (which is, after all, exploratory) may inhibit them from taking risks; it might even quash their imagination entirely. They may well start to second-guess choices they think will gain your approval. Patience is a virtue that a director must develop working through a process. However, if, after a reasonable period of time, you see the same worrying choices becoming increasingly insistent, then you can suggest that the actor is veering off-course. But you'll have to offer clear and objective reasons for your opinions. *Just saying you don't like something, or that it's wrong, is unhelpful, if not destructive.*

During later character sessions, you can approach actors and discuss quietly and briefly with them things you feel they should develop, things they might discard, things that have been neglected . . . You might have sessions where you specify for each actor an individual area of characterisation they need to investigate more thoroughly.

Again, this is a process and a journey and you must not expect polish or finish. A characterisation is never finished, not even by the last performance. This work pays off as, gradually and seamlessly, it blends into the work on text.

GROUP ÉTUDES IN CHARACTER

Later in rehearsal, when you feel that the characters have become more securely rooted, you can set up improvisations in which, preferably, they are not required to talk. (It's almost impossible for actors to improvise in the style and language of the original text with any conviction. Their language tends to remove them far from the reality they're trying to achieve.) If the play lends itself to such, you can set up études in which a family is preparing a routine meal, or a group is doing a routine job where any verbal communication can remain at the most rudimentary. This doesn't mean that they can't communicate by any other means. For example, I might suggest that the characters of *The Seagull* go to sit at the edge of the lake in the late afternoon after a heavy meal, when they're absorbed in their own preoccupations and feel no need to talk. The actors will find lots of ways to reveal aspects of character and relationships, and they'll have active time to broaden their thoughts about each other outside the frame of the play itself. Even without conversation, they can pursue objectives and play actions in the way they relate physically and spatially to one another.

HOT–SEATING

This is a technique in which the rest of the cast fire questions at the actor about her role. She can reply either as herself, talking about her character in the third person, or as the character, replying in the first person; or alternating both. The actor is perfectly within her rights to say, 'I don't know.' The session can reveal to the actor the areas in which she is secure and those about which she may not have thought at all. (Be careful that the questions don't become pointlessly 'scattergun'. Some questioners can get carried away by these sessions, asking Lady Macbeth how often she masturbates!)

TALKING THE CHARACTER

This is a process in which the actor, in front of her colleagues, talks about her character, trying as much as possible *to act out and physically fulfil what she's describing*. She can proceed in any sequence she wishes: autobiography, physical description, relationships, moving between aspects of her character as the process suggests to her. She should keep going, freely associating, so that what she eventually says and does will come more from impulse than conscious decision; she might then say and do things in our presence that have only just occurred to her. She should also be commenting on and editing her work as she shows it to us, e.g. 'I think she's intelligent, I mean *she* thinks she is intelligent, she's probably rather stupid, not stupid exactly but unable to see beyond her own needs because she probably indulges herself.' 'I think she lies around like this (demonstrates); well, no, more like this (changes her demonstration).' It's a challenging exercise; the actor has to get beyond initial self-consciousness and carefulness till she is inventively freewheeling with great abandon. It can be amazingly productive, and encourages the actor to realise and concretise what may have just been vague or unstructured ideas hovering in the back of her mind.

TELLING THE CHARACTER'S STORY

In this, once more in front of her colleagues, the actor tells her character's entire story, such as she knows it, from whatever is the earliest pre-action information the playwright has supplied, then describing what she does within a scene and also what she does between an exit and her next entrance. This last will be a mixture of whatever facts are available and what is conjectural; it does *not* require elaboration, just what is sufficient to get her logically and reasonably from exit A to entrance B. This should be done in the third person and is factual and objective, with occasional conjectures to flesh out the narrative. Its purpose is to ensure that the actor is clear about what happens to her.

For example: Masha, after setting up her background and backstory (she lives on the estate because her father is the estate manager; Medvedenko wants to marry her and she is in love with Konstantin . . .) might narrate her story in the first act something like this:

The household has just had dinner and she's managed to sneak a couple of shots of vodka. Medvedenko has asked her to take a walk with him, and having no reason to refuse, she agrees, planning to ensure their walk leads them towards the edge of the lake where Konstantin has built his temporary stage. She wants to be in touch with what he's doing and let him see how much his work matters to her. She enters with Medvedenko, who asks her why she wears black. He is so insensitive that he can't understand her when she talks about her unhappiness; he only see things in terms of financial happiness. She starts to debate with him that there are other things more important than money, but gives up, believing it will be quite pointless. He yet again tells her how much he loves her and wants to marry her, but she explains she cannot reciprocate his feelings. Konstantin and his uncle, Sorin, arrive. Konstantin asks them, rather brusquely to leave the vicinity of his stage as he wants to get things prepared for the performance in private. As she starts to leave, Sorin requests that she ask her father to stop the dogs barking all night. Upset by Konstantin's dismissal and determined to have as little as possible to do with her father, whom she finds coarse, she snaps at him that she has no intention of doing so. She and Medvedenko leave and, walking towards the house, meet up with the rest of the party on their way to the performance. This gives her the excuse to

join the group and return to the stage almost immediately. When
they take their seats, she tries to position herself where Konstantin
can observe her watching his play with great intensity . . . She
suffers for him when some of the audience talk while the play is
in progress. When, in a rage, he stops the play and then runs off
in tears, she offers to go and find him for his mother, Arkadina.
She runs off, calling his name. Konstantin avoids her and,
whenever he hears or sees her getting near, runs away from her.
She eventually returns to the stage where she finds him deep in
conversation with Dr Dorn. She delivers Arkadina's message that
she wants to see him. He yells at her to leave him alone and runs
off again. Dorn makes some banal generalisation about young
people that makes her snap that when people have nothing better
to say, they always say 'Youth, youth!' She starts to take some
snuff, but the doctor grabs the snuffbox and throws it into the
bushes stating that it's a disgusting habit. She suddenly burst into
tears, throws herself into his arms and confesses how desperately
she's in love with Konstantin and begs for help. Dorn can offer
her no advice or comfort and rhetorically asks her what she thinks
he could possibly do about it.

Techniques Towards Characterisation

There are many transformational techniques to help actors towards character-isation. Here are some that I regularly make use of. Several are the creations of others and you can find a fuller and more detailed description of them from their own writings. So I will merely sketch out their purpose and my use of them. I've found them to be helpful as alternative languages or tools to help the actor to-wards the creation of a role, especially in breaking them of patterns and ingrained habits. These techniques may not all work for every role or every play and some may stimulate some actors' imaginations more than others. But they're useful for actors to know, available as part of their battery of technical skills and as aids to creative work. They provide them with stimulation from different directions, a varied palette from which they can draw in developing a character. Essentially, they broaden the range of an actor's expressiveness. They are all initiated by physical work – from the outside in. They are the means to an end, *not* an end in themselves, and are *only useful inasmuch as they help an actor.*

Laban Efforts

Efforts are part of a much larger scheme of movement conceived by Rudolf Laban. I originally learnt about them from Philip Hedley, via E15 Drama School. I've used them for a good forty years and, each time I do so, I learn some new application for them. It's likely that during this period, they've shifted somewhat from Laban's original intentions; nevertheless, I offer my version of them for what they're worth.

What attracts me to efforts is that they're holistic: starting from the physical they lead to the mental and emotional. By moving in particular and different ways, actors will also *think* and *feel* differently. *Laban defined movement as the way in which we relate to the world.* I like this, too; it implies a focus both on relationships and intentions – and reinforces the system of actions and objectives.

THE INGREDIENTS OF LABAN

Laban analysed a movement as possessing three pairs of opposing elements or qualities:

Light or Strong

Direct or Flexible

Sustained or Broken

Some practitioners argue about what names they should be given and become very proprietary about the ones they've been taught. But, finally, these are only a means of identification and not literal descriptions, each element having many implications and applications. They could as usefully be called A, B, C, D, E & F. So avoid getting hung up on language and concentrate on what these elements actually do.

Efforts can only be understood by being fully explored physically. What follows is merely general guidance. There are several books available on Laban's work; ideally, you should study it with a Laban teacher.

DEFINING THE ELEMENTS

Light implies functioning with ease, without effort; there is no resistance to overcome, no barriers to break through; freedom from gravity, with all energy inclining upwards; helpful images might be: suspension aloft by balloons or feathers or wings; or by the support of some imaginary cloud-substance beneath your armpits, between your legs and under your feet.

Strong implies functioning at some level of intensity, there is always resistance to be overcome; a barrier to break through; a useful image is to imagine that you're moving through an environment in which the atmosphere around you is a substance of some density (like mud or sand) against which you have to apply a certain amount of pressure; what degree of pressure is for the actor to explore.

Direct implies that you have total focus and sense of purpose; you know what you want, you impose yourself on the world, you initiate, you give, you lead, you aim at what you want and know where you are going; *you make things happen.*

Flexible implies that you have no focus or purpose but are totally available, accessible, vulnerable, open to be affected, to be moved by impulses, energies and thoughts both from within yourself and from outside you; you receive, take in, absorb, follow; *you allow things to happen to you.*

Sustained implies continuous unbroken movement and energy, flowing seamlessly from one physical state to another; movement tends to be curved, rounded and soft; an image of underwater plants endlessly swaying in varying currents and tides may be helpful; there is nothing abrupt. It tends to be slow.

Broken implies constantly renewed energy, tending to be angular, abrupt, fast with the impulse refreshed from second to second; the image of any competitive sport is useful: boxing, tennis, soccer . . .

Technically, *Light* and *Strong* deal with *Weight*.* This does not have anything to do with personal avoirdupois (many heavy people can move with extreme lightness). It is more about relative levels of intensity and gravitational pull.

Technically, *Direct* and *Flexible* have to do with *Space*, how you move in it and relate to it directionally.

Technically, *Sustained* and *Broken* have to do with *Time* (tempo/speed).

THE EFFORTS

These three pairs of elements in different combinations create Eight Archetypal Efforts (the above warning about names applies here, too):

Light/Flexible/Sustained = Floating
Light/Flexible/Broken = Flicking
Light/Direct/Sustained = Gliding
Light/Direct/Broken = Dabbing
Strong/Flexible/Sustained = Wringing
Strong/Flexible/Broken = Slashing
Strong/Direct/Sustained = Pressing
Strong/Direct/Broken = Thrusting/Punching

All eight efforts are of equal value and *together make up the complete human potential of ways in which we function.* No one effort is better than another. Each effort has what one might call its positive and its negative qualities. We're all capable of experiencing *all of them*, and, in fact, to be well rounded, we should do so as we go about our lives. But our upbringing may unconsciously lead us to favour some at the expense of others. Often when actors start working on efforts, they find some uncomfortable, even unbearable; some make them feel constricted, others, out of control. Sometimes women baulk at thrusting, and men at floating; serious-minded people often become irritated by flicking. Eventually, by persevering with them, all actors will be able to break free from the trap of physical habits and patterns they have unconsciously developed over the years. They will now have potential access to a total range of expression and experience.

---

* One definition about which I do side with the word-police: don't be tempted to use '*Heavy*' for '*Strong*'. Heavy has a totally negative connotation and is not conducive to creativity.

Here is some general guidance to their tendencies. I hesitated to put down this list as it describes results, tells you what to expect, what to look for, rather than allowing you to make the discovery for yourself. However, I felt I should give some suggestion of the way they work, so I outline them here *with the serious proviso* that when you work on them for the first time, you dismiss from your mind any of these depictions and try not to anticipate where the physical work will lead you. Allow your body to inform you. With efforts, I've found, it's always possible to find fresh connections and areas of experience.

THEIR TENDENCIES

Floating tends to dream-states, meditation, spirituality, unworldliness, artistic creativity; to avoidance, denial; it is not about doing; possibly: religious people, daydreamers, 'poets', artists, people unconcerned with material values, impractical people; people avoiding any unpleasantness or the practical realities of life . . .

Flicking tends to playfulness, light-heartedness, permission to be silly; to superficiality, vanity, lack of concentration, fecklessness; possibly: party-goers, flirts, jokers, people having fun; people absorbed by their appearance, people who refuse to take responsibility . . .

Gliding tends to poise, confidence, elegance, wisdom, calmness, warmth, ability to advise; to snobbishness, arrogance, coolness, a sense of superiority; possibly: aristocrats, diplomats, people who have arrived and feel no need to strive, people born into money and social standing; possibly therapists, priests, advisors, counsellors; show-offs (models, poseurs . . .)

Dabbing tends to sociability, humour, extreme manual dexterity, multi-tasking, getting things done with ease, getting on with the daily aspects of life; lack of profundity or ambition; possibly: excellent PAs, gifted technicians, mothers of large families . . .

Wringing tends to indulgence; sensuality, giving in to pleasure in all sensory experiences (sex, food, fragrance, scenery . . .); giving in to anxiety, worry, depression; it is non-achieving; possibly: sensualists, gourmets, vacationers; the anally obsessive, the insecure, all worriers, brooders . . .

Slashing tends to abandon; total letting go, daring, recklessness, intense letting off steam; to paranoia, panic, unfocused violence and aggression; possibly: daredevils, adventurers, risk-takers (bungee-jumpers); wild hedonists; psychopaths, people with low self-esteem, people with grudges against the world . . .

(Note: Slashing is an exhausting effort and shouldn't be exercised for too long at any one time.)

Pressing tends to meticulousness, loyalty, thoroughness, reliability, seriousness; stubbornness, inflexibility, lack of imagination, lack of humour; possibly: excellent seconds-in-command, draftsmen, model-makers, perfectionists, people who go into great detail; bureaucrats, 'jobsworths', people who take everything literally, people who go by the book, follow the rules . . .

Thrusting tends to ambition, achieving, aspiring, acquiring, moving-and-shaking, building, creating, managing, alertness, enterprise, initiative, practicality; aggressiveness, competitiveness, acquisitiveness, ruthlessness; possibly: entrepreneurs, big business people, politicians, sports persons, stars, rulers, CEOs; dictators, conquerors, careerists, bullies . . .

Totally opposing pairs of efforts complement each other and, in a way, create a whole:

Dabbing/Wringing: coping/indulging
Floating/Thrusting: dreaming/achieving
Gliding/Slashing: in control/out of control
Flicking/Pressing: playful and irresponsible/serious and responsible

Note: *each effort has innumerable applications and implications.* Never, intellectually, try to confine them within boxes. Never limit them to a series of formulas. They have tendencies such as the ones I've described, but understand that these *are only tendencies.* They cover wide areas of experience and depending on the context, may move into unexpected areas and provide surprising possibilities.

THEIR CENTRES

Each effort has its ideal centre. This is their hierarchy, from high to low:

Floating: as high above the head and into the sky as you wish to imagine
Flicking: around the eyes and ears
Dabbing: mouth, jaw, shoulders (and by extension, hands)
Gliding: the centre of the base of the sternum, the chest
Thrusting: the solar plexus (the most centred effort)
  (Note: Thrusting is balanced between head and gut which allows great flexibility and initiative)
Wringing: stomach, especially where the ulcers grow
Slashing: hips, genitals, lower stomach
Pressing: as close to the ground as possible

The four *strong* efforts, with their lower centres, tend to be more engaged with passion, intensity, strong feelings.

The four *light* efforts, with their higher centres, tend to be more involved with the intellect, the spirit and feelings of sensitivity.

The four *direct* efforts are active and achieving.

The four *flexible* efforts are not doers or achievers, and are more involved with feeling, sensing, absorbing, experiencing and reflecting.

The four *broken* efforts allow for quicker adjustments and adaptations.

The four *sustained* efforts tend to be more cautious or careful.

The efforts can only be understood by initially being explored physically. The total involvement and commitment of the actor's body is the only way to lead to a change of attitude and feeling.

PRACTICAL WORK ON EFFORTS

To start with, you should work non-realistically, exploring all types of movement: rolling, circling, bouncing, crawling, moving sideways, backwards as well as forwards, on your knees, on your toes, low on the ground, high in the air, supine, prostrate . . . making sure that the whole body is firmly engaged, with special attention to the spine.

You should begin with the individual elements (*light, etc.*) until you understand them 'in your body' and only then begin to combine them, first in pairs, then in their full effort threesomes. It will take some time to learn how to blend them together. Each element must be balanced against the others, e.g. in thrusting, *strong, direct* and *broken* must each be fully and *equally* executed. (For example, take care that *sustained* blending with *light* doesn't render it *strong.*) No one element should dominate to the dilution of the other two. Each element should be carried out with total commitment to its purest essence. For instance, if working on *direct*, ensure that you discover what it really means to be *totally* focused, alert and aware of everything around you. *Work with intensity but never with strain.*

You should imagine that your stomach, breathing, brain, eyes are all equally engaged in the effort. Once you have mastered the efforts physically, you'll start to feel, think and see the world around you differently. With each new effort you learn, you'll begin to understand how totally it transforms your whole organism. For example, in moving from floating to thrusting, its total opposite, you should experience a one-hundred-per-cent change in your whole sense of yourself and way of functioning.

Fluency with efforts will gradually release you from the trap of largely unconscious physical patterns and habits. If you've grown up to feel comfortable and natural being, say, *light* or *sustained*, you're likely to have drawn all your characterisations towards those comfort zones. You may probably find it difficult, uncomfortable or even unnatural to express what is *strong* or *broken*. But with time, these elements will become part of your expressive repertoire. When you have learnt and absorbed all eight arche-types, you will have potential access to a total range of human expression.

IMPROVISATIONS WITH EFFORTS

Initially, the actors work on their own. Only, later, when they have some skill and understanding, should they start working together in different combinations. Here are a couple of improvisations.

AN EXERCISE IN PAIRS

The two actors choose different efforts and then – physically and *not* realistically (no speech) – try to relate to each other. In order to cope with each other, the actors may have to give up their pure effort and move through other efforts in order to adjust to their partner. They should, of course, try to sustain their personal effort as much as they possibly can. They may find that, counter-intuitively, the less likely of the pair may end up being the dominant one. This is a non-realistic, totally physical exercise. *The efforts must be used flexibly and imaginatively.*

A GROUP EXERCISE IN THREE STAGES

1. The actors all work individually on the same effort.

2. They each develop a character from that effort. This needs time.

3. Once established, their characters come together in a realistic impro-visation, a recognisable situation, in which they can explore and further develop their characterisations through action (for example, the meeting of a committee to discuss a new policy for their organisation . . .).

VARIATIONS ON THE ABOVE

A: Each actor makes their own choice of effort.

B: The director assigns a different effort to each actor.

Once a company has developed the language of efforts, it will find it quite easy to invent improvisations to explore them further.

WORKING WITH MORE THAN ONE EFFORT AT A TIME

1. SIMULTANEOUS DIFFERENT INNER AND OUTER EFFORTS

It is possible to use, simultaneously, conflicting inner and outer efforts: what we're experiencing on the inside and what we're expressing on the outside – how we really feel and how we want to be seen, *an inner state* and *an outer image*. This, of course, is how we lead much of our lives, hiding what we really feel and think and trying to project something quite different to the world. Solyony in *The Three Sisters* is essentially a slasher (paranoid, suspicious, insecure, dangerously aggressive) but tries to present himself as its complete opposite, a glider (cool, knowing, poised, detached). We are frequently wringing on the inside but covering it, or trying to cover it, with a different effort, possibly dabbing. This can happen both deliberately, knowing what we're trying to present, and unconsciously, when we instinctively, spontaneously, assume an image. Note that if, for example, you're trying to be a dabber (sociable, amenable, free of problems), the exact opposite of the worrying and anxious wringer you are trying to hide, the quality of the dabbing will be very different from dabbing executed on its own, without needing to disguise anything. This double-effort technique can be very useful for comedy if the struggle between the two efforts is not resolved and the inner effort keeps breaking through the outer effort. It can also create a disturbing, unsettling, dangerous atmosphere; for instance, a slasher lurking beneath a glider, as with Solyony.

2. SIMULTANEOUS DIFFERENT EFFORTS IN DIFFERENT PARTS OF THE BODY

It is also possible, technically, with practice, for different parts of the body to express themselves simultaneously with different efforts: e.g. a foot tapping (flicking) while the upper body elegantly reclines (gliding). Maybe this would 'read' as the character trying to appear at ease while actually distracted. Isolating one part of the body to express something quite different from the rest of one's physicality can be a usefully subtle revelation of psychology. This might occur spontaneously when working with conflicting inner and outer efforts.

VARYING THE PURITY OF AN EFFORT

It is possible to create variations on the eight basic archetypes: imagine floaters of different degrees of lightness, pressers of different degrees of strength. One can visualise a heavy-ish dabber, a light-ish wringer, a slow-ish thruster, and so forth. Once actors know an effort at its purest, they can play around with the composition of the elements that comprise it. *Efforts are there to be used imaginatively, flexibly.*

EFFECTING CHANGE WITHOUT PHYSICALISATION

Once the efforts in their purest form have been mastered by total physical commitment, actors will find they are able to change from one effort to another simply by thinking or imagining themselves into it – with no further need to physicalise, certainly not in any extreme form. It's something like clicking a switch in your mind. While appearing to be totally still, you are internally changing your entire organism; energy, focus, pulse, dynamic, centre . . . *This is probably the most useful, practical application of efforts for actors.* An actor can create an exciting and unexpected transformation in the atmosphere of a scene by an instant inner change of effort. Imagine a sudden shift of beat from floating to slashing.

Efforts and Characterisation

Efforts can help towards the construction of character. Although actors should endow their character with the possibility of all eight efforts, there is usually one that is clearly dominant – and it is a useful way for them to break patterns and find a way to get in touch with a person who functions very differently from themselves. Masha, in *The Seagull* for example, is largely a wringer, indulging in emotions and fantasies, never solving problems, not actually accomplishing anything in life. Arkadina is clearly a thruster. Dorn is probably a glider. It's useful to try to identify a character's main effort. In high farce, it's possible to build an entire characterisation from one effort. For example, in Gogol's *The Government Inspector*, the airhead Khlestakov, who is mistakenly taken for the inspector, might be totally created through flicking.

Efforts and Scene Work

Efforts are also useful for scene work. If a scene or speech is not working satisfactorily, applying some of the techniques of Laban efforts (e.g. playing less directly or more strongly, dabbing rather than pressing) may well solve the problem.

Reminder

Efforts are *tools* for stimulating the actor's creativity and for problem-solving in scenes, speeches or matters of characterisation. They do not represent a rigid formula that has to be 'got right'. They are there for actors to play with and work with. All these techniques require skill. To get their full benefit, actors must develop those skills. They should be used with flexibility and imagination. *Like all the techniques in this section, efforts are a means to an end, not an end in themselves.*

Psychological Gestures

In Oslo, there is a park filled with the sculpture of the artist, Gustav Vigeland.[*] His life work was creating there, in bronze and stone, human beings in all our familiar experiences from joy to grief, from childhood to old age. Some of his sculptures are carved in granite and slightly larger than life. They brilliantly capture essential, recognisable moments in our lives. The physicality of his men, women and children express entirely what they are feeling and thinking. I found them deeply moving and used to go and stand by them in the twilight, as the park was emptying, just before closing time. Their shapes emanated a physical energy and a intense, specific emotional state. I think they represent wonderful examples of psychological gestures.

> The psychological gesture is a technique conceived by Michael Chekhov. I think it is somewhat a misnomer, having more to do with the archetypal than the psychological. The purpose is to find the total physical 'gesture' incorporating the whole body that expresses the super-objective of the character. It must stem from a natural, human impulse to move, not an intellectually conceived physical contrivance with little connection to recognisable behaviour. But it *is* heightened. It is totally committed. It has intensity and although it's real and natural, it doesn't remain in everyday actuality but is closer to the sorts of 'gestures' that our bodies make at peaks of extreme emotions or situations; how people might move *in extremis*, when they've abandoned all caution and allowed their whole being to be totally given over to the expression of a need. For example, if your super-objective is *to avoid life's pain*, your psychological gesture might be to roll yourself up tightly into an embryonic ball; or, if it's *to embrace all that life has to offer*, your psychological gesture, in contrast, might be a running forward motion with arms wide open, reaching out. If you roll yourself up into an embryonic ball and sustain that position

[*] It is, in fact, called the Vigeland Sculpture Park!

for a while, you will find, when you have to unroll and stand up, that this physicality has created in you sensations of anxiety, fear, lack of confidence and vulnerability. The gesture of spreading wide your arms, quite the opposite, will give you feelings of great confidence, and you will find your energy filling the space you inhabit.

It is not an easy exercise; it can be hard to find the right gesture. The slightest deviation in the angle of an arm, the twist of a wrist, the distance apart of your feet can change the whole sensation and say something other than you intended. But once found and exercised, it will engender a very strong emotion in the actor – and it is this sort of emotion that I discussed (*see*: EMOTION – TWO LEVELS OF EMOTION) as the *long-term* emotional ground bass which leads towards a deep transformation of actors, in which they replace their own inner patterns of thinking, seeing, feeling with those of the character. Technically, it is a matter of repeating the shape with the utmost commitment until the inner sensations are invoked. To find the way into the technique, it might be helpful, at the start, to repeat *sotto voce* the words of the super-objective: 'I want to be loved, I want to be loved . . . ', 'I want to belong somewhere, I want to belong . . . '; it's possible that the yearning and longing of those words may move the body towards some pertinent physicality. As with the Laban efforts, once actors have firmly established a psychological gesture, it is sufficient for them *merely to imagine themselves in that particular shape/gesture* for the feelings and attitudes induced by it to be evoked in them.

———

Physical Centres

The physical centre, also created by Michael Chekhov, is that part of their characters' bodies from which actors imagine their energy might generate. I must stress that this is a totally imaginary technique; there are no objectively correct choices, and whether a particular choice works for an actor is its only criterion. Directors can make suggestions, but only actors can know whether it stimulates their imaginations.

Physical centres can be endowed with any quality whatsoever: hot, soggy, gritty, vibrating, feathery . . . They can be both within the body or outside it. They could possibly be within another character. Because of Konstantin's fixation on his mother, his physical centre might be within Arkadina. Masha's might be churning away inside her stomach. Irina, in *The Three Sisters*, might find hers outside her body, above and before her, drawing her towards some idealised future. Pianists' physical centres might be in their hands; labourers' in their backs. Sometimes the way to explore this technique is for the actor to imagine that the part of the body they've chosen is exaggeratedly large as in a caricature or cartoon (e.g. Nixon's nose, Blair's ears). Work on physical centres can be particularly helpful for bold comic characterisations – though not exclusively so by any means.

Again, by changing the way you use your body, a physical centre can affect the way you think and feel.

———

Inner Pulse

Another way actors can make a fundamental change to their whole being is by exploring variations in rhythm, tempo and dynamic. We all have a basic pulse, distinctive to ourselves, with which we normally conduct our lives, unless we're thrown into a heightened situation that temporarily changes it. We are very comfortable with this pulse; it's hard to let go of it and lose that natural comfort. We all know people whose energy is very high, fast and restless; and those whose energy is low, slow and who tend to take their time over the simplest actions. It can be as painfully difficult for the speedy person to slow down as it is for the slow person to speed up. But often the solution to character is exactly in changing to a very different tempo. I've experienced occasions when actors seem to have done all the right work on their character, are playing their actions and objectives with accuracy and truth, have defined clearly the social placing of the character, are physically and vocally appropriate – and yet something is lacking. Often that something is that they still haven't *relinquished* their own inner pulse. As soon as they adjusted this, the character immediately fell into place and became totally convincing.

I define a pulse as the rate at which a person ticks; the frequency with which they renew their energy-impulses and the degree of dynamic with which they occur – with greater or lesser intensity. Another, more imaginative device is to find a rhythm for the character. Is it a march or a Viennese waltz, salsa or heavy rock? Is it steady or erratic? Is it executed legato or staccato? These shifts from the actors' habitual pulse will effect all sorts of other changes in them: how they move, how they think, how they relate. Once more, it's a matter of actors practising these shifts until this new deployment of energy feels as natural and as comfortable as their own. Attainment of skills is no mystery. *If you want to acquire a craft, keep practising it.*

Animals

To use an animal (or bird, reptile, insect or fish), it's not necessary to appropriate its entire behaviour and movement. Only take those characteristics that are helpful. So the way an animal uses its paws or turns its head might be sufficient to open up an idea or give an insight into character. I recommend visits to the zoo – a rich source of ideas for character.

The Actor and the Role

Actor and Role

You are you, so how can you possibly embody Masha, Hedda Gabler, Phèdre, Viola, Blanche DuBois and Hamlet, or Pastor Manders, Lear, Willy Loman, Pinchwife, Estragon and Lady Bracknell? They are as different from each other as they are different from you – in time, place, culture and language, possibly age and sexual orientation, even gender, let alone their psychologies and the varied stylistic WORLDS they inhabit.

Are you going to bring the character to you or are you going to take yourself to the character? One of the problems with Method actors was that they opted for the former. It focused on the actors' experiences, how *they* felt, what *they* wanted. It ignored or denied the demands of the character and text if it conflicted with the actor's needs. Their performances could be strikingly 'real' but not necessarily relevant to the character; they were also self-indulgent and inarticulate. So, understandably, those American actors could only succeed in roles that were contemporaneous with their own lives. Whenever they attempted roles outside that experience, especially classic and foreign roles, they were appallingly inadequate, because they'd developed no means of going out and away from where they felt comfortable within themselves.

The writer didn't create you, he created the Macbeths and the Prozorovs, open as they are to wide interpretive possibilities. So of course, you, the actors, have to reach out to them, find out what they want, not what you want; *find them in yourself, rather than impose yourself on them.* The making of the five lists will give you a healthy, factual start. But those lists refer totally to the material of the text. *There is another pair of lists to make that are very much connected with the actor, with you.*

The compiling of this pair of lists – less comfortable to deal with than the previous five and whose objectivity is less easy to ensure, will probably be ongoing throughout rehearsals, if not your entire working life:

The first List: Everything that you, personally, share with the character.

The Second List: All those elements of the character that are alien to you or different from you.

THE FIRST LIST

In the first list, age, marital status, culture, nationality – all the factual details are easily dealt with. However, when it comes to the personal areas of psychology, behaviour patterns, life experiences, even appearance, you need to be pretty rigorous with yourself. The better you know yourself, the more honest your work will be – and the less painful. The more objective you can be about your own psychology, habits and appearance and the more you're able to admit to difficult areas in your own character, the easier it will be to transform yourself. As long as you labour under self-delusions and remain in denial about certain personal traits or qualities, you'll only confuse and distort your work on a role.

What you're doing, first of all, is identifying those aspects of yourself that are appropriate for the role and then eliminating those (especially comfortable and comforting performance habits and tricks) that are not. You are in fact distilling yourself according to the needs of the character. If you have to let go of those protective devices you've got used to – those devices you've contrived to get you safely through a performance – you will undoubtedly feel naked and vulnerable. *Being truthful on stage is an act of daring.* An actor should always start work clean and free from old habits, open and flexible, ready to move in whatever direction the play and production require. Once you've accepted a role, that is your job. It is not your job to throw up smokescreens and distress signals and indulge in diversionary tactics. If the role frightens you or is one you don't believe you can fulfil, don't accept it!

So: you have your personal identification with the character and your search for those aspects of the character that are not yours. The former needs as much work as the latter. It's not only content (*what*) you are looking at, but also form (*how*). For example, if you, like the character, tend to sulk when you don't get your own way, you can identify with the *experience* but possibly not the *manner* in which the character sulks. Although you can identify with the inner state, you'll have to replace your own patterns of expression with those of the character by means of observation and practice.

THE SECOND LIST

The second list involves a lot of research: into period, place, culture and stylistic WORLD. If you play a killer, you can discover a certain amount from your own homicidal tendencies (when you scream or mutter 'I could kill him!', the impulse, though not literally meant, will be coming from some dark corner of your psyche). Then try to explore the barriers that prevent your acting on them, find out about people who seem not to have those barriers. Stanislavsky's 'If' comes in very handy here. 'What if I were someone who . . . ?'

You have recourse to your knowledge and observation of other people. I'm often amazed how unobservant actors can be. Everyone you come in contact with, everyone you pass in the street, is potential material for future creativity. Actors should be ruthless scavengers of other people's behaviour. Perhaps actors are naturally so inner-directed, so preoccupied with themselves, that they can't focus sufficiently on others. I would earnestly recommend developing this faculty. This is where you'll find most of your material – not from exclusive absorption in yourself. Sit at an outdoor café table for half an hour every day and watch the passing crowds. I promise you, you'll gather a lot of material. You also have access to world literature, fiction and non-fiction, to paintings, films, television, theatre itself. You need to be selective, though, in recognising what is authentic and what stereotypical, otherwise you run into the danger that I've already discussed, of creating life at second or third hand.

These lists are no business of directors. They cannot, should not, ask to see or discuss them. They're the exclusive and personal business of the actor. Of course, actors can, should they feel it would be helpful, share whatever they see fit to impart to a director.

Empathic Imagination

The natural talent of some actors is the instinctive ability, seemingly on the instant, to imagine themselves as another person in another situation. I call this particular ability *empathic imagination*. From very few pieces of well-chosen information, such actors can extrapolate a very accurate account of a life that, in fact, they've neither experienced or known before. They are able to propel themselves towards a character with great flexibility and imagination and a corresponding absence of huffing and puffing about doing so. They seem to have no problem in shedding their own patterns and shaping those of someone quite different from themselves. They embrace the whole concept of characterisation with the utmost naturalness. The more that actors can find of others in themselves, and the more of themselves in others, the more they'll extend their human understanding and their capacity to characterise in any depth.

STRAND THREE:
THE WORLD OF THE PLAY
Discovering New Worlds

World v. Style

The third strand of rehearsal, running parallel with those on text and character, deals with worlds. I prefer the use of *world* rather than *style* to identify the particular reality of a play: its cultural provenance and its vision of actuality – how it reflects, distils, magnifies, heightens or distorts selected aspects of our life. Style, for me, has connotations of something decorative and mannered imposed from the outside, something both superficial and artificial, whereas a world is innate to its material.

Asking Questions

The world of a play consists of the particular values, qualities and elements which give it its *form of existence*, its – well – style! One of the first questions a director and actors have to ask themselves is 'What sort of world do the characters in this play inhabit?' What is its reality, not only in realistic terms – if applicable – of time and place (i.e. its cultural framework such as *fin de siècle* Russia, Restoration London . . .), but also in what way it departs from actuality? An opera posits a world in which it's natural (but *not* naturalistic) for the characters to sing; in a Feydeau or Ben Travers farce, characters live in a near-permanent state of mindless panic that hurls them into ridiculous situations. But then, what is the difference between the worlds of Travers and Feydeau, and then again, what is the difference between Travers's *A Cuckoo in the Nest* and his *Rookery Nook*? No two plays exist in exactly the same world. What is the departure from our everyday, recognisable actuality? How are the characters to speak? How move? How substantial, how suggestive, how literal, how metaphoric is their environment? What is their relationship to the audience? Do they acknowledge it? Ignore it? Imagine they are unobserved? And how do you want the audience to receive the work? We have rough guides under such generalised headings as Romantic, Expressionistic, Absurdist, Naturalistic,* 'In Yer Face' . . . But these categories have been created after the fact and can only give us an approximate nudge in a general direction. Plays are complex constructions and cannot be constrained

---

* Naturalism is as formalised as *The Country Wife* or *The Oresteia* and is as selective as any other form. I repeat my suggestion that you take a look at films from different decades of the last century to see how what seemed 'just like life' becomes increasingly artificial from generation to generation.

within neat compartments. Labels lumping things together in convenient blocks are generalised and formulaic (lazy), whereas our job is to discover what is particular and specific about each of the texts we bring to life (industrious). Every production has to create a world afresh. We're already prisoners of our own culture (it's impossible for us to see or think differently from the way we do) without further imprisoning ourselves in specious received ideas, many of which have always been false or which have now outlived their usefulness. We have no received way of playing Shakespeare, say, or Coward, only certain clichés – unlike the Comédie-Française where, until the middle of the last century, they pursued a manner of playing Molière in the supposed style of the original performances – and pretty sterile that was. Certain traditions tend to grow uncritically around certain writers and encrust them in false images or unexamined reputations. What is the world of the play? We have to find out for ourselves each time we embark on a new production.

Content and Form

The ultimate purpose of rehearsal is, in fact, to create a unique and cohesive world that embodies the material we're trying to bring to life; a visualisation as close as possible to our understanding of it; the realisation of the forms that (we hope) will best reveal its themes and system of values. *We have to discover the rules of the new game we're learning to play with a text – the rules of this specific world.*

A work of art is one in which form and content, manner and matter, style and substance, have seamlessly fused. In this section of rehearsal, accordingly, we're in search of the ideal form to express the content of the text: the appropriate *how* for the *what*.* This is the most open-ended of the three rehearsal strands and, unlike the other two, has no overall structure applicable to each and every production. However, it does have an endless series of challenging questions for director and cast to grapple with.

The world of the play of course involves the visual, physical aspects of a production and the technical structuring of how things occur (scene changes, use of technology), but most important is the particular reality in which the actors play. Too frequently, we see productions where a lot of time has been spent on *how* the show looks and now, thanks to the growing sophistication of technology, more often on *how* it sounds, but little or none on *how* the actors perform. Actors tend to get left to their individual devices in an area that needs collective development. This is another reason why, in so many productions, members of the same cast appear to be simultaneously inhabiting widely different realities.

---

* Because they usually evolve together, the form and content of a devised piece are likely to fuse together more seamlessly than the form that's created for an existing text. The performances that Robert Lepage has created himself, for instance, feel that much more fulfilling and fulfilled than his productions of other people's material.

Unfamiliar Territory

The further a text moves away from a realistic depiction of contemporary, local actuality, the further the actors have to move themselves into unfamiliar performance territory where they can no longer rely on the recreation of their own natural psychology and physical behaviour. If the text does remain more or less realistic, but that reality exists in a different culture, then appropriate research can help them to travel some of the way towards it. Obviously, the further away in time and distance that culture exists – especially once we travel back beyond the era of technological reproduction (photography, recorded sound), the more challenging it becomes to find useful material.* Then, because of ever-diminishing concrete evidence, we have to deploy an increasingly empathic imagination towards whatever material we do find. If the text moves away altogether from realism, then we have to extend our (re)search even further from the factual to sensitive conjecture and, then, to imaginative interpretation of what it seems to suggest to us about its particular reality. What, for instance, happens to the behaviour of characters who inhabit a world where their natural medium of expression is singing? What sort of reality do such people live in? We don't communicate in arias, duets or recitatives, so it can't be identical with ours. How do they move and in what sort of space? How do they gesture? How do they sound? What sort of clothes do they wear? What values are given to specific emotions in such a world? And are we talking about the world of Verdi or Monteverdi, of Berg or Britten, Lloyd Webber or Sondheim – or, to labour the point, the world of Sondheim's *Passion* or his *Pacific Overtures*? From a score and libretto, assisted by whatever factual research may be viable, we have to extrapolate clues that will imaginatively take us towards a form of expression that most appropriately releases and reinforces the content and becomes one with it.

Compound v. Mixture

There are times when a director deliberately imposes a violently incongruous form on a piece of familiar material. This may be for the excellent purpose of jolting the audience into looking afresh at material that's become deadened by repeated layers of cliché-ridden encrustations that hide rather than reveal its life, much like a painting made dim, its details obscured, by too many coats of varnish.

Sometimes, however, a 'bright idea' produces a form that enlightens some aspects of the material at the expense of the rest. A mix-and-match, anything-goes,

---

* Despite the continuous excavations of industrious scholars, we have virtually no knowledge of how, for example, Shakespeare's actors actually performed. We have to shift sideways into rules of rhetoric for ideas of delivery and gesture on the assumption that these might have applied to acting. The much-quoted holding of a mirror up to nature gives us no idea as to what degree of natural reflection was envisaged. As I keep pointing out, we've only to take another look at actors we once admired in old movies to see how much our idea of what's 'natural' changes with time.

never-apologise ('It's ironic, you know!') approach may well release a momentary frisson in the audience; but a production that shows off a whole gallery of forms and effects draws attention to itself rather than to its material. Self-regarding art inevitably provides an undernourishing experience. Audiences will be better sustained by a piece of work that presents a cohesively conceived world; a *compound* created from the imaginative transformation of separate components into *a totally new entity*, rather than a *mixture* of discrete elements that remain jostling against each other unchanged.

Now, when I go to the theatre, I often feel I'm crossing into the country of curates' eggs annexed by the forces of postmodernism. There may be excellent elements (a sexy costume, some witty lines, a well-played scene, an interesting theme, a surprising scene change, some ironic counterpoint), but they rarely add up to a coherent whole, an integrated sum of its parts. The work seems to be more about scoring points than establishing an intellectually and aesthetically sustained vision of a world. Each effect cancels out the last. Writers and directors indulgently shift the goalposts of conventions or change stylistic horses in mid-stream because they don't seem able to muster the necessary rigour to pursue any consistency. Arguments that theatre is ephemeral, that we no longer live in an observably consistent world, may attempt to justify such practices, but why spend weeks preparing a production merely to slap-and-tickle an audience that would rather be made love to? *Integrating many different elements into an edifying whole is the director's challenging job.* The pressure of constantly asking questions and struggling to solve the problems they throw up does eventually yield rewards.

Playing Fair with the Audience

The work of director, designers and actors is to share with the audience a unique world, a world referring to – but meaningfully different from – the one we live in. Each time they come to the theatre, audiences have to learn to interpret an unfamiliar system of signs, conventions and rules for the new world they're expecting to enter. If, however – through whim or lack of rigour – the signs are inconsistent, the rules broken, the conventions shuffled around, they're at first bewildered, then irritated and finally uncaring. Art should present a whole, a self-proving unity, even if that whole represents a world containing contradictions, fragmentation and discontinuity. One purpose of art is to give form to the shapelessness of life, some coherence to the chaos – not merely to echo it.

The Berliner Ensemble

The first time I truly experienced fully conceived worlds was with the last visit of the Berliner Ensemble to London in the mid-'60s. It was then considered internationally *the* company *par excellence*, a byword for brilliant theatre. I saw the five productions in their repertoire on successive days (or that's how I remember the experience). After almost twenty years of theatregoing, I at last saw – on each occasion – the artistic vision of a particular theatrical reality totally carried through in a way I'd seen no English company achieve. *The Resistible Rise of Arturo Ui* was played in bold slapstick, with a lot of acrobatic movement, and from the set to the mask-like make-up, every element in the production reinforced this form; *The Threepenny Opera*, revived by the director of its original 1928 production, created a world of raffish, thrown-off charm, a *dégagé* lightness of touch, insouciance – the characters had wonderful walks and great shoes; *Coriolanus* was harsh and hard, metallic and rock-like, even the delivery of the text sounded as if the actors were crunching granite; *The Little Mahagonny* was crisp, witty, playful and edgy, even camp; and finally *The Days of the Commune*, in which the company brought to naturalistic life photos of Paris in the 1870s. For each production, the same actors transformed themselves into its specific world; their performances all truthfully inhabited the same reality. Their technical skills seemed infinite. It was for me unutterably inspiring. It proved that such completeness of vision was entirely possible.

Starting Points

The following are suggested devices to kick-start the imagination in its search for *a new world*. Once again, our starting point, sensibly, can only be the text.

Text

The language of a text must offer clues as to the sort of world its speakers inhabit: not so much what it is saying (for the moment), but in what form it is saying it. Is it in verse or prose? If verse, what is the nature of that verse: lyric, epic or doggerel? Is it formal or free, blank or rhymed? If rhymed, is the scheme subtle or insistent? What is its metre? If prose, is the language ornate or laconic, complex or simple, playful or serious, witty or intense? Is it bawdy or decorous, demotic or mannered, rough or refined, circuitous or direct? Is it imagistic, rich with simile and metaphor? Does it employ rhetorical devices? Or contrivances like alliteration or onomatopoeia? Is there wordplay? Are there jokes? Does it employ references and quotations? Do all the characters inhabit the same verbal world? Does each character have his or her own voice? Do the characters express themselves intellectually rather than emotionally? Do they use accents or dialect; do they speak in slang or jargon, in patter or professionalese? What does the text look like on the page: are lines brief and broken or are there long tirades; is it heavily or loosely punctuated; is there emphasis by varying fonts and typefaces? And after you've answered these questions, you come to the critical one: in what form, *how*, are these answers to be interpreted in performance?

The answers should start to give you ideas about energy, attack, atmosphere, tone; and some thoughts about the cultural and emotional provenance of the characters: educated, close to nature, urban, satirical, fantastical; whether language is of conscious importance to them . . . All this information should stimulate your imagination into initial images of a world that might contain people who use language in this way. What is the physical impact of such language? What are the visual equivalents of such language? Are there visual artists whose work could be a source of inspiration? All this, of course, is ultimately a matter of interpretation; but if dialogue is short, sharp and overlapping, for example, it's unlikely that a production of autumnal moodiness is going to do the job. Explore the language with the actors – see how they respond to it, whether it organically changes the nature of their behaviour. In what way, if at all, does it shift them away from – or stop them resorting to – a comfortable, workaday naturalism.

Text and Subtext

And what is the text in relation to its subtext? Is the text dense, the subtext light, or vice versa? In Shaw's plays, the characters, whatever their class or occupation, are all articulate. He creates worlds in which characters hold passionately felt ideas and are admirably adroit at debating them. They say what they mean and mean what they say; consequently there is not much purpose for subtext. In Pinter, the language is compressed, elliptical, indirect, shaped with pauses and unnerving repetitions so that by contrast there is a sense that what is being said carries a huge freight of disturbing subtext. It's a world that wields words like weapons to fend off the revelation of feeling. In Chekhov's plays, his very natural but indirect speech resonates with depths of subtext that never seem to touch bottom.[*]

Just by looking at a page, we can see the virtuosity of Shakespeare's language: complex and clear, imagistic and rhetorical, demotic and vulgar, full of puns, jokes and neologisms, moving flexibly between verse forms and prose. In each play, it seems that he is trying to expand the possibilities of language, breaking out of traditional forms and closer to how people think and speak. No two plays sound the same and all characters have their own voice. Language is their dominant means of communication. Shakespeare's people live through the word and on the word. Frequently the same things are said twice, once in heightened speech, then in a simpler form, to ensure that members of the audience understand according to their cultural context. The characters speak in precise and elaborately imagistic detail because they want to say exactly what they mean.

---

[*] If you're working on a play whose original language is not English, it's a good idea to acquire some knowledge of what the form of the original text is like. Nowadays, sensibly, directors tend to commission new translations or versions of foreign plays they direct, and it's possible that working with the translator, you may be able to create a form of English that does echo something of its origins (*see*: TRANSLATION *in this section*).

There is little subtext, except in the prose. If characters are lying, they will have warned you of this in advance and the lies they employ are *precisely* what they want to communicate to their victims. From this we can see that the actors must inhabit a reality where the accuracy and vividness of words really matter in ways quite alien to our language-distrusting world of 'Know-what-I-means' and 'Innits'. This demands the highest degree of skilful verbal and vocal expressiveness. But what form should their expressiveness take? How, for example, should they handle the verse? Should they heighten or soften the structure of the verse line, acknowledge or ignore the rhymes of couplets? And how does the expression of such language affect an actor's physicality? And what are the texture, appearance and structure of an imagined physical world that contains people who use such language?

These examples are all, of course, generalisations. As I've said, there is no standard manner of playing the text of a particular playwright. Writers may have recognisable tendencies, but each of their plays is different from its predecessors: *Back to Methuselah* is not *You Never Can Tell, One for the Road* inhabits a vastly different world from *The Collection,* as does *The Cherry Orchard* from *Uncle Vanya, The Winter's Tale* from *Richard II* . . .

Confronted with the contrast between text and subtext, which are essentially the outside and inside of the characters – what the characters wish to show versus what they unwittingly reveal or deliberately insinuate – the actor has to find a particular physical, emotional and psychological life that engages with this dichotomy, the tension between the two and the relative importance of one over the other. As we've seen, characters in plays outside our contemporary culture do not necessarily employ the same psychology that we do; neither do they necessarily endow specific emotions with the same values, so that actors, moving further into the past or into the distance, have to search for forms of expression that are less and less familiar until they're *inventing the form* that seems appropriate to the text – *a form, a world, that has never been seen before.*

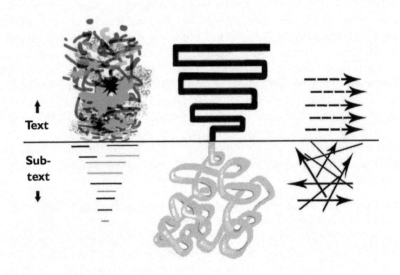

VISUALISING TEXT–SUBTEXT
(What is the relationship of text to subtext?)

What's the Subject?

We are complex organisms made up of many areas of experience, influenced by the continuous circumstances of our lives. We exist within the domestic and the communal, politics and play, religion and philosophy, sex and violence, vocation and career, money and idealism, psychology and fantasy, romanticism and realism, globetrotting and patriotism, friendships and rivalry, love and hate, selfishness and altruism, environments and space, science and history, medicine and faith, language and gesture, art and sport, and on and on . . . We play many roles: child, sibling, partner, spouse, divorcé, parent, grandparent, friend, enemy, lover, colleague, artist, labourer, boss, employee, athlete, gambler, dreamer, leader, follower, rival, victim, bully, client, patient, carer, fighter, failure, success, moralist, philosopher, hedonist, ascetic, deviant, conformist, devotee, mourner, celebrator, and on and on and on . . . Our friendships can be formed from the social world of our parents, from school, college, travel, work, nightlife, neighbours, hobbies, vacations, vocations . . . Our sexual relationships range through first gropes and first love, crushes, obsessions, experiments, marriage, cohabitation, pick-ups, divorces, commerce . . . With each person and in every circumstance we behave, to some degree, differently. As I pointed out when dealing with points of concentration, different people and different circumstances trigger different 'switches' in us that elicit from us what we sense to be appropriate responses to them. We are incredibly versatile!

But even the most determinedly naturalistic writing cannot convey the utter complexity of an actual life. The playwright, deliberately or by default, will inevitably have selected *specific areas of concern*. So when we approach a play, we need to identify a play's topics and subject matter. We are now talking about content, rather than form. Is its emphasis on the psychology of the characters, on their passions or on their social behaviour? Do the characters think or are they impulsive? Are they driven by appearances and social decorum? Are they linked by occupation or a belief system? Does the play deal with labour or art or politics or religion or money or fashion or illness or war or why we are alive? Does it deal with class and social structures? Does it inhabit a dream world or is it a slice-of-life? Are the incidents dramatic, violent or farcical? Is it a world of extremes? Is it erotic? Is it a play constructed on elaborate plot and physical action or on mood and atmosphere or on intellectual debate?

Equally important is to know what it does *not* deal with. So, essentially, you are recognising both the areas that need to be worked on and those to be eliminated. Actors tend to approach every role in the same way. For instance, it's a waste of time and 'stylistically' inappropriate for the actors to spend a lot of time, as I've known some Method-indoctrinated actors do, constructing a realistic offstage daily routine, say, for the Macbeths. It would be wasteful to explore a dense psychology for characters in a Feydeau farce where the main ingredients are the conflict between sex and respectability and extremes of physical action under pressure. It's fair to suggest – to be more specific – that a play of his offers us characters who do not think but function on impulse, who literally throw themselves in and out of situations, who have little self-awareness (otherwise his plays would grind to a halt!) and are trapped within their own tics and mannerisms. Feydeau's world suggests topics such as social and sexual hypocrisy, misogyny, even underlying violence. It's a very physical world, in which the actors need stamina and energy and even athletic dexterity. It deals with a very specific class, time and place (*fin de siècle* French bourgeoisie) and needs to be reinforced with all the appurtenances of that culture. You're unlikely to get the most out of a Feydeau play by placing it in a black box with the cast in leotards.* But there again, having said this, it may well be that some day someone will do just that and create something utterly revelatory. This is what's both maddening and thrilling about theatre: you never really know what you've got, till you've got it!

---

* The awareness that Feydeau's plays need a 'style' has somehow created a rather mindless 'tradition' about how they should be performed; a lot of bad acting habits and received mannerisms endow most productions; the actors rarely pretend to believe in their situations, they comment on their characters, demonstrating in a cod 'ooh-la-la' way a lot of clichés about being French. Basically, they 'mug'. A world with its own ethos, clear rules and reality is never realised. The plays are not taken seriously. Yes, I *know* they are farces, but comedy is a serious business, and there's nothing more serious than participants in farce. However much a play departs from actuality, we must still be able to recognise its humanity. The

The subject matter, the content of a play, needs to be carefully noted and then developed. Anything that's beside the point – however attractive, informative or amusing– must be firmly eradicated. Directors, at times, have to prise from the actors' jaws any inapposite material they've become inordinately attached to. Directors, too, have to ensure they haven't fallen in love with an inappropriate conceit of their own. Rigour!

LIFE PIE
(Which Slices of Life are relevant to the text?)

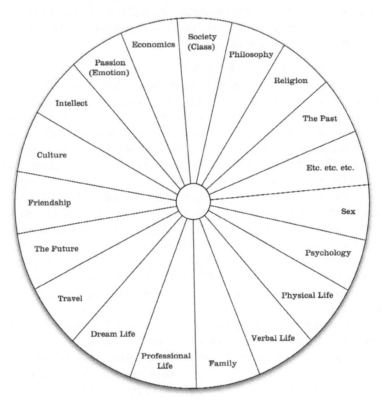

injunction to take comedy as seriously as tragedy is as old as the hills, but it's rarely followed. I directed *Private Lives* over what's considered an unusually long rehearsal period for such a play (eight weeks). We used the time to dig and search into the characters and their values. As far as I can remember, we never once talked about what was funny, or about getting laughs, or about 'timing'. We took the characters seriously and found the material allowed them considerably more complexity and expressive range than tradition has allotted them. (You must allow any character the potential for a full range of human expression.) When we finally performed, audiences laughed – a lot. They were also surprised, even shocked, and moved. We had created a world rather than 'done a number' on the play.

Departures from Actuality

We have dealt with the form of language and the subject matter of plays. Now we must look at the particular shift from actuality the writer is suggesting, not only through language, but also by the way the narrative unwinds, by the nature of the characterisation, and by how near or far the incidents of the plot stand in relation to what we recognise as our experience of life. If we establish naturalism as the theatrical form that most closely represents our actuality, the questions to ask here are how much does the play appear to move away from it, in what direction and in what way. As already noted, different material within various periods and movements has been consigned to convenient categories: baroque, expressionist, absurdist, kitchen-sink, and the like. These are, of course, extremely generalised groupings and merely indicate certain tendencies for a piece of work. There is absolutely no formula for directing all the plays gathered under one particular category. There's almost a quarter of a century between Wycherley and Farquhar, for instance, both categorised as writers of 'Restoration Comedy', but their plays have very different purposes and ingredients and need correspondingly different treatment. As a starting point, it might be helpful to try to decide in which of these general categories your text might be placed; and then to ask which of its elements identify it in that way, and which make it unique and true only to itself.

Do the characters behave 'naturally' within the context of their period? Are the characters individualised or theatrical stereotypes (interfering mother, bullying father, conniving servant) or types and humours (Miser, Hypochondriac, Pedant, Jonsonian characters like Sir Epicure Mammon) or representatives (Boss, Worker, Mother)? Is the play full of physical action and spectacle (Boucicault) or a courtly chamber piece in which passionate characters agonisingly debate ethical choices (Racine)? Is it comic, sentimental, tragic, and what do those categories mean specifically to the play in question? How are the scenes structured: a lot of short scenes or long, sustained acts? Does the play decorously observe the unities (Marivaux) or does it roam all over the place and time (Shakespeare)?

You cannot satisfactorily answer these questions with words. You can only offer suggestions, point out tendencies that will eventually become fleshed out by the actors as they investigate them in action, on their feet.

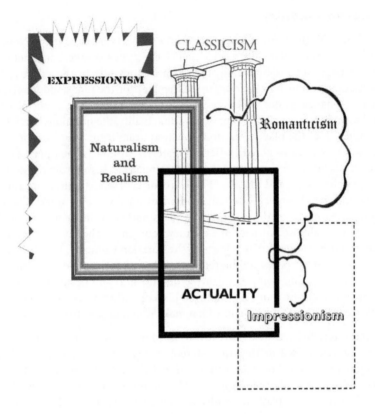

DEPARTURES FROM ACTUALITY
(How does the text depart from the reality of our lives?)

Relationship to the Audience

Is the production to be presentational or representational? In what way should this particular play relate to its audiences? Do they become eavesdroppers, peeking through holes in a 'fourth wall'? Do we acknowledge their presence? In what way do we do this? Does each character have a private relationship with the audience in which feelings and thoughts that cannot be revealed to the other characters are shared in confidential asides and soliloquies with them? Or do characters talk to an audience with the full awareness of the others? Or is it the actor rather than the character who communicates with the audience? And what are the characters'/actors' objectives towards the audience? And with what role are we endowing the audience: confidant, sympathiser, judge, evaluator, someone to be challenged? Do we relate to them from within the reality of the imagined world or do we make them complicit with a full awareness of the theatrical event? And what in the play guides us to make those choices?

Translation

If you're doing a foreign play, the creation of a world will be critically dependent on the nature of the translation you're using. We know that *traduttori traditori* – translators are traitors. A definitive translation is an impossible object; especially impossible – if that's possible – into English. English-speakers have an immense number of words at their disposal (far more than the French, say) because of a double vocabulary that's evolved from two parallel roots, Latin and Germanic. Consequently, we're spoilt for choice in the matter of synonyms, some of which have the most delicate shifts of meaning, and the selection of which is often a matter of personal taste and style, tone and mood, or of which audience we want to reach. This alone makes translation problematic. There is rarely a clear one-to-one translation; the 'same' word in different languages often has very different overtones. And there are some concepts that don't exist in all languages, even in languages with linked roots (Schadenfreude, Heimweh). Some Yiddish words are almost impossible to convey in English.

The preface by Stark Young, an American theatre critic of the 1930s and '40s, to his translations of Chekhov's *The Seagull* is instructive. To make his point about the distortion of most translations, he compared excerpts from four other translations then current. In all cases, the translators appeared to feel the need to explain what they were translating and so they added an enormous amount of text that is not in the original. At the same time, they had neglected to translate some of what *is* there. By means of capitals for what was added and italics for what was left out, he compared versions of the same dialogue that demonstrated the distortions to the text. It is a fact that those translations, especially those of Constance Garnett, were to a large degree responsible for the reputation that still vestigially clings to Chekhov, of being vague, static, moody, impressionistic, boring . . .

Clearly, foreign plays have to be translated into English to be performed for English-speakers, but what I take great exception to is an accompanying assumption that the plays themselves should be 'Englished', that is to say, turned into English plays, either put into local English dialects and accents with local references or put into current demotic speech. In the same way that I believe actors should reach out towards their characters, I believe they must reach out towards the culture in which those characters exist. I would suggest that translations should be in a sort of neutral English with, as far as possible, no choices that suggest English class and period and no English slang or idiom. (People in Ibsen simply do *not* say 'shit' and 'fuck'.) This distorts the accurate depiction of other places and periods, complete with their values and the expression of those values, and we end up in an unconvincing no man's land. By trying to make unfamiliar worlds familiar, we lose the mystery of those worlds. *What is thrilling is the difference between cultures that nonetheless reveals our shared humanity.* The intention behind the translation of a play should not be to produce a piece of literature but to provide a practical blueprint for performance. It should be the most self-effacing

of employments. As far as can be consciously controlled, it is not for the translators' personalities (with any tendencies to make their own jokes, indulge in inauthentic wordplay, slant the material in some politically preferred direction) to
get between the author and the actor and so between the author and the audience.

Plays need constantly to be retranslated. When I commissioned a new translation
of a Feydeau play, the translator of one already in circulation was upset I wasn't
using his. It was perfectly good, but it had been written thirty years earlier, so it
added the cultural complication of another – unintended – layer of 1960s English
to *fin de siècle* Paris. We need the text to be as clean as possible of alien resonances.
With a neutral text, the actors, as they evolve the world of a play, can vocally bring
the tone, sounds and colours of that world to their interpretation of the language.

My thoughts about translation were reinforced for me by James Fenton when he
was the theatre critic for the *Sunday Times*, and reviewed our Shared Experience
production of *The Comedy Without a Title* by Ruzante, an early sixteenth-century
Italian who wrote about peasant life. The original language is an unusual mixture
of Paduan dialect and a sort of poetic peasant idiom. Instead of turning it into
something familiar (predictably West Country or East Anglian), I tried to stay as
close to the original as long as it was satisfyingly sayable and playable and still
made sense. The actors spent a good part of the rehearsal period 'acquiring' the
language, making it their own until it became a natural component of their performance. This is part of what Fenton wrote:

> But how do they solve that question of translation and local flavour? . . .
> The solution will perhaps sound a little unpromising on paper; but it is
> wonderfully achieved. The idioms are allowed to stand, unchanged in
> all their rude weirdness. The lines are delivered in a style which very
> gently suggests Italian accents and mannerisms. The language corres-
> ponds to no form of spoken English. The actors speak in a way which
> has been invented for the production. And yet the whole manner of
> delivery contrives to conjure up the locality and the period, gently,
> easefully and truthfully . . . And it seems to me that Mr Alfreds has
> found the best possible solution to that nagging problem of the dialect
> play. Instead of saying, In order to understand Naples, think of
> Lancashire; or Don't think about Vienna, think about sex, he says:
> The genius of this work derives from the fact that a Paduan is talking
> to Paduans or presenting his fellow-countrymen to a Venetian audience
> who know them well . . . If a Caravaggio peasant stepped out of a
> canvas and began to talk, one imagines that he would sound something
> like this.

Accents and Dialects

The matter of accents carries on the same argument about problems of translation.

It is observable that actors develop and release their bodies with less difficulty (at times one can almost say less trauma) than they do their voices. The voice seems deeply connected with our most intimate sense of our identity. Many of us develop voices that try to cover up that deeply private area of ourselves. The letting-go of their uninhibited, 'real' voice can be a shocking and disturbing event for some actors. I've seen trembling and tears accompany such release. It's as though these actors fear they've lost control of some part of themselves; or they've uncovered something disturbing, never before acknowledged but kept firmly under subconscious wraps, something that shakes their very sense of themselves. This is especially noticeable with young women whose self-image is often linked to traditional ideas of gender, in this case having light and high voices. The discovery that their true voice may be much deeper (with an accompanying sensation of power) can be troubling for them. This is not how they've profoundly felt themselves to be, and they often resist or deny their own vocal reality. Sometimes it takes a long while to accept the need to adjust one's self-perception.

How we speak is intimately connected with how we present ourselves. It's also deeply connected to how we use our bodies. This is also true with accents. It is virtually impossible simultaneously to speak in RP (Received Pronunciation) and gesture like an Italian or shrug like someone French. Try it. If your physical image of yourself is a study in laid-back cool, it's hardly surprising if you have difficulty finding sufficient energy to get any words at all out of your mouth.

So how should actors proceed when playing characters of some other provenance and ethnicity than their own? As I've said, both in matters of translation and characterisation, I'm a great believer in actors reaching out towards the world of the play, rather than remaining in the one familiar to them; that's to say, rather than seeking to transform themselves as little as possible (lazy and arrogant), they should do so as much as the character seems to demand (industrious and modest). It's quite obvious that if an actor is playing a Glaswegian, he cannot stay with his own South London accent. In fact, most actors love using different British accents and – as long as they're accurate with them – they're usually transformed by their use. But I experience nothing but frustration when confronted with the inanities, inadequacies and inaccuracies of foreign plays performed as though the characters are British: Viennese *midinettes* as Estuary tarts, Russian peasants as Mummerset farmhands, or German industrialists as Yorkshire businessmen talking about 'brass'. As much as human beings are, *au fond*, the same, culturally we behave very differently. Geography, history, genetic predispositions all develop in us a distinct psychology and a unique set of cultural values. There is no neat one-to-one equivalent in shifting from one culture to another, any more than languages can neatly match up, one with the other.

When I'm working on the world strand of rehearsals for a foreign play, I will, at some stage, get the actors to play scenes in (their version of) the accent of that particular culture. *Inevitably, the actors are positively transformed: not only do they become free to move and gesture in a totally different way, their playing takes on a different temperature and temperament, considerably more appropriate to the material than their own cultural and personal mode.* In certain productions – for example, in *The Comedy Without a Title* that I just mentioned – the actors retained a faint residue of the Italian accents they'd employed in rehearsal. I took this procedure to its logical conclusion with my last production of *The Cherry Orchard* when, with the incalculable help and skill of Joan Washington, a brilliant dialect coach, I got the actors to perform with very accurate Russian accents. Both their inner and outer lives were vividly transformed by this. The critics, of course, reacted vitriolically, but audience members who had lived in – or were from – Russia assured me that they recognised these characters completely and found the world they created totally convincing. With the same group of actors, I created a production from several stories by Isaac Bashevis Singer and for this we worked on Yiddish accents, which language the characters would have been speaking in their Polish towns and shtetls. Interestingly – and ironically – not one peep of protest did I hear from any critic. But the convention was identical to that for *The Cherry Orchard*. (What can one deduce from this? Either that the English feel very proprietary about Chekhov – he's a surrogate Englishman, and only to be performed in a way that conforms to that – or that there's a vaguely anti-Semitic indifference to how Jewish material gets presented!)[*]

I believe that this is a rich area of work in need of examination. Currently, I don't think it's even given a moment's thought, certainly not in any productions I've seen. We're very preoccupied with the aesthetics of how things look on stage, but not at all with how the actors sound.

To solve these matters of translation and accent, similar sorts of questions have to be relentlessly asked of ourselves as those in the creation of a world. The sound of a world is as much a part of it as its look.

[*] In defence of the critics, I must admit I was briefly pulled up short when an Israeli, to whom I'd expounded my theory of accents on stage, asked me how I would react to a bunch of Israeli actors performing Shakespeare in Hebrew with English accents!

Self-Blocking

This is not exclusively an exercise towards the creation of a world, but rather, like basic voice and movement work, the continued exercising of fundamental skills that an actor needs for any work. However, as any world is certain to demand a particular way of moving through space, you might well incorporate its development into this basic work on self-blocking.

Most actors have an innate instinct about moving around a stage and quickly acquire a fluency. However, liberated from imposed blocking, especially if the physical life of the world is complex and there are several people simultaneously on stage, they may initially feel less secure and find themselves awkward and insensitive to their partners and the space. These exercises are ways in which the actor's instinct for spontaneous use of the stage space can be encouraged and developed to a high degree of skill.

A SERIES OF SELF-BLOCKING EXERCISES

Choose a section of text for the actors to play, then give them the following instructions:

A: MASKING AND UPSTAGING

Their point of concentration (POC) in this exercise is to make sure they neither upstage themselves nor mask anyone else.

The text is played *one beat at a time*. This is not dissimilar to FEEDING-IN in the TEXT strand of REHEARSAL.

The actor initiating the beat (playing the dialogue) must make a strong choice of action and do so with energy as a PROVOCATION to the others.

Everyone else in the scene, responding with an action, must find a justifiable reason *to react physically and move in response to every beat*.

When moving, they must ensure that they do not (a) upstage themselves and others, or (b) mask themselves or others. In other words, they must all endeavour to let the audience see their faces at all times.

The scene will inevitably not be played with fluency, as each beat will effect a sort of punctuation as everyone deliberately reacts to it.

VARIATIONS

Reverse the basic POC and instruct them to make sure *they are always upstaging and masking each other.*

Their POC now is to make sure their own faces are seen, while endeavouring to mask or upstage all the others.

B: FURNITURE AND PROPS

The POC is now on the actors justifying the use of a piece of furniture or a prop as part of their reaction to each beat.

The instructions for this exercise are the same as for A.

C: THE SPACE

The POC is now on exploring the use of space, how each actor uses it relevantly and expressively on each beat.

The instructions are the same as for A.

VARIATIONS

Specify certain areas or shapes to be used or established, for example:

>   Using only the four corners of the stage
>
>   Using only the periphery of the acting area
>
>   Moving only on diagonals
>
>   Moving only on curves
>
>   . . . and so forth.

D: DEPTH

The POC is on exploring their relationship to audience: near (i.e. downstage) or far (upstage); from stage left or stage right, etc.

The instructions are the same as for A.

E: LEVELS

The POC is on exploring height and levels: crouching, lying down, sitting, standing, standing on furniture or platforms, etc.

The instructions are the same as for A

F: AREAS

The POC is on exploring various areas on stage, for warmth, coldness, remoteness, power – find out what qualities an area endows the actors with.

The instructions are the same as for A.

G: OTHER ACTORS

The POC is on exploring how to interrelate physically. This is useful if you are creating a world in which there is a lot of dynamic group movement: people climbing on each other, carrying each other and so forth. Be specific in your instruction as to what type of group physical work you want them to explore. For example, you might limit the space in which they can move, which will inevitably force them into close physical contact.

The instructions are the same as for A.

H: BLENDING

You can blend some of the exercises accumulatively. For example, in all succeeding exercises after the first one (A), the actors could ensure that they are never upstaging or masking themselves or each other, or they could have to use a prop in all the variations . . .

ALTERNATIVE APPROACHES TO THE USE OF TEXT

(applicable to all the above exercises)

EITHER

The lines (and beats) can be played in their correct scenic sequence. For realistic material, this is probably more useful, ensuring the text moves on its natural journey.

OR

The actors, each in turn, can play a sequence of beats with dialogue taken from anywhere in their own text in any order. In this case, there will be no connection between the beats and each one is played for itself without any dramatic accumulation. This method is probably more productive if you're working on a very heightened piece, such as a melodrama or a farce, because it will force the actors to shift rapidly from one extreme state to another, without any logical, psychological 'softening'.

SELF-BLOCKING IN THE WORLD OF THE PLAY

Combining self-blocking with the creation of a world, you have once more to ask yourself a lot of questions, such as: How should the movement flow? Do the characters want to be kept physically isolated from each other or bunched up together? Does the world suggest curved or angular moves? Does it suggest levels? Do the characters need to cover a lot of ground fast?* When you have chosen what you think might be appropriate physical and spatial qualities to explore, make them the POCs of the self-blocking exercises.

NOTES

The purpose is for the actors to develop a trust in their ability to react *spontaneously* to each other's stimuli, and to move imaginatively and expressively.

If the actors are playing the scene in its natural sequence, they will be familiar with the text, so remind them that those 'receiving' the beat should not anticipate it, but allow the true moment of impulse to shift them; nor should they take time to think about how to react, otherwise the moment will have passed before they've reacted to it. The energy with which the beat is played should influence the reciprocal energy of the reaction. This can never happen if the actor goes into 'head' mode.

The actors should always be looking for imaginative ways to be expressive corporeally and spatially.

Using the Third Strand for Skills

This third strand of rehearsal can include any sort of training in special skills, such as acrobatics, should they be part of the performance language. If the production requires certain formal behaviour, such as the etiquette of a period, then bows, curtseys and specific manners should be worked on, not just technically, but with an understanding of their language, psychology and purpose. They should be exercised through improvisations so that in performance their execution looks totally natural, individualised and not something stiff, artificially imposed on the actors from the outside.

This strand also provides a useful space for any general group work that you feel necessary for the company. This may not always deal specifically with the discovery of a world; it may rather be about maintaining and enhancing basic skills of good theatre practice: body work, voice work, stamina, spontaneity and the like.

---

* For example, when I worked at Shakespeare's Globe, it seemed necessary – partially because of the width of the stage, but more relevantly, because of the heightened drive of the language – for the actors to cover ground fast. In the space of a couple of words they had to be able to get from A to B, a distance that would, in naturalistic mode, have taken them a few more syllables to accomplish. So finding the right energy that would allow the actors to move comfortably and naturally at speed became one of many exercises we devised to find a physical language for that particular space.

Practice

Worlds Evolve

Having answered the seemingly innumerable questions that have to be asked in the search for a world, we can start to respond conjecturally and more imaginatively. Is the material a piece of brutalism? Or a cartoon? What is its energy – erratic, flowing, buoyant? Does it indicate an open or closed world?[*] A light or dark one? Colourful or muted? Spatially formal or free? Curved or rectilinear, flat or uneven? Scattered or gathered? Soft or hard? Smooth or rough? Larger than life or intimately microscopic? Which end of the telescope *are* we looking through? These are still rather loose, approximate terms. The challenge, *our work*, is to translate all this into specific visual, aural, physical and emotional correlatives. We assume, of course, that while we're asking all these questions, our instincts will be coming up with a stream of increasingly tangible images, gradually pointing us closer to where we feel the production might go. Often, it's just one image that pulls all the ideas and elements together. A concrete and individualised world can only *evolve* through the trial-and-error of creative, exploratory rehearsals.

In the creation of a world, never aim for the precise reproduction of a preconceived image. You'll only experience the frustration of trying to shoehorn the actors into results that allow no room for discovery or any use of their imaginations – that is, no contribution from them. It's entirely possible that the actors, given the freedom to explore, will come up with something more appropriate, more expressive and wittier than whatever you, the director, have imagined. Several amalgamated imaginations are richer than one. You can reassure yourself that since you're always guiding and selecting what the actors offer, you need never be in danger of losing sight of your own initiating vision (assuming that vision stands up to the test of the company's explorations). In fact, the actors' contribution can only enhance it for you. So make your search *with* the actors, sustained by a sense of where you *might* be heading. Let freedom and discipline work hand in hand. If you truly do so, you'll find that you've evolved a form of playing unique to *this* particular production and *this* particular cast. You'll have created a world that's been distilled through *this* company, is true to *this* company and couldn't be realised quite like it by any other company. In the best cases, there's a satisfying inevitability as a world comes more and more into focus. Because the actors have been creatively involved in its evolution, they've developed

---

[*] Categories excellently defined by John Peter in his book, *Vladimir's Carrot*. An Open World functions in reference to the one we live in. A Closed World is self-referential and exists within its own rules. He cites *Waiting for Godot* as an example of the latter. *A Doll's House* is an example of the former.

a natural ownership of this world and will be able to display exactly the same freedom and spontaneity that they'd offer in the most naturalistic piece. This world both fulfils your vision and *at the same time surprises you*. Whatever image of the production you've envisaged before or early in rehearsals, *the reality is what you've arrived at by the end of rehearsals. A world cannot be neatly packaged and labelled in advance. It evolves.*

Two Productions

There's no one way, applicable to all material, of evolving the world of a play. To give concrete examples of how texts get translated into specific visual and physical forms and are embodied by the actors in a particular distillation of actuality, I can only describe how I've worked on particular texts. For this purpose, I've chosen two very different pieces of work: a novel by Evelyn Waugh and a play by Gogol.

A Handful of Dust

Here is the way I approached the world of Evelyn Waugh's 1934 novel, *A Handful of Dust*. The adaptation and the production evolved together. In fact, the adaptation proceeded from the approach to the production.

ANALYSIS

THE PLOT, THEME AND TREATMENT

The novel, set in the early 1930s, charts the breakdown of an upper-class marriage and, in its wake, the collapse of an English way of life. The action moves from London and the Shires to Brazil as the hero loses wife, son and ancestral home, ending up a prisoner in the Matto Grosso reading Dickens to his reclusive jailer. The novel, partly autobiographical (travels in Amazonia and a failed marriage), balances Waugh's satire with a more compassionate treatment of the main couple. He condemns equally the grasping vulgarity of café society and the incapacitating values of a more gentlemanly age that fail to recognise the enemy, let alone put it to rout.[*]

---

[*] The destruction of a refined but effete society by energetic and enterprising barbarians is a classic subject of drama: Blanche DuBois raped into madness by Stanley Kowalski in *A Streetcar Named Desire*; Olga and Irina, in Chekhov's *The Three Sisters*, ejected from their home by Natasha . . . Pertinently, Blanche and the sisters produce no children; Stanley and Natasha are fecund.

THE SUBJECT MATTER

The novel deals with the *mores* of two overlapping social worlds: country-house life and café society. The characters are ruled by the values of these worlds, which, in the former, stem from paternalistic tradition, one's position in the community and the dictates of *noblesse oblige*; in the latter, from the requirement to be amusing and amused, seen in the right places dispensing gossip, wit and elegance – a sort of early twentieth-century cool. In both cases, money matters. The action is marked by a series of social events: parties, a hunt, country weekends, the opening of a restaurant . . . The characters are not explained, but revealed through their behaviour. Thoughts and emotions are rarely disclosed except, on occasion, those of the main couple. The characters themselves never discuss feelings, nor analyse motives. In these worlds, this would indicate vulgar intrusion or lack of poise. The social banishment of emotion avoids any risk of vulnerability. This, in its turn, banishes any likelihood of intimacy or self-knowledge. People are judged by their manner and manners, their *savoir-faire* in fulfilling certain rules of conduct. This is reinforced by contempt for those who don't (know how to) conform to them.

THE STYLE AND STRUCTURE

The writing is precise, elegant and witty; the tone, for the most part, ironic, cool and dispassionate. It elicits painful laughter from the reader. Much of the economic text is unattributed dialogue, often as phone conversations. The action moves rapidly through short scenes and incidents.

RESEARCH

The main element of the material is the depiction of those very specific social worlds. Those worlds are observed from a slight distance with a very cool eye. The book creates a very selective realism with a concentration on behaviour and an avoidance of feeling. My main task was to get the cast to inhabit such worlds, almost no traces of which remain today. We had to rediscover them through literature and music, photography and art.

And film. We watched black-and-white English movies of the 1930s, especially those that dealt with the upper classes, to learn how they moved, wore their clothes, gestured, sounded and dealt with servants.

English of the 1930s is now almost a dead language – in vocabulary, slang, pronunciation and delivery. People then spoke with much more confidence and articulacy; they were louder and more emphatic. Vocal placement was further forward than it is today; delivery faster. Women's voices seemed pitched higher (though the distortion of period recordings may exaggerate this perception). There were distinctions between various upper-class accents: 'County', 'Mayfair', 'Oxford' . . . Speech ranged from the clipped to the drawled. There was, interestingly and surprisingly, very little inflection. The upper class felt no requirement to make any special effort to communicate. Sentences were thrown off rapidly, almost in a monotone. If you wanted to emphasise a word you leant on it with increased volume. Explanatory inflection was left to the middle and lower classes who felt obliged to make themselves understood.

We looked at lots of society photos and studio portraits of the period. What was striking was a sense of conscious posing, often in silhouette and wreathed in cigarette smoke. Everyone smoked. There was a culture of tobacco, evident not just in the accoutrements of matches, table and pocket lighters, cigar cutters, humidors, tobacco pouches, cigarette cases, boxes and holders, but also in the way people smoked. The way you lit, inhaled, exhaled and stubbed out a cigarette was part of your persona. Clips of an interview with Noël Coward show him wielding a cigarette as if it were an extension of his arm, a very expressive antenna.

It was an extremely elegant period. People were *soigné*, carefully groomed; their wardrobes contained specific clothes for every occasion and they changed throughout the day for whatever was next on their social schedule. They carried items of grooming around with them. Everything was in 'terribly good taste', rather small and neat. Both men and women bore their elegance with studied ease.

Women carried themselves with their shoulders rounded and their chests consequently rather collapsed. Their shoulders replaced breasts as a major erogenous zone. Evening dresses were cut very low in the back and skirts cut on the bias so that they flowed as their wearers moved.

Men were socially attentive to women: lighting their cigarettes, placing their chairs, opening and closing doors for them, helping them into and out of coats, capes and cars, and generally fetching and carrying for them. Women expected this attentiveness and waited for it to happen! Everyone had servants. No one did any sort of domestic work for themselves. Many of the men had inherited incomes and didn't work.

There was a lot of social dancing, in couples of course, and everyone knew how to dance. This was the period of the great dance bands, a period rich in highly sophisticated popular songs – some of the finest twentieth-century songwriters were at their peak in this period with their literate, witty lyrics: Porter, Coward, Berlin, the Gershwins, Rogers and Hart.

It was a time of nightclubs and great parties which went on into the small hours. People moved from one party to the next, ending up driving out of London to some roadhouse for breakfast before going to bed for the rest of the day. Women spent a lot of time entertaining from their beds – a sort of twentieth-century *levée*.

APPLICATION

The above behaviour and form had to be acquired by the actors. To find a theatrical correlation for the observational nature of the writing, we decided that the characters should be very much displayed and on display. So we worked to create very conscious self-images and for the actors always to have a sense of themselves in silhouette or profile, knowing exactly what shapes their bodies were sculpting in space. Every day, for the first few weeks, the actors had a 'posing' session, when, for half an hour, they would explore placing themselves into positions that revealed the whole sense of their bodies, working against walls, with furniture, in space, perched, seated and standing. The purpose was not for them to fix on any particular shapes or even to think specifically about their characters, but to understand the body language of this world, to teach their bodies instinctively to move appropriately in whatever situation they found themselves. They first started working on their own; then in pairs; then as a group, finding out what sort of social physicality and tactility was permissible between such people, always making sure that whatever they did had a natural elegance. Later we added to this the business of dealing with props, especially those connected with smoking. The men, especially, had to practise taking cigarette cases and lighters out of their pockets. The women became adroit at moving accessories to and from handbags. We extended the exercise to include wearing clothes of the period. The aim was to achieve a very relaxed self-awareness. The characters always looked totally at ease and, at the same time, very much in control, impervious to judgement or revelation. We carried this area of exploration into phone conversations; how you behave when you're alone at the end of the line: what you say and how you look may be two very different things.

All this meant using one's observation (from films, photos and paintings), and then having once found the *modus operandi*, to add one's own imaginative choices within this physicality. It was a matter of daily practice, quite simply exercising a developing skill. If, while watching, I felt that the physical choices were inaccurate, out of style, I would monitor them. As soon as the actors looked secure within the period, they then explored the physicality of their actual characters. The reason for holding off on the characters was that, had they immediately focused on them, they would almost certainly have limited their explorations and reduced their imaginative possibilities. ('My character is like this, not like that . . . ', 'My character would do this but not that . . . '). We did exercises/improvisations in which the women expected certain attentions from the men without having to state what they wanted. They waited to have cigarettes lit, chairs placed, coats removed. The men learnt to read what was required of them.

We did exercises in which the actors conducted conversations across wide distances so that they developed the ability to make vocal contact with effortless confidence. We also exercised their skills in overlapping so that the dialogue became sharp, tight and incisive.

The company had classes in ballroom dancing – foxtrots, quicksteps, rumbas – to be able to use them during the action, and to experience their unexpectedly vivid sexuality: to dance correctly, partners had to interlock thighs.

As we've established, the physical and the psychological are intimately and irreducibly interconnected, and this continuous, specific exercising of a physical life found its correlation in a naturally evolving view of life: looking out at the world with a cool irony; searching out weaknesses in others, but giving nothing away oneself; playing with one's cards very close to one's chest. Although the expression of emotion is so firmly avoided in this culture, we did not ignore the characters' inner lives; on the contrary, it seemed important to find out how the characters dealt with their feelings, how they suppressed them or found alternative outlets as a release or a cover for them: assumed boredom and weariness, denial, flippancy and the like . . . *

As there were no props used in the show – all that was on stage were ten high-back chairs elegantly upholstered in grey velvet and a similarly upholstered back wall – the actors had to develop skills in mime as well as in the smooth movement of chairs from one position to another with a minimum of distraction from the focus and flow of the show.

This is just a small example of some of the work we did on this particular material.

---

* Waugh entitles one of his chapters *Hard Cheese on Tony*, the schoolgirl slang used by one of the characters to indicate (while denying any real pain) the suffering that the hero experiences from his wife's infidelity.

Marriage

This farce is Nikolai Gogol's other full-length play besides his famous *Government Inspector*. It was written in 1835. Though hardly known in the UK, it's a staple of the Eastern European theatre repertoire.

ANALYSIS

THE PLOT, THEME AND TREATMENT

The simple action of the play takes place in St Petersburg in the 1830s and concerns Podkolyossin, a confirmed bachelor, whose friend is determined (with absolutely no ascribed motive) to get him married. A matchmaker who is trying to procure a husband for an aging young lady brings him and several other suitors together with the potential bride. She chooses Podkolyossin, and they agree to marry. At the eleventh hour, in a fit of panic, he climbs out of a high window and runs away. The material is concerned with the essential incompatibility of men and women. The contradictory urges of lust and flight are themselves in conflict with the social imperative for everyone to get married. Its deeper concern is with the terrors faced by most people in attempting to cope with existence: the fear of commitment to any relationship, the difficulty of actually getting out of bed in the morning or walking through a doorway. The play contains all the nightmare experiences of the characters in Gogol's short stories. Gogol writes with his peculiar blend of social satire and highly emotional farce.

THE SUBJECT MATTER

The characters come from the shabbier part of the bourgeois merchant class and include retired, low-ranking officers of the army, navy and civil service. They are lonely, isolated and, apart from the two matchmaking characters who violently drive the action along, totally unproductive. They are all eccentric manifestations of their fears and obsessions and all totally self-deluded. They see themselves as attractive specimens of humanity. They have developed a tenuous mode of conduct that just about passes for social behaviour. They exhibit extraordinary patterns of speech, with which they fail utterly to communicate. As they struggle to cope with the formalities of paying court, there is the feeling that, under this particularly thin social veneer, anarchic forces are about to erupt and confront them with their greatest terrors – sex, responsibility, loneliness, failure and loss of identity . . .

THE STYLE AND STRUCTURE

The action is tight, moving on the level of farce that threatens to explode into violence. The characters are drawn large without any breadth of complexity but with vast depths of feeling. Their highly selected traits are exaggerated in what European theatre identifies as 'the grotesque'. The play is a series of confrontations, studded with huge monologues that carry the emotional weight and passion of operatic arias. For the audience, laughter could, at any moment, turn to alarm.

RESEARCH

We looked at books of interiors for ideas about the *milieux* in which the characters lived and found examples that would lend themselves to heightening: shabby, underfurnished rooms for the men, and heavily cluttered, over-ornamented furnishing in the Biedermeier style for the women.

The main search, however, was for images that might connect with the extreme characterisations. We turned to nineteenth-century cartoonists and illustrators for inspiration and having looked, especially, at the works of Grandville and Doré, hit a bull's eye with some caricatures of French politicians by Honoré Daumier who specialised in satirising corrupt governmentarians. He had drawn a series of full-figure portraits, not dissimilar in principle from those by 'Spy', whose gallery of Victorian ruling-class males still tend to decorate traditional British barbershops. Daumier's work, however, is crueller, more exaggerated and more solid, a perfect entry point for the actors and designers into the world of Gogol.

The rest of Gogol's none-too-prolific fictional output – his great novel, *Dead Souls*; his shorter fiction including *The Nose*, and *Ivan Shponka and His Aunt*; his two short plays, plus several dramatic fragments – all reinforced the impression of the heightened, exaggerated world of *Marriage*.

Several years earlier, the Moscow Art Theatre had visited London. The repertoire they brought with them included Stanislavsky's productions (still in their repertoire in the 1960s) of Chekhov's *Cherry Orchard* and an adaptation of *Dead Souls*, in both of which some of the characters were played – and costumed – in a bravura style, unlike anything that I'd seen in English theatre: actors boldly conveying the essence of their characters by means of extreme physicality wedded to intense feeling. A miser, for example, was portrayed with a pinched voice that made it unclear what gender he was, and with a closed, bent body, permanently trembling from cold, layered in rags that he somehow hid behind while he shuffled cautiously amongst his shabby treasures as though he even distrusted the air around him. *Most striking, the actors played with total seriousness, without the least hint of comment or complicit winks at the audience.* My memory of these performances helped to guide me towards a possible world for Gogol's play.

We had to create an exaggerated world, but the exaggerations were of an actual world that wasn't instantly accessible to us – specifically, the psychological behaviour and emotional life of early nineteenth-century St Petersburgers. So we had sessions in which we pooled our collective knowledge of Russians. This knowledge was gleaned from films, literature, theatre, travel and our observations of any Russians we knew. We came up with some familiar generalisations that were affirmed sufficiently often to convince us of their genuine basis in actuality. In comparison to us, Russians were more open and liberated in the expression of their feelings; men were not ashamed to weep; nobody was ashamed to sulk or fall into moods; they allowed themselves to indulge in huge emotional swings and had the ability to shift with great volatility from one to another; they lived in a vast country that experienced extremes of climate and duration of daylight that seemed to invite a tendency to philosophise; they indulged in *Weltanschauung* and suffered from *Weltschmerz*; they talked about their souls (not as a religious concept); on the land, a great percentage of the population were, at the period of the play, still serfs; the bureaucracy and government of this vast country was Byzantine, hierarchical, incompetent and corrupt; obtaining justice was barely possible; they had a closer relationship to the arts; Russians were physically more tactile and demon-strative; their speech more sensuous, 'chewy', liquid; their language had no definite or indefinite articles that made them seem more direct, less 'polite': they were bigger-boned and deeper-voiced; their identity wavered insecurely between the Slavic and the European; they seemed to live at greater extremes of intensity . . . From all this, we had eventually to extrapolate what seemed useful and appropriate for our specific characters, play and period.

APPLICATION

The company had to create a world that was not only distant in time and place but also departed considerably from actuality. The actors had to discover both the 'Russianness' in themselves and then its exaggeration. Felicitously, the two somehow blended together quite early on.

I set up simple exercises for the actors to explore states such as profound boredom, despair in the present, longing for an idealised future, self-delusion as to personal qualities, fear of the opposite sex and desire for the opposite sex. These sessions involved the actors finding their own space in the rehearsal room where they worked alone, exploring in any way they could the particular experience. They did not at this early stage relate it to character. They could work from some personal experience, from something suggested by the play or from their own imaginations. I would coach them through these sessions (they stayed *inside* the exercise while I talked to them, from the *outside*, as it were), encouraging them to make sure they were being specific, that they were *not trying to feel emotion*, but allowing the release of whatever feeling might come to them from the specific thoughts and longings they were imagining and experiencing. I encouraged them to allow their physical selves to react to whatever impulses came to them, never to censor or inhibit them. I also urged them to develop the range of their expressiveness but never to demonstrate it, to allow their body (face, arms, breathing, any part of them in fact) to respond more and more spontaneously to their thoughts and the feelings.

Once they began to develop the ability to express, truthfully and fully – that is, without inhibition – states of emotion and thought that were not necessarily familiar to them, I would then coach them through a seamless sequence of changing situations and preoccupations that led them to move, often rapidly, from one emotional state to another. To help this volatility, I suggested the image that our 'Anglo-Saxon' emotional life lay buried deep in the interior of our stomachs, hard to access, but once contacted and released, hard to push back, whereas Russian emotions sat more availably on the outside of their stomachs and therefore were easier to access and manipulate. As with most techniques, the more this volatility was practised, the more skilful the actors became at achieving sudden bursts of feeling.

We also did a lot of work on their physical life: on their tactility, both touching themselves and others, stroking cheeks, caressing and kissing hands, hugging themselves, stretching and sighing, shrugging, pouting, stamping feet, throwing hands up in frustration, exploring different degrees of tearfulness; in short, allowing themselves to be in every way far more expressively self-indulgent than we permit ourselves to be. Many of these simple actions (e.g. pouting or stamping the foot) were unfamiliar to some of the cast and took a while for them to make their own!

When they knew the text, we played scenes with Russian accents, which released this repertoire of gestures almost instinctively.

As they became more and more comfortable with this work, the actors all observed that it was making them feel and think very differently. An inner life was being created from their physicality. They were seeing things in broad and vivid colours and thinking in equivalently broad, large thoughts. They found indulging their feelings became increasingly easy. Eventually, as they developed their characterisations, this work more and more informed their specific behaviour and psychology.

Working towards the heightening and intensifying of these characteristics, I set up sessions where they tried to take (without straining) a mood, a state, a situation, a feeling, to the extreme of its expressiveness. Slowly, their bodies dared to make larger, bolder and fuller expressions of how they felt and thought and yearned. At times, it looked as if they were pumping themselves up like giant inflatables. I used the characters' long soliloquies as a way into this level of work. I've described them as being the equivalent of operatic arias, and I indeed encouraged the actors to sing them until they were able to perform them with great release and expansiveness.

In the character work, the main concern was to find a level of playing that would encompass a huge physicality and a passionate intensity. We worked on psychological gestures, physical centres and on building a complete characterisation from just one basic drive or fear. In this way, each character became the walking-talking epitome of his or her obsession.

We created exercises to break down verbal and grammatical logic. We worked on unusual vocal deliveries. In the Russian text, the matchmaker totally distorts her language. As an equivalent, I created a pattern of repeated syllables within long words, so that she at times sounded like a jammed typewriter (secretari*ari*at, sensibili*lilili*ties, necess*essessess*ary); plus giving her a general confusion of language: '*I'm exerted from all my exhaustions*; *it's a scander to slandle me*' and so forth . . . It took time for the actors to master these unfamiliar patterns, but paid off triumphantly when they succeeded.

As with all our work, no external action was fixed, so we spent a lot of time building up their improvisational skills. The actors were encouraged to be brave, not only in the emotional heights they strove for and in daring vocal expressiveness, but, quite literally, in battling elements of the set and each other with a courageous physicality. We sought a huge vitality fuelled by powerful *but truthful* emotion; a comic physicality that hovered on the edge of violence.

The play is formally a farce, and a whole other area of work had to be developed, so that the playing of any situation could be extended to the last degree of its emotional logic (certainly not the logic of someone in command of their common sense – the characters being ruled by feelings and impulses rather than reason). Props, furniture, clothes and environment all became particularly important, and the actors' handling of these added to the heightened expressiveness of these moments. If the 'heroine' felt particularly shy or embarrassed or frightened, it was within the realms of truth and logical possibility for her to try to hide under the tiniest chair or inside a cupboard. One of the suitors, by the name of Friedegg, an immensely broad man who could only enter a room sideways, lost his violent temper when he learned that the 'bride' had rejected him and smashed up some of the furniture.

The set contained two double-hinged doors that were positioned so that the audience could see on both sides of them. They were equipped with particularly strong springs that automatically snapped them back vigorously from either direction to their closed position. The actors devoted a lot of time to discovering how these doors worked – in the first place making sure that they could handle them without being whacked in the back as they completed an entrance. Then they explored entering and exiting them at speed, slowly, confidently, insecurely, angrily, peeking through them . . . until they had quite literally made those doors dramatically and expressively their own, and every entrance and exit became a little drama of its own. For example, in keeping with the heightened playing of situations, the hero's friend, in his determination to see him married, would thrust Podkolyossin back into the room each time he tried to escape from his interview with the bride, literally hurling him through the door so that he sometimes arrived back at the lady's feet having slid all the way to her on his knees.

Working on heightened farce where the characters have a limited psychology and a strong relationship to the audience (as the characters do here), we felt a need to enlarge certain important moments of intense reaction, in keeping with the way we were elaborating situations. We extended such reactions by breaking them up into three separate impulses, three strong rapidly executed beats, so that the actors revealed the inner process of what happens instantaneously in psychological actuality. It worked as follows: first, a beat for the initial impulse of a reaction; second, a beat to consider what to do about it; third, a beat of taking action as a result of that consideration. An example: someone hits me; first, I express the immediate shock and pain at the blow; then, I consider whether this requires flight or fight; and finally, I decide to play for sympathy and cry. Or: someone proposes marriage; first, I react with maidenly coyness, hiding my face behind my fan; then, I fan myself while considering whether I should accept or not; finally, I avoid the wooer's eyes while asking for time . . . All those beats were clearly delineated – and all or any one of them could be shared with the audience. Because of the convention of the soliloquies, the audience could be party to the process of the characters' every thought. This tripartite reaction sustained a world where everything is heightened while remaining firmly based in psychological behaviour. For the actors to achieve this particular skill required a huge amount of practice, at first executed very technically and then, with familiarity, becoming more and more natural, spontaneous and not in the least mechanical. (I realised some time later that this triple reaction belongs to the language of *Tom & Jerry*.)

In this play the characters are essentially dealing with prime emotions – there's very little space for subtlety or much nuance. However, we still wanted specific and revealing detail. Even a relatively small reaction needed to be well shaped. The important thing was that it was performed with truth. This work resulted in performances of great precision and delineation. Not a moment was blurred or thrown away.

There were two sets: the bachelor's apartment and the bride's house. The guiding principle of the design was to create the opposing worlds of Male and Female. The former was a disorganised, messy, somewhat under-furnished dark brown bachelor haven where Podkolyossin lay umbilically attached to his chaise longue, indulging his natural inertia, abetted in his sloth by a servant who no more wanted him to marry than he did himself. The bride's home was a riot of ultra-feminine domesticity, crammed with furniture, overdecorated and overstuffed with ribbons, bows, cushions, anti-macassars and brightly coloured cloths through which it was difficult to manoeuvre without tripping over a frilly footstool or enmeshing yourself in fringe. An Everest of wardrobes (which were eventually opened to reveal the bride's vast trousseau in all its piles of glory) vanished into the flies. A little window high up towards the top of these wardrobes was the one from which Podkolyossin finally escaped, first having to mountaineer up the sides of the wardrobes to reach it.

Costumes and wigs, hugely exaggerated and with a vivid life of their own, followed the same principles, giving the actors even more material for expressive and revealing action. These were introduced into rehearsal early enough for the actors to have time to learn control over them and to inhabit them as their own.

The final image of the production was of matchmaker, bride, bride's aunt and hero's friend manically emptying the wardrobes, cupboards and drawers of their treasured trousseau, unfurling billowing sheets, pillows, tablecloths, table-runners, place mats, doilies and underwear amongst the smashed furniture, in a desperate search for the missing groom. The two sets were on a revolve that, as it slowly circled the stage, simultaneously revealed Podkolyossin safely back in his bachelor home, snuggling under a grubby blanket on his chaise longue, attended by his relieved servant.

There are as many formulations as the director and actors care to invent to help them to discover the world of a play. What I've suggested are just a few samples of an apparently endless number of areas that need to be questioned before you can confidently begin your search for the world of the play: *a detailed and unique world, true to its own rules and conventions, and not quite like any other world you've ever seen. You will eventually share those rules and conventions with the audience; and then you must play fair with them.*

———

The Actor's Creative Freedom and the World of the Play

A note of clarification. It must be clear that the actor's freedom is specifically defined by the conventions and parameters of each specific world. The 'rules' of the particular game create the form and discipline within which they find their freedom. Their areas of freedom will be very different from show to show. You can't apply the rules of football while playing cricket.

BRINGING THE STRANDS TOGETHER

The Final Stage of Rehearsal

The work up till now has been free of requests for results (and will continue to be so); you've been as non-judgemental as is humanly possible for a director to be in the rehearsal room. For most of the time you'll have given the actors – and they too will have contributed – a rich input of material to absorb, and it's only at the last stage of rehearsal that you can seriously observe its output: how the ingredients of the work on text, character and world have blended and now inform each other. Of course, you'll have been getting glimpses along the way of what is working, but the process up to this point involves a lot of trust: trust that if you make particular suggestions in a particular sequence, the actors will, in return, provide you with a developing vision of what the production might be. Now you'll be able to see what you've all created and, where necessary, to begin a sort of editing process: elaborating, eliminating and balancing elements. But, even now, if you become impatient and start pruning too early, you may nip some buds that are still some way from blooming. Process demands patience. I wait as long as I can before exercising any editorial function. You will, in fact, have been more or less 'editing' throughout rehearsals by your moment-to-moment judgements of what next needs to be done. Indeed, the more time the production has to evolve, the less need there's likely to be for any editing at all. *The whole process is largely self-monitoring* and the production, given breath, should evolve organically.

All things being equal, the work on text, character and world gradually filter into one another. But sometimes material you believed of value may not have been absorbed into the body of the production – that's to say, *literally* into the bodies of the actors. This rejection wouldn't have been a conscious decision on their part; it means the material in question didn't connect imaginatively with them in relation to the material that did. Then you have a choice: either to accept that it was probably inappropriate, in which case you graciously bow to that reality and let it go; or, should you feel the material is potentially too useful to be relinquished, your other option is to remind the actors of it by reintroducing it as a point of concentration. Sometimes good work fades because inadequate attention was devoted to it when it was first introduced; it wasn't planted to a sufficient depth for growth.

Runs

You'll start to discover the life and the world you've all created once you've done a few runs of the play. Runs should dominate the final period of rehearsal: first of scenes and acts, then of the whole piece. I'm a great believer in runs, and I'd advise setting them up as early as possible in the rehearsal schedule. From the very first week, I try to do a full run as a way of ending each week – even when the actors still need to hold their scripts. These runs function – not as tests – but as a celebration of the week's work. It gives the actors the chance, naturally and gradually, to shape the arc of their roles and to develop their stamina. Dealt with calmly, runs also give you, the director, periods in which to sit back, as it were, and watch the show with increasing objectivity.

If runs are left too late in the proceedings, they can acquire an undue importance, even induce a sense of panic, and several things can occur that militate against the purpose of all your work up to this point. Under last-minute pressure, the actors can feel that, abruptly, they have to come up with results, that they're going to be judged in a way they haven't experienced up till now; they may feel they need to 'get it right for you'; they may feel the need to 'perform'; they may feel safer reverting to old habits. You won't see your company functioning as they have done so far, but, instead, suddenly obeying a lot of former agendas that distract them from the spontaneous creativity you've been nurturing. And you, yourself, as director, may react to such runs with clumsy alarm that everything's going down the plughole, and you have to start fixing things – in fact, demanding results!

Whatever else you do, *you must under no circumstances change horses in midstream,* or unintentionally seem to be doing so. Runs must conform to the organic process you've established. They have to be set up creatively so that the actors can continue to explore, as indeed they must, *right up to the final performance.* Actors will almost instinctively anticipate a run as a sort of test. The earlier you embark on runs, the less likelihood of their reacting in this way. Your job is to discourage actors from putting false pressure on themselves, while encouraging a sense of challenge. You have to persuade them to see runs as a continuing development of the rehearsal process, not as a sudden gear change. *What you should be promoting and monitoring on all occasions is the creation of truthful stage life and a coherently imagined world.*

In this last period of rehearsal, it's advisable to have runs at different times of day. Our energy varies throughout twenty-four hours, and the actors, by sometimes doing a run early, sometimes later, will have to make adjustments that wouldn't happen if they always did them each day at the same time. They need to keep on their toes, rather than settling into patterns. Once they're in performance, they should be able to handle the circumstances of any show with the greatest flexibility.

It's unproductive to do run after run without intervening sessions to rectify moments that are thrown up as needing attention. And there's a point beyond which runs become tiring and de-energising, when the actors could do with some faces other than your own and those of the production team observing them for the umpteenth time. In fact, what we all need at this point is the response of an audience the better to understand what we've got. It's a good idea to invite a few people who have nothing to do with the production to watch some of the final runs. The actors can at least anticipate the stimulation of fresh reactions. They'll have the challenge of putting themselves well and truly behind the work they've been committed to for the past several weeks.

Within this final period dominated by runs, it's also a good idea to have daily sessions in which particular skills developed in search of the world of the play continue to be exercised and refined. When we were working on *A Handful of Dust*, we had, by some quirk of scheduling, the opportunity to do a dress rehearsal in front of an audience a week before we actually opened. It went encouragingly well. The actors of course felt tremendously confident. We took advantage of that following week to hone the form of what was a sophisticated and heightened production (*see*: PRACTICE in WORLD OF THE PLAY). Each day, we would run a section of the show with the POC on speed and attack, then on the characters' use of language, then on the way they wore their clothes . . . and so forth. Of course, the actors would always be playing their actions and objectives freshly and spontaneously, but the form of the world was being continuously reinforced and the execution perfected in a playful and creative way. By the time we opened officially, that world had been defined to an impressively high and skilful level. These 'technical' aspects of the show were not a burden, a limitation or an inhibition to the actors (as technical demands can sometimes be) but had become for them a necessary and natural expression of the world they inhabited.

Points of Concentration in Runs

Runs without clear purpose are counterproductive. A way of keeping them alive is with the use of points of concentration. They can deal with both given circumstances and technical skills. *Remember: at all times, whatever the POC, the actors must play their objectives (and situations) with absolute focus and commitment.*

TECHNICAL POC RUNS

In these runs, actors have to maintain a total subjectivity in the actual playing of the scene, whilst objectively exploring and exercising some technical aspect of their performances (as I've just described for *A Handful of Dust*). With technical preoccupations, the dual nature of acting will be very much in play: while, as characters, they are pursuing their objectives with full commitment, the cast will be exploring their POCs as actors. Set up your runs with very precise technical instructions for their POC.

For example, if you feel that the actors could move with greater speed through the performance, give them the POC to up the ante on their intentions; to find, at every moment, the greatest but justifiably motivated urgency with which to play their actions; to move the play forward with the utmost economy and focus. If you merely instruct the actors to play faster, they will tend to do just that – go fast, without purpose or motivation, rushing, gabbling and generalising. Some other examples:

To explore how the space might reveal character, theme and situation

To explore the expressive use of props and costumes

To reveal further aspects of character, such as profession, or status in the family

To explore the expressiveness use of the character's style of language and speech . . .

GIVEN CIRCUMSTANCE POC RUNS

You can also revive POCs or create new ones that deal with the given circumstances, in which case the actors would of course employ the POC subjectively, in character.

Playful Warm-Up Runs

These 'playful' runs or partial runs should be placed within the warm-up section of rehearsals and are about developing a general stamina, flexibility, playfulness and ease in handling the text.

PLAYING THE TEXT ON THE RUN

You instruct the actors to play a scene or act, or part of an act, *with full commitment*, while constantly running in the acting area. They should make sure they are really communicating with their partners and not haphazardly throwing their lines into the air without focus. They should work for verbal precision, sustained breath and supported voices so that the continuous movement and the effort of the lungs never for a moment interfere with the delivery of the text. If they can only just get the lines out accompanied by a lot of heavy breathing, they're not fulfilling the exercise. This exercise needs building up over time.

PLAYING THE TEXT ON THE RUN WITH VARIATIONS

This is an elaboration of the above. The actors continue running, but you add other things for them to do that you think useful, such as passing props to each other, changing clothes, their own and each other's, moving furniture, lifting and moving each other. They should never stop in order to execute any of them. None of this needs to be motivated. What it achieves is a great ease and naturalness with the text and an adroitness in dealing with physical matters; all in all, a greater fluency. And a sense that they can deal with anything that might occur during a performance. Ensure that the text is kept moving. In such runs, the actors are having to deal with the unexpected, while keeping the text flowing. It should counteract any tendency for them to get settled or cautious during the more formal runs.

Scene Work

Work on scenes should take place between runs. Up to this moment, the whole company will have been present for all rehearsals. Now, you may want to do some quite conventional, detailed scene work, in which case you can now call only those actors involved in a particular scene. Actors, however devoted to the idea of an ensemble, will always appreciate some period when your attention is exclusively on them. By this stage in the process, with their amassed knowledge and experience of their roles, they will be in the position to absorb any observations you have about their work. Earlier in the proceedings when, for lack of such knowledge, they're much more vulnerable, your comments will have less ground in which to take root. Actors may tend to reject ideas early in a process, when they're not yet sure of what they're doing. They may feel that the director is imposing on them before they've had a chance to make their own contribution. Later, with knowledge and experience, they're able to listen and weigh up your suggestions on a healthier, one-to-one basis.

I must stress that these 'private' sessions on scenes are not about asking the actors to make choices (fix results) as to how each moment should be played. *That will never be the case.* It is more about pointing out missed or blurred transitions, undernourished details of character or situation, maybe urging them to be more exploratory, more daring at particular moments or ironing out any inconsistencies of style or convention.

A Final Week's Schedule

Let us assume that we have six more days of rehearsal before the start of technical rehearsals, that the production is of *The Seagull*, a play in four acts, and that we have already done some full runs of the production.

	Monday	Tuesday	Wednesday	Thursday	Friday	Saturday
Morning	Warm-Up Runs; POC Runs; Scene work.	Warm-Up; Technical Exercises (voice, etc.); Run Acts 3 & 4.	Warm-Up Runs; POC Runs; Scene Work.	Warm-Up; Technical Exercises (voice, etc.); Run Acts 3 & 4.	Warm-Up; POC Runs or Technical Exercises; Run Acts I & 2.	Warm–Up; Full Run; Notes.
Afternoon	Run Acts I & 2	Full Run; Notes.	Run Acts I & 2.	Full Run; Notes.	Run Acts 3 & 4.	

THE TEXT EMBODIED

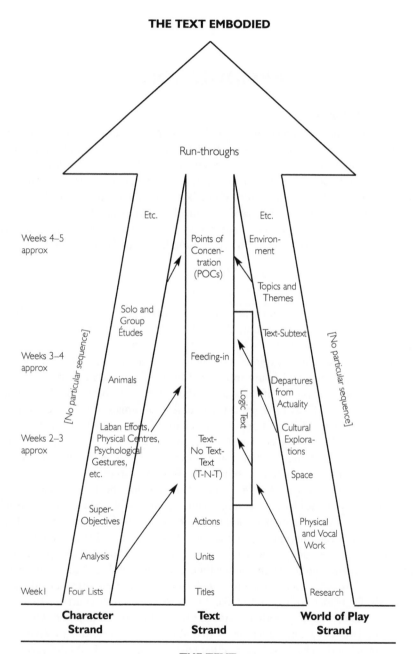

Run-throughs

	Etc.	Etc.
Weeks 4–5 approx	Points of Concentration (POCs)	Environment
		Topics and Themes
	Solo and Group Études	Text-Subtext
Weeks 3–4 approx	Feeding-in	Departures from Actuality
	Animals	
	Laban Efforts, Physical Centres, Psychological Gestures, etc.	Cultural Explorations
Weeks 2–3 approx	Text-No Text-Text (T-N-T)	
		Space
	Super-Objectives	Physical and Vocal Work
	Actions	
	Analysis	
	Units	
Week 1	Four Lists	Titles	Research

[No particular sequence]

Logic Text

[No particular sequence]

Character Strand   **Text Strand**   **World of Play Strand**

THE TEXT

THE REHEARSAL PROCESS

PRODUCTION

Actors and Designers

Design – and a director's relationship with a designer – is a topic in itself and not the remit of this book. However, wanting actors to have freedom in performance must inevitably influence the sort of designer you, the director, will choose to work with and the sort of design process you'll go through together. The purpose, always, is to ensure that the actors don't become trapped by any technical or design element over which they have no control or with which they can't create a relationship. So in order to give a comprehensive view of how to maintain the actors' freedom in every aspect of a production, let me make some points on this area of work.

Idealism

Of course, the ideal situation (which, on rare occasions, does happen) is to have the designer in the rehearsal room, observing and working with the company on a regular basis from the start of rehearsals, especially during the 'world' strand of the work. As the actors explore, the designer will be both influencing the evolution of the work and being influenced by it. The designer can offer suggestions for the organisation of the space and the flow of movement and can commandeer what seem likely to be appropriate objects and materials for the actors to experiment with (cardboard boxes, rope, chairs, balls, particular elements of clothing . . .). I experienced a wonderful example of this, working with the designer Rae Smith, who, unusual amongst her profession, dedicates a lot of her time to being with the company in rehearsal. We were working on the production of a play by Cervantes, *Pedro, the Great Pretender*, for the Royal Shakespeare Company. Most of the characters were Spanish country-folk. She excavated from the RSC's vast wardrobe stock a wide range of clothes, which were not all at first glance obviously reminiscent of peasant life. These were wheeled into the rehearsal room on clothes-racks. The actors were encouraged to hunt for the clothes that they thought would be suitable for their characters and to dress up in them. Over a period of days the company transformed themselves into their ideas of shepherds, farmers, gypsies and the like. I then set them improvisations. Rae took digital photos of them, individually and in groups, in action and posed. On these photos she later drew any adjustments that she thought necessary to what they were wearing, and from these, their actual costumes were made. Many garments that the actors had chosen found their way straight into the performance. There were two clear benefits from this process. The design could not be other than thoroughly integrated into the show. Let me put that more correctly: it wasn't a matter of integrating something into an entity that already existed; the costumes evolved organically along with the other aspects of the production. The second advantage was that in performance the actors had a creative relationship with what they wore – it belonged to them, and they had expressive control of it. I think this is a fine example of honouring everyone's creativity and the spirit of ensemble.

Realism

Unfortunately, there are practical reasons why such a situation can happen only occasionally. One is the usual four-week rehearsal period, inadequate time for designers to investigate possibilities with the cast, then to prepare designs and technical drawings and for these to be executed before the first performance. Another is the limited availability of designers, most of whom are so inadequately paid that they're forced to work on several overlapping projects at any one time and can't be at the exclusive call of any single production. They invariably have complicated schedules which necessitates your making claims as early as you can on whatever of their time is not committed. Periodically, you may discover your collaborators have disappeared to some distant part of the globe. A third factor is defined by the schedules of theatres themselves. Your show will probably be just one in a crowded programme, so they usually need designs and technical drawings well in advance of rehearsals in order to budget for the money and time required to build the design in relation to the other productions flanking yours.

Pragmatism

Working within the system that exists, director and designers have to decide how best they can achieve their vision of a show. You need to know well in advance the sort of restrictions likely to face you. Then you can find the best way of maximising your aspirations within them. For example, if it seems more important for the production to evolve in rehearsal rather than being pre-designed, you might give up any idea of heavily constructed scenery and negotiate instead on the basis of creating a physical space that needs less time to build. It becomes a matter of intelligent compromise. I admit that, often, limitations do create imaginative solutions. But constant restrictions do eventually become creatively numbing. Providing conditions for the designer to be a deeply embedded collaborator on the production is by far the best situation.

Process

I have no rules or patterns for a working method with a designer. This relationship is intensely personal and each one develops in its own way. I do try to involve a designer as early as possible in the process of my imagining a show. This, I hope, ensures that the designer can start contributing before my ideas have become too advanced and consequently too prescriptive. So as soon as I get the glimpse of an idea, I share this with a designer. We usually have a long, agreeably arduous period of getting to know each other (understanding each other's language, predilections, aspirations . . .) and trying things out (lots of drawings and sketches from the designer, research and looking at images together in books, museums, galleries, in the street . . .); then, as we get closer to where we seem to be aiming, we consider a series of models. This is extremely demanding on the designer; but by constantly questioning and shifting things around, endless trial and error, even going out on wild limbs with provocations to challenge the validity of our current ideas ('Let's have the actors hovering off the ground for the entire length of the show'), the design evolves, taking on a life of its own as it does so. Because we've kept discarding and simplifying along the way, by the time we arrive at the final image for the show, what we've ended up with seems absolutely 'right'. I don't remember ever having a set that was unworkable, unaesthetic or unsympathetic to the actors. Only once, quite early in my career, did I have a bad experience with a designer. After what I thought were several amicable and sympathetic exchanges of ideas, culminating in an agreement that the production (Goldoni's *Servant of Two Masters*) should be warm and earthy, he presented me with designs of ice-blue, silver and black. When I demurred, he indignantly said he'd managed to find some warmth and pointed to a little detail of red trimming! We soon separated.

The Actor and the Set: Two Approaches

There seem to be two basic ways of ensuring that the design is absorbed into the actors' creative journey. If the show has to be designed in advance, one is to insist that the design is also *constructed in advance* and brought into rehearsal so that the actors can develop a relationship with it and inhabit it practically, sensuously and emotionally; and, should something not work, there is still time to adjust it. This is what I did with the designer Paul Dart, with whom I've collaborated on about twenty-seven productions, for a National Theatre production of Goldoni's *Trilogia de la Villeggiatura* (*The Countrymania Trilogy*). The set was complicated: a series of small revolves on a large revolve. We managed periodically to get on the stage itself to habituate ourselves to the large revolve; the smaller revolves were brought into one of their large rehearsal rooms so that the actors could familiarise themselves with how they moved. The combination of revolves working simultaneously created logistical problems that we'd never have solved during a normal technical period. On another occasion, working on Philip Osment's *The Dearly Beloved* for Hampstead Theatre, Paul and I wanted to use a raked stage. But it was essential that the actors were able work on an incline in safety and comfort. Standing and moving on a slope for any length of time can often cause injuries; the body's weight becomes unevenly distributed, creating unnatural stresses that throw the spine out of alignment. This is even more critical if an actor is wearing high heels. The incidents are legion of actors, eager to please directors, letting themselves be persuaded onto rakes in unsuitable footwear and ending up with permanently damaged backs. (As much as actors can be 'difficult', they can equally go like lambs to the slaughter.) So, for this reason, we had the set, complete with raked floor, from the first day of rehearsal. A physiotherapist came into rehearsals to give advice. The actors were given specific exercises to strengthen their legs and stretch appropriate muscles. By the time we opened, the actors were using the rake naturally and imaginatively, without anyone having incurred, or ever incurring, the slightest twinge.

The other approach is to design a box of tricks, a set of building blocks that the actors can explore, play with, manoeuvre and put together in many different ways according to their scenic needs. So the set is not a fixed object but becomes a series of possibilities. I used this technique when I worked with designer Peter McIntosh, first for Method & Madness, then for Yale Repertory Theatre, on the James Ellroy thriller, *The Black Dahlia*, another novel adaptation needing numerous locations. We wanted to create the violent male atmosphere of a noir-ish 1940s Hollywood, in which the furniture could be kicked, shoved, pushed in such a way that it shot across the stage. The set was a steel frame, suggestive of the locker room of both an American police precinct and of a gym, lined with lockers which were movable and used to contain props and clothes. There was a smooth steel floor and very light steel furniture which slid easily and rapidly over it. (I say 'easily', but it took time and effort and trial and error to achieve this.) All these elements were brought into rehearsal and the actors discovered how to use them practically and expressively, how to push, pull, shove and kick chairs, desks, lockers, beds and tables around, so that at times furniture literally flew across the space by itself, creating instant transformations. This sort of work is a substantial and creative part of the main rehearsal period and would be impossible to achieve during the standard time scheduled for technicals. So, once again, I stress the need for adequate rehearsal time.

When a Set is Not a Set

A good set should feel incomplete until an actor steps onto it. The air within a set should vibrate with the *promise* of action. It should create a feeling of excited anticipation in the beholder. For the audience, the beauty of first facing an empty space is that it arouses in them a sense of something about to fill the void, an excitement as to what might appear. While it's empty, anything could happen. A chair placed in the space will instantly create an impatience in the audience for someone to be seated there. People who work in theatre will be familiar with the experience of coming upon an empty stage in a darkened auditorium, with just a work light left on. Some chairs may have been left, scattered around. The effect is often more beautiful and more suggestive of something thrilling and mysterious about to happen than any fully designed stage can create. A set, however beautiful, that looks complete in itself without people inhabiting it, is essentially static, lacking in vitality, deadly, dead.

The Ground Beneath Their Feet

The most important part of the set is the floor (despite the fact that in most class-ridden theatres from the past, the stage floor is invisible from several parts of the house). The design should emanate from the floor. It supports and gives power and energy both to the set and the actor. Viewed from above, as it is by the whole audience in most well-designed modern theatres (and Greek amphitheatres), the floor also frames the actor. The floor creates a dynamic space on which action will be played out. Concentrating on 'walls' (as most projected images do) merely creates flat decoration.

What is best for the action? What supports the actor? These are the questions to keep uppermost when thinking about a set.

———

Lighting

When I describe to other theatre people the spontaneity in performance that I pursue with the actors, their first response is frequently, 'But how do you light a show? If the actors are able to move anywhere?' Well, the simplest solution, initially, when I first embarked on this principle, was to have the whole space lit by open white lamps set at a constant level throughout – in other words, the lighting was to ensure the actors and audience were visible to each other, and had no other purpose but that. Despite its simplicity, it was not laziness that prompted the decision. There was a clear artistic purpose. As I've stated, my intention when I founded Shared Experience was to prove that all that was necessary for a full experience of theatre were actors and audience together in the same space at the same time with the material that provided the story that the first group would tell to the second. The source of that material could be an improvisation, the adaptation of some non-theatre text or a play. In those early days of the company, it came from the adaptation of stories and novels. One of the challenges posed by such material was for us to evoke its numerous places, spaces, times, clothes, objects and other environmental conditions in the imaginations of the audience by the imaginations of the actors. For this, we insisted on an empty stage. Anything placed in the acting area would intrude on both groups' imaginations. This included variations in lighting, too. I've already described the lighting effects that the audience imagined they saw in our *Bleak House* production.

Lighting is a temptation. It can do so much. It can also do *too* much. Its downside is that it instantly does a lot of the actors' work for them. It can't help but impose associations, images, moods and atmospheres on the audience, depriving them of their imaginative participation in the performance and pre-empting a vital part of the actors' creativity. Lighting, like sound – music especially – is a dominating medium that, if not curbed, can take over the proceedings. Many directors employ light, music and sound brilliantly, often to compensate for the inadequacies of the acting. Dynamically used, they can give the audience the sense that something is happening, even when the actors aren't making anything happen at all. They are partially disguising the essential emptiness. But lighting doesn't provide life. *An authentic theatre experience is created only when actors create it.*

So initially, constant open white light was a signature of the company's productions. Over time, I've allowed myself to broaden the scope of the lighting. In a realistic play whose action moves through a single day, the lighting might change slowly and subtly from early morning to evening, making its changes imperceptibly and with the whole space always in a lighting state that allowed the actors to move anywhere without being plunged into shadow. Then, as an experiment, first in *A Handful of Dust*, then in an epic *Arabian Nights* in Germany – with Paul Dart on both occasions – he designed a rig of open white light that was evenly balanced on four sides, from above and from below, with which we evolved a sequence of different states that always kept the whole space clearly lit, but created different effects by varying the intensity of the light from its different sources. We ended up with what was essentially a box of lighting possibilities. We then applied them *quite arbitrarily* to different scenes, the lighting states were programmed at random. It was revelatory to discover that all the states seemed appropriate to any scene they lit! The actors never had to concern themselves as to whether they could move into certain areas since the stage was always 'equally' lit. And the audience was getting visual refreshment.

Lighting is the element with which the actor has the least connection. Occasionally, if the stage felt too moody, actors from an earlier generation complained that the audience wouldn't be able to see them, or demanded to be lit in certain colours they believed were flattering to them. Sometimes actors, who are concerned with being able to make contact, complain (rightly) that they can't see the audience or each other because of lights focused at a level with their eyes. But, by and large, actors don't participate – and aren't invited to – in how they're lit. They're not even given a chance to see what the lighting looks like. (You can't see it when you're in it!) However, I try, whenever possible during technical rehearsals, to let the actors at least look at the lighting from offstage and then, if I can steal time, to work with it on stage, if only for half an hour. The lighting ideally becomes another means of their creative expressiveness. Owing to rapid developments in electronics and digital technology, lighting has become an increasingly sophisticated medium, and it's rare to see a show that isn't interestingly, even beautifully lit. Even stronger reason for the actors to collaborate with it, exploit it and enhance it.

Some forty years ago, Grotowski led the way by placing on the floor of his acting spaces rather primitive lamps (he *was* an exponent of Poor Theatre) that allowed the actors, by where they moved and stood, to vary the intensity of light or to cast shadows. They were in rather limited control of how the lighting affected the space.

Since then, there have been productions in which the actors used handheld lamps to light each other. I used them on one occasion but found that technological restrictions limited their effectiveness. To avoid the problem of cables trailing all over the stage, lights were battery-operated; the problem *then* became the unwieldiness of batteries large enough to provide sufficient intensity for long enough before they needed recharging. More recently, I did a production of *A Midsummer Night's Dream* for Shakespeare's Globe in which lights, much like those nowadays designed for Christmas trees, were sewn into the costumes of the fairies with controls strapped to their wrists so that they could light themselves up in a variety of speeds, rhythmic patterns and intensity. But even for the short stage time they were needed, the relatively small batteries were quite heavy and difficult to place on the body without limiting the actor's physical performance. And despite constant recharging between performances, there were discouraging occasions when a fairy's lights would die on her in mid-scene . . . Exhorting the audience to call out that they *did* believe in fairies wouldn't have solved the situation at these moments. Technology and faith don't naturally marry.

When I worked at the Cameri Theatre in Tel Aviv, they had a very large rehearsal space away from their main theatre in which they had set up facilities for lighting. For at least the final two weeks of rehearsal, the lighting designer was able quietly to work on lighting the production while, simultaneously, the actors and I got on with our work. The results were, of course, tremendously satisfying – detailed, complex and precise. In such a situation, I could give the actors time to work creatively with the lighting: first seeing how the stage looked in its various states; then exploring how they could exploit the use of shadow, warm and cool areas, backlighting and so forth to reinforce – or more sophisticatedly, to counterpoint – a dramatic or psychological point. It obviously gave the designer and myself more opportunity to try things out, rather than having to make rapid decisions under the usual pressure of technical rehearsals. As with everything else in the preparation of theatre work, *time is the element essential to achieve best practice*.

Introducing the Physical Production into Rehearsals

The traditional way for actors to meet their set, lighting, props and even their costumes for the first time is at the technical rehearsal, which often takes place only two or three days before they meet their first audience. Suddenly, under pressure of time, the actors are thrown into an abrupt and usually stressed encounter with the technical and design elements of the show – the environment in which the life they've been gradually evolving in rehearsal is at last supposed to come fully into bloom. Nothing ever prepares them for this encounter. Despite having been shown sketches and models, probably on the first day of rehearsal, nothing is quite what they expected. Coloured tape marking out the set on the rehearsal-room floor does not have the same dimension as the solid objects that suddenly intrude on what was once open space. The clothes for which they've had fittings look and feel unrecognisable in their final form. Props are either larger or smaller than their rehearsal substitutes, have different textures and weights and function differently. Chairs and sofas are suddenly awkward to get in and out of; costumes collide and tangle with furniture; shoes come into conflict with stairs; lighting frequently blinds them or it is so intense that it makes them sweat in their heavy costumes. All the work of the preceding weeks that have been devoted to the delicate process of nurturing their spontaneity and creativity is pushed unceremoniously to one side as they juggle under limited time with items that seem to have been designed specifically to subvert their performances. Within this pressured period, there is rarely (if ever) time set aside for them to come calmly and creatively into a relationship with this new environment, to familiarise themselves with what they are wearing or handling or moving within, and to make this physical world their own, an organic part of their creative language.

So, frequently, the physical elements of the production end up being imposed on the actor, a situation from which some performances never recover. I can't begin to count the productions I've seen where the actors have absolutely no spatial, emotional or even realistic relationship with their environment or with what they're wearing, both of which become obstacles rather than enhancements to their performances. Sometimes actors can to all intents and purposes disappear beneath the wigs and costumes that are little better than dumped on them. This situation means that previews are spent not only adjusting to the reality of audiences but also of the physical production. This is also true of the technical aspects of the production: sound and lighting cues are usually completed only just before the 'curtain goes up' on the first performance, sometimes not even then. So first performances become an extension of dress and technical rehearsals. It is a poor and unproductive tradition based entirely on economic grounds (few theatres feel they can afford to remain 'dark' for more than two or three days for these rehearsals). It has nothing to do with providing the best conditions for creative care.

To avoid this situation, I establish my requirements for the physical production well before the start of rehearsals. I find out what might be the theatre's limitations of time, space and budget and then push for whatever amounts of these I can claw back to incorporate the physical elements into the actual body of rehearsal. Initially (as in the examples I've given of working with designers), I ask for the set to be in the rehearsal room from the first day of rehearsal and then negotiate from that position. I want the costumes available for the actors for at least two weeks before we start technicals and I establish deadlines for the actual props and furniture (not substitutes) to be fed into rehearsals. If the actors have to deal with very specific technical aspects of the production, such as moving the set, I'm even more insistent on these elements being brought early into the rehearsal room so that they can be organically woven into the fabric of the play's world, in fact, contribute to the making of that world. This is clearly of mutual benefit to both actors and designers.

I also make sure that the entire sound score is ready and being used in rehearsal so that, once more, the actors can have time to incorporate it creatively into their performances. Lighting is the one element that usually has to wait until the production has moved into the theatre. Even here, as I've said, I try, whenever possible, to fight for the actors to have time to get off the stage and, at very least, see how they're being lit.

So, in the best of all possible worlds, the set, costumes and technology are gradually introduced into the actual rehearsal process and are given the creative time to become an integral part of the world under creation. This allows for problematic elements that in a pressured technical rehearsal are rejected by the actor in a sort of hysteria ('I can't wear this!' 'I'm not working on *that* rake!') to be more diplomatically examined, tried out and, if necessary (and it's usually not necessary if you avoid last-minute confrontations), adjusted to the benefit of both designers and actors. Often, the actors can make a contribution to the design of the show. When the company does finally arrive at the technical and dress rehearsals, these proceed more fluidly. Most technical matters will have already been absorbed during the preceding weeks. The inner life of the production has not been crudely disrupted and therefore the designers and technicians have the benefit of more uninterrupted time to do *their* jobs. Then, technical rehearsals become genuinely for them, just as they should.

I know that some people do actually love the unnecessary panic and pressure, the blood, sweat and tears of a standard technical rehearsal. They superstitiously believe this to all be part of the magic of creating theatre. 'A bad final dress rehearsal means a great first night' and so forth . . . I've no time at all for such theatrical mumbo-jumbo. I stop whistling backstage only to say 'Macbeth' very firmly before starting to whistle again.

PERFORMANCE

Postnatal Care

Once the production is in performance, my goal is to ensure it remains flexible, that the actors are constantly 'in the moment', alive and living, open to change, and never drifting onto auto-pilot. The goal of most directors is to ensure that their production stays close to how it was when it reached the press night. Even if there are details that they'd have liked to change, the moment has passed and everything connected with that show is done and dusted. This may be dictated more by convention and tradition than by any artistic criterion. Contractually, most directors are required to keep a periodic eye on a production, but that depends on their availability which is often non-existent as they go off to work on a new production elsewhere. This is the consequence of an economically pressured, freelance profession. Many directors, like designers, only earn a reasonable living by running from one production to another. So the maintenance of the production becomes the responsibility of either the stage management or an assistant; and their remit is to make sure things stay pretty much as they are. A few directors may be conscientious and responsible. Most, I think, read the reviews and, if good, they dine out on them and show up at the theatre trailing clouds of glory and people they wish to impress; if they're bad, they forget them as fast as possible and move on. I've frequently heard actors lament, 'After the press night, we never saw him (the director) again!' If a show is successful, the main danger for actors is that an aura of self-congratulation can creep into the performance. In the opposite situation, out of a sheer instinct for survival – after all, they're the ones who have to go out there and face the audience – the actors usually remain admirably committed to a show. Indeed, they may well believe in their production, despite the reviews. But the effort to stay positive can be emotionally draining in the face of dwindling audiences. Knowing one thing and pretending another for as long as a show continues to run its course can take a heavy toll on an actor's psyche.

Recidivism

Once before an audience, some actors, new to an open-ended way of working, may instinctively clutch at what feels like security and revert to old habits, repeating those moments that clearly please the audience. Lindsay Anderson, in his *Diaries*, complains of the audience-pleasing intransigence of his stars, Celia Johnson and Ralph Richardson, once they were performing *The Kingfisher*. He writes of 'gross takes' and 'stylised gestures' that the audience loved, but 'each laugh,' he records, 'is like a sword in my side.' Presumably there had been no trace of these during rehearsals. Once, just before the first preview of a production, as I was warning the cast of such traps and reminding them to stay open and alive to change and growth, I was stunned by the surprised comment of an actor who, after weeks of rehearsing in much the process I've been detailing in these pages, exclaimed, 'Oh, I didn't really think you meant it!' I did. And I do.

Watching a Show: the First Eighteen Months of Shared Experience

One-Night Stands

In the first few years of Shared Experience, I watched almost all our performances. I toured with the actors, was the main minibus driver and ensured the venue was ready for performances. We did a lot of one-night stands in a variety of spaces originally never intended for performance: classrooms, dining halls (with the smell of stale cooking still present), small community centres and the like, most with limited technology and improvised seating. In those days, our boast was that we could perform anywhere at any time for anyone. We offered workshops, discussions and demonstrations of our work as part of the package. So I felt it more than beholden to me to be there to oversee such events. To be fair, the actors, after some initial sessions, would have been perfectly capable of dealing with them on their own – as well as driving the bus! But I believed that this was what the creation of a true company demanded. I was trying hard for a sort of democracy: if I, as director, expected actors, often in uncomfortable circumstances, to undergo a gruelling schedule away from home and family in order to present the fruits of my ambitions, I should be prepared to be part of what was going on, too. However, my reason for being there, beyond wanting to show willing, was to continue working on the shows. We seemed to be discovering so many new levels of playing in those storytelling days that, however far we progressed, there was always further and deeper to go. So, in addition to travelling, giving performances and workshops, the hard-pressed actors were also rehearsing in whatever time was left.

The First Six Months

And, of course, I was also curious to see how the shows developed in performance. In the company's first eighteen months, which included five different productions of stories from *The Arabian Nights* (three for adults and two for children), I learnt a lot. The initial six months were spent watching the actors, adjusting, clarifying and, I hope, enriching their performances.

The Second Six Months

My confidence and trust in the actors being utterly secure, I found myself, over the next six months, observing the audience and the spaces we were in. This was not something I'd planned. This is where my focus seemed naturally to want to go. I could see how both these – audience and space – could be creative in helping us to play freshly. Part of our development of the performances was learning to take artistic advantage of what was happening and what was there. So a lot of our daytime work became not so much about working on the material, but dealing with the nature of the performance itself, devising ways of adjusting perform-ances to possible audience reactions and to the space. If, for example, we played in an unusual or uncongenial environment (one of our boasts being that we could perform anywhere), instead of bemoaning the difficulties and fighting against them, we learnt to make the peculiarities of the new space a positive condition of that night's performance, something to exploit by means of stimulating POCs, such as 'the limitation of the space' or 'the distance of the audience'.

With regard to audiences, we tried to develop a group sense of how they were reacting and an ability to adjust to them collectively as the performance went on its course. If the audience was a little nervous (we were frequently very close to them, sharing the same open lighting, using direct address and making eye con-tact), the actors as a group developed the skill to slow things down and allow the audience space and time to get on a wavelength with them. When faced with a cold or unreceptive audience, an actor's instinct for self-protection is to think 'Fuck you!', close off and get through the performance as fast and painlessly as possible. The company had to un-learn this almost autonomic reaction and, in-stead of getting tense, learn to relax and open up. It always worked. If, on the other hand, the audience was bright, quick and threatening to get ahead of them, they learnt to speed up.[*]

The Final Six Months

In the final six months, my focus returned to the actors and the production. And something rather uncanny had occurred. By this time, the actors had played each moment of the play in so many different ways (no two performances had been identical) that their performances had by now acquired a sort of multi-dimen-sional resonance. A moment or scene – irrespective of how it was consciously being played on that occasion, or of what choices the actors were spontaneously making in the heat of performance – seemed simultaneously to release the ghosts or vibrations of many other choices that had been made in the past. I've no idea if the audience sensed this. It wasn't something you could ask them; what they were seeing was for them their first and sole experience of the show. But they

---

[*] Instructively, there was a distinct difference between audiences north and south of Watford: the former were quicker on the uptake, more direct, frequently less used to going to theatre and therefore, it seems, more open to see and accept what was there; ironically, the South-erners, more used to theatre, were warier and at times had difficulty understanding the simplest conventions, presumably because these weren't part of what they'd grown to expect from previous experience.

were clearly engrossed by these richly resonant moments. Comic moments were poignant, thought-provoking and sour; dramatic moments were ironic and tender. In fact, it was hard to define any one moment. *This was a great realisation: potentially, any moment could contain anything and everything.* The actors had reached a level where their knowledge and experience of the material had grown very deep within them. I think they felt, at those moments, a rare sort of fulfilment. Something like a current of electricity passed between actors and audience. The warmth and intensity of communication between the two groups seemed to make them one. On those occasions, theatre seemed totally to validate itself, to become the theatre I dreamt of. All the deadness, the difficulties, the disappointments of so much theatre, my own as well as other people's, were wiped away. In that period, in some of the most unlikely circumstances, I experienced my most rewarding moments of theatre.

———

Keeping the Performance Alive

A show, fixed and repeated for that length of time without any fresh input or exploration, would, by contrast, have become increasingly slick and unfulfilled. You have only to see most West End performances after a couple of months to sense that the actors are on professional automatic in their well-oiled machine.

My presence on tour ensured that a show stayed fresh. Between us, we discovered more and more nuances and ideas in the material, more aspects to relationships, more shape to situations. The cast, if they felt in danger of getting stale, would themselves decide to use a POC for a particular performance – either reviving an old one (though not recreating old results) or inventing a new one. Or each actor might choose one individually. They did serious warm-ups before every show, despite their demanding schedule. In some venues, we had to do a lot of pleading and insisting to get stage time for this, to keep the house closed till as near to the start of the performance as possible.

The Director's Presence

Eventually, I realised that my continual presence at performances was possibly becoming a form of benign oppression for the actors; periodically freed from my gaze, they might feel released from a subliminal need to do what they thought would please me. They might take *even more* chances. So I lessened the number of shows I watched. They'd always report that the shows I hadn't seen had been terrific, exceptional . . . ! I believed them.

Heightened Levels v. Comfort Zones

When I started running Cambridge Theatre Company (later renamed Method & Madness), I no longer travelled with the company. The conditions for touring had changed: no more one-night stands, people travelling under their own steam, fewer workshops. Besides, I had more 'office' responsibilities with this larger company – and, to be honest, I'd become less infatuated with my own work. Each week, I'd visit the show in its latest venue, usually midweek when the actors had already adjusted to the peculiarities of the new space, so I could watch the show without having to take those into consideration. I would arrive in time for a performance, give notes and do some work on the following afternoon, watch that evening's performance and leave the next morning. What could happen to a show in which a heightened level of playing had evolved during rehearsals was that imperceptibly, as the actors grew more comfortable within the performance, the degree of heightening began dropping from its intended level back to their own more personal comfort zones. The show remained detailed, spontaneous and alive, but it had become slower, more naturalistic and was beginning to lose its aesthetic logic. It seems that a company, however astutely self-monitoring, does periodically need a director's eye to point out something that is imperceptibly slipping – something that, understandably, it might not notice happening. However, it's possible that the performance might have eventually fallen to a level at which the actors themselves *would* have noticed it.

A Snowy Night in Lincolnshire

During the period I taught at LAMDA, the school had a policy of sending some of their third-year-student productions on a short tour. I had directed a production of *The Servant of Two Masters*, in which the ten students had excelled themselves, especially in their improvisatory skills and spontaneity. We toured to Lincolnshire during a bleak January week of heavy snow. One evening, we arrived at the school where we were due to perform, only to discover that not just the snow but also a local election had left us with an audience of nine. There was much discussion as to whether we should proceed with the show. There's a rule (whether it's merely a tradition or has contractual validity, I've never checked) that if the cast outnumbers the audience, it's permissible to cancel the performance. To the ten students' credit, they insisted on going on with the show. It was a happy decision. I had foreseen having to sit dutifully through a heavy-going night; after all, a lively comedy needs more than an audience of nine. All I know is that I had one of the best times I've ever spent in 'theatre'. In that dank and shabby classroom, with the audience seated on school chairs in a single row right in front of them, the actors were so released, so free of tension or nervousness, that they transcended themselves. They were witty, brave, surprising, inventive and generous. So were the nine hardy spectators who, instead of exhibiting, as I'd gloomily anticipated, that mixture of embarrassment and pity that tends to afflict very small audiences, responded with warmth and energy. Between them, audience and actors created an evening of intense joyfulness. Perversely, some of the most eagerly awaited performances in far more glittering circumstances turn out to be a disappointment, such as final performances that we all want to be the best ever! So! You never know *when it's going to happen.* You keep travelling in the faith that every so often you'll arrive for a brief and glorious sojourn, before you move on again . . .

5
UNCLOGGING THE WORK

Clearing the Decks for Action

When I describe a way of working, I'm visualising a process that moves with fluency and harmony from one step to the next. The reality, however, rarely works that way. Some directors might say that what's considered the rehearsal work proper (transforming words from the page into action on the stage) turns out *not* to be the main part of their job, which is, *rather*, clearing away the obstacles that hinder its progress. Even theatre isn't immune from the problems of leaves on the track, transport strikes, unreliable babysitters, illness, accidents, death even; all the vicissitudes of messy life can intrude on the enclosed order and sanctity of the rehearsal room. But they might add that more of their energy is absorbed in dealing not so much with these external obstructions as with the internal blocks that, in their hydra-headed manifestations, at times clog up the work. These give rise to an additional strand of 'work' that travels in parallel to the work I've been detailing throughout these pages and, in a sense, ghosts its progression.

We're simultaneously on two journeys: the one, overt, concerned with the life of the text; the other, subtextual (unless and until it thrusts itself to the surface), concerned with the life of the company. The two are inextricably interdependent. The well-being of the text affects the company, and the company's well-being affects the text. Naturally enough, the text is always the object of everyone's concern, but the health of the company is frequently overlooked. This allows unnecessary difficulties to seep into work which is sufficiently hard as it is. To rehearse creatively requires complete trust all round. Because our best work flourishes when our defences are down, that trust can easily be shaken. As I noted when I worked in Cincinnati, *I came to understand that directing was as much about dealing with people as with texts.* What follows is about unclogging the work and clearing the decks for action.

Bad Behaviour

Once Upon a Time in the West End

About thirty years ago, the musical that I earlier mentioned having written and directed for some students in their final year at LAMDA, eventually came into London. I indicated that it had been an unedifying experience, dragging on for two unhappy years before it came to an abrupt end in the West End. Exhuming a few bits of ancient gossip from this saga may render it more edifying than it was at the time.

At LAMDA, the musical got a good notice in *The Times*, which in those days reviewed the occasional drama-school production. From this, a year later, it found its way, in a production by Edinburgh University students, to the Festival Fringe where again it was well received, this time more widely. Its performing rights were bought by a West End management, who, the following year, gave it to a provincial theatre to tryout for London.

After my initial meeting with the director, I conscientiously carried out the re-writes he'd prescribed (my big break and so forth . . .) and sent them to him. In due course, a smartly bound copy of the revised script was returned to me. Flicking admiringly through the pages, I was alerted to lines that looked unfamiliar. On closer inspection, I discovered that the script was littered with dialogue I'd never written. In some indignation, I enquired why I'd never been consulted or, at very least, warned. He retorted that Iris Murdoch and J.B. Priestley had always accepted his changes. Well, I didn't, so some rather rancorous negotiations ensued, from which I emerged shaken but back in control of my material – or so I thought. A retrospective laugh doesn't come totally amiss. A steady erosion of both script and production was to spread itself over those next two years. However, I want to focus on how the management treated the actors and how the actors dealt with this: how two groups of human beings interacted.

It began, naturally enough, at the auditions, which took place at Wyndham's Theatre. Ironically, under the circumstances, *Oh, What a Lovely War*, an inspirational show that I'd seen three times, happened to be in the middle of a long run there and the backstage notice board was covered with the notes of its director, the formidable Joan Littlewood. For a young director, it was a revelation to read the imaginative and outrageous advice she had for her company as I passed through the stage door each day on my way to join a very different theatrical ethos.

From the start, I was embarrassed and then depressed by the inept ways in which the actors who paraded out of the wings onto the stage to sell themselves tried to cope with the indignities of auditioning. This they did by adopting unwisely artificial personae that a child of three could have seen through. Over a couple of weeks, I noticed that they fell into certain categories. Some of the women assumed a 'Grande Dame' manner: 'I'm afraid my agent only just reached me. I had to rush to get here, so I don't have any music with me. Actually, I rarely audition these days', all said rather breathlessly, with much acting out of how exhausted the lady indeed was from having had to rush to get there, much circular pacing of the stage to regain composure and flicking out of dishevelled hair. Or there was the predominantly male 'Sub-Method' method: 'I need a few moments to find my way into . . . mumble, mumble, mumble', followed by a lot of drifting about, shoulders hunched, hands in pocket, in an effort, no doubt, to find their way into mumble, mumble. There was the gender-free 'Jokey' approach: 'D'you want me funny piece or me serious?' usually delivered in a mock North Country accent and accompanied by a physical jerk of comic enquiry. On and on it went, day after day, with the actors becoming less like members of the human race (or even of Equity) and more like grotesque puppets, posturing and posing before my appalled gaze as I sat observing events from the back of the stalls where I'd been firmly installed out of the way. Very infrequently, human beings would appear, come straight down stage and say simply, 'Good morning', give their name and itemise what audition pieces they had to offer. But they didn't cut any more ice with the auditioners than the puppets did. For their part, director and producer (from now on identified as 'Management'), seated in separate rows, one behind the other, spent most of the auditions deep in private conversation, the one in the front twisting round over his seat to talk to the one behind, totally blocking the latter's view of the stage, with his own back fully turned on the auditionees. These, nonetheless, kept dispensing whatever aspect of their talent they hoped might win them the attention of these conversationalists. I longed for just one actor to stop and ask whether there was any point in continuing. But no one ever did. After they'd left the stage, Management would usually throw some snide, dismissive comment after them. I don't know which was worse: the way in which Management demeaned the actors or the way in which the actors demeaned themselves. Occasionally, actors with some claim to star status would be obsequiously ushered into the auditorium, on which occasion Management leapt from its seats and rushed to surround these luminaries, flatteringly sycophantic, literally dancing attendance as they bowed and scraped, while lackeys produced cups of tea and biscuits, smiles and genuflections. Once they'd left, Management discussed them with almost as much contempt as they'd thrown at the nobodies, while at the very same time weighing up their commercial usefulness to the show – a procedure of breathtakingly self-defeating contradiction.

I wasn't around for rehearsals – probably just as well for the state of my health, reasonably assuming that their conduct wouldn't radically differ from what I'd already witnessed. I and the composer were busy elsewhere writing, at the command of Management, what finally amounted to some forty additional numbers. I also did five more drafts of the script, each one moving it further and further away from any semblance of what it had been originally. By the time the production had its out-of-town tryout, the show had become a pretty glum shadow of its former self. When one of the cast was incapacitated by an accident and the London run aborted, I gave a sigh of relief, happy for it to sink without trace. I looked forward to putting the whole thing down to experience, but this was not to be. Who knows what streak of sadism drove Management, some six months later, to resurrect the show to go directly into the West End. It was as though everyone involved in the show owed Management a debt that might just about be paid off in this way. The original director, wisely, was no longer interested. When I offered myself in his place, I was looked straight in the eye and told, 'But what control would I have if you wrote *and* directed!' So, more auditions, rehearsals, rewrites . . . I was bullied – I won't honour the process by saying I was persuaded – into combining two vastly different characters into one role, ' . . . otherwise we may not be able to see our way to put the show on', and was made to feel responsible for a future life of deprivation for the entire cast, crew and management and the closure of the West End in its entirety if I didn't play along. I was young. I was alone. I gave in.

Dress rehearsals and previews were conducted with much abuse of the cast (insult, sarcasm). On the afternoon of the very first preview, no doubt by way of encouragement, Management accused the attractive and conscientious 'ingénue' of looking and moving like Richard III. (There were some potted plants on the set. I'd have heaved one at him; she merely stifled her tears.) The actors, in the only way most actors can, retaliated against their treatment with petty sulks and stupid dramas about costumes and wigs and complaints about the set. During previews, Management, with cohorts in tow, held daily meetings, ostensibly to 'discuss' the previous night's performance, but, in actuality, to issue more and more wilful decrees, resulting in further rewrites and numbers passing through the show like doses of salts. These meetings wouldn't have been out of place through the looking-glass. Conversations went something like: 'But yesterday you agreed.' 'No, I didn't.' 'Yesterday you said "Black".' 'No, I didn't. I said "White".' A song threatened with the axe was permitted one more performance so that the audience reaction could decide its fate. The audience liked it. Next morning, when this was noted, Management snorted, 'What do they know? They're just shop girls!' I only wish I'd had had the sense to keep some record of the barefaced assertions and denials that daily left me increasingly wide-eyed with disbelief. When I besought support on some issue or other from the bevy of assistants and associates, some of whom had indeed agreed with me in private, they cravenly advised me to listen to Management because Management *knew*! I gradually realised that it was pointless to fight, and comforted myself with the thought that if Management really *did* know and the show *was* a success, it might buy me some credit for the future. In the event, it got what I'd anticipated – and justifiably: the worst reviews possible ('Of this ghastly farrago, the less said the better'), was kept running the necessary period contractually required for Management to retain the performing rights for a few more years – and that was that.

The experience over the two years was like a nagging sore that wouldn't heal. But, to be fair, it did actually prove salutary for me – in fact, was a turning point that shaped my future. It made me think long and hard about the nature of the profession I was struggling to find my way in and how I wanted to lead my life. Nobody connected with that enterprise came out of it with much credit. Work your way through the alphabet: abuse, betrayal, cowardice, dishonesty . . . They all played their role. I was perplexed as to what Management thought it would achieve by throwing its weight around other than bolstering its need to be right at all costs, even at the cost of being wrong. It was so clearly counterproductive. Probably it didn't think at all, but was behaving as it was accustomed to behave, as it had no doubt been allowed to behave for years. Or perhaps it was just some elaborate scam to write off the show as a tax loss!

Negative Means – Positive Ends?

Theatre is the most immediately human of all the arts, the one closest to the experience of living, so the justification for its existence must be in the unique ability of actors to embody that experience as truthfully as possible. Presumably, to attain this, the professional conduct of theatre practitioners should in some way reflect this honesty, both between themselves and in their relation to their audiences. Simply asked, can a director guide actors towards truth by manipulation, bullying and bluff? And can actors touch the audience in any depth if they're cheating? Here's what playwright John Whiting had to say about pulling the wool over the audience's eyes:

> No form lends itself more easily to the meretricious and the cheap than
> the theatre. No other art can provide such immediate and extensive,
> though ephemeral, gratification to the practitioners. There have been
> those – and their names often rank very high in theatrical history – who
> have used theatre and the credulity of large crowds to practise what, in
> the end, proved to be nothing more than the tricks practised by the
> experienced on the innocent . . . It must be remembered that workers
> in theatre possess enough trickery to deceive even the very discerning.

Nonetheless, I'm convinced that deep in our (audience's) guts, we can sense the truth of something, despite the sad fact that our reflexes have been conditioned to accept certain substitutes as the real thing.

Ends do not justify means. Taking short cuts is merely applying sticking plaster to matters that need fuller attention. Cutting corners for expediency never creates good work. Nor is forcing a performance from actors by any means whatsoever a path to creativity. There are anecdotes of directors exploiting intimate knowledge of actors to 'get a performance out of them' or, in movies, tricking them into unexpected situations and filming their reactions. This denies actors any autonomy in the execution of their profession, and turns them from artists into puppets – things. Short-term results ignore eventual debt; your actions can return to haunt you. Any one show, important as it may be, is only part of your career, only part of your life. Your behaviour is accumulative. Over time, moral wear-and-tear can be damaging to the psyche. *Good conduct invests in the future.*

To do their job properly, actors have to be honest about themselves, with themselves, with their colleagues and, ultimately, with their audiences. This can only happen when they feel secure enough to be so without fear of abuse or exploitation. Actors' raw material is themselves, and therefore their sense of success and failure must touch them that much more profoundly. After all, their appearance, intelligence, taste, sensitivity – *their whole being* – is constantly under scrutiny. Directors must remind themselves that they are usually making demands of people at the most intimate level of experience. Only assorted therapists and counsellors, after several years of training, get to deal with people so intimately, and even then, can still do harm. Some directors, with very little training in any aspect of their chosen vocation, let alone dealing with other people's psyches, plunge in with two left feet – and strew a lot of human damage along their career paths.

Decadent Times

We live in decadent times, an era of bread and circuses. Gladiatorial combat is more or less with us; throwing people to lions just a matter of time. On TV, people are routinely humiliated for our entertainment, hardly for our enlightenment. Holidaymaking Brits on Mediterranean islands, looking like carcasses of raw meat, have been popular Friday-night viewing as they enjoy themselves, vomiting and falling down drunk. Celebrity chefs abusing their kitchen staffs are seen at very least as amusing, even worthy of emulation. Indeed, many people consider it a virtue, wholly admirable, to display vanity, ruthlessness, and the ability to get away with things. Candidates who've just been fired from *The Apprentice*, preening themselves on its thirty-minute appendage, *The Apprentice: You're Fired*, bear witness to this as they smirk at the clips confronting them with their poor behaviour on that show. The first word on Westministerial lips is 'Resign!' A collective *Schadenfreude* rejoices in the destruction of reputations. But the possessors of destroyed reputations no longer feel the need to redeem themselves à la Profumo with lives anonymously dedicated to good works; rather, they're encouraged to celebrate their notoriety, generously rewarded with offers to become cheque-book journalists and television presenters. Our values are totally confused. First we're prurient ('Did they? Actually? Do that?'), then censorious ('Shameful! Disgusting! They ought to be punished, fined, fired . . . '), then concedingly adulatory ('Well, you have to hand it to them . . . '). Were we ever so absorbed by such worthlessness? Since Diana's death I've somewhat shocked myself by gradually coming round to the idea that there might be something to be said for stiff upper lips.

While we live in a culture of such distorted values, this diatribe leads me to query whether it's even reasonable to expect people in an exposed and competitive medium like theatre to behave any differently: honest rather than false, vulnerable rather than ruthless, modest rather than boastful, generous rather than selfish, willing to admit failure rather than bluffing, taking responsibility rather than blaming others; in short, behaving decently. Of course, my answer is that it *must* be a reasonable expectation for people working in theatre to behave differently if they're going to create good work; in fact, it's a necessity.

We know that history is littered with instances of artists who behaved appallingly and produced masterpieces. We often struggle with the conflicting emotions evoked by this disparity: how can I admire the writings of an anti-Semite or the paintings of some feckless, drunken womaniser? Well, we can admire the work; the work is not the person.* I'm not of the school that believes that someone capable of lying to their partner is incapable of telling the truth under any other circumstances. Human beings are not quite so simplistically predictable, goats and sheep not so easily categorised. But here I'm not concerned with people's private behaviour. That's their business.

I'm concerned with the behaviour involved in collaborative creation. Putting words on paper or paint on canvas is very different from putting people on stage. The creation of a piece of theatre relies on the mutual trust and interdependence of a group of people from very different disciplines, something that a novel, poem or piece of visual art need never require. So whatever theatre practitioners do in their private lives, they ought, when they come together creatively, to treat each other with *care* – in every meaning of that word.

Damaged Goods

It's inevitable that in most workplaces there's likely to be some difficult relations amongst co-workers. But in some quarters of theatre (and in film even more so – *pace* the Weinsteins**) there seems to be an unspoken agreement that bad behaviour is *de rigueur*, a necessary part of the creative state where infantile tantrums, broken promises, moral cowardice and abuse of power are more or less accepted, even grudgingly admired, facts of artistic life. To give a couple of fairly low-level instances: after they've auditioned, actors can deliberately be kept

---

* Daniel Barenboim, in one of his 2006 Reith Lectures, justifying his introduction of Wagner's music into the Israeli orchestral repertoire, made the point that the music is of importance in itself and in no way expresses the anti-Semitism Wagner espoused in the non-musical side of his life.

** The behaviour of the notorious Weinstein brothers, Harvey and Bob, is described in no uncertain detail in *Down and Dirty Pictures*, Peter Biskind's book about the rise of independent film-makers in the '90s.

waiting to hear whether or not they got the job (they never hear) or are lured into companies to play small roles with the promise of bigger roles to come (they never come). Actors repeatedly experiencing this lack of consideration (to characterise such conduct at its most benign) grow both in resentment and an ever-hardening paranoia that they never get told the truth until they've assumed the unattractive role of victim. When you, the director, arrive, unknowing, ready to work with them, you discover that, before you can do anything else, you have first to break through this carapace of suspicion they've constructed to protect themselves from further hurt. Sometimes the wounds are so deep and the scars correspondingly so thick that there's little likelihood of any breakthrough.

Actors Without Whom Not . . .

An activity whose ultimate expression is mediated through the sensibilities of a particular group of people – people on whom other people are totally dependent for their own fulfilment – would seem to demand collaboration of the utmost sensitivity. Playwrights, directors, designers, composers, technicians, producers are all *totally dependent* on actors for their professional existence. Actors, though they seem unaware of their potential independence, need no one.*

Directors, Playwrights and Designers, but no Actors = *No Theatre*.
No Directors, Playwrights or Designers, but, yes, Actors = *Theatre*.**

Of course there are good collaborators and examples of inspiring collaborations; but many people who work with actors do, in their heart of patronising hearts, think of them as unintelligent children, high-maintenance egotists, tedious obstacles to directorial vision . . . and so on. Actors, of course, sense very well what people think of them, and retaliate, living up to the portrayals assigned to them. So the work becomes a struggle between competing egos rather than the collaborative struggle it ought to be in the search for truth – truth that transcends ego.

Happiness All Round

How we lead our lives, I'd presume, is guided by some rules of conduct we've evolved for ourselves from our observations of life. And I'd presume that the

---

* It is not totally surprising that actors have never really exploited the innate power they possess. The reality is that (a) they tend to rely for their work on the people who misuse them, and (b) there are so many actors available, that they know – and know that their would-be bosses know – that they're replaceable, expendable. Only the most starry of stars can exploit their uniqueness. I've often been hugely disappointed when an actor I'd set my heart on for a role couldn't or wouldn't do it. I've grieved for twenty-four hours, self-dramatisingly declaring, 'I can't do the show without them', then resigned myself to the fact that 'somebody's going to have to play it' and ended up with an actor even more suitable than my original choice. *Everyone's unique, but nobody's indispensable.*

** *Commedia dell'Arte* troupes, for example, were essentially companies of actors who, where necessary, took on other functions as a natural extension of their acting.

precept of not knowingly pursuing an action that will harm any other person would be a part of most people's moral systems. As art *is* a part of life, not separate from it, those involved in its practice are in no way exempt from this common morality. Consideration doesn't exclude rigour; you can be both fair and demanding. I call upon John Stuart Mill to support the conviction that treating people with respect creates better conditions for all involved. What's good for the Individual is good for the State! Happiness all round.

Conflicting Perceptions

It could be, it should be – in fact, *it is* – inspiring, nourishing, to be an actor, especially in the theatre. To share with all sorts of people the experience of our common humanity, to be an agent of understanding between us, to draw us closer to each other across time and space seems to me a noble purpose in life. It should bring out the very best in its practitioners – and in some, of course, it does. I have a vision of actors, no doubt unrealistic and unrealisable, as potentially superb human beings: open, available, generous, alert, risk-taking, sensitive, curious, creative, collaborative – knowing when to lead and when to follow, imaginative, knowledgeable, playful, witty, responsible, expressive, enterprising, compassionate, indefatigably full of good energy, physically and emotionally healthy and modestly appreciative of their innate gifts, understanding that they are the medium for something much larger than themselves. This is a huge burden of expectation to lay on anyone. But I can think of no other vocation that requires all these attributes – ideally demands them – and indeed provides the context for their practice. Throughout their careers, actors are expanding their range of physical and vocal expression, their empathic knowledge of others, their knowledge of themselves and – each production being a new world to discover – expanding their knowledge of the world. Then, they share all this with their audiences in a vivid and pleasurable form of communication: an exhilarating job that, deservedly, can reward its many rigours with a sense of great fulfilment.

So why are the dictionary definitions of words connected with theatre so pejorative, and theatre people tainted with a reputation so far removed from this, to wit: affected, artificial, camp, egotistical, exaggerated, insincere, out-of-touch, precious, self-indulgent, self-obsessed, selfish, shallow, spoilt, temperamental, theatrical(!)? Why – when the practice of their profession should lead them to be seen as committed, compassionate, hard-working, informed, natural, rooted, self-challenging, skilled . . . ?

Art v. Biz

One reason is the dichotomy between art and business (theatre and showbiz). As a reaction to the charge of elitism levelled against the arts, there's been a tendency to blur the distinction between art and popular entertainment, to knit high and low brows closer together. This, of course, can't really succeed in any balanced way. Art and commerce are virtually incompatible, indeed irreconcilable; their aims are so different. Art (high) is defined by what the artist needs to express; business (low) by what the punter is willing to buy. One aspiration has to lose out. And of course, commercialism, which means popularisation, has inevitably been the winner. The more you patronise people's ability to appreciate the arts, the steeper your descent to where the simple and familiar take precedence over the complex and unknown.

One rarely hears much about the rewards of a life committed to art, being, as they are, hard-to-define feelings of inner growth and creative fulfilment. (Of course, creators of 'high' art are far from impervious to material rewards, but these are not necessarily a prime motive.) The rewards of commercial success are far more observable (if seldom achieved) and endlessly trumpeted: unlimited fame, money, adulation . . . sex, drugs and rock 'n' roll. No wonder that each year – despite the paucity of days worked annually by the average Equity member – acting schools are inundated by an increasing volume of applications.

Nina

At the top of the book, I quoted from two speeches by Nina in *The Seagull*, in which she expresses contradictory views of what it means to be an actress. In the first, she's almost delirious at the thought of fame. In the second, she explains how acting has enabled her to face life. In the two years between she has learnt about life and art the hard way. That is her journey: *from the outside of acting to the inside of acting*. Her radically conflicting visions of what it means to be an actor perfectly exemplify the dichotomy many actors experience, especially nowadays when they are treated more and more as a commodity: the conflict and contradictions between business and art, career and craft, public acclaim and personal fulfilment. It's given to very few to have the best of both worlds. (I have a hunch that those who do never set out to achieve both; the commercial success came as a serendipitous by-product.) Some actors who deliberately try to accommodate both goals can become lost in confusing compromise. Confusing, because each goal makes totally different demands. Both require determination and energy, but there are few other points of overlap. Career requires the confident packaging of yourself as a fashionable image, the exploitation of only those qualities that 'work', the banishment of any seriously examined self-doubt and absolutely no risk-taking. Art requires nakedness, endless self-questioning, total commitment to what you believe in, and the acceptance of failure as part of the search for excellence. The former is for as long as it lasts; the latter is for a lifetime. Acting feels as though it has 'thinned out' over the last twenty years or so. Small wonder. With such conflicting goals and rewards, even the most seriously motivated actors can become totally bewildered about what they want, what is wanted of them and what they stand for.

Actors and Directors

The Critical Relationship

Fear is the cause of most bad behaviour in both actors and directors. How that fear can be exacerbated or diffused is very much dependent on the relationship between the two. If directors and actors are going to approach each other as more than professional technicians politely accommodating each other as they get on with their respective jobs (much as I gather was done in the past, when some directors did little more than direct onstage traffic and arbitrate between hysterical leading ladies and their dressmakers), their relationship has to be treated as the most critical in the creation of a production. All other contributions founder or thrive on its failure or success.

Dealing with others is never easy, nor is it easily taught. There are no neatly formularised solutions to apply to the infinite possibilities of personal friction. Of course, you can learn a lot through experience. But you *can* be made aware of areas of potential conflict, alerted to problems you might not anticipate. I might have made fewer mistakes early in my career if someone had pointed out the naivety of my assumption that theatre-folk were all happy, well-adjusted people who just wanted to put on a show.

The relationship between each cast and director is different from every other cast-and-director relationship, just as that between any couple is particular to them: all unique, all individual – but also, *all the same*. There are generic, semi-automatic patterns of behaviour that any of us can fall into under the right (that is to say, wrong) circumstances. And these are worth considering.

Director Power

We directors are in a position of immense power. That may well be what attracted some of us to our choice of profession. Others of us are quite unaware of how much power we do exert. With no need to demonstrate any proof – just by virtue of our job title – we start out automatically endowed with authority and credited with omniscience! Flattering and pernicious attributions, not to be taken seriously, nor for granted, nor advantage of, but only with huge pinches of salt. However, when actors reinforce the idea of these endowments by automatically relating to us as all-powerful and all-knowing, making little Gods of us in fact, it's a short step to our own complicity in the belief that we do indeed possess these qualities. Power is an intoxicant. You've only to observe people in positions of power going a little bit mad as over time they come to believe their own PR.

Director Image

Early in their careers, most directors are very self-conscious about the kind of impression they make in the rehearsal room. Some deliberately try to perform in a manner that they hope conveys some chosen self-image. But even if you're not consciously imposing a performance of yourself on the proceedings, you're going to be – in fact, cannot avoid – exuding character traits that the actors will anxiously be trying to divine in order to know which way to jump. This happens at an instinctive level. Your status automatically alerts actors to accommodate themselves to you as they sense they should. It took me a long time to realise that, without doing anything – just by being there and being me – the fact of my function combined with the fact of my personality imposed a particular atmosphere on the environment. You, from whom it's impossible to detach yourself, cannot avoid conveying your specific temperature, energy, level of concentration and the like. Unless you've developed a foolproof, impermeable persona, what you are will inevitably bleed through what you may be trying to present. It's not easy to sustain an assumed role for several hours a day, several weeks at a time. And as you and the company begin to relax together, you may well find you've somewhat dropped your guard and let your image slip. *Even by doing nothing at all*, you have an effect on the way rehearsals are conducted and – inevitably – on their outcome.

After a rehearsal period, during which I thought I'd been displaying great calm, I was disabused of that illusion by an actor letting me know he'd been worryingly affected by the anxiety I'd transmitted during the later stages of the work! On reflection, I had to admit that, despite denying so to myself, I'd become increasingly uneasy about the production. I thought I'd been hiding my concerns very well. So be alert to the fact your subtext *will* 'read': if, say, you're of an inwardly impatient disposition, the actors, picking up on this, may well feel required to rush for results; if your attention span flags, the actors are likely to drop to a comparable rate of commitment. Once again, these modes will probably pass unremarked, the actors adjusting instinctively to whatever unspoken input they're receiving from you, the director. At a subliminal level of communication, you're defining the conduct of rehearsals. The problem comes exactly when you're not conscious of what it *is* you're defining. Setting the tone of every rehearsal is your responsibility. Rather than performing your idea of a director or your image of yourself as a director (precisely what you don't want the actors to do with their roles), you should try to eliminate what, to quote the sociologist Erving Goffman, is least helpful in your 'presentation of self'. Encouragingly, once you start to recognise certain unhelpful patterns in yourself, your organism, almost unprompted, will embark on a slow but sure process of change. Ignorance and denial, of course, change nothing.

Tough Love

Some directors desperately seek their actors' approval, indulging their whims, constantly in conciliatory mode. This doesn't get things done. A touchy-feely environment induces no rigour. The need for approval, even disguised as concern and goodwill, translates as weakness. Actors may accurately interpret an overly-ingratiating director as one lacking in self-confidence. This may inspire in them a mistaken feeling of power.* Being a good and fair director doesn't mean being a soft one. Your role is to inspire your company to excel, to exceed their normal levels of achievement, which means, at times, administering tough love. Most important is to be honest with them. Don't try to comfort them by pretending poor work is good (describing their efforts in a scene as 'promising', 'on the way', or whatever other euphemisms you might employ). This will merely confuse the actor when, later, you criticise them for doing the very same thing. Then they'll end up distrusting anything you have to say to them.

Roles for Directors

What is a director? Virtually anything you want the job to be. A director has as many roles are there are relationships. I would immediately discourage those of dictator and guru. They deprive actors of any independence, though those actors who insist on remaining in a needy state of infancy will often try to lay them on you. Nor should you try to be their mate. This will hobble you. By all means be friendly, but it's a mistake to believe you can be one of the cast. You have such very different artistic lives. Actors need to bond together in the life of a production that they'll have to sustain long after you've departed the scene. They should, for their autonomous health, maintain a certain degree of separation from you. You have enough involvement with them without totally taking over their lives. Besides, it's not easy to administer tough love to mates. What's more, directors should be even-handed with every member of a cast. Face it: directing is a lonely business.

I like to think that in the ideal situation, directors and actors come together, not hierarchically with the director descending from above towards a group of eagerly

---

* Actors aren't too good at power, they get so little practice! From years of playing victim to directorial bullies, there may be a vengeful, reciprocal bully lurking resentfully inside some actors, waiting for any sign of a crack in a directorial facade in order to retaliate. Then their sense of power often takes the form of settling old scores with the profession in general, for which you may, unfairly, bear the brunt. From inexperience, too, they're apt to miscalculate the relative importance of grievances, complaining about something relatively trivial to the neglect of something about which it's well within their rights to be heard. Or they bottle up whatever's upsetting them, missing a suitable moment to broach the matter, letting it eat away at them until it's built up such a head of emotional steam that it gets blurted out at precisely the moment when they're in the least appropriate state to make a coherent case for themselves.

uplifted faces waiting for instruction, but meeting on the same plane, the actors bringing their particular talents with them and the director theirs, ready to work together, understanding that they each have skills that complement the other's and with which, together, they'll be able to create a piece of theatre. Within this, you, the director, function as a guide, stimulator, challenger, arbitrator, enabler, mid-wife, encourager, coach, adviser, synthesiser, company lover, lay priest and analyst (careful!), counsellor, daddy, mummy, sibling, colleague, court of last appeal – if necessary – and ultimately buck-stopper. Apropos the last, your shoulders must be broad enough to accept *whatever happens in a production* as your responsibility. (Even if an actor does something reprehensible, not at your instigation and out of your control, you are nonetheless the one that chose that actor!)

Someone Has to Decide – Or Do They?

Pierre Boulez sees his role of conductor as 'a colleague who decides'. There are particular occasions when somebody *does* have to decide. (I believe it's not beyond possibility for a small group without a director to work at some level of equality – but it would need not only equality of opportunity and commitment, but also of talent, especially the talent to know when to open one's mouth and when to keep it shut.) Ultimately, theatre can never be completely democratic. Talent is not a product of or a means towards democracy. Talent is elitist. It doesn't get handed around in equal shares. If you try to make art by vote, you may end up with lowest-common-denominated compromises that can smother creativity, as happened within some theatre collectives of the 1960s and '70s, where everyone was supposedly equal. Hours were frittered away as a group bickered over some-one's erroneously perceived infringement of some artistic or personal belief before coming to an unsatisfactory vote.*

When we launched our first Shared Experience project, *The Arabian Nights*, I had defined the artistic brief for the company to the effect that the actors (and their text) would be the sole creators of whatever happened on stage. There would be no scenic or technical aids whatsoever. What the actors couldn't create from themselves wouldn't be there. This meant, in simple terms, they were working in an empty space – a totally unfamiliar experience for all of us. About three-quarters of the way through rehearsals, the actors began to feel a little lonely, and, very gently, suggested that perhaps they might have a few (Arabian-type) pillows scattered around on the floor to keep them company. From their point of view, this was understandable. Of course, I couldn't be too certain how my 'vision' would work out, so I, too, was feeling vulnerable. I remember agonising over the issue: to cushion or not to cushion. After all, what difference would a few pillows make if the actors felt less exposed? Nonetheless, I clung to the purity of my

---

* In *Taking Stock*, Max Stafford-Clark recounts the difficulties the Joint Stock company experienced in democratic decision-making while creating their early productions, especially in trying to cast by consensus. However, they survived the experience triumphantly.

belief in the absolute sufficiency of the actors to create a total theatre experience with *nothing* beyond their own skills. The pillows seemed like a dangerous breach in that belief, possibly the thin end of the wedge – if pillows got through, what else might follow? I argued the logic of my case perfectly well, but I experienced the issue at a more visceral level of conviction; the actors, however much they understood the concept of the piece, couldn't possibly feel what I felt in my gut. Someone had to decide. I decided it was me. If the issue had been put to a vote, the pro-pillow lobby would probably have won. And I'm glad, in this case, I stuck to my guns. The pillow-free show made a totally unambiguous statement – and, of course, as the actors finally acknowledged, pillows would only have got in the way!

However, having said this, I must contradict myself. In the daily process of rehearsal, there's really no reason to make decisions. I approach the creation of a production in the same way that I try to allow a play to reveal itself: through active work on it with the actors, letting it tell me rather than my telling it, withholding choices, refusing to make decisions until as late in the process as possible, and only then if absolutely necessary. *Ideally, the world of the play evolves.* People are trying things out. Those that work tend to get absorbed into the body of the production; those that don't, disappear. But with every choice, every decision, a door slams shut against possibility, against revelation and, indeed, against process. Decisions are blocks. Apart from the rare, one-off situation such as I've just described, where *matters of first principle* are threatened, *the director's role should not be to decide, but to guide.*

Don't Talk, Do

When actors want to discuss things in rehearsal, I encourage them not to tell me but to *show* me what they mean. In that way, you avoid the stasis that occurs when actors leave their bodies, rely on their tongues and lock themselves inside their heads. I suggest that you urge them to express their ideas in concrete – physical, active – terms. Discussing ideas that cannot eventually materialise as something seen and done – however enjoyable the discussion – is more often than not a waste of time and energy.

Never block an actor's request to try something. If they want to show you an idea, encourage them to do so, even if everything in you is screaming out that it can't and won't work. If you reject their offers, you may well inhibit their making any more. Unwittingly, you'll have eroded their confidence, their goodwill and their energy; even aborted their creativity. Reassure yourself that any good process of work is self-monitoring: actors, once they've tried something out, know very well whether it has legs or not. If it doesn't, you won't see it again. But if you deny them that chance, you're in danger of providing a bone for them to chew on, a grievance that confirms everything they've always distrusted about directors. They will then either brood or – one way or another – find a way of forcing their idea into the proceedings. And, having done so, they'll continue to do so. They'll have pushed the situation to the point where they cannot, without losing face, acknowledge their idea's a non-starter, even if, in their heart of hearts, they know it to be so. If you had initially encouraged them to try out their idea, the matter would have been amicably diffused.

Don't Do, Talk

I was once content to leave to themselves those actors who appeared to be quietly getting on with their work, and it might be that for several days I said very little to them – sometimes even nothing at all. When there were actors new to me in the cast, whom I wanted, naturally enough, to ease into the rehearsal process, I'd focus on them, confident in the knowledge that those actors I'd worked with before were more than capable of functioning for a while without assistance from me. Neither of these procedures was good practice. It resulted in anxious faces peering at me at the end of the day, hoping for feedback and reassurance. Committed actors are bound to feel exposed and to need recognition of their commitment. They are likely to interpret your inadvertence as a sign that you're displeased with them, or think them so inadequate that you've given up on them. Actors with whom you have a long-established collaboration can sometimes become possessive of their relationship with you, and resent too much of your attention devoted to a new face. An actor I regularly worked with once said to me, with an ironic curl of the lip, 'I know – I'm like a comfortable old sock you can pull on when you feel like it.' On the other hand, avoid letting actors with a tendency to demand attention monopolise your energies; and at times, it's productive to let an actor struggle for a while before you intervene. A big part of a director's intuitive sense is allowing that high-grade computer constantly alert in your head to advise you when which actor needs what sort of help.

Periodically, I *do* set up an official 'talking' session, say every couple of weeks, to check if everyone has a sense of where the production seems to be heading, if anything needs clarifying. For those actors, who so far haven't found the opportunity, it's a useful occasion to bring up any concerns they might have about the process, and for you to learn, if you haven't already been able to decipher it from their work, precisely where their thoughts are. These talking sessions should be exclusively about the work on the production and not allowed to meander.

What you must do is ensure that every day you have some personal contact with each member of the cast. I don't mean that you should invent comments just for the sake of having something to say about their work (you don't have to mention the work at all), but that you continue to develop your particular relationship with each one of them and convey your constant awareness and appreciation of them.

Actors' Fears

Sensitive Assessment

Most problems that you, the director, are likely to encounter with actors stem from fear. In your position of power, you must never increase those fears. Stimulate, challenge, but never intimidate. Never mock. Never reject. Never blame. Never reproach. Never harangue (a weakness of mine, I fear – possibly one that's all too evident). This forbearance can be difficult, especially when you're provoked! But you simply cannot allow yourself to become impatient or irritated – certainly ever to show it. What can it possibly achieve, apart from inhibiting the actors further? As long as they're trying to fulfil what you've asked of them, all you can do is give them encouragement, support, time . . . You cannot demand of actors to be more emotionally free, more perceptive, more imaginative (that is, more talented) than is within their capacity. One never knows, of course, at what point that capacity is reached. Every person's potential is unknowable, so – theoretically – infinite. It could burst into flower at any time. Your role is to help actors to realise their potential, to exceed their own expectations and break the limitations they may have imposed on themselves ('I'm no good at "funny"'). Not only time, but *timing* influences this. What actors cannot grasp at one moment, they may well be able to absorb at a later date. This doesn't mean that you handle them with kid gloves, or indulge them; this will do nothing but reinforce a natural inclination to remain within their normal comfort zone. On the contrary, you should be demanding.

The exception to your forbearance may be in cases of selfishness, thoughtlessness, tactlessness – any conduct that disturbs the work of the group. This usually occurs when actors are more concerned with their status than their role. Then you're entitled to be as appropriately critical or admonitory as you feel the situation warrants. When you're establishing a working method for the company that's built on trust, you need, early on, to discourage any behaviour that seems likely to sabotage it. This, however, needs to be filtered through an astute assessment of what anxieties might be causing such conduct.

Finding Out and Being Found Out

What are these fears? Mainly fear of exposure. This may seem perverse in a profession whose *sine qua non* is displaying yourself to an audience. But exposure means vulnerability – to mockery, contempt, rejection, unwelcome self-knowledge, low self-esteem . . . *Actors are frightened of being found out* to be untalented, to be uninteresting, to be unattractive to an audience, even dislikeable; or *they're frightened of finding out* what they'd rather not know about themselves.

For many actors, the desire to act and the fear it elicits seem to go hand in hand. A reason that they've chosen this way of life may be a longing to escape from their perceived sense of themselves (they don't like themselves). They may long to escape from the implacable routines of daily existence (they don't like their lives). So they find themselves in the double bind of wanting to assume other identities, but having to expose their own identity to do so. Some people dismiss acting as living life at one remove, commenting on it rather than experiencing it. A psychologist once gave me his opinion that actors never reach emotional maturity and are unable to sustain relationships. He argued that they've chosen a way of life that gives them permission to change roles and move from place to place with no responsibility to commit to anything with any degree of permanence. I would argue that many of an actor's best attributes *are* a child's: enthusiasm, endless energy, the readiness to play, unfettered imagination, a perennial innocence, a healthy naivety (that is, a lack of cynicism), curiosity . . . Indeed, one wants actors who've retained these qualities in adulthood, one wants them to be childlike. (What one *doesn't* want them to be is child*ish*; but maybe you can't have one without the other!) But these are generalisations. An actor is just one more human being, motivated by a complex of drives and desires, who shouldn't be pigeon-holed with simplistic psycho-babble labels.

Actors are Their Own Instruments

Acting is both an ordinary human impulse and an extraordinary phenomenon. What is unarguable: acting, unlike any other profession, requires its practitioners to use themselves in their entirety, to withhold nothing, especially those most intimate areas of themselves that the rest of us spend our lives trying to keep well hidden and protected. Directors have to recognise this. And respect it.

Actors' instruments are themselves. Unlike other artists, they have no objective external element on which they can ever focus (a manuscript, a piano, a block of marble). Like athletes, they have to develop the ability to objectify their bodies, which means, for instance, being able to locate and control muscles some of us don't even know we possess; more to the difficult point, they have also to objectify their intentions, feelings and thoughts, hard to achieve, at times almost impossible. Actors can never pull back from what they're doing to examine the means of their expression or skill (such as a violin, a tennis racket, a paintbrush); they can't touch them or look at them or test them, nothing of what they use is outside them (props and costumes, in this context, are very much secondary elements; mirrors are misleading). Everything they use is part of them, *is* them. Many actors, I suspect, don't grapple with this dilemma sufficiently, and that's probably why so much acting tends to be, as I say, thin, both in its inner content and outer form.

Permanent Judgement

I can think of few careers whose practice is accompanied by – in fact, depends on – continuous evaluation, judgement and criticism. Actors are judged in the casting process for both their professional abilities and personal qualities. (Can you imagine the psychological stress on the average person if, like actors, they had continuously to chase after jobs for which, most of the time, they were turned down?) They're evaluated by the director all through rehearsals – and by their colleagues; then by audiences through the period of performance; to say nothing of public judgement by critics and, worse, by arts and gossip columnists. (Few people have to suffer the indignities of discovering in a gossip column or magazine article that they look awful, aren't sexy, are too old for the part, have big bums and a collapsing relationship, or are failing to fight a drink or drug habit . . . and then go out and perform in front of the public.) And the structure of theatre practice being what it is, this pattern is repeated again and again throughout their careers. Success hardly ameliorates the process. The more you succeed, the more there is to lose. Because actors are using themselves to such an intense and intimate degree, it's almost impossible for them to separate the professional from the personal – not to take professional comment as personal attack. So you can understand if sometimes they feel the need to be safely in control of their performances and are frightened to take what they perceive as risks.

Control v. Danger

Actors who do try to stay firmly in control prefer to discuss how they're going to play their role, rather than to find out on the hoof. It's safer to plan what you're going to do before you do it. No chance of falling on your face or getting egg on it. But if you don't give yourself permission to make mistakes, don't occasionally risk your face meeting some egg on the floor, you'll never make discoveries. And rehearsals should be the safe place where actors feel they can take chances without reproof or mockery. But some actors are terrified of putting themselves into unpredictable situations where they might be confronted by what they'd rather not encounter. Nevertheless, actors should *not* be totally in control. Performances planned in every detail may be perfectly correct, but they'll be perfectly dull. They eschew any semblance of life. They avoid danger at the loss of spontaneity. Good acting involves the possibility of having to enter danger zones. The actor who proceeds in a controlled and controlling manner not only never learns anything, but in fact works from a decreasing base of knowledge and ability. If you don't go forwards, you go backwards. Unused muscles atrophy. If you (try to) stay in the same place, you stagnate.

Thick and Thin Skins

Some actors develop thick skins and an assumed indifference to criticism. But actors who become thick-skinned also become insensitive and unavailable. They lose vulnerability. And without vulnerability, they lose half their humanity. As acting, good acting, is about being human, this becomes something of a liability. So actors who try to remain vulnerable probably have to live throughout their careers in a permanent state of raw nerves. Serious actors will tell you that although they grow more skilful with the years, acting never gets any easier.

It's a director's responsibility to take away, as much as possible, an actor's fear. Actors need a balance of challenge and reassurance. When an actor creates difficulties, there's usually some basis of anxiety that is causing the behaviour, even if it comes across to you as vanity or self-indulgence or competitiveness. Realise that actors who do risk opening themselves in rehearsal to genuine experiences may, rewardingly, release brave, exciting, often disturbing moments. But they do so at a cost. Such release can leave them feeling exposed, shaken and for the moment a little destabilised. In that state, coupled with tiredness, they may, under insensitive pressure from you, the director, become atypically upset or aggressive. You must respect the fact that when you ask actors to put themselves on the line, you're asking them to strip themselves personally and emotionally naked.

A Partial Taxonomy of Fear

Actors, like everyone else, are complex individuals, never completely knowable. Therefore, the more they can release their true individuality (rather than regurgitate old habits and mannerisms) makes them exciting to work with and special to an audience. Their individuality means, obviously, that they each come equipped with their particular skills, perceptions, frames of reference, speeds of comprehension, the levels of which you can never know until you've actually worked with them for a while. I've described a process of work that ideally flows in smooth sequence from stage to stage, strand to strand, but since each member of a company cannot and doesn't work with the same level of absorption or technical ability, rehearsals are inevitably steered through these variations. I've made the point that we share neither a serious professional language, nor a basic training to help keep us together on some common track. So individual difficulties surface along the journey. Most of the time, this is not a problem, just a natural part of rehearsing. *The majority of actors work enthusiastically, positively determined to get the most out of a rehearsal process,* supporting each other and trusting that they'll eventually understand the concepts and acquire the techniques that currently escape them. And so the work proceeds with reasonable fluency. This is, in fact, my dominant experience: *a creative, committed atmosphere where personal struggles are accepted as part of the natural process.*

But there are times when something in the process meets something in the personality of some actors that causes them to feel inordinately threatened, so much so that they no longer take things in their stride. They become suspicious, resentful, anxious or impatient and, depending on their awareness of the needs of the group – more to the point, their *lack* of awareness – they can fall into certain stereotypical patterns that do nothing to lessen the stress they're experiencing and, in fact, make things worse. These range from the tedious to the irritating, the foolish to the downright nasty. They can develop on a scale from unhelpful to obstructive, until they ruin things for the rest of the company. These are syndromes that over the years I've come to recognise, some of which I'll identify, not out of malice, but to make the point that fear, not recognised and dealt with, can be disastrous, not only for the person concerned, but for everyone else involved.

THE COMPANY CLOWN

This is the actor – and ninety-five per cent of the time it's a man – who is talented, but frightened of revealing himself, while at the same time desperate to be admired and accepted. His most comfortably available talent is being funny. So the difficult journey of rehearsals is accompanied by his jokes and clowning, irrespective of whether they're appropriate or not. He usually has lots of wonderful (but misplaced) energy. Of course, his craven colleagues (the other actors) laugh at his jokes and feed his habit. Even after completing a scene that he's played well and seriously, he abruptly sends it up ('Very emotional! Can't let that happen too often or I'll have to ask for a raise!'), promptly devaluing what he and his partners have just achieved. For him, admitting seriousness would automatically expose him to judgement. While he jokes, he projects an attitude that nothing's worth taking *that* seriously and this – he believes – lets him off the commitment hook. Probably, a director's best approach is to appeal to the adult in him rather than the child. Give him responsibility. Seek his advice. Upgrade him! I have to admit that none of those tactics worked with a hugely talented but irrepressible actor in my Israeli company. Throwing books at him was the only thing that shut him up – for about half an hour. I don't advocate this approach. But, hey, that was Israel . . . !

THE 'I'M INTELLIGENT, TOO' ACTOR

More often a male tendency, this pattern's becoming increasingly bi-gender. These are the actors who, whatever's being discussed, have to let you know that they know all about it, too. They function by waiting until a topic has been thoroughly aired and then paraphrase everything that's already been said as though the ideas are theirs. They drop names and references that have little to do with the matter in hand. They tend to keep talking when everyone else wants to move on. They contribute nothing to the debate, waste time and, over time, bore the rest of the company rigid. Their misguided attempts to impress are compensation for feelings, often quite unjustified, of educational and intellectual inadequacy. This is tricky to handle because any criticism will only reinforce the inferiority they feel. Maybe the way to boost their ego is pre-emptively to seek out their opinions. This gives them status and may diffuse their arias.

THE AGENDA-IST

Twenty or thirty years ago, this role had a strong gay manifestation. Today, it's predominantly played by women. They make an issue out of some material in the text (in terms of racism, say, or feminism or the environment), having hunted down every suspect reference. (To be fair, the impulse usually stems from a justified sense of injustice; but it often coincides with some current, high-profile cause, so, at times, their convictions can seem less personally held than fashionably embraced.) Such issues may indeed be of concern, but of no relevance to the work in hand. For instance, if you're working on a text from a past culture in which women's role in the society is objectified in a manner totally antipathetic to present values, unless the play and production are conceived specifically for the purpose of tackling this theme, to make an issue of it is a distraction. Agitprop theatre apart, the stage rarely deals with simplistic moral decisions (this is right, that is wrong). Agenda-ists are guilty of the arrogance of hindsight in the presumption that the writer should have thought and felt as we think and feel now. They often demonstrate a lack of empathy with other periods and cultures. This tendency often goes hand in hand with a lack of imagination and a limited sense of humour. The director can try to waylay this during the casting session by making clear the nature of the text and the approach to it. If you then both decide you still want to work together, you'll do so with an agreed understanding of the terms.

THE TEACHER'S PET

This pattern is familiar in both genders, more frequently so in women. These actors come to you, the director, after rehearsal or in a break, to seek the reassurance that you've *already* given them *in* rehearsals, or to let you know that they understand what you said in rehearsal, to tell you how wonderful they find the work, to ask if they can talk to you. (They talk to you about talking to you!) Of course, there's absolutely nothing wrong with an actor wanting to talk to you about their work outside rehearsals – in fact, it's considerate to the rest of the company. But, repeated, it becomes more about begging for attention, approval and a special relationship with you. These actors listen oh, so attentively to every word you say, and express by sound and look that they absolutely understand and agree with what you're on about. It is dangerously flattering to unwary directors. These actors have a generous capacity for masochism – they appear to take a lot of criticism with earnest enthusiasm. This seems like a strategy to contain it by embracing it. It's best not to reinforce this behaviour. It eventually gets up the collective nose of the company. Try politely and gently to minimise such encounters and keep encouraging such actors to believe they're more than qualified to stand on their own two feet.

THE AVOIDER

If relationships get difficult in rehearsals, this actor, usually male, keeps a very low profile and disassociates himself from any unpleasantness, keeping his nose very firmly in his script. I'm reasonably sympathetic to this – after all, actors have to continue to work together, perform together and share dressing rooms, so they want to protect their future well-being. But this is short-sighted, as non-confrontation with recalcitrant colleagues doesn't necessarily pay off. Unchallenged, the latter only increase their misdemeanours. One irritating tendency of the Avoider is to condemn his difficult colleagues to you in private, while saying nothing in public – sometimes even mildly supporting them. All you can do is try not to take this two-faced behaviour personally. You could, should the Avoider complain to you in private, take the opportunity to suggest that, if that's the way he feels, maybe he should take his complaint to the offending colleague.

THE WEEPER

Totally female. This is the actor whose eyes are filled with tears for large periods of rehearsal. The tears implicitly say, 'I can't do it', 'I'm no good', 'You must think I'm useless'. This is a very genuine case of total collapse of confidence (possibly connected with matters other than theatre) and a plea for help. It might cross your mind that if the actor feels so insecure, she had no right to accept the job! Alarming for the director, it can occur at the least expected moments – when you're actually praising the whole cast for their prowess. Don't reinforce this trait. Don't indulge her. Be sympathetic but firm and, above all, encouraging. Make her acknowledge her achievements.

THE SUFFERER

This also tends to be a female trait. These sufferers believe that their work cannot possibly be good unless they go through agonies to achieve it. If it comes easily, it's suspect. This of course is nonsense – sometimes the work *can* flow smoothly. This trait is, sadly, a genuine artistic urge that has somehow got distorted; possibly it's developed as an implicit criticism of directors who, in their opinion, don't work seriously enough. It's certainly a ploy to gain status ('I'm serious about my work and I'm not going to be fobbed off with your facile encouragement'). So the director is confronted with a lot of emotional writhing and unhappiness which alternates between self-deprecation ('You must think I'm lousy, you made a boo-boo when you cast me!') and attacks on the way you're working ('I found that exercise utterly unhelpful, quite eroding in fact'). The director who tries to solve the problem is on a hiding to nothing, because the problem doesn't want to be solved. If you praise the actor's work, more likely than not you'll get a response along the lines of 'Nonsense! I was terrible'. If, on the other hand, you dare to offer criticism, you may get something like 'Oh? I thought I was finally getting somewhere. Well, I'll just dump that then, shall I?' Sympathy gets you nowhere. Ignoring them doesn't help much either, because the rest of the company gets pulled into their sufferings and want you to deal with it. A difficult one. In the last resort, if driven to it, you may have to be sharply confrontational and administer the verbal equivalent of a brisk slap in the face! These actors are usually talented.

THE COMPETITOR

These actors, male and female, decide that they should be running the show, and try to compete with you, the director. This manifests itself in their being helpful to other actors with suggestions when it appears you've failed to solve a problem, in assuming the self-appointed role of company spokesman, in undercutting many of your suggestions ('We think it would be more helpful if . . . '), in criticising the way in which a rehearsal is set up and in challenging the validity of a particular exercise or improvisation. The cause of this competitive behaviour seems to be a need for status, which they test by challenging the most powerful person in the room. Or it could be the outcome of a complicated relationship with you, the director, that they've developed in their head, totally unknown to you. They feel their commitment to you deserves your constant appreciative acknowledgement; they need to know that you rate them above the rest of the company – unrealistic and unlikely when you're trying to build an ensemble! You have two basic approaches here: one is, as unobtrusively as possible, to feed these actors' craving for the reassurance that you really do think them special by selecting them for areas of responsibility, consulting them outside rehearsals – and see if that calms them down. They may be happy to be seen as your semi-official lieutenant. But this can grow tiresome, and it's not entirely honest. The other approach is to challenge them head on and head things off before they go too far.

THE SABOTEUR

This is usually a function of male bitchery. These actors never go in for direct confrontation, but by look and tone imply that everything you, the director, have to say, is crap. They're very good at emitting quiet little snorts of contempt while you're trying to deal with another actor. When you talk to them, they rarely look you in the eye, but maintain their secret, scornful smile. They never refuse outright to do anything but offer comments such as 'If that's what you want . . . ', 'If you think that will help . . . '. They rarely give an opinion. That would lay them open to fallibility. Giving sardonic glances to other actors behind your back is their effective technique for feeding directorial paranoia; like small children, they often have an instinct for sniffing out your areas of greatest insecurity. You end up thinking that every glance between actors in rehearsal is a put-down or send-up of you. They're difficult to challenge because they don't quite do anything wrong. When alone with you (though they rarely allow that to happen), they behave impeccably, charm itself. If you can ever catch them out and justifiably challenge them, they respond by going into a violent sulk. These actors are terrified of revealing anything about themselves, but have usually developed rather brilliant external acting skills. They fight tooth and nail for survival. Other actors are a little in awe of their cool. They're usually very bright. Anything that smacks of craven attempts by you to woo them over will merely increase their disdain. This needs, first, a private confrontation, to let them know that you're on to them, but with sufficient acuity to avoid the retort that you're imagining things. Then, as they're bright, you might engage their intelligence in accepting the fact that, in the end, you all have a show to put on together. If that doesn't work, you may have to, deliberately and with great control, lose your temper with them in front of the whole company. They really should leave. Their ego's defence system is so strong, there's probably no way for you to release it, especially since you and your process of work are the very things that threaten them.

THE DESTROYER

This designation should alert you to a deadly presence in rehearsals. The trait, gender-free, can manifest itself when you least expect it – even in someone with whom you've worked well in the past. It has several bases. It can be caused by dis-illusionment, a profound sense that you, the director, have betrayed values they presumed you espoused; it can be a huge panic from the sudden (unconscious) fear that the work is going to threaten them (usually male in this case) with the ruthless exposure of their most intimate anxieties; it can be a desire (and this is frequently female) to be bullied and beaten down by you until you've proved you're convincingly in command. These motives result in them challenging the director at every point of rehearsal, never satisfied with what's happened, never conceding that anything's worked. Appeasement just adds fuel to the flames. It's a battle and it's to the death. Other manifestations of this syndrome can be an inability to concentrate (the eyes drift about in panic) or a total collapse of energy. One such actress used to insist on lying on the floor from which vantage point she watched the others rehearse with an expression of scornful malevolence, dragging down their energy to the floor, too, and sucking it in like a vampire. She had a powerful presence. (*Never* let actors lie on the floor!) These actors subtly infringe basic discipline – always *just* being late, not being *quite* off-book on schedule . . . They're unrepentant and irreclaimable because once they cross the border of social conscience, that is, once they're no longer concerned about how they're affecting their colleagues or what their colleagues think of them, they've defined for themselves a role which, from that moment, must be their identity. To pull back from that position would lose them status; they've reached the point of no return. So they armour-plate themselves against any sense of guilt with self-justification, often on high artistic and ethical grounds, and become increasingly defiant. Offers of understanding or rapprochement only intensify their sense of power. If they've been 'bad', that's the way they're going to stay. The other actors' time and energies are debilitated by misguided attempts to appease or accom-modate their colleague. The only action for the director is to get rid of them. They infect the rest of the company like one rotten apple in a barrel of good ones. These actors are often very talented, but intensely unhappy.

Once, in Germany, I suffered from an extreme version of this syndrome. The actor was deeply resentful of an English director coming to tell him what to do and, with that curiously provincial pomposity one finds in some German actors, announced that he had been a star of the Bremen Theatre. (A bit like an English actor telling me he'd been a star in Southampton.) He had the other rather pusillanimous male members of the company under his thumb and tried to set the agenda for what they would or would not do (certainly not improvise) and sneered at any sort of exercise. He was deeply insulting in the most barefaced male-chauvinist-pig manner to the women in the company, all of whom *did* want to do the work, and there would be screaming, abusive rows between them that ended in rather alarming hysteria on both sides. I finally mustered the energy and courage to confront him with his behaviour. Much to my surprise, he broke down and sobbed. I was curious as to where this would take him, whether he would return purged and ready to use his not inconsiderable talent positively. No such luck! At the next rehearsal, he had certainly changed, but not for the better. He was all compliance, but in terms of 'Just tell me what to do and I'll do it', totally passive and non-contributive. This was worse than what had gone before, so in the end I had to get rid of him. As soon as his replacement arrived, warm and enthusiastic, the rest of the male company were totally transformed and got on with the work. But until I wielded the axe, rehearsals were a misery for everyone.

Open Conflict

Sometimes, rightly or wrongly, actors interpret criticism from you, the director, as personal antagonism, and retaliate accordingly. I would advise you not to get drawn into confrontations with actors about what they think is your relationship with them. Avoid the trap of being thrown on the defensive. Don't be lured into trying to refute their accusations that you're deliberately out to get them, are trying to crush their independence, are always picking on *them*, are regretting you cast them (if you aren't already, they're doing a pretty good job of shifting you in that direction!) and so on. Try always to move such disagreements away from the personal towards the professional: what, in the circumstances, would best contribute to the good of the production.

Some directors thrive on conflict and even go out of their way to generate it in their belief that something creative will come from the tension. Whatever does come tends to be hysterical and inauthentic, deriving from personal circumstances rather than those of the material. It is a form of manipulation. I myself find it hard to work with negative energy in the room. So much so, that I used to take the opposite approach, making the fatal mistake of denying any signs of trouble in the hope that the problem would quietly tiptoe away by itself. It rarely does. You have to deal with it – if for no other reason than the rest of the cast rightly expect it of you. It's better to handle the situation early, before it becomes too convoluted for resolution. There's a good sense of achievement if you can reclaim actors before they reach the point of no return, and restore them to health, as it were, and the bosom of the company.

Things Change

On occasions, I've come to the end of a production, swearing to myself I'd never work with a particular actor again. *But never say never again.* Time's a great healer and *people change – including you.* Over time, some actors, admirably, have made contact to say that despite the difficulties, they'd learnt a lot and wanted belatedly to say sorry and thanks. Or we've met and mutually made it up. And subsequently worked together again in perfect harmony.

If much of what I've said here sounds harsh towards some actors, it stems largely from frustration. Sometimes I feel that I'm more ambitious for actors than they are for themselves. Their vulnerability often blinds their ability to see what a wonderful vocation they've chosen for themselves, and consequently they fail to grasp in both hands its potential to empower them in totally positive ways rather than by the misguided behaviour patterns I've described. They seem unwilling to embrace their undoubted creativity, when the release and development of that creativity would be the life-enhancing experience they must surely have longed for when they first dreamt of becoming actors.

Directors' Fears

Omniscience

Directors should keep their awareness of actors' fears firmly in the front of the mind. We have our own fears, too, which can render us insensitive to the real cause of an actor's lassitude or tantrums or tears. Preoccupation with our own vulnerabilities can lead us to handle matters clumsily. What are directors frightened of? Equally: *of being found out.* As I've said, we're often credited with absolute knowledge. Since the theatre deals with the whole of life, this puts us in the false position of being supposed to know everything about everything (I can think of no other job where the required knowledge is quite so extensive – actually without limit). So a major fear is that we'll be found out not to know very much at all about anything! Opinions are one thing, but real knowledge and real techniques may well be in short supply. So any implicit criticism of our knowledge of facts or processes is a threat to our position. If ever challenged, we may well retaliate with bombast, bluff, high-handedness or placatory oversolicitude. For me, the great day of liberation arrived when I could actually bring myself to say to a group of actors, 'I don't know! I don't know what to do! I don't know how to do it!' Suddenly the weight of self-oppression lifted from my shoulders. I was free. And the world hadn't collapsed around me, nor the ground beneath my feet. I go hot under the collar when I think back to those occasions on which I tried to pretend I did know about matters for which I really didn't have an answer. But my job description said I was meant to, had to, and therefore couldn't be seen not to. I blush at the bluff and double-talk I indulged in while the actors stared at me with stony disdain. Certain actors, of course, will tend to push you into the corner of omniscience – they will want to relieve themselves of any responsibility by saying, 'Well, that's what the director wanted!' Don't let yourself get painted into that corner.

Omnipotence

Directors are also automatically endowed with authority. But do we have natural authority? Will we be able to deal with actors who are out to challenge us, test us or tease us, and see how much they can get away with? Will we be found out here, too? Many directors need to be adored, admired or unquestioningly obeyed. This leads them into patterns of behaviour which take them beyond the true concerns of the work into the dangerous area of image and relationships. It's far healthier if both parties forget about status and remind themselves why they are there in the first place. As I say, I always try to diffuse perceived issues of status by constantly throwing the focus back on the work with questions: 'Does this help the production?' 'What's best for the production?'

Directors Can Learn

I remember how foolishly I used to behave if an actor was late (maybe, at unguarded moments, I still do). I'd take it as a personal affront, but, not having the courage to say anything, I'd become extremely tight-lipped and tight-jawed, projecting offended dignity and betrayed trust. All this did was create tension for everyone in the room. Eventually, an actor had the courage (and intelligence) to point out that (a) I should know them and their commitment to the work well enough to realise they were neither being late out of indifference, nor in order to annoy me; and (b) my attitude only intensified whatever guilt they already felt about being late and the defensiveness that went with it. A tense mouth achieved nothing. I gradually learned to relax my jaw.

This was in the early years of Shared Experience, when I worked intensively with a small group of actors over long periods. I have them to thank for teaching me a lot about other counterproductive behaviour of mine. I had the habit, for instance, of rushing backstage in the intervals of early performances of a new production to load them with fussy notes that I'd already given them earlier in the day (of the 'Don't forget to . . . ' variety), or to give judgements on how they were doing so far. After the show, before the actors had time even to get offstage, I'd already be in the dressing room, waiting for them with more notes in my hand. This went on until an actor who worked with me steadily over the first five years of the company sat me down and gave me a lecture. 'Look, Mike, you've got to understand that when we're in the middle of the show or just at the end of it, our adrenaline is high. Whether or not we've given a good show, we've been out there working hard and seriously – and we're in no fit state to absorb anything you have to say. You must realise that when actors are performing, especially in the way you ask of us, we're extremely vulnerable. And getting notes when we're in that state only makes us resentful and defensive – and angry with you. What we want now isn't notes, but a drink! Give us the notes tomorrow when we're in a receptive frame of mind to appreciate them.'

A Partial Taxonomy of Fear for Directors

Some directors develop ways of behaving to compensate for a sense of some inadequacy or other, and, in doing so, frequently exploit their position of power. I want to make it clear, as with the preceding list of actors' syndromes, that I'm not saying all directors always behave in all the patterns I'm about to describe, but that any director might fall into some of them at some time, and that some directors fall into some of them more often than not.

THE ENTHUSIAST

This director kills with kindness; it's usually a he, and he's full of good intentions. He exudes more energy than the rest of the company put together and bombards the actors with a plethora of ideas and suggestions. He conducts rehearsals rather like a soccer coach, encouraging and exhorting while the actors try to get on with their work. With him, the start of rehearsals go swimmingly, but the law of diminishing returns kicks in early: the actors feel deprived of space, initiative and energy, even oxygen, and if they don't say so, they probably think, 'Why don't you do the whole thing yourself!' The pity is that his ideas and intentions are actually good. But his need to be popular, to be seen to be a conscientious director, stemming from a certain insecurity, exceeds his perspicacity as to when to shut up. Actors should firmly but nicely insist on being allowed space to find some things out for themselves. If challenged too directly, he deflates like a balloon. Directors, by all means generate good energy, enthusiasm and excitement, but let these flow from a basis of calm.

THE ENTERTAINER

This director, very much male, treats rehearsals as a showcase for his own talents. He is full of theatrical anecdotes and reminiscences; he's terrific with the jokes; he's a performer in his own right and acts out all the roles with great flair. He's the unspoken star of the show. Rehearsals are full of good-humoured laissez-faire and usually finish early – and nothing much gets achieved. There's something of the dilettante about him. He probably has many abilities. Directing is not necessarily his main profession. Actors, you'll need some clever tactics to manoeuvre him into letting you actually do some work.

THE TALKER

A possible adjunct to the entertainer, he talks and talks and talks and talks, in love with the sound of his own voice and what he has to say. He's erudite and intellectually sharp. Lecturing on ideas is his strong suit. But what he has to say remains largely in the world of theory, interesting in other circumstances, but in rehearsal, something of an energy-sapper. Actors need practice rather than theory, and he has little knowledge of how actors function, nor how to translate theory into practice. He can only ask for generalised results and probably compensates for this by spending far too much time discussing their moves with them (because that's what directors do – he's really an amateur). Directors who devote most of their rehearsal time to matters of blocking aren't going to provide much else. Actors, once again, you'll have to find ways of encouraging him to let you get on your feet.

THE DESPISER

Another male type, probably more from the past, who rarely if ever moves from his chair. Well protected behind his table, languid and effete, he gives very few instructions – often on the level of 'Well, then, what are we waiting for?' 'Let's see what you've got to offer.' He works from a basis of weariness and unutterable boredom. He provokes actors with withering scorn: 'Oh, that's what you've decided to do!', 'Is that the best you can come up with?', 'We'll have to settle for that, I suppose!' If asked by actors for help, he may imply that that's their job – to solve their own problems. He may well concentrate on externals, how things look and sound, fussing with minutiae of blocking and line-readings; he is a sort of aesthete. The occasion on which he might stand up is in order, rather grumpily, to show a stupid actor how to place a chair. He frequently chooses a junior member of the cast as his whipping boy. With his sarcasm and his wit, he does frighten actors into results, and he's not without talent. His productions are slick, tight and often successful. But they're also cold and loveless. These are shows in which the actors, once in performance and with the director absent, may revert to naughty-child behaviour, getting their own back by rather pettily subverting minor details of the production, changing blocking, not wearing certain pieces of costume (hats are a big item here) . . . The main thing for you actors is not to be undermined or allow yourselves to (be made to) feel small. Keep your own sense of yourself and calmly get on with your work.

THE DIVIDE-AND-RULER

This director, male, is rather quiet, slow and very thoughtful. He gives his instructions *sotto voce* to his leading actors, strolling with them into corners to conduct private conferences away from the rest of the cast, who are left to kick their heels. He treats actors hierarchically, devoting a lot of time to his leads – totally indulging those who demand his attention – and almost no time to those playing smaller roles, whom he may use as scapegoats for his frustrations. There is no sense of a company or an ensemble. Everyone is left to stake out their own territory according to status. All an actor can do here is to make as much good contact as possible with other members of the company to override the effects of this procedure.

THE PROBLEM-SEEKER

This director, usually female, functions insidiously and damagingly. She has a need to possess the actors, to make them totally dependent on her, not just for this production but for as long as the spell holds. They will credit her totally with their salvation. So she seeks out problems that aren't there or magnifies those that are into psychological blocks. 'Darling/Love/Whatever, I *see* what your problem is. I think we should find time to talk about it.' Actors can easily be seduced by the promised comfort of an understanding mummy (or daddy), so they fall for it. Most actors tend to depend on directors more than they probably should. This approach totally erodes their independence. It works on mutual neuroticism and it's unhealthy. True, it's hard for directors not to find themselves at times in the role of therapist, but most of us aren't qualified as one, nor is it our job. We have to find other, less pernicious ways, to unblock the actor – better by subtly leading actors to recognise and try to solve such problems for themselves. Actors, don't let your vulnerability seduce you into this sort of relationship; politely decline the invitation.

THE BULLY

This is a syndrome of both sexes and speaks for itself. They abuse, shout, use a lot of the Despiser's techniques without his weariness. They contact the actors at home at all hours to threaten, reproach and make demands. They exploit their personal knowledge of them and employ emotional blackmail. Perversely, many actors repeatedly agree to work with these directors and then unfailingly complain about them. They are clearly actors who want to be bullied. So both parties become mutually locked in a vicious circle. However, as soon as an actor stands up to these directors, they instantly move into disingenuous appeasement mode; bullies, as we know, are cowards. So, actors, answer back. This may disable them for a while, but at some later date, they'll probably bounce back with a new angle of attack. Bullies are pretty irrepressible. They have to be 'in control'.

THE BLUFFER

This director (mainly male) doesn't do his homework, comes unprepared, doesn't plan his rehearsals and spends a lot of the time demanding the actors keep repeating the same scene while he stares at the text he doesn't really know and has few ideas about. He's made himself extremely vulnerable, so a lot of bluffing ensues. When challenged about something, he can become very aggressive and dictatorial. To cover himself, he displays a great deal of busy-ness, arriving a little late and breathless, with piles of scripts and documents (he has a lot of other projects demanding his attention!). He will tend to take phone calls during rehearsals and have hasty meetings with other members of the production team ('Run over your lines, shan't be long'). The one strength of this approach is that the actors, out of sheer desperation and a strongly developed instinct for survival, band together to work on the production outside rehearsals. Their smiles are, to say the least, wry when they read reviews praising the director for his production. Actors, keep demanding his help, advice and suggestions, keep him on his toes. But never do so to the degree that even hints at his ignorance or laziness. Best acknowledge that for any serious work, you are to all intents and purposes on your own.

THE ABSENTEE

This is the careerist, almost exclusively male, more excited about what is to come rather than what is happening now. He lives in the future. Once he's got the job, rehearsals become a hindrance to his networking. He's usually late and instructs associates and assistants to keep the actors busy until he shows up. He's full of superficially exciting ideas, but has no staying power or discipline to carry them through. What doesn't happen quickly, won't happen. His interest is in his next string of projects. Getting work is his talent – he's a persuasive talker – and, with long-suffering actors and good collaborators, he can get away with being seen to do a good job for a certain period. The actors, once more, out of an instinct for survival, get the show together more or less on their own. And once more, the show gets reasonable reviews and he takes the credit. Actors, have the courage to challenge him either to stick around and do his job or to stay away permanently.

As with actors, these directors' syndromes are not fixed characteristics, but patterns that directors adopt, not deliberately, but instinctively, as a survival mode to cope with an inner panic that they're losing control or don't really know what they're doing. I was not immune from some of these patterns (Problem-Seeker, Enthusiast, Talker, Bully). I can still fall into old traps when I'm thoughtlessly off-guard. Quite late in my career, at a period when, through years of complacency, I'd developed, I suppose, an unspoken assumption that it could never happen to me – indeed, no longer even conceived of the possibility of myself in such a situation – I experienced, through my own blindness, a whole production exploding in my face. I was never able satisfactorily to solve the ensuing problems, but kept trying, inadequately, to patch things up over a long and painful period. It was another sobering lesson in 'Never Assume'.

But over time, as I've described, I learnt, usually from actors, that certain behaviour just wasn't helpful. As confidence in our ability deepens, it should become obvious that 'bad behaviour' is pointless. This is about growing up and learning to face ourselves. It's hard and unending – it goes on all our lives. But living should mean learning, and theatre is a permanent school. The effort more than earns its rewards. We can learn and we *can* change.

Rigour

The Austerity of Theatre

Theatre makes exceptional demands on its practitioners – and its audience. Despite its reputation in some quarters as a repository for flamboyant self-indulgence, it is, in fact, a surprisingly austere medium of severely restricted parameters. Of all forms of writing, a play is the most challenging, with its limitations of length and means of expression (dialogue and stage directions) and its ultimate form as a performance. It has none of the flexibility of a novel. A production is similarly restricted in time and space and by the fact that it's live. To make maximum impact, both playwrights and directors have scrupulously to observe the form in which they're working.

In many ways, theatre is closer to sport than to other arts. I've likened actors to athletes, indicating that they need particularly high levels of stamina, energy, and concentration, self-knowledge and the many skills necessary to release their natural talents to their fullest. Once a performance begins, it is relentless, unstoppable. Both audiences and performers have to keep up with it. There's no possibility of pausing to reflect or going back to make a correction. You can't flick through the pages, skip tracks, rewind or fast-forward. There's no 'back' icon to click on. To create and appreciate theatre demands rigour. Rigour has its basis in self-discipline, but it also means meticulousness, specificity and severity in the pursuit of excellence.

Heightened Awareness

There are many routines (brewing coffee, brushing our teeth, putting out the garbage, letting in the cat) that we carry out daily without any need to consider them. Almost unconsciously, we execute the actions that maintain the basic patterns of our lives. This of course is a mercy. Imagine the exhaustion of having to think about each and every activity you performed between waking and sleeping. Recall how time-consuming it was, how demanding on your concentration and energy, when you were learning to master unfamiliar skills that are now second nature to you (playing a musical instrument, driving a car, operating a computer). Actors, despite frequently repeated performances, cannot allow themselves to fall into such routines. Everything that happens on stage should be filled with meaning well beyond the habitual, even when the characters are carrying out observably everyday actions. Throughout rehearsals, and certainly in performance, actors need sustained awareness of their surroundings, and especially of their colleagues, ready to adjust spontaneously to whatever happens. Their awareness has to be sharper, more intense than the average. They must function like competing athletes, like people engaged in high-risk activities or those caught up in an emergency. For the period they're on stage, actors need a highly developed state of alertness that Antonio Damasio, a professor of neurology, defines as Extended Consciousness. They need to attain a level of performance that Kenneth Tynan admiringly described as having High Definition, *his* definition of what makes a performance great.* Actors are constantly having to fight against the automatic patterns into which muscle memory and the deadening repetition of fixed results can lead them. (I've already mentioned actors in long runs not knowing which scene they were in.) Actors cannot rely on the adrenaline rush of a performance to keep them continuously on the *qui vive*. They need the utmost rigour to sustain such heightened awareness.

Parts Without a Sum

It's not unfair to say that people, on the whole, are becoming more impatiently self-indulgent. Instant gratification and effective results being very much the order of the day, ends tend to justify means. This inevitably filters into theatre; theatre is, after all, a microcosm of the society that creates it. If what we've done makes an acceptable effect, there's an unwillingness to examine sufficiently what we actually *have* done. There's a sense that it's wasted time to question too scrupulously the what, the why and the how: whether we *really are* saying what we mean, whether what we mean *is relevant* in the overall context of what we're doing and whether we're expressing it by the *most appropriate* means.

What theatre too frequently offers us is a string of moments that may be individually effective, but collectively don't add up to a complete world. Without the integration of its parts, it's almost impossible for an audience to get deeply caught up in a performance. We remain on the outside, as it were, maybe titillated from moment to moment, but rarely captured by a complete experience. In describing the process of creating worlds, I was at pains to stress the rigour with which you must keep asking yourself questions until all your ideas combine in a satisfying whole (not the least of which is that all the actors look as though they belong in the same reality). I sense that such questions don't always get asked, and, if asked, aren't always answered with sufficient rigour. Theatre needs rigour to hold our attention. *To sustain our engagement, everything that happens on stage must contribute to the creation of the world it's offering us.*

---

* I seem to remember Albert Finney in a TV interview – I think with Kenneth Tynan – talk about watching Laurence Olivier from the wings when he was understudying him in *Coriolanus* at Stratford. He described his performance as taking each moment just that much further than anyone might believe it could reasonably go.

Patience

Few people any longer take a job in the anticipation that it will be for life, with its attendant expectation of going through an apprenticeship and slowly but surely moving up the promotional ladder. Nowadays, a job is seen as a stepping stone to the next one; you take out of it whatever you can and then you get out of it as fast as you can. But some things do need time and due process. And these include the development of the actors' skills and the creation of a piece of theatre, the reason being that human beings, the raw material of theatre, can only learn and develop, change and grow in their own time, not according to a preordained schedule of expected results.

So, despite the fact that we live in a society that demands everything *now*, directors and actors have to dance to a different piper. You shouldn't expect work conceived as a process to produce quick achievements. One of the most valuable assets for a director is patience. There's enough time if you learn to use it properly; even if you do have a tight schedule, you have to create around the actors an atmosphere of sufficient time and breathing space. Otherwise your anxiety to get through one scene in order to get to the next in order to get to the next will transfer itself to the actors. Wait for the right moment to say something to an actor. You don't have to blurt everything out as soon as it comes into your head. Either your impatience will create an atmosphere of unease in the cast or your eagerness will overwhelm them with more information than they're able to process at any one time. Patience creates a better state for creative work. *Impatience implies judgement*. Patience expresses tolerance for what the actors are trying to do – a better quality for developing their trust and their work. However, patience does *not* mean lack of bite or energy. You can push the actors hard; get them to work with high energy and vitality. But you must be patient in waiting for what is eventually released. Just as it's counterproductive, while learning a skill, to keep checking as to whether you're improving, so, too, is looking anxiously for results in others. This will only inhibit the actors. Of course, if a sequence of work is clearly not going anywhere and all that the actors are achieving is frustration both with themselves and with you, it's perfectly sensible to acknowledge this, neither with feelings of reproach towards them nor of incompetence in yourself, and move on to something else. Patience is very much a part of rigour, it encourages rigour, it allows rigour.

Failure

It's a commonplace that we learn from our mistakes, but a useful one and possibly one to ease the feelings of distress that accompany failure. With success, you push away your own doubts, all too ready to believe in the nice things people say, even if there's a part of you that knows the praise is not completely deserved. Failure – unless you've developed the thick skin of denial – causes you to brood. At first, you defensively reject the criticism and cling to what straws of support do come your way; you run over the work in your mind, justifying to yourself all your choices; but, over time, the pain of the rejection forces you to examine your work more objectively and you begin to see that some of the criticism might be justified, until eventually – often when you're working on another piece that unexpectedly throws the previous work into perspective – you come to accept what was not good about what you did.* Not necessarily what others thought was not right, but *what you now see* was not right. Failure does hurt, but it can also develop a strong faculty for the rigour of self-criticism, whereas success lets you off the hook, allows you to avoid any confrontation with your achievements. Ultimately, you're the one who *really* knows, albeit subliminally, the truth about your work. Success can take you somewhere very unreal – not least into an area where *being seen to be successful* is more important than what you actually achieve. Some forms of success cancel out others. Public and critical acclaim can sometimes award you success for second-rate work. When this happens, everyone's values get confused. You have to stand by what you stand for. Failure at least keeps you in the real world.

Freedom

We know that only by perseverance and the rigour of practice can we attain a skill. On a day when we're not checking for signs of improvement, not looking for results – just practising, not even consciously trying – we suddenly find that we're no longer the slave of those techniques we've been so assiduously struggling to acquire. At long last they've been absorbed into our psycho-physical system and we've begun to master them. The reward for rigour is creative freedom. *Rigour is freedom*. The greater the rigour, the greater the freedom. There's no freedom without it. How can you feel free if you're not quite sure what you're doing? It's a tedious platitude, no doubt, but the more you put into something, the more you get out of it.

Love

I do believe that good directors love – have to love – actors. That is to say, love the potential creativity in them, love the way they embrace their vulnerability, love their generosity of spirit, their willingness to reveal themselves, even to take themselves by surprise. I love their courage to go wherever the material sends them: to the dark, to the light, to ugliness, to beauty, to pain, to joy. I love the deep wit of really imaginative actors. Coming into a rehearsal room in the early morning where actors are quietly warming up – their bodies, their voices, their entire beings – I feel calmed and nourished by their concentration as they prepare for whatever the day will bring. I talk specifically of actors who really love acting,

---

* I've been deeply wounded, cut to the quick, roused to the heights of indignation by reviews that, looked at again some time later, turned out to be not that bad at all!

not in any sentimental or narcissistic way or with one eye on what this or that role is going to do for their careers – a pointless preoccupation anyway: it will do whatever it does! – but with a profound inner understanding of what acting might be. They seem able to embark on their work without fuss or prevarication, instantly taking on a life and a situation through innate empathic imagination.

The main reason I've directed with such happiness for so many years is for the intense pleasure of being party to the release of this creative imagination in actors, of watching them bloom before my eyes, of being someone who helped them to express that creativity. At times, the exhilaration has been indescribable. It seems a wonderful job to have, a privilege both to assist and be witness to such moments.* Audiences are most of the time deprived of these thrilling and revelatory occasions. By the time the fruits of that pure, raw creativity reaches them, it's become tamed, smoothed out, diffused and knowing.

My joy in directing is not about putting on a show – that's the literal, formal aspect of the job. It's in enabling a group of people to exercise their imaginations collaboratively as well as individually, watching them grow, develop and extend themselves until together they coalesce as a unique creation, a world true to its own specific existence and only possible because of these particular people. For me, one of the greatest satisfactions of being a director is to return to a show that I've been involved with and find that it's developed *a particular and real life of its own*, one that I might never have foreseen. I experience a gratifying sense of fulfilment, a pride in the positive growth of something in which I once participated.

Creativity can only come through process, process that enables that creative imagination to evolve like everything else in this universe, changing, transforming and growing as it more and more defines its uniqueness.

---

* For what it's worth, the French *'assister'* means both to witness as well as to help.

6

CODA: SUMMING UP

RECAPITULATION

Theatre is a live medium. Everything to do with theatre must exploit that fact. This book has been about the justification for the actor to remain spontaneous, creative and truly alive in performance and about the ways and means by which all elements of a production can support this aim. Life on stage can only be created by and between actors. Every performance should be a freshly created event.

The actor is the *sine qua non* of theatre. There can be no theatre without actors. You need only actors with a story to tell and an audience to tell it to in order to create theatre. Everything and everyone else is an elaboration of that circumstance and therefore fundamentally inessential.

The actor is also the theatre's *raison d'être*. We go to theatre, not to see plays, but to see actors *in* plays. We go to theatre to experience actors acting out our lives and giving meaning to them. We go to theatre to confirm our humanity and our extraordinary potential as human beings. *Actors are the representatives of our humanity.*

Plays and their interpretation are not the reason for theatre. Plays serve actors with the material with which they can serve theatre. Some of the best theatre has not always been created from plays or by playwrights. However, when the playwright is a writer of genius, you have the best possible material for the theatre.

Since actors, in order to play with spontaneity and therefore with truth, have to tap their creativity at its most intimate, directors must serve this process with the greatest sensitivity. Theatre is not about directorial concepts. Directors should create the circumstances in which actors can flourish. They are midwives.

Any form of design or technology should also serve the actors and not dominate or stifle them. Anything that blocks actors' creative freedom is working against the nature of theatre. Any scenic, physical or technological element in a production should be within the expressive control of the actor. Rehearsals should ensure that these elements are blended into the performance.

Theatre is comprised of three groups of people: audience, actors and characters. What makes theatre unique is that the actors transform themselves into other people in front of the audience. Together, actors and audience in an act of complicity create the third group of people – the characters. They share in an act of imagination in which they agree to believe in something that really isn't there. Actors and audience exist simultaneously in two realities: the reality of being in a theatre (or some spatial equivalent) experiencing the phenomenon of the actors doing their work; and the reality of the imagined world being materialised by those actors.

All members of an audience should be free, individually, to create their own performance within the context and frame of their own lives. A production should never tell the audience what to think or how to feel.

The less literal and the more suggestive the production, the greater the creative space for both actors and audiences. The less there is on stage, the more the audience's imagination is stimulated. On a continuum from a stage filled with scenery and technology to an empty space, the audience shifts from passive consumer to active participant.

Theatre has its own language and its own purity. It is neither a subsidiary of other disciplines, nor a dumping ground for the techniques of other disciplines. Theatre practitioners must employ the greatest rigour in all areas of their work to ensure they are using the pure language of theatre to its fullest expression. Rigour results in creative freedom. There can be no freedom without rigour. The *what* of a play provides its discipline; the *how* provides the freedom.

Truth in the theatre is not necessarily about whether audiences believe in the interpretation of a character ('The character would never have done that' – or 'done it like *that*'), but whether they believe in the *execution* of that interpretation, i.e. *how the actors act!* In the former case, such an opinion is personal, subjective and open to debate; in the latter, there are techniques that can be objectively observed. This book has been largely about them.

No production can be the definitive version of a play. Nor should any performance strive to be the definitive version of a production. As theatre is live, its main element should be its live-ness. As we live with areas of freedom and choice, as we have to behave with spontaneity in order to survive (things do happen beyond our control), *so* we should function in theatre. Every performance should be a unique event, open to permanent change – the reality of our lives – and to discovery. Fixed performances make deadly theatre.

Beyond a certain point, theatre cannot be controlled. That is to say, neither should actors be controlled, nor should they be wholly *in* control. Competent actors *make* things happen. Good actors *let* things happen. That's why theatre always has – or should have – the potential for danger, for the unpredictable. A performance should be a disciplined improvisation.

Theatre is the most human of all the arts, its raw material being the three groups of human beings designated. It is the art closest to the actual texture and experience of life. The theatre that embraces the spontaneity, immediacy, unexpectedness of life together with our ability to change, grow and develop, will create the truest and purest form of itself. This depends totally on the creativity – the humanity – of the actors.

Two Quotes

One from Athol Fugard defining 'the pure theatre experience':

The full and unique possibility of this experience needs nothing more than the actor and the stage, the actor in space and silence. Externals, *and in a sense even the text can be one*, will profit nothing if the actor has no soul. (*My emphasis.*)

And from myself:

The actor manifests our capacity to be vulnerable and daring, sensitive and strong, perceptive and compassionate, to be expressive and to be beautiful. The actor not only stimulates our empathic imagination but also reminds us of our inexhaustible potential as human beings. We all have something of everyone else within us. When actors transcend themselves, so will the audience. The purpose of theatre is the revelation and confirmation of the breadth, heights and depths, the multi-dimensional richness, of our shared humanity.

GLOSSARY

Action Actions are what actors play and characters do in order to achieve their OBJECTIVES. Actions give theatre its life. Theatre is the art of action. Actions are tactics. The semantically pedantic distinguish between an 'inner' action (*coaxing, threatening, apologising, rejecting, denouncing, praising*) and an 'outer' or physical action (*pouring a drink, shaking hands*) by calling the latter an ACTIVITY. Others call OBJECTIVES actions and actions ACTIVITIES! That's fine by me. It's not important what things are called. It's understanding what they *are* that matters. I repeat: actions are what characters *do*. We, the audience, watch them doing them. We watch characters in action. Actions are what actors play. Technically, actions are all they *can* play (*see*: BEATS).

Activity A routine physical ACTION like peeling potatoes or painting a wall that has little dramatic value in itself. It is, of course, made expressive by means of a character's inner ACTION, as a vehicle for revealing what the character is thinking or feeling. The activity is informed by HOW the character performs it. The actor endows the activity with meaning.

Actors Actors have the ability to transform themselves into other people, acting out other experiences in other places and other times; bringing the *there and then* into the *here and now*. Actors create THEATRE. PLAYS do not create THEATRE. PLAYS serve actors. Actors do not serve PLAYS; they serve THEATRE. THEATRE cannot exist without actors. All human beings are potential actors.

Actuality Our REALITY. Our lives as we actually experience them (*see*: REALITY).

Anticipating This occurs when an actor reacts to something before it's happened, such as replying to a question before it's been completely asked. This occurs with RESULT-orientated actors who are clearly not IN THE MOMENT. It's hard to avoid totally in a production that's been fixed, especially one that's been playing for a long time, when the actors know exactly what's coming next. Their MUSCLE MEMORY tends to take over, influencing them to play on automatic.

Art An aesthetic construct that engages our empathy, stimulating a combination, variously, of our emotions, senses, intellect and imagination. Great art moves us on all levels. Perfection occurs when content and form are indistinguishable.

Beat The smallest, most precise ACTION. Any TRANSITION however small, any shift of thought, attitude or ACTION initiates a new beat. There may be several beats within larger ACTIONS. Beats are, in effect, indivisible ACTIONS. A beat is what the actor *actually* plays. A sequence of beats is the detailed score for an actor to play.

Blocking The term for fixing how and where the actors move during a scene. It is also known as 'plotting'. This may be worked out by the director in advance of rehearsals or evolved during them with the actors. I am totally against either procedure. Blocking is indeed *le mot juste*; it blocks possibilities of creative change, of spontaneity, of life itself.

Centre In order for actors to play truly and freely, they must play from their centres. Their energy should flow from the centre without restriction, which means the body must be totally free of unnecessary TENSIONS. The centre is about two centimetres below the belly button. It is connected with the gut where emotions are most 'felt', with the pelvis which supports the torso, and balances the body, with the sex organs, and with the breath. There is nothing arcane about the concept of being centred. It is site specific. Being totally centred makes one totally vulnerable to all possible FEELINGS. Because of this, many actors avoid or deny their centre, creating TENSIONS as barriers to its access. Strained voices, physical TENSIONS, lack of spontaneity are symptoms of being off-centre.

Coaching A way of guiding the actors through an improvisation which allows them to remain concentrated *inside* the exercise while simultaneously taking in from *the outside* the director's periodic instructions.

Commenting This occurs when actors demonstrate crude value judgements to make sure we can see that their characters are wicked or good or stupid; that is, not allowing us to discover for ourselves or make up our own minds, but telling us what to think. This is pretty flat theatre (*see*: INDICATING, DEMONSTRATING, RESULT, SHOWING).

Conflict What theatre cannot do without. There cannot be story without conflict. There is no DRAMA without it. Conflict is the result of clashing OBJECTIVES. It creates our excitement, our need to know what will happen next or how events will unravel. Though the major conflict in drama is between characters, characters can struggle with conflicting OBJECTIVES within themselves (*see*: COUNTER-OBJECTIVE). In agitprop or other provocative forms of theatre, there can be conflict between actors and audience.

Counter-Objective A major OBJECTIVE that pulls in the opposite direction from the character's SUPER-OBJECTIVE. These two objectives are OBSTACLES to each other's attainment and cause CONFLICT *within* the character.

Curiosity If you're only interested in yourself, don't work in the theatre. Actors and directors need genuine curiosity. Curiosity is one of the many attributes of childhood that the best actors retain in adulthood.

Demonstrating A crude form of playing a RESULT, when actors illustrate what they would be doing if they were really doing it. Actors who are able to produce tears to order without earning the right to cry, not having actually played the situation, are guilty of this. They present rather than represent (*see*: INDICATING, COMMENTING, DEMONSTRATING, RESULTS, SHOWING).

Drama The body of literature that provides material for theatre (*see*: PLAYS).

Dramatic Essential and integral to theatre; a situation whose tension or excitement arouses our desire to know what will happen next, creating suspense and curiosity through the vivid use of conflicting OBJECTIVES and ACTIONS. It is *not* the same as THEATRICAL.

Effect Playing for effect is when actors try to charm, amuse or move us for their own personal needs, rather than for those of the characters in the situations of the play.

Effective A derogatory word implying that something makes an effect without substance or truth – something which works at a superficial, extrinsic level, or gives a false appearance of truth; very much the tool of 'deadly theatre' (*see*: THEATRICAL, INDICATING, COMMENTING, RESULTS).

Emotion Actors cannot play emotions. Actors experience emotions as a result of their success or failure in achieving their OBJECTIVES (*see*: WANT! DO! FEEL!). If they play their OBJECTIVES truthfully – really trying to affect their partners and allowing themselves to be affected in turn – feelings will be spontaneously aroused without any effort on their part. In fact, actors should be in a fluid state of FEELING for the whole length of their performance. If in our own lives, we are incapable of turning our emotions on and off on demand, like water from a tap, why should an actor be expected to fall madly in love at 8.20, suffer pangs of jealousy at 8.45, seek vengeance at 9.30 and die of despair at 10.00? Emotions come from our unconscious and have to be evoked or encouraged to manifest themselves by the playing of OBJECTIVES. There are two basic states of emotion: situational – when we feel something in response to a specific occurrence or circumstance, such as a quarrel; and ingrained – the basic emotional ground bass of someone's existence, such as being prey to depression or anxiety (*see*: EMOTION; CHARACTER DEVELOPMENT).

Empathic Imagination This is the natural talent of a true actor. Such actors can instinctively identify with other people in other situations and enter into that belief without having to agonise through every step of the way. It is allied to Francis Ferguson's *histrionic sense*. These actors may have no actual experience of what they're required to play, but have such empathy towards other people that they can imaginatively put small pieces of observed knowledge to an accurate understanding of a complex situation. (I'm always amazed by couples who, after the birth of their first child, discover to their bewilderment that they're no longer free to come and go, that they don't get enough sleep, and that the responsibility is terrifying. 'The best-kept secret in the world,' they announce. They lack Empathic Imagination!)

Energy Energy is the *appropriate* amount of flow of purpose that is needed at any moment in order to fulfil an action. A much abused word. Energy is not about being as frenetic on stage as you possibly can, which is usually accompanied by tremendous TENSION. That is actually blocked energy. Directors scream for 'More energy! More energy!' and the actors hurl themselves around the stage like demented puppets, losing any sense of what they are playing. They only achieve loudness and coarseness – and strain.

Feeling I use this word in two senses: (i) passion, EMOTION, mood – we are always in a state of feeling – 'I feel relaxed, preoccupied, a little anxious, pensive, wistful, bored, irritated, offended, curious . . . ' ; (ii) the intuitive sense which leads to understanding.

Form This is the external (physical, behavioural, expressive) realisation of the content: the themes, ideas and inner life of a performance. This is achieved by means of design, dramatic structure and the actor's manner of playing. When the form is imposed from the outside, it can distort the content. Mannerism occurs when the form draws attention to itself, rather than revealing the content. True form emanates from the content. Content without form is incommunicable. In the best art, form and content are indistinguishable. We also talk of manner and matter, style and substance (*see*: STYLE, WORLD).

Given Circumstances All the facts that influence the situation in which the characters find themselves. These can range from the time of day, year, weather, location to past histories, the preceding scene, anticipation of events to come, relationship to the other characters, the culture of the WORLD that the characters inhabit. Given circumstances affect and inform HOW the characters pursue their OBJECTIVES and ACTIONS.

How The interpretive element of a production. How is the creative freedom. WHAT is the discipline.

Imagination There are two sorts of imagination, one that comes from the head and one that comes from the 'gut', that is, from instinct, impulse, from the unconscious. The former I would tend to call inventive, clever. The latter is where actors are at their most creative. The former is made to happen *by* the actor, the latter happens *to* the actor. Good acting is Zen-like. You don't act the scene – the scene acts *you*. By which I mean, instead of actors believing that they must *make* things happen, they *allow* things to happen. With the head, actors are using their INTELLIGENCE, they are relatively objective and somewhat outside the role; with the 'gut', they are allowing their instinct into PLAY, subjectively from within the role. And with instinct comes deep imagination.

Indicating This occurs when the actor chooses an obvious and repetitive piece of business to make sure that we understand what we would have understood anyway.

For example, gyrating the pelvis to let us know the character's a prostitute; continually rolling sleeves up and down to tell us the character is a manual worker (*see*: INDICATING, COMMENTING, SHOWING, RESULTS, DEMONSTRATING, which are all virtually synonymous).

Intelligence/Intellect Actors often confuse intelligence with intellect. Some allow themselves to feel inadequate if the director is disposed to discuss the production in intellectual terms. (It's not much help telling an actor that their character symbolises the decline of Christianity or is a metaphor for *nostalgie de la boue*.) Ideas – absolutely vital to the coherence of the production – have nevertheless to be translated into organic, active, playable choices for the actor. However, an actor has to be intelligent. Actors have a very particular intelligence – what Francis Ferguson calls *the histrionic sense* and closely allied to what I called EMPATHIC IMAGINATION. By this, I take it to mean that they have an immediate, instinctive grasp of character and situation and the implicit dramatic shape of a scene. Actors cannot work by letting the head dominate. Discussion and analysis have their place, but they are not conducive to creative acting, which has to treat the head as just another part of the body. Some actors promote their intellectual abilities to avoid their emotional exposure.

Intensity/Tension Intensity good; tension bad. Intensity is the degree of commitment an actor invests in a moment; the greater the intensity, the greater the excitement and interest for the audience. The amount of power needed is gauged by the importance of what is happening for the character. You should instruct actors who are playing with insufficient intensity, not with exhortations for more ENERGY or intensity (which creates generalised TENSION) but to raise their stakes in the outcome of a scene, to up the ante, to endow their OBJECTIVE with greater urgency.

Main Line of Action (*see*: THROUGH-LINE)

Moment: Playing the Moment, Being in the Moment This is the simple concept of dealing with what is actually happening at any particular moment in a performance, irrespective of how you might have played it yesterday or a month ago in rehearsal. It reinforces the idea of process rather than result and demands instant, spontaneous response.

Muscle Memory This is the innate ability of actors to learn a pattern rapidly so that it becomes almost a reflex. It is both an advantage and a liability. In the latter case, it can take over from actors' autonomy and cause them to go into automatic mode, destroying any chance of BEING IN THE MOMENT.

Naturalism (*see*: REALITY)

Objective The objective, intention, mission, goal, destination, purpose, longing, hunger, desire, target, aim, problem, need, task, drive, stake of a character. *What* *the character wants to achieve.* Why the character enters a scene. The objective motivates and initiates the character's ACTIONS. Objectives are the fuel that drives the motor (the ACTIONS) of the DRAMA. Objectives drive the story forward. Objectives are the strategies for the ACTIONS' tactics. Objectives do not have to be achieved. In fact, in good drama, they rarely are. If an objective is achieved, there's no more drama. Conflicting objectives create DRAMA. Actors don't so much play objectives as immerse themselves in them, physically, mentally and emotionally – holistically. There are different levels of objectives, a hierarchy of them – momentary objectives, scene objectives, some that cover the length of the play. Objectives and ACTIONS should not have to be thought about during performance. They form a score and should be as absorbed and personalised in the same way as the text (*see*: SUPER-OBJECTIVE, WANT! DO! FEEL!).

Obstacle A barrier, block, obstruction, whatever impedes the achievement of an objective; whatever characters have to overcome to get what they want. There are three types: external circumstances (war, snowfall, illness, traffic jams . . .); the opposition of other characters (they don't want to give you what you want, or you don't want to give them what they want); and conflict within a character (opposing drives: SUPER-OBJECTIVE and COUNTER-OBJECTIVE).

Physical Physical means the involvement of the actor's *entire being*, not just a vigorous movement of muscles. If the physicality is truly committed, it embraces the emotional and the intellectual. Physical means holistic. Speech is physical.

Physical Theatre A tautology. All theatre is physical. The physicality may be better or less well executed or more or less obvious, but the actor who sits expressively in a chair creates better physical theatre than that created by the actor who charges all over the stage badly. Being hectically physical is not necessarily good theatre or even active theatre in the profoundest sense of ACTION. The committed playing of inner ACTIONS is what makes a performance truly physical. All theatre is physical but not all theatre is verbal.

To Play Two meanings. (i) To be playful. Play is vital to theatre. The good actor works playfully and plays seriously. The actor is playing a game, both as a child and as an athlete. Theatre is about using your IMAGINATION. (ii) To engage in ACTION. I keep making the point that the *only* things an actor can play is a BEAT (ACTION), the only thing an actor can actually *do*. Actors *cannot* play EMOTIONS or moods or character – or objectives. EMOTIONS are released by ACTIONS; mood is established by the collective ACTIONS in a scene (one dominated by ACTIONS like *celebrating, congratulating, roistering, revelling* will evoke a 'happy' mood, one with ACTIONS like *comforting, condoling, commiserating, consoling* will evoke a 'sad' mood); character is created by the actor's ability to transform; OBJECTIVES are activated by longings, needs or wants. Actors who try to play these only INDICATE or DEMONSTRATE . . .

Plays The richest, most efficient source of material for the theatre, the most fit for purpose. If actors were playwrights (and directors), theatre would be close to perfect. See Shakespeare and Molière! We are told Sophocles acted. Theatre is not about the interpretation of plays. It is about realising them, bringing them alive. Plays provide actors with the material to perform their function as the living force of theatre. Plays serve actors. Actors do not serve plays; they serve theatre. Plays do no create theatre. Actors create theatre.

Points of Concentration This is a technique for integrating the GIVEN CIRCUMSTANCES into the performance. GIVEN CIRCUMSTANCES should influence HOW you play your actions. Using GIVEN CIRCUMSTANCES as points of concentration gives the actor infinite possibilities of HOW a scene can be played. A point of concentration is, technically, a preoccupation with a GIVEN CIRCUMSTANCE that accompanies the playing of ACTIONS throughout a scene and influences the manner in which the ACTIONS are executed, in fact defines the HOW. Another way of thinking about POCs is as filters through which a scene is distilled. A very simple example: you can easily visualise very hot weather as a point of concentration affecting the playing of a scene very differently from a point of concentration on icy weather. Points of concentration do not just work from the head, but must be absorbed into the depths of the character's life and the actor's performance.

Professional This has two implications: (i) positive – having the skills to do one's job in a practical, efficient, organised way that releases creativity; (ii) negative – producing something that is slick, efficient, secure and eschews risk, doubt, questions or search.

Provocation An offer (that you cannot refuse), stimulation, choice or challenge made by actors, either in a scene or an improvisation, to stimulate their partners to react. It is totally positive and has none of the negativity implicit in the word. It is intended to heighten a partner's imaginative response.

Realism (*see*: REALITY)

Reality/Actuality, Realism/Naturalism The first two are words to describe our life as we see and understand it, the reality we perceive we live in; the latter pair are the labels given to categories of plays which aspire as closely as possible to the former. To be more specific, I would use ACTUALITY to describe the world we live in and REALITY as a generic term for discussing constructed WORLDS ('What REALITY are we in?'). Some actors believe that only playing realistically is truthful. So their work is reductive. Realism, as a form, is just as 'unreal' as, say, Romanticism. Naturalism aspires to a sort of photographic reality that hides its structure whereas, in Realism, the organisation of a play is more apparently structured. (Crudely, it's the difference between plays by Chekhov and Ibsen.)

Results, Playing a Result Playing a result occurs when actors play a moment without going through any of the inner processes that would actually bring them to that moment – a sort of jump-cut. This means the actors don't allow themselves to be effected by the other actor-characters on stage. The moment being played is not being fully experienced internally. It's a form of INDICATING, even ANTICIPATING. This, in my book, is very bad acting, however skilfully executed. Results can often be highly polished, but they make acting a matter of scoring points ('Here I cry, here I laugh') rather than the natural flow of experiencing a situation. Playing a result means that actors know what's going to happen before it's done; therefore, they can never be spontaneous, creative or, indeed, alive. Playing results is a series of little deaths (*see*: INDICATING, DEMONSTRATING, COMMENTING).

Showing This occurs when the actor is not fulfilling an action and allowing us to interpret it, but is explaining it to us, spelling out the SUBTEXT or the character's feelings (*see*: DEMONSTRATING, INDICATING, COMMENTING, RESULTS).

Style Another dangerous word. It tends to label a performance as having had something decorative and artificial imposed upon it. Sometimes it implies that an actor has flair or elegance – or a particular quality, which is, actually, a series of mannerisms refined into a system. An actor's style can function like a theme tune. It is sometimes applied to give the erroneous idea that there is one particular way of playing a period or a playwright ('Are you doing it in Restoration style', 'In the style of Noël Coward'). It is, for me, like THEATRICAL and EFFECTIVE, a pejorative word which implies all manner and no matter; a triumph of form over content, in short, superficial. I prefer, for serious purposes, to use the word WORLD (*see*: FORM, WORLD).

Subtext Literally, what is going on under the text – the unspoken implications that lie beneath the dialogue or ACTION. It is frequently the opposite of what is being said and is often a device for irony. Subtext can be both deliberate on the part of the speaker or unconscious. There is also the subtext of a play as a whole, which implies its metaphorical and thematic levels.

Super-Objective The overall drive of a character that defines and contains all their life choices. This is not playable because it is couched in broad, generalised terms (to succeed in life, to avoid life's vicissitudes, to belong, to dominate the world). It is more a guide to the specific choice of SCENE OBJECTIVES. It is a way of giving coherent shape and intellectual structure to a role, however inconsistent or contradictory the character may appear in the text. It should be an imaginative stimulus to the actor's work. A super-objective can be explored physically. Once actors have discovered a super-objective, they should find the playing of every scene much clearer. It is different from the THROUGH-LINE (MAIN LINE OF ACTION) which is plot-driven, whereas the super-objective is character-driven, The super-objective influences the THROUGH-LINE. A character's super-objective exists before the play begins and, assuming the character is still alive at the end of the play, continues afterwards. There is also the super-objective of a play, which is the sum of all the characters' super-objectives.

Tension/Intensity Tension bad; intensity good. Tension means that the flow of energy, oxygen, breath is distorted and impeded. Watch actors who should know better straining after 'emotion'. Most emotion is the *uninhibited* release of expression. Because we live in a culture where we inhibit most emotion, we confuse the inhibition with the real thing. Tension stops you from functioning. You cannot think, hear or see properly if you're tense. If one part of your body *has* to be tense (e.g. a fist) make sure that it alone is tense and the rest of the body free. And don't hold on to the tension after its moment of necessity has passed. It's bad for business and health. (Observe the exercise of power without tension in martial arts disciplines.) Art should be executed with lightness. I am turned off by performers who show you how hard they're working. Intensity, on the other hand, is the degree of commitment to a moment and the greater the intensity, the greater the excitement and interest for the audience. Tension can, I suppose, be used positively to describe the audience's state when caught up in dramatic conflict and wondering how it will work out.

Text The written play or the material you are working from.

Theatre One group of people watching a second group of people becoming a third group of people, the first two groups collaborating with their shared imagination to create the third. Theatre is about people in action and is always telling a story. The performers transform themselves in the presence of their audience. If there is no CONFLICT, there is no DRAMA; if there is no DRAMA, there is no theatre. Forms of performance that use all the elements of theatre except drama (*see*: THEATRICAL) probably have more to do with the visual arts. Theatre appears to be attractively vulnerable as a dumping ground for almost anything that anyone might want to do with it. It is the most available of art forms because it appears not to require special talents or specialised skills. It can attract people who have an artistic urge but no specific artistic talent. However, theatre *does* have its own nature, its own purity and can be true to itself. Theatre by its nature is essentially rough and unreliable, uncontrollable, potentially dangerous and unexpected. This is because its raw material is fallible human beings and its condition is immediate and ephemeral – and therefore difficult to contain.

Theatrical Everything that is externally attractive or EFFECTIVE; extrinsic, superficial, somewhat pejorative as in its dictionary definition of *exaggerated, false*. Used at its best, the theatrical supports and reinforces the DRAMATIC. At its least good, it replaces the DRAMATIC with the externals of theatre (lights, costumes, sets, music . . .).

Theme/Topic People ask what a play is about. You must distinguish between a play's theme and its subject matter. Syphilis is not the theme of Ibsen's *Ghosts*, nor is women's position in society. These are two topics in the play. The theme of *Ghosts* might be something like: 'Lying to retain your status and position in a repressed, conformist society will eventually destroy you.' The topic is the material used; the theme is the idea that informs the play. The theme utilises topics for its own clarification. Directors need to decide what they believe the theme of a play to be in order to create a coherent production. Some plays may have several themes but there will usually be a dominant one that is in fact the SUPER-OBJECTIVE of the play. A theme may be deliberate on the part of the playwright, but it's more likely to be instinctive, implicit in the writer's vision of life. Themes that are too deliberate tend to be didactic. In a good play, the sum of the characters' SUPER-OBJECTIVES will reveal the theme – or the super-objective of the play; e.g. in *The Three Sisters* all the characters are motivated by a need to belong somewhere other than where they are. Their drives range from changing their social position (Tuzenbach, Natasha) to something as simple as having their own room (Anfisa). Irina moves from job to job; the sisters yearn for Moscow; the soldiers move from camp to camp . . . I would say the theme of the play is: 'In a time of social change, people are searching for the security of a place where they feel they (can) belong.' It's useful and focusing – and not at all limiting – to be able to state the theme in a single sentence.

Through-Line The characters' main purpose or ACTION in terms of the plot. What they are trying to carry out throughout the play. The main thing they are trying to do: to (find the cause of and) end the plague (Oedipus); to have influence over Eilert Lövborg (Hedda Gabler); to become an actress (Nina). This is not the same as a SUPER-OBJECTIVE which in these cases might, respectively, be: to be seen to be a good ruler; to exert some influence in the world; to live life to the full. SUPER-OBJECTIVES are motivated by character; through-lines by plot (the situation in which the characters find themselves). A through-line may also be called the main line of action.

Time ACTION moves us through time. Time, possibly more than space, is the profound dimension of theatre. As the characters move forward in pursuit of their goals, we not only move with them, we are also moving through our own lives. The ephemeral nature of theatre gives it its poignancy. The performance cannot be rewound. And can never really be repeated. In this sense, theatre is like life. Another reason for not trying to repeat a performance.

Transition Any shift or change from one thought to another, one OBJECTIVE to another, one ACTION to another, one BEAT to another. Transitions fully executed give shape and dynamics to the playing of a scene; the more transitions there are, the greater the variety of expressiveness (range, colour, texture, mood . . .) and the greater the vitality of the performance.

Truth Truth in the theatre is not necessarily about whether you believe in the interpretation of a character ('The character would never have done that' – 'or done it like *that*'), but whether you believe in the *execution* of that interpretation, i.e. how the actors act! In the former case, truth is personal, subjective and debatable; in the latter, there are techniques that can be objectively observed. This book is largely about them. REALISM is not the exclusive domain of truth.

Unit A unit is the portion of a script in which one event occurs in which every character in the scene is involved; that is to say, every character in the scene must understand what the event is. The length of a unit is immaterial. It can cover several pages of text or be one line of dialogue – or even a single stage direction. Units should be titled. The event of a unit should be identified at the simplest possible level. It is not interpretative, it merely observes what appears to be happening: 'They argue about money', 'They greet their guests', 'He persuades her to sleep with him', 'He spills the milk'. The sum of the titles should tell, at a very surface level (that is, without any concern for the motives of the characters), the incidents that go to make up the plot of the play. A unit is similar to, but not identical with, a Stanislavskian 'bit'.

What The factual, unarguable elements of a play. What provides the discipline. HOW provides the creative freedom.

World The particular values, qualities and elements of a play which give it its form of existence. One of the first of many questions a director and actors have to ask themselves is 'What is the REALITY of this play? What sort of world do the characters inhabit? Not only in realistic terms of time, place and culture (*fin de siècle* Russia, Restoration London . . .), but also in what way its elements depart *from* ACTUALITY (a simple example: an opera posits a world in which it is natural – but *not* naturalistic – for the characters to sing). No writer's total work exists in one world: each play is a world of its own, though a playwright's body of work will of course have certain similarities and repeated themes. How should the world look? How are the characters to speak? How move? What are their values? What is their relationship to the audience? How do you want the audience to receive the work? We have rough, generalised guides in such overall categories as Romanticism, Expressionism, REALISM and NATURALISM . . . But labels are only an approximate nudge in a certain direction. They try to link together what is similar, whereas our job is to discover what is particular and specific about each piece of work we create. Each production has to create a new world. We must not imprison ourselves in received ideas about certain plays, many of which were always false or have now outlived their usefulness. There is no received way of playing Coward, say, or Shakespeare or Restoration Comedy or Pinter or Feydeau, only certain clichés. What is the world of the play? To find out is our job.

FURTHER READING

The English-speaking world has never been particularly thorough or comprehensive in publishing the written works of major theatre practitioners. Despite our reputation for creating possibly the best theatre in the world, our readership for books on the subject (which must largely include people who work in the profession) seems to put no demand on publishers to make such material available. Possibly our reputation convinces us that we have nothing to learn, especially from foreigners. More likely this lack of curiosity reflects that anti-intellectual Anglo-Saxon pragmatism that's suspicious of theories and systems concerning the crafts we profess to practise. If you're fortunate enough to speak a foreign language, your access to major writing on theatre will be greatly broadened. In Germany, as one might have predicted, the complete works – and I mean *complete* – of the great dramatists are readily available in paperback. (I name, at random, Hugo, Calderon, Schnitzler, Jonson, Marivaux . . .) In France, large, handsomely produced volumes in a series called *Les Voies de la Création Théâtrale* have been appearing almost annually since the 1960s with detailed analyses, descriptions and production notes of the work of notable contemporary directors (Strehler, Kantor, Lyubimov et al.). In Paris, I was able to buy a French translation of the first volume in a set of the Collected Writings of Meyerhold. His written work and that of other innovative directors – Copeau is an example that comes to mind – may, at best, appear here only anthologised and highly selected in expensive academic editions (usually American) that soon disappear from their publishers' back catalogues. In the 1950s and '60s, for instance, the University of Miami published a series of theatre writings by, amongst others, Appia, Antoine, Sabbattini and including Desmond MacCarthy's contemporary account of the original (Royal) Court Theatre company (1904–7) under Granville Barker and Vedrenne. I doubt these are any longer available. You will probably have to scavenge around to find material on people, productions and periods that interest you.

The titles below are of books that either heightened my longing to work in theatre or were revelatory and strongly influential on how I worked. Many of them were read a long time ago and may by now seem dated.

Acting

You can find numerous books by and about Stanislavsky in any store that sells theatre books. Apart from his own, I would recommend *Respect for Acting*, a very practical down-to-earth explanation of his main techniques by a fine American actress, Uta Hagen. For a comprehensive and definitive analysis and categorisation of his work, there's Bella Merlin's *The Complete Stanislavsky Toolkit*. David Mamet's *True and False* is a stimulatingly confrontational focus on the playing of actions as the actor's only serious responsibility. A wonderfully funny antidote to the distortions and excesses of The Method is Robert Lewis's *Method – or Madness?* Michael Chekhov's writings on acting, considerably less prolific than Stanislavsky's, can be found, somewhat confusingly, in different editions and titles: his seminal *To the Actor* appears, considerably revised, as *On the Technique of Acting*. Jerzy Grotowski's *Towards a Poor Theatre* is by now a classic work on a very different approach to acting that should be in any theatre person's library. This goes for Jacques Lecoq's *The Moving Body*; and, indeed, for *Impro* by Keith Johnstone and Viola Spolin's *Improvisation for the Theater*, both of which are inspirational and gratifyingly practical expositions of their authors' belief in the natural creativity of all human beings and in encouraging the release of imagination and spontaneity.

Voice

Books on voice by Patsy Rodenberg, Cicely Berry, Barbara Houseman and Kristin Linklater are excellent. They relate to the whole person, stressing natural processes rather than the artificial distortions and mumbo-jumbo that can accompany a lot of vocal training. Again, they're immensely practical.

Movement

There are several books about Laban's techniques, some of which I find somewhat indigestible. I suggest that you browse amongst them to find those that you respond to. One of the best is Jean Newlove's *Laban for Actors and Dancers*. Lecoq's book I've already referred to. *Movement for Actors*, edited by Nicole Potter, is an anthology covering a wide range of physical techniques for theatre. It may point you in new directions.

Theatre Theory and Practice

These are some of the books that over the years have influenced me or confirmed me in my ideas about theatre. Peter Brook's *The Empty Space* defines theatre in terms that are as fresh today as when they were first written. In Eugenio Barba's *The Paper Canoe* and his *Dictionary of Theatre Anthropology*, he uncovers universal principles underpinning widely different forms of theatre throughout the world. George Bernard Shaw's writings for the *Saturday Review* during the four years he was its theatre critic cut through the incompetence and pretensions of English theatre in the 1890s and exhibit a clear-sightedness that is applicable in any period.

When I embarked on a directing career, my ideas about theatre were excitingly extended by the books of three early twentieth-century Broadway designers: *The*

Dramatic Imagination by Robert Edmond Jones, *New Theatres for Old* by Mordecai Gorelik and *The Stage is Set* by Lee Simonson. In *Stanislavsky Directs* and *The Vakhtangov School of Stage Art*, both by Nicolai Goncharov, he describes in detail the rehearsals of these great directors which opened up worlds that I'd never known existed. Any books about the work of the Stanislavsky, Vakhtangov, Meyerhold, Tairov, Tovstonogov – in fact, any of that extraordinary profusion of talented Russian directors who were also working mainly in the first half of the last century – are worth reading; many of the theatrical techniques hailed today as innovative had already been discovered and employed by them some seventy or eighty years ago. Fortunately, their rehearsals were documented in great detail. This is also true of Brecht's productions. Amongst the voluminous writings by and about him, you should search out descriptions of his work with actors. Some of these can be found in the compilations, translations and books of John Willett, a major authority on Brecht. Contrary to his reputation for a somewhat cold didacticism (stemming mainly from his own theoretical writings), his productions were warm, lively and immensely theatrical. You should find huge stimulation from anything you can learn about the work of the following directors: Ariane Mnouchkine with Le Théâtre du Soleil, Joan Littlewood with Theatre Workshop, Joseph Chaikin with the Open Theater, Peter Stein at the Schaubühne am Halleschen Ufer, Elizabeth LeCompte with The Wooster Group and Ingmar Bergman in Swedish theatre. These directors vigorously throw rehearsals around in their search for the precise skills to fuse form and content and to embody their ideas of theatre.

In a different tone, I would recommend Albert Hunt's *Hopes for Great Happenings* and John McGrath's *A Good Night Out*, two inspiring and joyful books that espouse a genuinely popular (as opposed to populist) theatre. To inject a healthy sense of modesty and self-irony into anyone's pursuit of a career in a capriciously unreliable medium like theatre, I heartily recommend any or all of playwright Simon Gray's six (so far) funny-sad diaries/memoirs centred around the productions of some of his plays.

If you can locate Stark Young's preface to his translation of *The Seagull*, you will find revealing examples of the vagaries of translation. Francis Ferguson's *The Idea of a Theatre* and Michael Goldman's *The Actor's Freedom*, through their intellectual analysis of dramatic texts, bring supporting evidence to my belief in the centrality of the creative actor. Routledge have published several anthologies on theatre (*The Performance Studies Reader, The Twentieth-Century Performance Reader, Re-Direction, The Intercultural Performance Reader, Twentieth-Century Theatre: a Sourcebook, Twentieth-Century Actor Training* – and there are more) that might introduce you to unfamiliar names and ideas that intrigue you sufficiently to pursue them further. There are also two really splendid American anthologies edited by Toby Cole and Helen Krich Chinoy, *Directors on Directing* and *Actors on Acting*, the latter making its way through world theatre from the Greeks and Romans.

Beyond Theatre

I am a great enthusiast of popular science and have found within some books, especially those dealing with consciousness, scientifically based ideas about emotion that are wonderful correctives to the subjective indulgence with which this topic can get slopped around in the rehearsal room. Two are by Steven Pinker: *How the Mind Works* and *The Blank Slate*. He has also written an exhilarating, eye-opening book on language and speech, called *The Language Instinct*. Antonio Damasio, a professor of neurology, also deals directly with consciousness and emotion in a trio of books, *Descartes' Error: Emotion, Reason and the Human Brain*; *Looking for Spinoza: Joy, Sorrow and the Feeling Brain* and *The Feeling of What Happens: Body, Emotion and the Making of Consciousness*. These might, in places, become too technical for a layperson, but are well worth pursuing for the insights they yield up. Dylan Evans' *Emotion* is a helpful, more accessible introduction to the subject. The title of sociologist Erving Goffman's *The Presentation of Self in Everyday Life* speaks for itself.